Conditioning Democratization

Anthem Series on Russian, East European and Eurasian Studies

The **Anthem Series on Russian, East European and Eurasian Studies** publishes original research on the economy, politics, sociology, anthropology and history of the region. The series aims to promote critical scholarship in the field, and has built a reputation for uncompromising editorial and production standards. The breadth of this series reflects our commitment to promoting original scholarship on Russian and East European studies to a global audience.

Series Editor

Balázs Apor – Trinity College Dublin, Ireland

Editorial Board

Conditioning Democratization

Institutional Reforms and EU Membership Conditionality in Albania and Macedonia

Ridvan Peshkopia

ANTHEM PRESS
LONDON · NEW YORK · DELHI

Anthem Press
An imprint of Wimbledon Publishing Company
www.anthempress.com

This edition first published in UK and USA 2015
by ANTHEM PRESS
75–76 Blackfriars Road, London SE1 8HA, UK
or PO Box 9779, London SW19 7ZG, UK
and
244 Madison Ave #116, New York, NY 10016, USA

First published in hardback by Anthem Press in 2014

British Library Cataloguing-in-Publication Data
A catalogue record for this book is available from the British Library.

Library of Congress Cataloging-in-Publication Data
The Library of Congress has cataloged the hardcover edition as follows:
Peshkopia, Ridvan.
Conditioning democratization : institutional reforms and EU membership conditionality in
Albania and Macedonia / Ridvan Peshkopia. pages cm
Includes bibliographical references and index.
ISBN 978-0-85728-325-2 (hardcover : alk. paper) – ISBN 0-85728-325-1 (hardcover : alk. paper)
1. Democratization–Albania. 2. Democratization–Macedonia (Republic) 3. Albania–Politics
and government–1990– 4. Macedonia (Republic)–Politics and government–1992– 5. European
Union–Albania. 6. European Union–Macedonia (Republic)
7. European Union–Membership. I. Title.
JN9689.A15P47 2014
320.94965–dc23
2013049288

ISBN-13: 978 1 78308 422 7 (Pbk)
ISBN-10: 1 78308 422 7 (Pbk)

Cover image: "Europe on the Open Seas" © Agim Sulaj 2012

This title is also available as an ebook.

To Drita and Edmond Peshkopia
with love, humbleness and promise…

CONTENTS

PREFACE

In April 2007, I presented the paper "Institutional Reforms, Membership Conditionality and Domestic Needs," co-authored with Arben Imami, at the Midwest Political Science Association (MPSA) Annual Conference in Chicago. Later, our panel chair nominated it for the Kellogg-Notre Dame prize as the best paper in comparative politics. Ever since, on my own or co-authoring with Arben, I have continued to develop an interest in the effects of political conditionality and, specifically, European Union membership conditionality, on Eastern European institutional reforms with a number of publications, conference presentations and working papers. I consider this book to be a culmination of those efforts to date.

Institutional reforms intrigue me even more now, as I view them from a research perspective. Mine is a different view from the one I developed 22 years ago, inexperienced in politics and equipped only with a revolutionary zeal "to make Albania look like the rest of Europe," when I was first elected in the Albanian parliament. As a revolutionary interested mainly in the overarching goal of regime change rather than power struggle, I could not imagine why Albania, our "special case," could not successfully break with its past and adopt the institutional frameworks that have worked elsewhere. Apparently, lacking a personal political agenda, I was not aware of others' legitimate personal political agendas. My learning process was painfully tricky, and continues to this today.

Since the initial years of postsocialist transformation, sometime around the year 1994, a single question still pinches my brain: why do different postsocialist Eastern European countries gear toward EU membership at different speeds? Why is the process of drafting and approving a constitution so difficult and divisive? Why does it take so long for regional governments to get rid of the burdensome control over local government and allow communities to efficiently run their own affairs? Why is it so difficult to free the judiciary from government control? Why do countries establish refugee protection regimes when they have no refugees, and resist making the system work when they begin receiving refugees? Why do countries that share so many similarities pursue such different reform pathways? This book tries to reflect a theoretical assessment of what I've learned during the last 22 years in politics and academia combined.

The process by which I learned what I have learned cannot be easily comprehended and remains outside of the scope of this book. However, now that I mention it here I recall that a surprisingly large number of people contributed to my development, some intentionally, but most of them inadvertently. I feel obliged to thank those who have intelligibly contributed, directly or indirectly, to my learning experience and, ultimately, its conversion into this book.

I will begin with my parents, Drita and Edmond, whose unwavering support in everything I have undertaken thus far has set for me moral obligations that can be fulfilled only through succeeding. Beyond them, a list of wonderful scholars and dedicated friends persisted, against my stubbornness, to positively impact my work with this project. Professor Karen Mingst has her input in this work as much as in most of my work thus far. My joy at having been her student both inspires in me the legitimate pride of having worked with one of the best international relation scholars alive, and burdens me with the dilemma of whether or not I am living up to her expectations. As I mentioned earlier, my lifetime friend and colleague, Arben Imami, a brilliant Albanian politician and scholar, has been my co-traveler in much of this research, and we are currently continuing our work on a few other projects.

Another great friend, the late soft-spoken philosopher of the contemporary Albanian nationalism and skillful politician of Albanians in Macedonia, Arbën Xhaferi, has served as a source for frequent consultation related to the views of Albanians in Macedonia regarding constitutional and local decentralization reforms. Our long conversations helped me to better understand the struggle of Albanians in Macedonia to reconcile their dreams with reality. Revered by Albanians and respected by Macedonians, Arbën Xhaferi had the ability to always look at the events through his original lens. His untimely death in the summer, 2012, brought to an end a productive life and our common research plans. D. Stephen Voss of the University of Kentucky has been a loyal supporter and friend, and has commented on several drafts of this project. Being one of the most methodic researchers I know, Steve has been able to contribute significantly to this work through his typically parsimonious comments, dropped sparingly here and there during our conversations. With meticulous copy-editing and stylistic suggestions, his wife, Kathleen Elliott, turned this manuscript to a piece worth submitting for publication. Also, Lola Adebiyi has provided much help with copy-editing and comments during the earliest stages of the project.

During the seven years of my work with this project, I have spent time in several universities in three countries: the United States, Albania and Kosovo. Everywhere I have been, I have met talented professors and students as well as dedicated college administrators eager to help with the research and facilitate my work. I have a deep emotional attachment to the University of Kentucky's Department of Political Science where I received my doctoral degree, and where I spent some of the most inspiring years of my life. There, my childhood dream of living among some of the smartest people in the world came true. Only there could I meet scholars like Horace Bartilow, Charles Davis, Don Gross, Karen Mingst, Herbert Reid, Steve Voss, Lee Walker, Richard Waterman and Ernie Yanarella. Outside this department, professors from other disciplines were as supportive as could be: David Leep from Mathematics, Cidambi Srinivasan from Statistics, Suleiman Darrat from Modern and Classical, Languages, Literature and Culture, John Stempel from the Patterson School of Diplomacy, Ed Jennings from the Martin School of Public Policy and Administration, Robert Olson and David Olster from History, and Ted Schatzki and Harmon Holcomb from the Department of Philosophy.

Other people with the University of Kentucky did not need to be academicians in order to offer me priceless logistic and inspirational help so very needed to go through the process of preparing a manuscript. A short list of them would include William Arnold, Pat Bond, Charlene Leach, Mary Marcum, Karen Slaymaker and Mike Wilson. Outside the University of Kentucky, I remain grateful to Daniel Hulker and James Sturtevant, two close friends who always stood by me during the dark days, as well as my fellow countrymen Besnik Gojani, Shaqir Vula and their lovely families who live in Lexington, Kentucky. My cousin Bardhyl Peshkëpia, my friend Arben Bejleri and their families in Sterling Heights, Michigan, provided me with warm friendship and brotherly care anytime I needed it. I am sure that I am leaving outside of this list many other people who deserve recognition, but the fact that I am not mentioning them here does not mean that I am less grateful to them.

I have been collecting data for this research since 2006, but wrote most of it during the 2010–11 academic year, which I spent as a visiting/postdoctoral fellow with the Institute for European, Russian and Eurasian Studies (IERES) and the Elliott School of International Affairs at George Washington University. My IERES year turned out to be one of the most productive periods of my life due to the outstanding scholarly and intellectual environment that the institute consistently provides to its fellows. I feel deeply indebted to the IERES director, Henry Hale, the current director Peter Rollberg, its assistant director Robert Orttung, Hugh Agnew and other faculty members, administrative staff and fellow researchers from all over Europe, East and West, who have managed to maintain and further develop IERES as one of the few places in the world where one can engage international scholars from around the world in daily interdisciplinary exchanges on Eurasia.

Equally pivotal in my development and preparation in writing this book has been my special relationship with two of my closest friends: Rajan Kumar and Satoshi Machida. Our friendship grew out of the unlikely terrain of cultural differences, warmed by the sun of common love for our colorful humanity. Even though we live now on three different continents, we still feel as close as we were in our doctoral studies. So, too, do I feel about Saikat Boliar, Nilesh Raut and his wife, Smita, and Abisheik Tiwari with whom I spent wonderfully productive years at the University of Kentucky. For few years, my fellow countryman Genti Kristo and his wife, Fioralba, were with me in Kentucky while they worked as interns with the University of Kentucky Chandler Medical Center; both them remained supportive as they moved to the Harvard University hospital system in pursuit of their careers. Another graduate student, John Davis from the Department of History, and his growing knowledge on Russia, impacted my interest in and knowledge of the region. My friends Fredline McCormak-Hale and her husband, Aaron Hale, have been for long now invaluable pen pals, unwavering in their belief in this project.

Similarly, I owe thanks to Lars Kristensen, another pen pal and collaborator with whom I have already co-authored an article and with whom I am now preparing a co-edited book proposal; Lars has been quite patient while I shirked my responsibility to our project to return to this book through the different stages of its publication. My gratitude extends to Agim Sulaj, as well, a wonderful Albanian painter and caricaturist who lives and creates in Italy. I came to admire his paintings during the 1980s when Agim managed to distinguish himself among a crop of ambitious and talented young painters of late communist Albania. Now in Italy, Agim has established a wonderful international career as a caricaturist, and I am grateful to him for offering me the permission to use his prize-winning caricature, *Europe in the Open Seas*, for the front cover design of this book. Last, but certainly not least, I must mention my best friend, Ilir Butka, the outstanding Albanian painter, film director and the director of the Tirana International Film Festival; we've never managed to collaborate on common projects even though we have planned to do so many times. It seems that we have come to the conclusion that we are better in inspiring creativity for one another than joining forces. This book holds much of that inspiration and support that I received from him and his wife, Artes, a press official with the European Commission Delegation in Tirana, Albania, who has periodically proof tested my arguments.

Warm thanks go to colleagues at my current institution, Universiteti për Biznes dhe Teknologji (University for Business and Technology, UBT), Kosovo, especially Halil Bashota, Lulzim Beqiri, Belul Beqaj, Naile Demiri, Ardian Emini, Edmond Hajrizi, Alban Lauka, Lirigzona Morina, Naim Preniqi and Artan Tahiri. I joined the UBT during the publication process of this book, which turned out to be overwhelming. It would have been hard for me to succeed with copyediting comments and indexing without the tremendous support that I received from everyone on campus. The free time that my colleagues opened up for me so I could concentrate on my work is a testimony of our institution's commitment to research and development, a feature that sets us apart from many other universities in the Balkans.

I received valuable expertise in both Albania and Macedonia. In Albania, among others, I am grateful for the help of Bledar Çuçi, Arben Imami, Skënder Minxhozi, Sokol Nako and Ali Rasha. In Macedonia, I received help from Sadi Bexheti, Židas Daskalovski, Orhan Ibrahimi, Blagoja Markovski, Biljana Popovska, Maria Risteska, Vlatko Danailov, Riste Tanaseski and Tane Tanaseski. While all their contribution was invaluable, I am especially grateful to my Macedonian friends who were infinitely patient in explaining me their views on developments in Macedonia, thus helping me not only to understand the country better but also to avoid any ethnic bias, which once in a while kept creeping in. Zoran Drangonski, a bright young activist and scholar from the Young Lawyers of Macedonia Association read some of the chapters in different stages of their development. I am so grateful for his time and efforts to help me improve my research with his information and suggestions.

Some of my work for this project was supported by the University of New York, Tirana, and I thank Deputy-Rector Konstantinos Giakoumis, for his unceasing endorsement. Later, I transferred to the American University of Tirana where I had the opportunity to meet a crop of talented young scholars such as Klodjola Dhamo, Genc Gjonça, Aida Hoxha, Mirva Hoxha, Klejda Hudhra, Greta Hysi, Arben Malasi, Erika Melonashi, Ajola Mesiti, Lulëzim Ndreu, Tefjol Pllaha, Ervin Ramollari, Elsid Sulaj, Rihana Terziu, Erisa Xhaxho and Skerdi Zahaj, as well as more experienced professors such as Engjëll Bejtaj, Luan Gjonça and Gjergji Minga with whom I established a special bond based on common research interests and worldviews. By and large, the AUT offered to me a comfortable academic and intellectual environment, which played a very important role during a crucial stage of this project. Also, I am grateful to the University for Business and Technology in Kosovo and its rector, Edmond Hajrizi, for supporting me with a research grant in the very final stage of this research.

I want to specially thank here all my former colleagues at the Universum College Kosovo, namely Alban Asllani, Burim Asllani, Alejtin Berisha, Arlinda Berisha, Ardit Berisha, Armend Berisha, Gentiana Berisha, Sedat Berisha, Suat Berisha, Besiana Buzhala, Kujtim Bytyqi, Mërgim Cahani, Festina Balidemaj, Violeta Dema, Uranela Demaj, Agon Demjaha, Amira Gabrrica, Elisa Hajrullahu, Ilirjana Hajrullahu, Burim Haliti, Visar Kastrati, Joseph Madden, Bekim Muçolli, Nita Luzha, Fitore Pacolli, Dorina Ponosheci, Rinor Qehaja, Uran Rraci, Bashkim Rrahmani, Arianit Sahitaj, Fidaim Sheholli and Flamur Sopa. Their pride over the publication of this book and the support that some of them provided, often by taking over my responsibilities so that I could have enough time to focus on the manuscript, served as a source of inspiration, but also provided me with a strong sense of obligation to meet their expectations. Meanwhile, I received endless support from the entire student community of the Universum College. Some of the students, imagining the grueling work needed to go through different publication stages, kept asking me about my progress, and encouraged me to best represent myself and their school through this book. Others empathized with me when I delayed their grades so I could meet the publisher's deadlines. I will always feel humbled and inspired by all the support, empathy and cheerleading that I received from the Universum College.

Readers might still find errors and/or inconsistencies throughout the book. The enormous help that I received notwithstanding, the persistence of these infelicities remains my own responsibility. They will remind me of the long journey ahead toward becoming a better scholar and a humbler human being.

Ridvan Peshkopia teaches political science courses with the University for Business and Technology, Kosovo. He received his PhD from the University of Kentucky's Department of Political Science. From 2010–12, he was a postdoctoral fellow with the Institute for European, Russian and Eurasian Studies and the Elliott School of International Affairs at the George Washington University. During the 2011–12 academic year, he was Dean of the College of Sciences and Humanities with the American University of Tirana.

ABBREVIATIONS

AP:	Accession Partnership
APMI:	Aleanca për Punësim, Mirëqënie e Integrim (Alliance for Employment, Wellbeing and Integration)
ASE:	Aleanca për Shqipërinë Europiane (Alliance for the European Albania)
BDI:	Bashkimi Demokratik për Integrim (Democratic Union for Integration)
CARDS:	Community Assistance for Reconstruction, Development and Stabilization
CEAS:	Common European Asylum System
CEECs:	Central and Eastern European countries
CLRA:	Congress of Local and Regional Authorities
CoE:	Council of Europe
CRPM:	Center for Research and Policy Making
DKK:	*Dispozita Kryesore Kushtetuese* (Major Constitutional Provisions)
DPK:	Drejtoria e Policisë Kufitare (Directory of the Border Police)
DShR:	Departamenti për Shtetësi dhe Refugjatë (Department for Citizenship and Refugees)
DRN:	Drejtoria për Refugjatë dhe Nacionalitete (Directory for Refugees and Nationalities)
EAR:	European Agency for Reconstruction
EASO:	European Asylum Support Office
EC:	European Commission
ECLG:	European Charter of Local Self-Government
EE:	Eastern Europe
EECs:	Eastern European Countries
ERF:	European Refugee Fund
EU:	European Union
EURALIUS:	European Assistance Mission to the Albanian Justice System
ECLSG:	European Charter of Local Self-Government
Eurodac:	European Dactyloscopy
FYROM:	The Former Yugoslav Republic of Macedonia
HLAD:	High-Level Accession Dialogue
ICMPD:	International Centre for Migration Policy Development
ICTY:	International Criminal Tribunal for the former Yugoslavia
IDP:	Internally Displaced Persons
IOM:	International Organization of Migration

INGOs: International Non-Governmental Organizations
IOs: International Organizations
KKR: Komisioni Kombëtar për Refugjatë (National Commission for
                Refugees)
KU: Kolegji Universum (Universum College)
LAMP: Land Administration Project
LAOS: Laikós Orthódoxos Synagermós (People's Orthodox Rally)
LATP: Law on Asylum and Temporary Protection
LDP: Liberalno-Demokratska Partija (Liberal Democratic Party)
LSI: Lëvizja Socialiste për Integrim (Socialist Movement for Integration)
MPC: Makedonska Pravoslavna Crkva (Macedonian Orthodox Church)
MB: Ministria e Brendëshme (Ministry of the Interior)
MCVBR: Mechanism for Cooperation and Verification for Bulgaria and Romania
MLS: Ministerstvo za Lokalna Samouprava (Ministry of Local Self-
                government)
MNR: Ministerstvo za Nadvoersni Raboti (Ministry of Foreign Affairs)
MP: Ministerstvo za Pravda (Ministry of Justice)
MPVD: Ministria e Pushtetit Vendor dhe Decentralizimit (Ministry of Local
                Government and Decentralization)
MRP: Ministria e Rendit Publik (Ministry of Public Order)
MTSP: Ministerstvo za Trud i Socijalna Politika (Ministry of Labor and
                Social Policy)
MVR: Ministerstvo za Vnatresni Raboti (Ministry for Internal Affairs)
NATO: North Atlantic Treaty Organisation
ND: Nea Dhimokratia (New Democracy)
NGOs: Non-Governmental Organizations
NSDP: Nova Socijaldemokratska Partija (New Social Democratic Party)
OA: Oddelenie za Azil (Unit for Asylum)
OSCE: Organization for Security and Co-operation in Europe
OSCE/ODIHR: Organization for Security and Co-operation in Europe/Office for
                Democratic Institutions and Human Rights
PA: Politiki Anixi (Political Spring)
PASOK: Panelinio Sosialistiko Kinima (Panhellenic Socialist Movement)
PBDNj: Partia Bashkimi për të Drejtat e Njeriut (Party Union for Human
                Rights)
PD: Partia Demokratike (Democratic Party)
PDK: Partia Demokristiane (Christian Democratic Party)
PDP: Partia Demokratike Popullore (Democratic People Party)
PDSh: Partia Demokratike e Shqiptarëve (Albanian Democratic Party)
PHARE: Poland and Hungary Assistance for Restructuring their Economies
PP: Partia e Punës (Party of Labor)
Pp D: Paqe përmes Drejtësisë (Peace through Justice)
PPD: Partia për Prosperitet Demokratik (Party for Democratic Prosperity)
PS: Partia Socialiste (Socialist Party)

QKA:	Qëndra Kombëtare për Azilkërkues (National Center for Asylum Seekers)
QKPVT:	Qëndra Kombëtare për Pritjen e Viktimave të Trafikuara (National Reception Center of Victims of Trafficking In)
RSD:	Refugee Status Determination
SAA:	Stabilization and Association Agreement
SAP:	Stabilization and Association Programme
ShKGj:	Shoqata Kombëtare e Gjyqtarëve të Shqipërisë (National Association of the Judges of Albania)
ShPSh:	Shoqata Kombëtare e Prokurorëve të Shqipërisë (National Association of the Prosecutors of Albania)
SPC:	Srpska Pravoslavna Crkva (Serbian Orthodox Church)
SIDA:	Swedish International Development and Cooperation Agency
SMK:	Svetski Makedonski Kongres (World Macedonia Congress)
SDSM:	Socijaldemokratski Sojuz na Makedonija (Social-Democratic Union of Macedonia)
SDSM–BDI:	Socijaldemokratski Sojuz na Makedonija–Bashkimi Demokratik për Integrim (Social-Democratic Union of Macedonia–Democratic Union for Integration)
SDSM–PDSh:	Socijaldemokratski Sojuz na Makedonija–Partia Demokratike e Shqiptarëve (Social-Democratic Union of Macedonia–Albanian Democratic Party)
SFRY:	Socijalistička Federativna Republika Jugoslavija (Socialist Federal Republic of Yugoslavia)
ShAV:	Shoqata për Autonomi Vendore (Association for Local Autonomy)
ShIK:	Shërbimi Informativ Kombëtar (National Intelligence Service)
UBT:	Universiteti për Biznes dhe Teknologji (University for Business and Technology)
UÇK/KLA:	Ushtria Çlirimtare e Kosovës/Kosovo's Liberation Army
UÇK/NLA:	Ushtria Çlirimtare Kombëtare/National Liberation Army
UNHCR:	United Nations High Commissioner for Refugees
UNHCR BoT:	UNHCR Bureau of Tirana
UNPROFOR:	United Nations Protection Force
UT:	Universiteti i Tetovës (University of Tetovo)
VMRO:	Vnatrešna Makedonska Revolucionerna Organizacija (Internal Macedonian Revolutionary Organization)
VMRO–BDI:	Vnatrešna Makedonska Revolucionerna Organizacija–Bashkimi Demokratik për Integrim (Internal Macedonian Revolutionary Organization–Democratic Union for Integration)
VMRO–DPMNE:	Vnatrešna Makedonska Revolucionerna Organizacija–Demokratska Partija za Makedonsko Nacionalno Edinstvo (Internal Macedonian Revolutionary Organization–Democratic Party for Macedonian National Unity)

VMRO–NP: Vnatrešna Makedonska Revolucionerna Organizacija–Narodna Partija
                (Internal Macedonian Revolutionary Organization–People's Party)
VMRO–PDSh: Vnatrešna Makedonska Revolucionerna Organizacija–Partia
                Demokratike e Shqiptarëve (Internal Macedonian Revolutionary
                Organization–Albanian Democratic Party)
VSEP: Vladiniot Sekretarijat za Evropski Prasanja (Government's
                Secretariat for European Affairs)
ZELS: Zaednicata na Edinicite na Lokalna Samouprava na Republika
                Makedonija (Association of the Units of Local Self-Government of
                the Republic of Macedonia)
ZpR: Zyra për Refugjatë (Office for Refugees)

Chapter 1

INTRODUCTION

Today, after more than two decades of democratization and economic liberalization in postsocialist Eastern Europe, one wonders at the extreme variation of its outcomes. Eastern European postsocialist pathways have led to results as different as democratic stability and economic development, on the one hand, and authoritarianism and economic backwardness, on the other; North Atlantic Treaty Organization (NATO) and European Union (EU) membership coupled with vicious ethnic conflicts; and vibrant societies alongside painfully slow national revival. Research related to Eastern European democratization has developed along two divergent lines, one holding a mainly inward outlook, the other predominantly outward. Some of the most prominent theorists have attempted to explain Eastern European democratization by applying theories built to explain the Latin American transformations of the late 1970s and 1980s. Existing theories were well positioned for studying democratization, since its third wave originated in Latin America; adding Eastern European cases would give scholarly efforts a comparative advantage (Bunce 2003). As a consequence, work conducted during the early and mid-1990s was an extension of models built to explain the Latin American and South Asian experiences. The latter claimed universality by discounting the contextual background of the political transformation process and perceiving democratization theories as applicable to any world region. Therefore, explanatory models related to Eastern European democratization mimicked the dominant characteristic of 1980s democratization literature: an ahistorical approach to transition and democratization (Lijphart and Waisman 1996; Haggard and Kaufman 1995; Karl and Schmitter 1991; Przeworski 1991; Di Palma 1990).

An alternative approach, however, emerged around the second half of the 1990s, and represents the current dominant trend among those studying Eastern European democratization. The contributors to this literature try to explain the processes that occur under specific historical conditions and find among those conditions potential explanatory variables. Efforts to expand the explanatory power of democratization theories have led some authors to highlight the similarities in the postsocialist world rooted in the peculiarities of communism. These peculiarities represent factors that set democratization in former communist countries apart from democratization in other world regions. For other authors, any comparison of nation building in 22 European postsocialist countries to other cases of the third wave of democratization would be inappropriate. Arguably, the most useful comparisons are those within the universe of the 27 postcommunist and post-Soviet countries, which share basic characteristics but differ in important political details (Bunce 2000a). Differences among Eastern European countries (EECs) and former Soviet Union sub-regions, as well as among individual countries, explain various postsocialist pathways, as they can show whether or not a socialist past helps produce a consensus about the political and economic successor regimes to state socialism.

The historical background of the region demands that we define peculiarities of postsocialist democratization. Elster, Offe and Preuss (1998, 1) categorize these conditions as (1) the material legacies, constraints and sets of habits and cognitive frames inherited from past socialist regimes; (2) a turbulent configuration of new actors and new opportunities for action; and (3) the foreseeable newly consolidated institutional order under which agency is institutionalized, as well as the measure of sustainability (or consolidation) of those agency-shaping institutions. Since the authors are able to distinguish these phenomena in a time axis, their suggestions can offer an accurate explanation of what is happening and expected to happen in Eastern Europe and its sub-regions as it undergoes reformation. Moreover, those authors have set a baseline for studying institutional reforms in the region. First, they employ the *tabula rasa* notion to describe the institutional and authoritative vacuum that succeeded what they call the communist abdication of power (see also Laar 2002). Second, in the case of weak institutions, agency chaos and chaotic gravity centers, deceptive and inapplicable Western models, rather than autochthonous preparatory work performed by the opposition upon the old regime, often dominated the public scene. Third, the *tabula rasa* notion applies to authority alone, not to power; and lack of agency refers to the lack of effective institutional and legal parameters, not to the individual actors along with the material resources attached to them, their formal and informal ties to other agents, political memories, habits, frames, feelings of guilt and pride, loyalties and hostilities and fears and hopes (Elster, Offe and Preuss 1998).

Rupnik (2002, 2000, 1999) suggests several factors that affect the pace of democratization in former communist countries in Eastern Europe: the nature of the old communist regime and the depth of its imprint on society; market and civil society, specifically the willingness of countries to embark upon radical economic reforms rather than postponing market reforms and privatization while simultaneously supporting the development of civil society; a tradition of the rule of law and the Habsburg factor, i.e. the influence of the Habsburg administrative and institutional political culture; nation-state building and an obsession with societal homogeneity, i.e. difficulties that democracy faces from deeply entrenched fears that democratization might endanger national sovereignty; the cultural argument that connects democratization with religion; and the presence of an international environment that favors democratization.

However, even though Rupnik's model encompasses most of the key variables that would explain differences in the pace of democratization between Central and Eastern Europe with countries from its southeastern peninsula, the lack of systematic empirical work leaves his theoretical argument untested.

A critical assessment of Rupnik's model using the model suggested by Elster, Offe and Preuss will help to distinguish some relevant contextual elements as prerequisites for determining successful transition from communism to democracy. Most of these preconditions have focused on theoretical debates and empirical work, but other factors have not attracted the same scholarly attention.

The Legacies of Communism

The Leninist legacy stands as one of the most distinguishable features of a postsocialist society; Leninist structures led to similarities among countries and regions as diverse as Central Eastern Europe, Baltic countries, the Balkans, Russia, post-Soviet republics of Central Asia, Cuba, China and Indochina (Bunce 1999; Fish 1999, 1998a, 1998b). That legacy includes one-party (communist) rule; state-run economies oriented toward satisfaction of population needs rather than consumer desires; little or no private property; state monopoly of mass media, extended but mediocre quality health care, education, transportation, energy, retirement funds, housing and other public services; hostility toward the individual and its rights and liberties in favor of community-friendly attitudes and policies; distrust of the army and high reliance on the secret service to suppress dissent; control over internal population movement and travel abroad; inefficient institutions characterized by a stifling bureaucracy subordinate to the rigid communist party structure; and lack of political legitimacy of the ruling elites caused mainly by sham elections that rubber-stamp communist party decisions (Peshkopia 2010, 2008a; Bunce 2000b).

Pre-communist Legacies

As mentioned earlier, other literature related to postsocialist transformations tries to establish causality with the pre-communist history of Eastern Europe (Janos 2005; Tismaneanu 2000; Crawford and Lijphart 1997). While Rupnik's (2002, 2000, 1999) model combines variables from the recent communist and distant pre-communist history of the region, other authors tend to view that tradition from a political culture perspective (Tismaneanu 1995). Yet others authors highlight the correlation between pre-communist economic development and reform performance in postsocialist Eastern Europe (Bunce 2003; Verdery 2000). Careful consideration of all these cases reveals that, since this literature finds a connection between pre-communist underdevelopment and communist dogmatism during the communist monopoly of power, the communist legacy becomes an intervening variable between the pre-communist legacy and the pace of postsocialist democratization in Eastern Europe. While this discourse helps us to understand different sources of various communist traditions, only the latter bears significant relevance for understanding and explaining different postsocialist pathways.

Nation-State Building and Ethnic Homogeneity

Findings about the negative effects of ethnic heterogeneity in nation building, social cohesion and democratization remain inconclusive (Gerrits and Wolffram 2005; Fish 1999; Stavenhagen 1996; Diamond and Platter 1994; Horowitz 1985; Rupnik 2002). Rustow (1970), one of the earliest contributors of this research corpus, has listed the settlement of national and state questions as a prerequisite for successful democratization. Nation building is seen as related to the legitimacy of the territorial framework of democratizing countries, and the latter clearly remains the first prerequisite for democratic transition.

Such legitimacy is related to ethnic identity as a supportive culture, a prerequisite for every durable form of political system (Berg-Schlosser and Mitchell 2000, 9). Twentieth-century European history seems to redeem John Stuart Mill's (1861) pessimism about the prospect of establishing representative governments in ethnically divided societies, and to reject Lord Acton's (1862) claim that "diversity preserves liberty." Even the most optimistic authors note that though cultural homogeneity, or cultural heterogeneity pacified by consociational arrangements at the elite level, might not be a prerequisite or condition for democracy, it certainly helps (Gerrits and Wolffram 2005; see also Newman 1996). The debate over whether or not antagonism between ethnic divisions and democracy is reconcilable remains unresolved.

Kaufman (2003) views ethnic conflict as contingent upon deeply ingrained fears of extinction carried by ethnic groups; politicians who want to use such fears for power interests; and the contextual conditions that would allow those politicians to resort to violence. If elites are patient and committed to negotiations and political means, ethnic conflict is avoidable. However, from a rationalist perspective, it is very possible that those who prefer accommodation would be stigmatized as too soft to protect their ethnic groups from imminent threats from other rival ethnic groups, whether perceived or socially construed. Such politics would lead to a radicalization of the political stage and, potentially, to ethnic conflict (Shoup 2008; Diamond and Platter 1994; Milne 1981; Rabushka and Shepsle 1972). Whether it is a matter of political survival, as rational choice advocates suggests, or physical survival, as the region's history from the last two centuries indicates, political leaders resort to ethnic conflict as one of their most viable options for continued political existence.

However, the relationship between democracy and ethnic conflict can also proceed the opposite way. Eastern European democratization showed that, while cases exist in which nationalism and ethnic conflict undermine democratization, some of the most successful democratic experiences in Eastern Europe were not only efforts to change regimes but also to build new nations. Bunce (2003) provides the distinction between protests against the regime and protests against the state, with popular protest in both the Czech lands and Poland targeted towards the regime, while Baltic and Slovene demonstrations displayed both liberal and nationalist features. Differences exist, though, between countries in the northern sub-region of Eastern Europe and the Balkans. Bunce (2003) explains these differences as relating to whether the nationalist discourse preceded or succeeded regime transformation: the first case explains the Yugoslav wars; the second explains the peaceful stories of secession, Czechoslovakia and, to a certain extent, the Soviet Union.

Nodia (2002, 2001) tries to bring identity politics into the equation as a variable. The question, suggests Nodia (2002, 205; 2001, 31), is whether an ethnic group looks "up" or "down," in other words, whether "the other" is perceived to be better or worse than one's own ethnic group. Moreover, another powerful reference concerns whether that "other" exists within the same country or in another country, that is, "outbound" versus "inbound" nationalism. The claim is that democracy coincides with capitalism, that its development by Westerners represents the source of a perceived cultural correlation between democracy and the West. Eastern European ethnic groups who look down on their fellow citizens from other ethnicities consider themselves Westerners while perceiving the "others" as Orientals. As for the role of outbound nationalism in democratization, Nodia (2002) argues, aversion toward less Westernized neighbors might cause a country to introduce at least a minimal form of democracy. In such a case, an increase of the mobilizational capacity and a consensual character of nationalism might occur, embodied in a rational desire for national liberation from the domination of a backward neighbor. However, nationalism oriented against a more modernized hegemonic country, whether or not the nationalists are willing to admit that they are looking up at their target, contains a seed of weakness.

This discussion advises caution when considering democratization in ethnically divided societies. Evidence of the destabilizing effects of ethnicity and nationalism as well as their liberating and enfranchising effects exists. Most of the aforementioned literature tries to build bivariate correlations, oversimplifying the social and historical conditions of the ethnicity–democracy nexus in the process. Obviously, the effects of multi-ethnicity as an independent variable need to be analyzed in the presence of other variables; for instance, the level of social development of the country, combined with ethnic heterogeneity, might become a basic factor in establishing and maintaining democratic regimes (Berend 2005).

Elites and Masses in Democratization

One of the major challenges that the democratization literature of the 1970s and 1980s experienced during the revolutions of the late 1980s in Eastern Europe was mass mobilization. Contradictory to models suggesting elite pacts, some of the most successful transitions in Eastern Europe began with mass mobilization (Mastnak 2005; Bunce 2003; Smolar 2002). Mass mobilization forced elites to negotiate, increased the leverage of opposition leaders outside the system and reformatory forces within the system, radicalized the negotiation agenda and legitimized promises and subsequent radical policies for political and economic transformations (Bunce 2003). However, as that literature suggests, since mass mobilization emerged out of the need to overthrow the old regime, the vanishing of the former might also mean the curbing of mass mobilization altogether. Indeed, the rapid demobilization of postsocialist societies returned research focus to the role of elites in postsocialist politics, especially during the democracy consolidation phase, by pointing to elites' ability to prioritize their power-driven interests.

Arguably, the international dimension of democratization contains some of the most relevant causal factors of the Eastern European transformations. One of the thorniest issues in this democratization process is the relationship between power-driven elites and international actors interested in the region's democratization. Some authors assert that the former outweighs the latter (Saideman and Ayres 2007; Brusis 2005). However, others argue that postcommunist leaders tend to embrace normative behavior and to position themselves in student–teacher relationships with the IOs they aspire to join (Gheciu 2005). This argument rests on the conceptualization of postsocialist transition as continuity rather than a revolutionary break with the communist past. In such a case, the inter-elite struggle might be less severe due to an inter-elite pact, an acceptance of electoral competition norms and either power sharing or peaceful power rotation. However, such results can be achieved only under circumstances of moderate elite continuity; in the Soviet Union and the Balkans, the high levels of elite continuity have undermined democratic reforms (Higley, Kullberg and Pakulski 2002; Reisinger 1997). Other authors (Balcerowicz 2002; Laar 2002), aware of the perils of elite competition during periods of "ordinary politics," call for key reforms during periods of "extraordinary politics" that immediately succeed regime change.[1] In order to shield reformatory elites from electoral backlashes caused by the harshness of radical economic reforms, Laar (2002) suggests beginning the postsocialist transformation with political reforms; only a legitimately formed consensus for change achieved through accountable democratic structures and free and fair elections could make a country adhere to reforms despite the short term pain they bring.

While it is not difficult to notice historical differences throughout the socialist and postsocialist world, postsocialist societies resist giving up their similarities (Howard 2003; Rose, Mishler and Haerpfer 1998; Mishler and Rose 1997; Rose 1995). These persisting similarities make us wonder whether we need to begin our research with the elites, with institutions or with the masses. Such a need to define our ontological approach bears epistemological import, since it represents our basic assumptions on how society works. It also bears methodological ramifications; in order to assess the effects of the international dimension of Eastern European democratization, cases from countries with different historical legacies would suffice to establish a credible comparative ground even though the similarities between Eastern European societies continue to persist.

The International Dimension of Democratization and the EU Impact on Eastern European Democratization

One problem with the aforementioned literature is its sole focus on the role of domestic actors in countries' democratization and institutional reforms. While early democracy theorists downplayed the role of international actors in democratization, it is difficult today to find any research on democratization that does not reference the effects of the international climate on democratization, except in cases where that research has been exclusively dedicated to domestic dynamics of democratization (see the edited volume by Peter Nardulli 2008). Still, scholars do not always agree on the relevance of international actors on domestic affairs, even if they include the international climate as an independent variable. Disagreements range from defining mechanisms employed by international actors to encourage democratization (Pevehouse 2002; Grugel 1999; Whitehead 1996) to the real effects of the international situation on democratization (Schimmelfenning 2007, 2005; Saideman and Ayres 2007; Kelley 2004a, 2004b). Some of those disagreements stem from definitional fallacies, while others reflect inappropriate research designs.

Most of the democratization literature developed during the 1990s followed and further built on Huntington's (1991) research question: what are the major causal factors/ mechanisms that lead to the toppling of authoritarian/dictatorial regimes and create opportunities for democratization? A major breakthrough of that literature occurred in the form of renewed emphasis on the international dimension of democratization, an element only reluctantly tackled by the democratization literature of the 1980s (Janos 2005; Pridham 2000; O'Donnell and Schmitter 1986; O'Donnell, Schmitter and Whitehead 1986). The literature of the 1990s discussed regime change and democratization as more than mere outcomes of domestic causal factors. Theories regarding the international environment's impact on such events and processes unveiled the role of international actors and international organizations (IOs) in domestic affairs. This literature reflected the unparalleled impact of international factors on Eastern European democratization (Rupnik 2002, 2000, 1999).

Traditionally, studies of IOs' impact on domestic politics have been dominated by mainstream literature building on the rational choice assumption. Whether from an institutionalist angle such as Gourevitch's (1978) second image reversed, Putnam's (1988) two-level game or Goldstein's (1998, 1996) tying-hands approach, this literature assumes that leaders pursue a rational quest for attaining and maintaining power. However, democratization theorists disagree on the nature of the international actors' tools to expand and impose their preferences. Thus, Schmitter (1996) maintains that international actors enforce democratization by rational, deliberately communicated, demands. Developing this argument further, Pevehouse (2002, 519) has identified three potential causal mechanisms through which IOs can influence regime change: first, pressure generated from these IOs in combination with internal forces; second, the acceptance of liberalization by certain elite groups; and third, liberalization either through hand-tying or socialization of domestic elites. From a social constructivist perspective, Pridham (2000, 298) points out that this enforcement is not deliberately sent to recipient countries, but is a democratic spillover from international democratic institutions to democratizing countries. The flow of democratic values from democratic to democratizing countries occurs only because, through that spillover, democratic countries reassert their democratic identity.

Whitehead (1996, 5) has pinpointed two other mechanisms by which democratic principles can be unintentionally transmitted and/or intentionally enforced: contagion and control. Democratization through contagion does not imply any enforcement; it just leaks through borders within a predefined region. Control might be seen in Whitehead's (1996) metaphor "as a vaccine," that is, an intentional imposition of democratic norms, rules and principles on democratizing countries by another power; it does not exclude military intervention even though its absence may not necessarily generate the best results. Schmitter adds conditionality to these mechanisms: the term implies the stipulation of certain conditions from IOs that would force countries that aspire to join these organizations to change their behavior. Although coercive enforcement is always undesirable, this method creates the best incentives for inter-state and intra-state negotiations and bargaining, brings to the forefront different domestic actors with different inclinations, sets up compromises and generates what Whitehead (1996) calls consent and Pridham (2000) calls convergence. While Pevehouse's mechanisms are perceived to be consecutive steps toward regime change, and Pridham's democratic spillover rests as a causal mechanism isolated by other domestic and international factors, contagion, control, consent and conditionality are perceived to work both concomitantly and independently, thus allowing their study as both collinear and independent causal mechanisms.

Schmitter (1996, 30) defines conditionality as "the deliberate use of coercion—by attaching specific conditions to the distribution of benefits to recipient countries—on the part of multilateral institutions." Unlike control and contagion, which are mainly produced by unilateral actors' policies, conditionality emerges from multilateral international relations. In contrast to contagion and consent, which result from voluntary actions of democratic states often supported by private actors, conditionality explicitly involves coercion backed by IO member countries. However, while in Schmitter's concept these notions are sharply divided, the borderline between them might be less clear. In terms of Whitehead's metaphor, a vaccine is composed of weakened bacteria, but it can still lead to an invasion of the body; hence, could not control lead to contagion? Is consent not an acquired trait, hence a dependent rather than an independent variable? Is conditionality not a form of control over democratizing societies that have consented to take the vaccine despite their initial pain?

The purpose of these questions is to allow us to focus only on conditionality as the most relevant political tool for behavioral change. When we meticulously probe into seemingly inseparable contagion, control and consent, the study of conditionality can help us to uncover the aggregate effects of these factors. Increasingly used during the last three decades as a political tool more consistent with international norms than direct control and with much sharper expectations than the blurry contagion, conditionality continues to generate foreign policies and academic research. While such an increasing preference shows a growing consensus that conditionality yields results, the controversies that conditionality stirs cause politicians to appeal for corrections. As we attempt to unveil its presumed causality, we need to focus on the ultimate goal of conditionality: to change the political behavior of actors, whether they are political leaders or institutions, or both, according to the wishes of those who dispatch those conditions.

From political conditionality to EU membership conditionality

Initially, the notion of conditionality was related to attempts made by international financial institutions (IFIs) to change the political behavior of developing countries, which required international financial support in their structural adjustment efforts. The notion emerged around the early 1980s from a study of the World Bank that suggested placing conditions on African countries for disbursement of financial aid to assist them with the implementation of economic liberalization reforms (World Bank 1981). The policy reflected consensus among the Bank's major donors that economic success depends upon open market and liberal economic policies. Moreover, these prescriptions acquired an institutional dimension in later decades when the World Bank advocated the need for institutional reforms in recipient countries in order to enable them to successfully implement economic reforms, thus emphasizing the need for good governance as a *sine qua non* for economic development (World Bank 1997, 1996, 1992, 1989).

Scholars of development policies have focused mainly upon whether or not foreign financial aid helps promote economic growth and whether conditions placed by the

IFI have been effective in generating policy change in recipient countries (Spraos 1986; Bartilow 1997; Santiso 2001; Bulíř and Lane 2002; Vreeland 2003). Indeed, this literature has often been embedded in ideological arguments with mixed empirical results (see, for instance, Hibou 2002, 1998; Easterly 2006, 2002; Stiglitz 2002; Bhagwati 2005; Sachs 2005). This body of literature is characterized by four related debates: first, whether or not conditionality works (Easterly 2006, 2002; Vreeland 2003; Bulíř and Lane 2002; Stiglitz 2002); second, whether domestic or international factors are the main determinants of reform success (Easterly 2006, 2002; Sachs 2005; Bulíř and Lane 2002; Stiglitz 2002; Santiso 2001); third, how conditionality affects different domestic constituencies; and fourth, whether we can really speak of conditions at all (Hibou 2002; Bartilow 1997).

Much of this problem haunts EU membership conditionality as well. The conditions imposed by the EU on countries aspiring to gain membership include stipulations for implementing reforms and pursuing policies in the direction prescribed by the EU. The EU first applied membership conditionality in the wake of its second expansion, which included Greece in 1981 and Spain and Portugal in 1986. In these cases, although a statement by the Copenhagen European Council warned the new applicants that "respect for and maintenance of representative democracy and human rights in each Member State are essential elements of membership in the European Communities," little attention was actually given to the democratic institutions; the focus instead was on applicants' economic performance (Smith 2003; Haughton and Malová 2002).

European identity, democratic status and respect for human rights were laid out initially at the Lisbon European Council of June 1992 as conditions for membership. Yet, the European Commission did not further elaborate upon these criteria. Instead, it turned its attention to shielding the achievements of the European Community from potential dangers stemming from enlargement (Smith 2003). In the cases of Greece, Spain and Portugal, the EC did not apply membership conditionality consistently, and political considerations won over its strict imposition. When it came to the latest wave of expansion, however, the European Commission insisted that applicant countries had to accept the existing EC system, the *acquis communautaire*, entirely. From here, the Commission suggested conditional policies toward new applicants mainly to preserve the existing achievements of the European Union, as well as to ensure its further integration and enlargement: "widening must not be at the expense of deepening. Enlargement must not be a dilution of the Community's achievements" (European Commission 1992, 19).

Finally, EU membership conditionality took shape at the Copenhagen European Council, June 1993. It focused on the economic and institutional adaptations that EU membership–aspiring countries needed to perform in order to meet the EU criteria. Such conditions required the applicants to: (1) build a functioning market economy with the capacity to cope with competitive pressures and market forces within the EU; (2) ensure the stability of institutions established to guarantee democracy, the rule of law, human rights and respect for and protection of minorities; and (3) bolster capacity to take on obligations of EU membership, including adherence to the aims of economic and political solutions. In December 1997, the Luxembourg European Council recognized strengthening and improving the operation of the institutions in the aspirant countries as a prerequisite for membership.

The European Commission's "Agenda 2000: For a Stronger and Wider European Union" (hereafter Agenda 2000) further aimed at sharpening the very general notion of "stability of institutions guaranteeing democracy, the rule of law, human rights and respect for and protection of minorities" (European Commission 1997) by defining a functioning democracy as a political entity with: (1) a constitution that guaranteed democratic freedoms, such as political pluralism, the freedom of expression and the freedom of religion; (2) independent judicial and constitutional authorities; (3) stable democratic institutions permitting public authorities (including police forces, local government, and judges) to function properly; (4) the ability to conduct free and fair elections and recognize the role of opposition; (5) respect for fundamental rights as expressed in the Council of Europe's Convention for Protection of Human Rights and Fundamental Freedoms, including acceptance of the protocol allowing citizens to take cases to the European Court of Human Rights; and (6) respect for minorities, which includes adaptation of the Council of Europe's (CoE) Framework Convention for the Protection of National Minorities, as well as Recommendation 1201 of the CoE's Parliamentary Assembly. Meanwhile, the practical implementation and scrutiny of the fulfillment of EU conditions were included in the frameworks for the Accession Partnership (AP) of 1998 and the Stabilization and Association Process (SAP) of 1999.

EU membership conditionality can be defined as the set of conditions sent from the EU to EU membership–aspiring countries for implementing reforms and pursuing policies in the direction prescribed by the Union. Applied in the Balkans, EU membership conditionality serves as a multidimensional and multipurpose instrument geared toward reconciliation, reconstruction and reform; it is regional, sub-regional, bilateral and project-specific and relates to economic, political, social and security related criteria (Anastasakis and Bechev 2003). Arguably, these negotiations concern the process of preparation for EECs to join the EU and are not about give and take; hence, applicants from Eastern Europe have little power to argue against EU demands, since that there is a preset EU agenda on which aid is already conditional. The Accession Partnership presents conditions as a package that is difficult to take apart in negotiations (Grabbe 1999, 19). The pre-Accession Partnership and pre-Stabilization and Association Process negotiations show that EECs should demonstrate political will toward reform as a prerequisite for involvement in negotiations with the EU. On the other hand, it has been argued that these programs rest on the assumption that EU accession and EECs' transition to democracy and market-oriented economy are parts of the same process, and that preparation to join the EU is conterminous with overall development goals (Grabbe 1999). Moreover, the Eastern European elites and public alike view postsocialist transformation as a "return to Europe," a concept which weaves together the processes of democratization, marketization and Europeanization (Henderson 1999; Dimitrova 2004, 4).

Two views define the purpose of EU membership conditionality. The first, the demand-side viewpoint, portrays conditionality as mainly concerned with minimizing the risk of new entrants becoming politically unstable and economically burdensome to existing EU members. These conditions serve to minimize the risks and costs of enlargement (Grabbe 1999, 2002). Unfortunately, as the number of member states expands, fears that it will be much more difficult to come to an agreement grow, particularly in relation to the scope of integration, adding new policy areas to the process and the level of integration, such as increasing the use of qualified majority voting (Smith 2003).

Other scholars tend to view EU conditions from the supply-side approach. For them, EU conditions and the programs attached to them provide material support for implementing reforms (Moravcsik and Vachudová 2005); shield moderate politics from populism and nationalism (Vachudová 2001); strengthen democratic forces in the face of authoritarian downturns (Schimmelfenning 2007); and serve as instrumental justification for domestic policies that Eastern European leaders need to implement in order to attain their own rational, power-driven goals (Brusis 2005). The conditions provide EU membership–aspiring countries from Eastern Europe with political and economic objectives, as well as guidelines for achieving these objectives. All in all, the possibility of membership in the EU has created powerful incentives as transition states shape their reforms (Pridham 1994; Smith 1997; Kubicek 2003).

Recognizing EU membership conditionality as the most powerful instrument available to the EU in dealing with candidate and potential candidate countries (Anastasakis 2008; Anastasakis and Bechev 2003), some authors credit an obvious asymmetry of interdependence in EU conditionality as an important factor that enables the latter to be effective (Knorr 1977; Grabbe 2003; Hughes, Sasse, and Gordon 2003a, 2003b; Dimitrova 2004). This asymmetry stems both from the fact that EECs consider EU membership their highest foreign policy goal, thus putting the EU in a strong position to influence the internal politics of these countries (Kopecký and Mudde 2000); and the generally low public support for enlargement in current EU members and candidate countries (Cameron 2003). Eastern Europeans, captured by the return-to-Europe psyche, perceive a link between democratization and accession to the EU (Dimitrova 2004). Whereas EU member states and EECs will both benefit from EU enlargement, new members are expected to benefit more, thus putting the latter at a disadvantage in bargaining (Moravcsik and Vachudová 2005, 2003). Grabbe (1999) argues that, since the negotiations are over the process of EECs' preparations to join the EU and not about give-and-take, applicants have little power to argue against EU demands, especially given that there is a preset EU agenda on which aid is already conditional. In addition, the Accession Partnership presents conditions as a package, which is likely to be difficult to separate in negotiations. Generally, this literature agrees that such a power asymmetry causes strong convergences of EECs' policies with the EU and also a greater domestic convergence toward such policies compared to current EU member countries (Grabbe 2003). The economic and political benefits gained by Eastern European leaders, the lack of equivalent alternatives for postcommunist EECs, and the lack of interest from the EU in eastward political enlargement make EU membership conditionality a particularly powerful tool in the hands of the EU during its negotiations for eastward expansion (Brusis 2005; Janos 2005).

Rationally speaking, EECs ought to ask for Western assistance; the possibility of membership in the EU has created powerful incentives as transition states shape their reforms (Kubicek 2003; Smith 1997; Pridham 1994). The reforms conditioned by the EU shore up democratic standards, improve the functioning of the state and increase aggregate economic welfare (Moravcsik and Vachudová 2005). On the other hand, the prospect of Western Balkans countries' membership in the EU has remained distant for over two decades, weakening the strategic effectiveness of EU conditionality as an instrument of EU influence on their institutional reforms (Anastasakis 2008; Anastasakis and Bechev 2003). By the same token, the EU is increasingly facing the dilemma that its instruments do not provide incentives sufficient for reforms. Even when membership is available, purely external leverage may be insufficient to bring about the required domestic changes (Flynn and Farrell 1999).

Approaching our main concern, it has been argued that countries with statehood problems are more susceptible to international influences on their democratization process; in some ethnically divided societies, a strong EU presence limits their sovereignty (Noutcheva 2006). In such cases, the EU can be more intrusive, as it suggests a redefinition of statehood. The sovereignty-linked EU membership conditions constitute an additional layer of conditionality distinct from the Copenhagen criteria requiring democratic and economic standards. Under such conditions, domestic politics hold the key to compliance with sovereignty-sensitive conditions. The presence of external actors in domestic authority structures undermines political bargaining and has an impact on the way local actors define their interests in the politically constrained space. The existence of sovereignty-linked EU conditions, however, causes divisions in the domestic political community and, in some cases, brings about serious opposition to EU demands. The political fragmentation of these societies, in turn, affects the sustainability of compliance decisions and carries the risk of non-implementation and even the reversal of some reforms when a switch of the ruling elites occurs.

However, this argument misses two important logical ramifications: first, it downplays the capability of EU mechanisms to affect all major sections of those presumably "semi-sovereign" countries similarly; second, the EU idea itself can serve as a unifying factor for the entire society. If EU membership has become such a powerful attraction for Eastern European countries, the EU can easily use that attraction to impose consociational behavior upon ethnically and politically divided societies. Moreover, it is not clear how much of a buffer to the Copenhagen criteria those sovereignty-linked EU demands would provide; it is easily perceivable that reforms aimed at improving socioeconomic conditions of marginalized ethnic groups cannot but help improve those conditions for the entire society. Finally, a more detailed, and perhaps less politically correct, conceptualization of the nature of EU leverage would help in better understanding EU success in taming ethnic conflicts in some Eastern European countries.

Explaining the Effects of EU Membership Conditionality on Membership-Aspiring Countries' Institutional Reform

Most of the debate related to EU membership conditionality occurs over whether or not membership conditionality is effective. Authors separate into camps: those who cautiously count conditionality as the primary factor that drives policy changes in EECs (Grabbe 2001, 2003); those who admit that membership conditionality works under certain conditions (Schimmelfenning 2005; Kelley 2004a, 2003b); and those who argue that it is secondary to either domestic structure composition or to domestic leaders' power calculations (Saideman and Ayres 2007; O'Dwyer 2006). Haughton and Malová (2002) point out cases in which reform outcomes occur as the result of domestic politics' dynamics, while in other cases they are the result of pressures from the EU. Elsewhere, I have contributed to this debate by arguing that the effects of EU membership conditionality are contingent upon a tug of war between domestic, EU and EU member country leaders who perceive the outcomes of reforms in EECs as a means to promote their power-driven interests (Peshkopia 2005d). Cautioning against the vagueness of the political message sent by the EU to the EU membership–seeking Balkan countries, some authors point out that conditionality can function successfully only as one element in a well-defined relationship with the Balkan states; therefore, it is essential to establish clear links between the reform process and its outcome (Anastasakis and Bechev 2003). Usually, this research corpus tends to measure the effects of EU membership conditionality against accession, and thus consider those cases when countries have been accepted in the EU without fully complying with the conditions imposed upon them as failures. Against such an approach, one should heed Dimitrova's (2004) warning that the moment of entry to the EU is only one stop along a long road to transformation for the new members.

This discussion leads to the legitimate question: if the EU could make membership conditional with democratization, how much, and under what conditions, can the EU affect democratization and democratic consolidation? What are the mechanisms employed by the EU to affect reforms in countries escaping authoritarian/dictatorial rule? What causes these mechanisms to succeed or, alternately, to fail? What is the interplay between leaders' power-driven interests, the domestic constrains on their preferences and the international context? We generally agree about the relevance of the international environment's influence on domestic affairs, yet the expanding wave of democratization continues to challenge the research community with the complexities of such an influence and its outcomes. National and regional idiosyncrasies, historical legacies, demographic compositions, economic developments, time framing and even geographic locations prohibit us from having a general theory of democratization and democracy consolidation that would allow us to understand, explain and possibly foresee the democratization dynamics of particular countries and world regions. Yet mid-range theories might provide at least some answers for many looming and newly emerging questions. While the democratization research community is engaged in an energetic enterprise to find answers for such questions, this book is an attempt to respond to some of them.

The aforementioned categorical evaluations suffer from two major problems. First, they overlook the major purpose of EU membership conditionality, that is, successful transformation in the EECs that involves EU accession as only a distinct milestone rather than an ultimate end. Second, they lack a scale of measurement and do not account for reform progress in cases where EU membership conditionality is absent or the EU factor appears only as a set of loose and soft recommendations. In addition, in a typical biased interpretation, authors often downplay or circumvent policy sectors where conditions are fulfilled. Hence, most of the literature so far has missed the main question: does EU membership conditionality help the EU membership–aspiring countries become more democratic? In other words, does EU membership conditionality minimize the risk of new entrants becoming politically unstable and economically burdensome to the existing EU members? Does it shield moderate politics from populism and nationalism? Does it strengthen democratic forces in the face of authoritarian downturns? At a glance, we can see that for each of the eleven new entrants from Central and Eastern Europe, namely Croatia, Czech Republic, Bulgaria, Estonia, Hungary, Latvia, Lithuania, Poland, Romania, Slovakia and Slovenia, the answer is "yes." Yet, the jury is still out as to whether this progress has been made because of the conditions imposed by the EU, the willingness of these countries to progress in the direction prescribed by the EU even without conditions imposed, or a combination thereof. Projecting this question onto the framework of the international dimension of democratization, Pridham (2000) questions whether these factors are dependent variables or not, or whether variations in the external environment itself can impose a set of confining conditions for internal regime change.

Many of the problems plaguing research related to the widening and deepening of the European Union afflict research into democratization, as well as into the EU accession of former communist countries as a tool for democratization. The most severe methodological breach is a persisting tendency to overlook the endogeneity problem that haunts research on conditionality in general and membership conditionality in particular (Vreeland 2003). This problem consists of the difficulty in assigning causal and consequential statuses to membership conditionality and reform results; while one can claim that membership conditionality can propel reforms, one can also claim that an initial willingness, on the part of leaders, to undertake reforms, as well as some early results, might elicit offers of help from the IO with which the country seeks membership. The very aspiration to join the EU unveils aspirant countries' willingness to embrace EU laws and norms, and therefore, to undertake domestic reforms that embody similar laws and norms. In order to resolve such a problem, I follow King, Keohane and Verba's (1994, 188) suggestion, and parse the dependent variable in different policy sectors and inquire in which of those sectors (or periods of reforms in those sectors) membership conditionality is either a cause or an effect. Therefore, rather than studying membership conditionality as an overarching policy, I study it as a set of policies directed to specific sectors and inquire whether they affect or, in turn, become affected by reforms in those particular sectors. This methodological solution suggests the study of sectorial institutional reforms.

Studying such political phenomena requires research designs that best fit the study questions (Johnson and Reynolds 2008). Following advice from Schimmelfennig and Sedelmeier (2005), research on the eastward enlargement of the EU needs to expand its comparative focus. This suggestion maintains validity even when we study the effects of eastward enlargement policies on countries aspiring to join the EU. Indeed, most of these policies are intended to affect structural changes in EU membership aspirants from Eastern Europe, but they cannot be the only factors that affect these changes. Structural contexts that reflect historical and demographic conditions, along with strong individual power-driven preferences of new ruling elites in the presence of institutional vacuums, might either enhance or constrain their roles. All of these variables should be taken into account, for such factors differ across countries. When inserted into the same equation in which EU membership conditionality is a presumed independent variable, they help us build some degree of confidence in our explanations of the outcomes of institutional reforms in some of the former communist countries that have yet to become EU members.

However, aside from the social context in which Eastern European reforms occur, we have another set of actors, namely EU leaders and institutions. They, too, act in response to their structural background. This situation calls for an overarching theoretical framework that would enable us to follow the same epistemology for building an argument that explains the effects of EU membership conditionality on Eastern European institutional reforms. I argue that consociational theory serves as an overarching approach to processes of EU internal integration and eastward expansion. As a research program, consociational theory emerged by the end of the 1960s and owes much of its reputation to the work of Arend Lijphart (1969, 1968) as well as a number of authors interested in small Western European countries (Butenschøn 1985; Daalder 1989, 1974, 1971; Huyse 1970; Lehmbruch 1974, 1968, 1967; Steiner 1987, 1974, 1970). While originally its contributors merely wanted to explain the establishment and survival of democracy in severely fragmented European societies, they soon realized that the theory could help explain political developments, as well as prescribe solutions for other deeply divided societies around the world (Chehabi 1980; Dekmeijan 1978; Dew 1972; Dix 1980; Lijphart 2004, 1999, 1996a, 1996b; McGarry and Noel 1989; O'Leary 1989; Pappalardo 1981, 1979; Tindigarukayo 1989; Tsebelis 1990).

Contributors to consociational theory claim to have established an elite theory of democratization that bears universal validity. According to them, while maintaining social cohesion in deeply divided societies is difficult due to centrifugal factors that tend to destroy the social fabric, elites who are willing to cooperate in order to keep their countries together might be able to replace majoritarian practices and institutions with consociational ones. The latter represent political arrangements that would accord veto power to each of the groups in the society, allowing them to block the actions of other groups that endanger their own interests. These social groups, called segments or pillars, manage to waive internal cohesion and delegate power to their representatives so as to enable them to conduct negotiations and forge arrangements with representatives of other segments. Close-door negotiations and under-the-table political deals produce what has come to be known as "consociational democracy," the epitome of stable democracies in deeply divided societies.

Since the days when consociational literature first emerged, some of its contributors have become interested in applying its toolkit to explain institutional arrangements at international levels (Lehmbrusch 1974, 92; Lijphart 1975, 123, 131). Other authors (Costa and Magnette 2003; Hix 1999; Gabel 1998; Taylor 1998, 1996, 1991; Chryssochoou 1994; Steiner 1974, 281), including Lijphart himself (1999), have tried to see the EU as a "consociational democracy." Even though such efforts have attracted criticism (Andeweg 2000), I argue that, contingent upon reconceptualization and, indeed, returning to its original claims and goals, the consociational research program helps to explain the motivations of EU institutions in shaping institutional reforms of EU aspirants from Eastern Europe. In order to reach such a goal, however, we need to resolve the tautological relationship between consociationalism as practice, that is, independent variable in the explanation of democratic stability in deeply divided societies, and consociationalism as a definitional category of stability. I argue that eliminating the concept of "consociational democracy" in favor of "stable democracy" in segmented societies will be practically cost free. In addition, we gain a priceless theoretical framework that will help us employ the same epistemological, ontological and conceptual framework to explain both the EU internal integration and its eastward enlargement.

Building on Costa and Magnette (2003) and equipped with consociationalism as an elite theory of democratization, I analyze EU membership conditionality as a set of consociational practices that aim at expanding EU democratic stability in Eastern European countries that aspire to EU membership. If, as Gabel (1998) suggests, EU member states parallel various social segments of a stable democracy, this notion can be expanded to EU membership–aspiring countries. Both EU and Eastern European elites negotiate and employ consociational practices to build and/or reform institutions in a way that conforms to the existing EU model and contributes to the democratic stability of the Union. By the same token, EU elites apply consociational practices preemptively to expand democratic stability to potential members beyond existing EU borders. These conditions reflect the political preferences of EU elites, but differ from one policy area to the other. At this point, elites of the different "segments," that is, EU countries and EU membership aspirants, enter negotiations, and we expect the outcome of these negotiations to define the pace and quality of institutional reforms in those countries.

While the proposed analytical framework will help us understand the EU's motivations behind membership conditionality, as well as why it works the way it works, we also need to know why the sectorial reforms in these countries produce the outcomes that they produce. In order to explain the varying pace and success of different institutional reforms in Eastern Europe, I propose a mid-level theory that comparatively analyzes such reforms in two democratizing countries in Southeastern Europe, Albania and Macedonia. Since this theory aims at explaining the role of the EU and domestic leaders' quest for attaining and maintaining power, its key interacting variables are EU membership conditionality, that is, the set of conditions the EU places upon those countries wishing to attain EU membership, and sectorial reform outcomes. Indeed, EU membership conditionality offers an excellent analytical opportunity since most EU conditions focus on distinct institutional reforms, thus engendering a wide range of comparative cases. Often the conditions represent general policy principles, but sometimes they represent specific policy preferences of the EU main and/or leading actors. The dynamics of reforms are discussed on the background of a set of assumptions of both the EU and Eastern European ruling elites' changing political preferences regarding different reforms over time and the fact that some reforms openly fall on areas perceived as sensitive to countries' cohesion and security, especially in ethnically divided societies.

I call this model a *sectorial contextual* approach to democratization; it serves as an alternative to the impossibility of a global, and even regional, theory of democratization. Theoretical explanations of the effects of EU membership conditionality on institutional reforms in EU membership aspirants cannot hold universal validity because of the unique nature of the EU and its relationship with neighboring EECs. Therefore, a sectorial contextual approach relies on a mid-level theory of democratization built on an elite approach to democratization and a rational assumption of political actors' motivations. Moreover, ample evidence shows that, often, the EU requires specific conditions, with different intensity and continuity, to different countries, which countries obey to various extents. The same conditions may produce a variety of policy changes and institutional reforms in different countries. I argue that whether or not a country has already consolidated its statehood represents a major factor that determines the nature and intensity of the EU conditions fulfilled by that country in order to become closer to achieving EU membership. Nations at an earlier stage of the state-building process are more likely to follow EU policy prescriptions than states with a longer history of independence and statehood.

I develop in detail the cases of Albanian and Macedonian institutional reforms. These countries share similarities that stem from their ideological affiliation with the Soviet Bloc and/or a Soviet-style society. Both these countries conformed to the nationalistic socialist systems, with loosened ties with the Soviet Union. These similarities, albeit with different nuances, might serve as a good explanation of these countries' state organization during communism, reforms that they needed to adapt and institutions that they needed to build during their transition to democracy and its consolidation. For Albania, there was no walk of life that did not need reforms. Macedonia began its institution building from scratch as an independent state through a process that included both state-building and democratic institutional reforms. From an economic perspective, communism, with disputable success, tried to transform these countries from agricultural economies of the pre–Second World War period to Soviet-style mega-industrialized nations. Meanwhile, the agricultural sector varied from totally nationalized in Albania to mostly private in Macedonia.

These similarities notwithstanding, the two countries have fared differently during various periods of their transformation from communist dictatorship and socialist economy to pluralism and open market economy. If we set progress toward EU membership as a standard, Macedonia would be much closer to joining the EU than Albania. Macedonia, after having negotiated the Stabilization and Association Agreement (SAA) with the EU in the summer of 2001, gained candidate status in 2005, applied for full membership in 2008 and was qualified for accession talks in fall 2009, but was repeatedly denied due to its standing issues with Greece, a EU member country. Macedonia also took a major step closer to the Union in fall 2009 when it signed a visa liberalization agreement with the EU.

As for the laggard Albania, the EU finally agreed to open negotiations for the SAA in January 2006, and the visa liberalization agreement was reached in fall 2010. However, since 2010, the EU has rejected Albania's requests for the status of EU candidate country not once but thrice, making its applications the first ones to have been rejected by the EU thus far, based mainly on the lack of progress in institutional reforms and a notorious lack of willingness of opposing parties to cooperate on those reforms.[2] The purpose of this book is to help explain the variety in outcomes that have resulted from institutional reforms in Albania and Macedonia, and thus understand the role that EU membership conditionality, on the background of the assumed EU and domestic leaders' political preferences, and aggregate structural factors play in these reforms.

With the collapse of communism, these countries are undertaking reforms in all sectors. In this book, I focus on only four: the constitution, local decentralization, judiciary and asylum reforms from 1991 to 2012. The very nature of each of these reforms helps to expand the factorial variance; constitutional, judiciary and, to a certain extent, local decentralization reforms involve policy sectors with significant implications in power struggle, while asylum reforms do not directly affect power competition. Such a variance would help understanding sectorial policy outcomes in the context of varying policy preferences across sectors of both the EU and Eastern European leaders. Analyzing reform process will require historical process tracing.

This book proceeds as follows: Chapter 2 establishes the theoretical framework and develops my model, which I call a sectorial contextual model because variables need to be analyzed within the context of a given reform; yet these reforms need to be studied together in order to account for reform spillovers. Chapters 3 to 6 provide empirical analysis of these reforms. Chapter 7 expands the analysis beyond reforms to power struggle, its impact on reforms and the role that EU membership conditionality as a set of consociational practices plays on such a process. Chapter 8 summarizes the findings and suggests future research projects.

Chapter 2

A SECTORIAL CONTEXTUAL APPROACH TO THE EFFECTS OF EU MEMBERSHIP CONDITIONALITY ON EASTERN EUROPEAN INSTITUTIONAL REFORMS

I am trying to study the dynamics of Eastern European reforms as an outcome of political actions by domestic leaders under pressure of EU membership conditionality. These developments suggest the need for a cross-level analysis of EU institutions and Eastern European leaders as the primary actors in the political theater. Ample evidence exists in favor of claims, raised by institutionalist authors, that the highly structured EU imposes strict constraints on its leaders as well as member countries. However, a different approach tailored for a loosely institutionalized Eastern European decision-making environment is needed (see, for instance, the *tabula rasa* argument of Elster, Offe and Preuss 1998). In these societies, traditionally low regard for institutions and the highly *personalistic* political style of communist elites suggest that the main actors in reforming postsocialist countries are not institutions but leaders as rational actors with clear power-driven interests.

Epistemologically, the assumed rationality of the Eastern European leaders derives directly from methodological rationalism. "Leaders' interest in attaining and maintaining power" means that reforms that improve their chances for power are preferable to reforms that do not, and the latter are preferable to reforms that hurt their chances for power. Even though this view simplifies leaders' human nature, it reflects powerful assumptions about their motivations, especially in loosely institutionalized societies, where domestic norms are scarce and leaders' appropriation of certain political behavior, as proposed by international organizations, might not have occurred and/or been consolidated yet.

Assuming EU motives behind policy preferences requires more elaboration. The highly institutionalized EU political environment suggests that leaders' quests for power are always under constant checks and constraints from institutions able to set their agenda, which allows for little maneuvering. Logical consistency requires us to assume EU leaders are as rational as those of Eastern Europe. Yet, presumably, the embittered European political experience of the twentieth century has forced them to search for other means of attaining and maintaining power. Rationally, European leaders might have already reached the conclusion that democratic stability would be better for their political careers. Institutions and norms were established to achieve such a democratic stability, and consociational practices have been employed to establish and run those institutions. Therefore, EU leaders are interested in safeguarding and promoting the European Union's democratic stability. I view the latter as having been built upon consociational practices, and suggest that the same practices guide the EU's eastward enlargement. New members should be acquainted with these practices and prepared to adapt quickly in an institutional setting built and run by such practices. The institutions of countries aspiring to EU membership should be shaped in a way that they can adjust easily and quickly within the EU institutional setting. Therefore, EU membership conditionality can be seen as a set of policies that drive EU aspirants via the implementation of policies that lead to institutions receptive to the EU's consociational practices. This process is simpler in EU membership–aspiring countries with unified societies, as domestic homogeneity helps them arise as unified pillars within the Union. In this case, the EU simply sets conditions to establish institutions that would be able to function in line with the EU consociational practices.

However, in EU membership–aspiring countries with divided societies, simply ensuring that their national institutions are receptive to EU consociational practices will not suffice. One of the preconditions to the successful application of consociational practices is the existence of societal pillars, and a divided society cannot serve as a unified pillar. Consociational practices would serve to unify such societies to the point that they would emerge as unified pillars, ready to negotiate EU democratic stability with representatives of other pillars. In this case, the EU requires the establishment of institutions receptive to consociational practices at two levels: the national level and the EU level. The EU demands aspirants with divided societies to implement some of the same practices that have brought democratic stability in some of its member countries that have similarly divided societies, as well as to the Union itself. Therefore, a divided national society should first emerge as a single pillar, and its institutions should become ready to function according to consociational practices at another level: the EU level.

In his article "Consociational Democracy," published in 1969 in *World Politics*, the Dutch social scholar Arend Lijphart promised to provide an elite theory of democratization that would shift the explanatory focus from the structural factors of pluralist theorists to the rational choices of the ruling elites. The article was a culmination of scholarly efforts during the late 1960s to walk away from the structuralism of the 1950s and early 1960s, which claimed to find sources of a society's regime choice among its socioeconomic and cultural features (Lipset 1968, 1960, 1959; Lipset and Bendix 1959; Smelser and Lipset 1966), and embrace individualist and institutionalist approaches that view policy change as a result of elite's behavioral change (Connor 1967; Bluhm 1968; Lehmbruch 1975, 1968, 1967; Lijphart 1969, 1968; Rogowski and Wasserspring 1969; Rothchild 1970). Consociational theory has tried to reconcile, on the one hand, the simultaneous emergence of "primordialist" sentiments, where parochial loyalties are able to disrupt modern democracies and, on the other, a turn from socioeconomic determinism toward elite voluntarism. All in all, consociational theory has been able to displace other elite-centered concepts and theories that preceded it (Lustick 1997) and became a fashionable elite theory of democratization for more than three decades, before its decline by the turn of the century.

Consociational democracy serves to describe "government by elite cartel designed to turn a democracy with a fragmented political culture into a stable democracy" (Lijphart 1969, 216). It has been depicted as an effort "to refine and elaborate Almond's typology of democracies" (Lijphart 1969, 207). Lijphart suggests a new category for democracies that manage to remain stable even in deeply divided societies: consociational democracy. This definition simultaneously highlights the stability of these democracies in segmented societies and provides a means of achieving such democratic stability. In cases where political parties, interest groups, media, schools, youth and other voluntary associations identify with subcultures, the concentration of social interests in the subcultural social segments exacerbates political conflict along the lines of segmental divisions. As the consociational argument suggests, in these societies, contending groups, after having achieved internal homogenization, rise as pillars with the elites at the top. The major novelty of consociationalism is its suggestion that decision making by these elites relies on compromises rather than majority rule; they reach out to each other and forge agreements and deals that will assure social cohesion. Other authors argue that, in order to reconcile incompatible and transitive preferences that characterize deeply divided societies, compromise should not serve as an intermediate solution, but as a packaged deal with each social segment winning on some issues and losing on others (Lehmbruch 1974).

Consociational theory has drawn severe criticism. Its critics have pointed to its conceptual, methodological and empirical pitfalls. Brian Barry (1975a) has highlighted the tautological character of Lijphart's concepts of accommodation and consociationalism, offering them both as explanatory variables and as descriptive categories, while van Schendelen (1984) joins Barry in dissecting the empirical pitfalls of consociational theory. In addition, Barry (1975a) points to the tautological relationship between Lijphart's claim that consociational democracies are fragmented but stable democracies and countries governed by an elite cartel. Arguably, this claim represents a shift from consociationalism as an independent variable to consociationalism as typology, hence allowing Lijphart's typology to substitute for Almond's; while the latter ruled out "any 'fragmented but stable' democracy," the former ruled out any "fragmented but stable" society not ruled by "government by elite cartel" (Barry 1975a, 481; see also Lustick 1997). Other authors have pointed to the tendency of the theory to degenerate, after continuous additions of other variables, in order to accommodate persistent empirical rejections of its claims (Bogaards 1998; Lustick 1997). Still other critiques have targeted its unclear division between dependent and independent variables, as well as between the theory's explanatory character and its normative claims.

Critics have also pointed to consociational theory's conceptual and definitional problems. They point out its lack of definitions for crucial terms ranging from "democracy" and "stability" to "plural society," "segmental cleavages" to "crosscutting cleavages." Lijphart (1977, 4) attempts, finally, to offer democracy "as a synonym of what Dahl calls 'polyarchy,'" not as "a system of government that fully embodies all democratic ideals, but one that approximates them to a reasonable degree"; yet this did not satisfy his critics. They point to the fact that his definition of democracy seems impossible to operationalize and have raised questions about the meaning of "reasonable" and "democratic ideals" (Lustick 1997, 104). Moreover, it is questionable how much of a polyarchy a consociational democracy can be when, in the former, competition between the elites is, more than anything else, essential, while in a consociation, the opposite, namely intense cooperation, is essential (Schendelen 1984, 32). As for the concept of stability, critics have noted that Lijphart's definition of it as something multidimensional that jointly and independently combines ideas such as system maintenance, civil order, legitimacy and effectiveness is imprecise and makes difficult the development of rules for distinguishing "unstable" from "stable" cases (Lustick 1997, 105). Even more criticism has addressed Lijphart's concepts of "plural societies" and "segmental cleavages." Many items on his long list of cleavages that define a segmented society characterize almost every society, making them generally useless. As one critic (Schendelen 1984, 31) asks, "can one say that some division is not a cleavage and that cleavage is not segmental?"

"Favorable factors" have been among the most criticized features of consociational theory, and the theoretical and empirical attention paid by consociationalist theorists in addressing such criticism has contributed to unveiling and exacerbating the theory's logical inconsistencies and, ultimately, its degeneration. A list of fourteen favorable conditions, as counted by Bogaards (1998), has been amended by Lijphart over the course of 17 years, obviously reacting to criticism or trying to adjust the theory to new empirical data generated from other countries and continents. The favorable factors lack theoretical coherence since they were not deductively acquired from the theory, but were inductively obtained from empirical tests (Bogaards 1998, 476; Steiner 1981b). Other contributors to the theory have added demands as they fit their case studies, resulting in a long list of ad hoc favorable conditions (Steiner 1981a, 315); some have noticed the static nature of the favorable conditions and their inability to affect change in elite behavior (Dix 1980; Bogaards 1998); still others have revealed serious mistakes in the quantified values of these requirements (Bogaards 1998, 484). Also, the lack of distinction in consociational theory between the favorable factors for transition and those for consolidation have generated criticism, since the factors that impact transition might differ from those that affect consolidation (Rustow 1970; Bogaards 1998). Lehmbruch (1975) tries to tackle this issue by defining those that generate consociational democracy as "generic conditions," and the ones that are conducive for its maintenance as "sustaining conditions." Lijphart (1985, 119) responds to the criticism by pointing out that "a factor that is favorable for the establishment of a consociation will also be a positive condition for its maintenance."

Consociationalist theorists have never managed to untangle the web of favorable factors as social structures and elite decisions at an individualist level, hence the theory's current tension between determinism and voluntarism. As Bogaards (1998) notes, consociational theory treats the favorable factors as given: fixed parameters of political life, the relationship between favorable factors and elite behavior, with the former affecting the latter (see also O'Leary 1989; and Dix 1980). Here consociationalist theorists split between the "orthodox" who consider the favorable factors as conditions, and the "latitudinarians" who consider them no more than helpful circumstances (Bogaards 1998, 487). Lijphart (1977, 54) himself has described the deterministic role of conditions as "helpful, but neither indispensable nor sufficient in and of themselves to account for the success of consociational democracy." That has prompted Schendelen

(1984, 114) to scoff: "the conditions may be present and absent, necessary and unnecessary, in short, conditions or no conditions at all." Later in his career, Lijphart (1984) increasingly inclined toward determinist factors, turned to other structural variables, namely pluralism, population size and the cultural inference of a British heritage.

Bogaards (1998) equates consociational theory's conflict between determinism and voluntarism with the conflict between the empirical and normative value of the theory. Indeed, other authors have pointed to dangers that the normative application of consociationalism might represent: as Barry's (1975b, 395) sarcastic apposite of the Irish saying "Live horse, and you'll get grass" goes, "[h]ave proportional representation and a grand coalition, and you'll become Swiss or Dutch." Lijphart's critics have warned against his inclination to focus more on the normative potentials of the theory than its explanatory ones (Barry 1975a, 1975b) or, as Lustick (1997) puts it, Lijphart's shift from good science to good politics.

Consociational theory builds on three types of variables: a sociological variable (the division of society into pillars or segments); an institutional variable (a proportional electoral system with some protection mechanisms for minorities); and a behavioral variable (the inclination of elites to negotiate compromises) (Costa and Magnette 2003). Implicitly, consociational practices apply simultaneously in three different worlds and result in the same conclusion for all of them: one of these worlds is run by social structures; the other by institutions; the third by elites. This is, indeed, how the consociationalist theorists have developed their hypotheses thus far: when elites fail to make decisions needed for a stable democracy, consociationalist theorists search for social structures or institutions to explain elites' choices. This is a logical fallacy since it searches for structural or institutional determinants within the actions of leaders who are assumed to be power-driven. One has the choice to remove elites from the explanatory equation and rely only on deterministic social structures as necessary and/or sufficient factors; however, consociational theory would then provide nothing new from the existing pluralist theories it claims to address. Consociationalism was thus born as an elite theory, and only there would its scientific vigor rest.

However, in face of such criticism, consociational theory has shown surprising resilience and, with disputable success, has even managed to expand its influence over international relations, especially as it relates to efforts to explain EU political system with a consociationalist model (Lijphart 1999; Bogaards 1998; Gabel 1998; Chryssochoou 1994; for a critique, see Andeweg 2000). Though initially interested only in how domestic factors affect consociationalist solutions for deeply divided societies, around the mid-1970s consociationalist theorists became more aware of the impact of international consociationalist models on domestic politics. Some authors became interested in demonstrating how stable democracies implement patterns of international decision making that could be considered concurrent with consociational practices (Lehmbruch 1974; Lijphart 1975). The case is too tempting to resist, and Lijphart (1999) himself has explored and endorsed the similitude of the EU with his archetypical consociational democracy. The EU was founded by its member countries' elites in an effort to promote stability and democracy in a war-torn continent; most of its activity continues to be conducted behind closed doors, secretly and with little to no accountability to citizens

(Hix 1999; Gabel 1998). Bargain-style negotiations are the dominant way of making decisions, and minorities are empowered by veto power. Since the Single European Act, 1987, unanimity among member states is no longer required for as a criterion for decision making, except in areas of high salience; yet both the Council of Ministers and the European Commission, which represent intergovernmentalism and supragovernmentalism, respectively, continue to apply consensus in decision-making. Some political scholars go as far as to propose consociationalism normatively, as a remedy against the "democratic deficit" of the EU (Weiler, Haltern and Mayer 1995).

Although those who offer a consociational interpretation of the EU claim that all four of Lijphart's consociational characteristics can be discerned, sometimes they offer different consociational features in exchange for each of these characteristics. Building a strong case in favor of the consociationalist nature of the EU, Gabel (1998) parallels them as follows: (1) grand coalitions rest within the European Parliament, and the considerable autonomy of EU member states in some policy areas substitutes for segmental autonomy; (2) proportionality, or even overrepresentation of the smaller member countries, lingers in the composition of EU institutions; and (3) the continuation of consensual decision making, even after the introduction of qualified majorities, constitutes mutual veto.

Moreover, the EU enjoys better prospects for developing consociationalist democracy because it has what most segmented societies lack: the European Commission as an integrative entrepreneur. Potentially, even the European Parliament can emerge as an integrative entrepreneur since, as Gabel (1998, 472) points out, one minor reform that would increase the agenda setting power of the European Parliament might also promote crosscutting cleavages. Arguably, the power to initiate legislation might promote transnational coalitions in order to lobby the EU agenda. In turn, these movements might successfully attract public allegiances and overarching loyalties (Gabel 1998; see also Chryssochoou 1994). Lijphart (1999, 34) viewed EU institutions as very close to the model of consociational democracy only when the EU is seen as a federal state: the Council substitutes for a high chamber, the treaty for a "rigid constitution," and the Commission for a "coalition government." Those who oppose that view either dismiss the topic altogether or point out the originality of the EU and the impossibility of its reduction to some variations of the federal model (Costa and Magnette 2003). The latter view the EU as a new form of consociationalism distinct from both the classic federal and unitarian versions; hence they promote it as a general analytical framework rather than an item to be incorporated into other paradigms. Costa and Magnette (2003) consider the transposition of the consociational model to the EU as conceptual overstretching and propose a separate category for the EU in the existing typologies of democracy. The very nature of social segments determines these arrangements.

In my view, promoting consociational theory as a general analytical framework holds significant potential in explaining not only the internal integration of the Union but also its negotiations with membership aspirants from Eastern Europe. The question is whether practices that brought the EU into being and keep it in business are consociational practices; I contend they are. The case of the EU offers a great opportunity to observe how elites seek to expand the institutional model for a stable democracy by proposing other polities adopt many of the same consociational practices that have been applied to their own political system; that is, proposing Eastern European countries (EECs) take on the same consociational practices that have helped the Western European countries to establish a stable, democratic EU. The purpose remains the same: to create a stable continental democracy out of a segmented continental society of states. We can view conditions placed upon candidate countries by the EU as efforts to homogenize the pillars of a given society and to strengthen, by grand coalition, popular attitudes favorable to the government.

Of all the criticism against consociational theory, the only one that we need to address for the purpose of this research is the question of a tautological relationship between consociationalism as a set of policies that aim to help establish a stable democracy in deeply divided societies, and consociational democracy as a definition of a stable democracy achieved through consociationalism. First, I suggest replacing "consociational democracy" with "stable democracy"; after all, that is the ultimate goal of leaders who want to keep together deeply divided societies, an already asserted goal of the EU leaders. Then I suggest replacing "consociationalism" with "consociational practices." These practices are not always the same, not exercised with the same intensity and not all of them are implemented in all cases. Consociational practices might be considered a toolkit for establishing stable democracies in deeply divided societies, but leaders might decide to implement only as many and as much as they need to achieve that goal. Such a move not only saves us from the epistemological confusion between causality and definition, but also alleviates our concerns about the normative burdens of consociational theory. If consociational practices help to establish a stable democracy, but the type and intensity of those practices remain contextual, then it would be almost impossible for anyone to assess in what cases which type of consociational practices should be implemented and to what an extent in order to achieve a stable democracy in a deeply divided society.

Hence, we need a separation between what Barry (1975b) calls "consociational practices" and the definitional term "consociational democracy," thus eliminating the tautological relationship between the definition of the phenomena and its cause. This implies that we talk about consociational theory but not about consociational democracy. Lijphart himself (1969) equated consociational democracy with stable democracy. His definition of democracy clearly states that it remains an ideal to be realized rather than something countries have experienced. It includes the democratic ideal and, implicitly, stability. Therefore, consociational democracy is simply a stable polity achieved through consociational practices. If stable democracies promote, as has been professed, crosscutting cleavages, this would "depillarize" segmented societies and thus increase the potential for social cohesion even under majoritarian political institutions and practices; under this logic, the term "consociational" becomes unnecessary. I argue that the cost of getting rid of the definitional features of consociationalism, namely "consociational democracy," is practically nothing when compared to more clarity in causality.

Gabel's (1998) argument in favor of the consociationalist character of EU democracy helps to reveal two facts: the EU can be persuasively interpreted as a deeply divided society; and the EU is a stable polyarchy. Moreover, its leaders have employed consociational practices to achieve that level of democratic stability. Yet the difficulty of transitioning from a postsocialist state to a democracy proves a great challenge to the stability of EECs.

Some of these difficulties originate in fierce power struggles between strong leaders, weak or absent institutions, deeply entrenched habits of mind, cultural legacies, or nation-building problems; these situations are very likely to produce instability, if they have not already. Assuming that EU elites are rational actors, we should expect them to seek to ensure that such instability does not spill over into EU member countries. It remains within EU's rational interest to resolve this problem by incorporating these potentially unstable countries into its political body. Thus, EU membership conditionality can be regarded as a set of consociational practices that aim at influencing institutional reforms in aspirant countries so the institutions that result can be compatible with those within the EU. However, before implementing such a theoretical framework for explaining the effects of EU membership conditionality on Eastern European institutional reforms, some conceptual clarifications are needed.

Obviously, Eastern European societies are interested in democratic stability, too; pragmatically, it has worked in the neighboring countries of the West, and they hope that it will work for them as well. For this reason, they assign to their rational leaders the task of negotiating accession into the EU. In these negotiations, Eastern European leaders are in a disadvantaged position. It is very likely that they will be required to implement consociational practices in order to address sources of political instability in their countries, but these may not be the only practices that the EU will suggest and/or hold them accountable for; after all, democratic stability, not the oxymoronic "consociational democracy," is the goal. Whether or not Eastern European leaders implement recommendations from EU leaders as policy prescriptions, during institution building or the reformation of institutions already in place, requires a consideration of their rational preferences.

Consociational practices are, thus, those practices that help to forge a stable democracy in a severely divided society by establishing government by grand coalition, proportionality in representation and mutual veto power. The purpose of EU membership conditionality toward the EECs, both those with unified societies and those with divided societies, is to establish institutions that will be receptive to consociational practices. The difference rests with the intensity of the conditioning: in the second case, EU conditions stretch over policy areas where EECs with unified societies do not feel much the pressure of conditionality, but in other places conditionality is equally severe on unified and divided societies. It should be expected that the EU conditions are more intensive in sectors where the application of consociational practices is particularly relevant in establishing and maintaining a stable democracy.

A consociational approach to the rationale of EU membership conditionality maintains that, pragmatically, the EU is expected to transfer its own practices to EECs; after all, what works for the EU should also work for its aspirant countries. Arguments outlined above point to the consociational practices of the EU. However, not all of the EU institutions are built upon consociational practices. This returns us to Costa and Magnette's (2003, 6) argument that "the nature of the institutions set up to reach compromises depends on the nature of the segment." Building such institutions requires negotiating between pillars, which in our case means between the EU and countries aspiring to EU membership. In an elite theory of democratization, "the nature of the segment" reflects elites' political preferences specified by that particular policy sector. Whether reforms in a particular institution will require consociational or majority rule, practices depend on the political preferences of both EU and Eastern European elites in that particular policy sector.

The EU offers conditional consociational practices to its membership aspirants at two levels. The first level is the EU level, which means establishing such institutions that will be receptive to the EU consociational practices. This is the case in countries with mainly unified societies, which are able to provide their elites with clear and legitimate mandates to negotiate with the EU during the process of EU accession and integration. In other words, building domestic institutions receptive to EU consociational practices prepares the countries aspiring to EU membership for the political life within the EU. The second level consists of mandating consociational practices at both domestic and EU levels. This is true of aspirant countries with deeply divided societies. At this level, EU conditions simultaneously establish democratic stability in these countries as well as institutions receptive to EU consociational practices. The first step aims at molding these countries into "pillars" and unifying them around their elites by providing them with a clear and legitimate mandate to negotiate with the EU. The second step is the same as the process implemented in countries with unified societies aspiring to EU membership: it consists of the establishment of institutions that will be receptive to EU consociational practices during negotiations of accession and integration. However, in both cases, EU membership conditionality should assure cohesive elites on the top of their society pillars so that in the end society pillars, already EU member states, deal with a single interlocutor.

This reasoning opens the way to my next point: theorization of the effects of EU membership conditionality on institutional reforms in EU membership–aspiring countries from Eastern Europe. Now that we have defined the nature of EU membership conditionality, established a plausible assumption about EU motivations behind it and laid out expectations about Eastern European leaders' policy preferences at each stage of sectorial reforms, we can build expectations for reform outcomes. Thus, the sectorial contextual argument consists of scaffolding a set of hypotheses about possible sectorial reform outcomes from a variation of possible policy outcome preferences on the part of both the EU and domestic leaders. Before that, however, let us have a quick look at how the EU and Eastern European leaders negotiate.

Negotiating Conditions

Europeanization literature maintains that EU conditions are not able to produce convergence in domestic policy structures and institutions, but rather result in "domestic adaptation with national color" (Dimitrova 2004, 7; see also Héritier 2001; Risse, Green, Cowles and Caporaso 2001). Yet this argument cannot help explain why, in only some cases, EU conditionality has been able to elevate EECs' policies and institutions to levels required by the EU (Peshkopia 2005a, 2005b, 2005c, 2005d). A plausible answer might be the inaccuracy of considering EU conditions as a whole package, without parsing out specific conditions in various sectors. The holistic view of EU conditionality highlights the dilemma of whether the reform results are the best EECs can achieve in situations created by a lack of resources and human capabilities, or whether Eastern European leaders purposely distort EU policy prescriptions in order to produce policies that will help them maintain power.

The often vague EU goals that cite a need for "increasing capacity" or "improving training" rather than stating detailed institutional preferences (Grabbe 2001) leave room for Eastern European leaders to maneuver and make tradeoffs among their countries' development agenda, their own rational power-driven preferences and the priorities imposed by the EU. Thus, since the EU's advice is specifically designed to promote particular aspects of governance rather than taking a holistic view of how administration should develop (Grabbe 2001, 1,023), Eastern European leaders enjoy a wide range of opportunities to negotiate not only the shape of their institutions but also the timing of their reforms, resources allocated to them and their impact on the life of the country. As O'Dwyer (2006, 221) puts it, despite the incentives that stem from significant development aid from the EU when EECs comply with EU conditions, the practice of regional governance reform in Eastern Europe has proven much more elastic than the expectation of convergence would suggest. In the case of the Balkans, the EU emphasis on conditions varies from rigorous assessments of compliance to more adaptable and pragmatic assessments for the sake of preserving peace and avoiding security risks, thus affecting the consistency of the process (Anastasakis 2008). Moreover, although the asymmetry of interdependence allows the EU to set the rules of the game of membership conditionality, the candidate countries have an opportunity to temper to some extent the impact of the EU's influence on the way they implement the *acquis* (Grabbe 2003).

The range of that opportunity might be widened by the fact that, arguably, conditionality only works as a carrot, not as a stick; hence, rewards for compliance are effective but simple, whereas noncompliance with EU conditions leads only to being excluded from external resources and delays in accession (Schimmelfenning 2007, 2005; Grabbe 2003). This particular feature of conditionality allows more room for Eastern European leaders to maneuver between compliance and delay, while implementing policies built around their own rational goals; and it can also balance somehow the aforementioned effects of asymmetry between EECs and the EU *vis-à-vis* the accession. When receiving carrots is more rewarding than delaying, Eastern European leaders will comply with EU conditions. The obvious result is that reforms have been implemented because of the desire to become an EU member rather than from a genuine support for the goals themselves (Kopecký and Mudde 2002; Gerskovits 1998). Obviously, we need to update the carrot-versus-stick notion, as well as better differentiate between carrots and sticks.

EU membership conditionality involves more than the EU simply counting how membership-aspiring countries have scored in reforms. EU membership conditions are unavoidably elastic, creating room for Eastern European leaders to maneuver during negotiation and thereby circumvent conditions or water down EU prescriptions, resulting in incomplete reforms. One such circumvention strategy focuses on making rhetorical commitments and not living up to them. Moreover, sometimes policy makers may be slow in implementing EU-prescribed reforms if they do not fit well with other demands or if they feel that there is time to implement them later (Grabbe 2001). The growing gap between word and deed among EU membership–aspiring countries is a source of constant frustration in Brussels (Checkel 2000; Grabbe 1999). As Brusis (2005) points out, the explanatory power of EU conditionality is limited to only those cases where the EU prescribes determinate rules that might then be transposed or rejected by a membership-aspiring country. Reducing the process of EU–EEC negotiation to merely checking items off a to-do list removes the focus from important parts of accession politics. Hence, we must refocus on assessing important institutional reforms that have been left outside the conditionality package or that have attracted only soft and inconsistent recommendations from the EU.

EU membership conditionality raises uncertainties that affect EU–EECs interaction during the process of preparation for EU membership. According to Grabbe (2003), there are five dimensions in this process: (1) uncertainty about the policy agenda that should be undertaken by applicants, due to the fact that it has not been fully determined for member states either; (2) uncertainty about the hierarchy of tasks due to EU's frequent shifts of priorities; (3) uncertainty about timing, stemming from a big gap between the period of reforms and the time when EU membership will be acquired; (4) uncertainty about whom to satisfy, a concern caused by the juxtaposition of its short-term dimension (which leaves Eastern European leaders guessing who the veto players in the EU are and what priorities they advocate) with its long-term dimension (which puzzles Eastern European leaders as to who will be the next emerging veto players and what their priorities will be); and (5) uncertainty about standards and thresholds, such as what counts as meeting EU conditions, which rises out of the EU's unclear definition of progress toward accession. These thresholds, or at least how they are perceived by Eastern European leaders, play an important role in reform performance but also increase ambiguities about EU expectations from EECs, particularly in areas where EU and Eastern European leaders' preferences clash. These ambiguities result in intense negotiations because they allow the EU to tighten or relax conditions according to the emerging communal and/or major actors' preferences; however, it also leaves countries aspiring to EU membership with "considerable discretion over their implementation policies" (Brusis 2005, 298).

Considering Vreeland's (2003) argument that assessing the performance of countries involved in IMF programs requires an understanding of the IMF's selection of countries that participate in such programs, one might ask: why does the EU impose certain conditions on some countries but not on others? Is EU membership conditionality an exogenous factor that leads those countries toward democracy and economic development? Or, in turn, is the political will of those countries toward institutional and economic reforms the factor that encourages the EU to consider their membership, hence triggering membership conditionality? It is difficult to distinguish whether and to what extent the progress of EECs toward democratic reform and market economy is a result of their efforts toward democracy and economic development or whether it is an effect of EU membership conditionality. In other words, the EU engages in membership conditionality only those countries that manifest willingness to develop in a direction compatible with the EU policy prescription; on the other hand, it has been widely argued that Eastern Europe emerged from communism by aspiring to the Western European/EU democracy. Obviously, resolving such an endogeneity problem should be a primary task of research on EU membership conditionality.

The surprising underestimation of such a problem in the existing scholarship unveils a bothersome misbalance between concerns about conceptual advances and methodological meticulousness in studying conditionality, with efforts to conceptualize the phenomenon and overshadowing empirical work to test related hypotheses. Most of the scholarship takes the causal role of membership conditionality at face value, thus underestimating the powerful role that domestic leaders' preferences for reform play in democratization. While dissecting the endogenous relationship between conditionality and democratization requires additional empirical work, King, Keohane and Verba (1994, 188) offer the methodological tools to perform such a work. According to them, we can parse one of the variables and analyze whether other variables precede in time various elements of that variable. I follow a slightly different path and parse both variables simultaneously: democratization becomes operationalized as a set of sectorial reforms, and EU membership conditionality becomes operationalized as a set of conditions sent to domestic leaders to address sectorial reforms.

The Sectorial Contextual Approach

The EU–EECs negotiations are more than a process of checking that the candidate countries have adopted EU law, chapter by chapter, page by page (Moravcsik and Vachudová 2005, 201). EU membership conditionality serves as a framework for these negotiations. While the EU has a vested interest in eastward enlargement, mainly nurtured by the general belief that it will bring peace and stability to the continent, arguably EECs have no choice but to join the EU (Dimitrova 2004). Since the asymmetric interdependence in EU–EECs relations makes bargaining-style negotiations difficult, sometimes these relations are characterized by a tug of war between their clashing priorities. The greater the incentive received by EECs for compliance to EU conditions, the easier and faster their socialization becomes.

EU membership conditionality does not apply uniformly over all policy sectors in all countries. The EU and domestic leaders vary in their political preferences over different policy sectors. In addition, it is easily conceivable that independent structural factors would have varying influence across the institutional reforms. Thus, theoretically, the interplay between causal factors for one reform will differ from those for another. Therefore, our methodological need to operationalize democratization as a set of policy sector reform outcomes suggests the subsequent need to analyze the impact of EU membership conditionality on Eastern European democratization at a mid-level theory; in other words, I propose theorizing its effects on sectorial reforms. I call this a sectorial contextual approach. It entails a separate analysis of the relationship of EU membership conditionality with each type of reform, followed by a comparison of sectorial results.

Rather than an overarching analysis of Eastern European democratization, the sectorial contextual approach considers a series of cases of institutional reforms.

For the sake of simplicity, I evaluate both EU and Eastern European leaders' preferences on reform progress in each sectorial reform as positive (+), negative (–) or null (0), thus excluding a wide range of other potential preferences over the related reform. I am aware of the limitations that such a simple assumption will impose on the theoretical outlines that I intend to suggest. Assigning values to EU policy preferences is easier, since the latter states those preferences openly. However, assigning Eastern European leaders' policy preferences is more difficult, and I have assigned these values only after a theoretical interpretation of what rational leaders' preferences in a certain reform area have been during a certain period of a given reform. A detailed empirical elaboration of institutional reform progress in some EECs will provide a much better and deeper understanding of the dynamics of such reforms, and from here we can obtain a better explanation of policy outcomes during the process.

Eastern European governments might undertake reforms mainly because of the domestic need for them (Elster, Offe and Preuss 1998). Zürn and Checkel (2005) acknowledge that membership can be used as an incentive only after a decisive change has already taken place in the country. In this case, national elites will have initiated reforms prior to EU conditionality and the sectorial priority of those reforms has been determined by domestic needs rather than EU conditions. Eastern European governments are more prone to undertake reforms regarding issues of major domestic concern despite the level of foreign assistance offered. Sometimes elites are proactive in implementing reforms that would bring their institutions in line with EU standards (Johnston 2001, 488). Presumably, a high level of government commitment to reforms should allow leaders to maintain power, hence the claim that *EECs that aspire to EU membership advance reforms, even if these reforms are not conditioned by international actors but address major domestic issues* (Hypothesis 1).

In later stages of institutional reforms, especially in cases that represent sectorial reforms known in advance to conform to EU models, aspirant countries might ask for technical assistance. Eastern European leaders are often constrained by limited resources and knowledge, especially in dealing with specific sectorial reforms where technical experience might be needed; Eastern European governments also cannot afford the luxury of concentrating on one reform at a time, but are forced to work on several different tasks simultaneously (Elster, Offe and Preuss 1998, 19). If EU institutions share the same preferences with EECs, then EU assistance to these countries further encourages and legitimizes reform. Therefore, *the implementation of reforms that satisfy the preferences of both Eastern European and EU leaders provide the best chances for the most successful outcomes* (Hypothesis 2). This is the ideal situation from which to observe the negative effects of communist legacies on Eastern European reforms when leaders work to mitigate, rather than to exploit, these legacies.

However, sometimes governments implement reforms that do not have any domestic impact but merely satisfy the preferences and needs of international actors and donors, especially when these reforms are financially backed by the latter and do not threaten leaders' hold of power. In this case, insofar as domestic governments lack any preference in issues addressed by these reforms, they remain *à la carte*; the resulting institutions wind up feckless. The fact that the prospect of Balkan membership into the EU remains distant weakens the strategic effectiveness of EU conditionality as an instrument of influence for the region, especially when combined with the lack of tangible benefits. This line of reasoning suggests that *reforms undertaken under EU pressure, but which neither satisfy nor oppose Eastern European leaders' preferences, are not viable and sustainable; institutions established by these reforms are weak and non-functional* (Hypothesis 3).

Some EU rules appear to be ill conceived, ill suited to transitional economies, inappropriate for particular countries, or excessively costly for economically and politically vulnerable countries. As applicant countries might need to divert funds from social programs in order to implement the EU *acquis* (Moravcsik and Vachudová 2005), painful reforms may result in serious threats to a country's stability. Economic restructuring affects the lives of millions of people who, as a result, may rise up in demonstrations, strikes and riots. Violent protests or regular elections could overthrow reformist governments and halt reforms. In such cases, in order to mitigate the pain of reforms and to pacify contesters, governments might slow down the pace of reforms. Such a deceleration may conflict with EU conditions as well as with the geopolitical and security interests of some of the major EU actors (Skålner 2005).

In the final round of negotiations, the EU might also impose some self-interested conditions; it pushes candidate countries to accept unfavorable terms for their accession, that is, to sacrifice some portion of the benefits stemming from membership over the short and medium term (Moravcsik and Vachudová 2005). As Sedelmeier (2005) points out, previous enlargement episodes suggest that a lack of flexibility by the EU can cause severe problems for the candidate countries and leads to disgruntled new members. Political tensions might rise from these clashes, thus jeopardizing reform. Therefore, we can expect *EU and Eastern European leaders' opposing preferences on reforms to cause political tensions and slow the pace of reforms* (Hypothesis 4).

Yet certain reforms remain outside of the immediate interests of both EU and Eastern European leaders. It is not that either party necessarily opposes these reforms; they are simply indifferent toward them. Of course, the 80,000-page communitarian *acquis* includes norms and procedures that cover almost every aspect of EU functioning. Aligning with them would require EECs to undertake reforms in all political, governmental, social and economic fields. However, cases exist in which the implementation of certain reforms might not be an urgent priority and/or might bring neither immediate harm nor quick benefits to either the EU and Eastern European leaders. In this case, we can observe a greater number of Eastern European and Brussels bureaucracies, which, unburdened by leaders' preferences, manage successfully to push forward these reforms (Grabbe 2003). This is more a case with policy sectors where EU member countries may have adopted different models of that specific institutional design, and the EU might not have been able to embrace a single model of institutional arrangements. In such cases, the EU may simply emphasize the need for institutional reform in that sector, but not impose a specific condition with measurable results. The EU also refers to conditions and technical assistance coming from other regional IOs. Hence, *reforms that remain beyond the EUs' immediate prescriptive conditions, and beyond domestic leaders' political preferences, might be either successfully carried out by Brussels and domestic bureaucracies, or else be conditioned and assisted by other regional IOs* (Hypothesis 5).

Some domestic reforms might fall outside of EU interest and be opposed by domestic ruling elites. This scenario may involve policy areas that do not directly affect political and economic liberalization, human rights or issues related to domestic and/or regional security and stability. The very technical nature of the sector might be the common reason for the lack of EU interest in that reform, while domestic leaders might prefer the status quo in that sector. Conversely, the opposition of domestic leaders toward such reforms might stem from either the need to hold onto administrative power in that particular sector or from the lack of unity among ruling elites for that reform. Sometimes, slow progress might occur, but often this may simply represent unsteady efforts to respond to the pressure of interest groups rather than to a political will to undertake the reform. *Reforms that are not within the preference range of the EU and that are opposed by Eastern European leaders will not proceed, or, if they have already begun, will be halted* (Hypothesis 6).

These hypotheses are compiled in Table 2.1 The positive preferences and outcomes are marked with (+); negative preferences with (–); and the lack of any evident preferences by foreign and/or domestic agents with (0). The policy dynamics are not the same across policy sectors. As we have seen thus far, across two decades, both EU and domestic leaders' sectorial preferences have changed and shifted from highly prioritized sectors to sectors that have been previously neglected. Policy dynamics in each of the sectorial reforms can be explained with one or more of the outlined cases. Thus, Hypotheses 1 and 2 best explain early constitutional and economic reforms, as well as their spillover to other sectorial reforms. Also, Hypotheses 2 and 3 might be helpful in explaining reforms in the asylum and immigration system; its early dynamics are more accurately explained by Hypothesis 3, while its later developments are better explained by Hypothesis 2; Hypothesis 4 explains most stages of judiciary and local decentralization reforms, as well as constitutional reforms that relate to them; Hypotheses 5 and 6, meanwhile, help to explain different stages in welfare, education and health care reforms.

Table 2.1. Hypotheses

Hypotheses	Interests of EU Institutions	Interests of Domestic Leaders	Outcomes
Hypothesis 1	0	+	Good results
Hypothesis 2	+	+	Excellent results
Hypothesis 3	+	0	Good but uncertain results
Hypothesis 4	+	–	Tensions and uncertain results
Hypothesis 5	0	0	Uncertain results
Hypothesis 6	0	–	No reform

Research Design

Assuming elites' role

I have developed my elite-centered argument on the assumption that elites are divided, and that their competing political preferences lead to their different policy preferences regarding institutional reforms. This view is consistent with the foundations of transitology literature as established by Rustow (1970), and with some more recent literature on democratization that empirically tests its hypotheses on EU enlargement and Eastern European transition (Mansfield and Pevehouse 2006; Moravcsik 2000) as opposed to Prewitt and Stone's (1973) concept of unified elites (see also Finer 1966). Under the conditions of divided elites, their preferences will determine the course of reforms. However, in some cases, there exists national consensus over the general need for reform and/or distinct sectorial reforms. In other cases, elites are so divided that no decisions can be taken, especially in cases when those decisions require qualified/reinforced majority (I turn to this issue in Chapter 7). Sometimes, the ruling elites fail to receive the opposition's consensus for introducing reforms stipulated by the EU. In those cases, by not being able to concede to the opposition demands/offers, the ruling elite prioritizes reform failure to EU membership. The terms "elites" and "ruling elites" are used interchangeably, unless specified.

The empirical test and data

To test my cases, I develop a process tracing analysis of four institutional reforms in Albania and Macedonia. I trace every step of those countries' institutional reforms, while, in the concluding chapter, I employ the case of Bulgaria and Romania to present a general assessment of the institutional transformations in these countries, focusing on a comparative view between the pre-accession and post-accession development. The process tracing analysis focuses on highlighting moments of policy shift and queries the role of causal factors on such a change.

Selection of cases: Reforms and countries

Welsh (1994) lists institutional reforms necessary for resolving the main issues of political conflict, focusing on the following areas: the reform of electoral system; the reform of the government structure (including issues of decentralization); the selection of a new political elite; the development of political parties and interest groups; constitution writing; the prosecution and purging of communist party officials and members of security apparatus; the restitution of past injustices; and the reform of the media sector. However, in order to test my cases, some institutional reforms that go beyond those mentioned by Welsh must be considered. Usually, policy sectors able to attract fiercer political competition generate either positive or negative preferences by leaders. Thus, I also analyze cases in which domestic leaders might not have any specific preference for a particular reform. Only sectors that usually do not produce conflict would fall outside domestic leaders' range of political preferences. Hence, I find it necessary to test cases of sectorial reforms that fall outside of those mentioned by Welsh.

Scholarly attention to democratic reform has been skewed toward those reforms that most openly and dramatically affect political competition, justice, freedom and equality, often downplaying the role that other sectorial reforms play in the quality of democracy and good governance. Reforms in education, health services, asylum and immigration, public administration and local decentralization have always attracted less interest than constitutional, economic, electoral and judiciary reforms. Such an approach leaves gaps in our understanding of the role that domestic and international actors play in institutional reforms because it leaves out of the picture significant comparative cases where leaders' political preferences differ from sectors more closely linked to the power struggle. Moreover, studying sectorial reforms separate from wider domestic and international contexts has often created a number of methodological errors, some of the most acute of which are the inability to observe spillover effects of some reforms on others and the contextual conditions that factor into such spillovers. Those contextual conditions would also impact the outcome of international assistance to democratization. Hence, the balance between the domestic and international contexts in which reforms are taking place, as well as the roles and interests of international and domestic actors, must be taken into consideration.

Empirically, I focus on two reforms that have attracted intense interest within research on conditionality, namely constitutional and judiciary reforms, and on two other reforms not often elaborated upon empirically, namely local decentralization and asylum reforms. Thus, my empirical test covers only constitutional, local government decentralization, judicial and asylum reforms. These reforms might not be sufficient to test all the cases; to test Hypotheses 5 and 6, for instance, I would need to inquire into heath care and/or education systems. However, as long as those hypotheses hold logical consistency, I see no need to discard them and hope that future research can empirically explore their validity.

The countries themselves, starting with similarities that stem from their ideological affiliation with the Soviet Bloc and Soviet-style society, both conform to the nationalistic socialist system that was developed by Josip Broz Tito in Yugoslavia and Enver Hoxha in Albania during most of the second half of the twentieth century as a tool of legitimacy in compensation for their break with the Soviet Union. Postcommunist Albania came out of a severe and isolated communist dictatorship, and began introducing economic and political reforms by the beginning of 1991. And yet, despite the fact it had been out of the Soviet orbit since the early 1960s, Albania never abandoned the Soviet-style state system. Similarly, Macedonia, a state newly independent out of the Yugoslav breakdown, comes from a maverick, nationalist communism, yet with a more liberal tradition.[1]

These similarities might serve as a good explanation of the institutional arrangements of these countries during communism and the reforms they required in order to adapt and build institutions to assist them during the transition to democracy. For Albania, no walk of life existed that did not need reform, while Macedonia, as a new independent country, had to start most of its institutional building from scratch. From the economic model perspective, socialism has tried to transform these countries from pre–Second World War agrarian economies to systems of Soviet-style mega-industrialization, while the agriculture sector varied from being completely nationalized, as was the case in Albania, to mostly private, as in Macedonia. Notwithstanding their different ideological nuances and geopolitical orientations during communism, both countries implemented Soviet-style governments and, from this perspective, they share more institutional similarity than difference.

From a cultural perspective, both countries come from the Ottoman tradition as opposed to the Habsburg tradition of Central Europe or the tsarist tradition of the rest of Eastern Europe (Rupnik 2000).[2] Even though the Habsburg Empire was not a liberal democracy comparable to the British model, neither was it a royal autocracy like tsarist Russia; rather, it was a *Reichtstadt*, a state run by the rule of law. Accordingly, the tradition of the rule of law has been inherited by some of the Eastern and Central European societies that succeeded the Habsburg Empire (Rupnik 2000). Although Rupnik does not discuss the consequences of the Ottoman tradition on institution building and the establishment of the rule of law, his observation implies that countries that inherited this tradition do not share the same view of institutions. However, categorizing countries according to this criterion might not necessarily be easy, let alone accurate. Albania gained independence in 1912 and has had enough time to build its state structures; Macedonia existed as part of Yugoslavia, first as a Serbian region (1919–45) and then as a republic (1946–91), but Yugoslavia itself inherited both the Habsburg values (Croatia, Slovenia and Vojvodina) and an Ottoman tradition (Bosnia and Herzegovina, Macedonia and Kosovo), as well as a longer exposure to independence (Serbia formally since 1868 and Montenegro formally since 1878). However, constant interaction with Soviet institutional values for 45 years might be considered enough to erase the effect of the previous institutional traditions in both countries.

From the perspective of pre–Second World War development and postcommunist economic reforms,[3] both countries share similarities and differences, with the latter prevailing. Albania became an Italian colony, while Macedonia ended up simply the most underdeveloped part of Serbia and Yugoslavia itself.[4] After the collapse of communism, Albania embraced a shock therapy program of economic reform, while Macedonia has proven reluctant to undertake radical reforms and remained laggard at least until 2002, when it began pursuing more aggressive economic reforms.

Another factor that, according to Rupnik (2000), has defined the success of transition in Central and Eastern Europe compared with Southeastern Europe is the ethnic homogeneity/heterogeneity of society. Here both countries differ significantly. A highly ethnically homogenous society, Albania is composed of 95 per cent ethnic Albanians, 3 per cent ethnic Greeks and 2 per cent Vlachs, Roma, Serbs, Macedonians and Bulgarians. In the highly heterogeneous Macedonia, the 2002 census showed that ethnic Macedonians represented 64.2 per cent of the population, ethnic Albanians 25.2 per cent, Turkish 3.9 per cent, Roma 2.7 per cent, Serbs 1.8 per cent and other ethnic minorities 2.2 per cent.[5]

And, finally, there is the international environment factor. Indeed, for this research, it represents a key independent variable. Four international organizations directly affect the region: the EU, North Atlantic Treaty Organization (NATO), the Council of Europe (CoE) and the Organization for Security and Cooperation in Europe (OSCE), but only two of them, the EU and NATO, can offer sufficient economic and security incentives to affect reforms substantially. As Grabbe (2001) points out, such an influence goes well beyond EU official competencies in current member states; it affects the reform speed, domestic elite adaptation with EU norms and the inescapability of EU membership conditionality for countries that aspire to EU membership. The process of EU enlargement toward these countries has developed through two different programs: European Agreements for Bulgaria, Romania and Slovenia, and the Stabilization and Association Process for Albania, Bosnia and Herzegovina, Croatia, Macedonia and Montenegro. However, although these countries might receive requirements of different intensity for different sectors, normatively EU membership conditionality indiscriminately affects their reforms.

Variables

I consider domestic leaders' preferences in a reform to be positive when the development of a specific reform helps them gain and/or maintain power and negative when the reforming process might harm their power positions. As my argument states, often leaders either undertake reforms or stop them based on power calculations. Some existing blueprints can serve as guidelines, though. Generally, we should expect leaders to be more focused on reforms during the revolutionary periods of "extraordinary politics," that is, the initial period of regime change when a broad consensus exists among both the political elite and the public on the need for reform. However, the rhythm of reforms slows during periods when politics become routine and therefore become "ordinary politics." In the former period, swift and sweeping reform can be undertaken without much delay as the large involvement of the public in politics overshadows power politics. This is usually a short period: four years in Poland, around three years in Czechoslovakia, sixteen months in Albania and about two years in Macedonia. Moreover, we should expect smooth reforms during the first one or two years after the return to power of a formerly deposed party, for example, a party that has lost power in previous elections, as usually those parties scramble to show a new image to domestic public and international partners. One should expect their return to power politics during the second part of their term in office. Moreover, the zeal of reforms wanes during any second ruling mandate. However, the EU might manage to change leaders' preferences for certain sectorial reforms by using specific "sticks and carrots." This was the case during the EU visa liberalization agreements when the EU managed to change, overnight, the preferences of Albania's and Macedonia's leaders in asylum reforms from neutral to positive.

Measuring EU preferences in Eastern European institutional reforms is easier since the EU states its preferences in official documents. Indeed, the very release of such documents for specific countries shows a positive EU preference for reforms in those countries. Therefore, before the release of the Stabilization and Association Programme (SAP) we can generally assign EU preferences in the Albanian and Macedonian institutional reforms as neutral. However, the launching of the SAP did not mean that the EU became equally interested in all the institutional reforms of both countries. In that case, I use documents and historical contextual analysis to map out EU preferences in specific Albanian and Macedonian institutional reforms. I assume EU preferences in some reforms to be positive, as when EU institutions openly and forcefully condition those reforms. By the same token, I assume EU preferences in certain reforms to be neutral when the EU remains ambiguous about the level, shape

Table 2.2. Albanian and Macedonia historical contexts

Country	Ideologic. Legacies	Institutional Legacies	Habsburg versus Ottoman Legacies	Economic Legacies	Ethnic Homogenity	International Engagement
Albania	A Stalinist, nationalistic, communist regime isolated from the rest of the world	Has inherited institutions totally incompatible with transition requirements	Gained independence from the Ottoman Empire only in 1912: long-lasting Ottoman legacy	A totally nationalized, centralized, isolated and backward economy	Highly homogeneous: Albanians: 95% Greek: 5% Vlachs, Roma, Serbs, Macedonians and Bulgarians: 2%	1) June 19, 1991: Joined OSCE; 2) 1992: Agreement on Trade and Commercial and Economic Cooperation with the EU; 3) July 3, 1995: Joined the CoE 4) June 12, 2006: Signed the SAA 5) April 1, 2009: Full membership in NATO 6) April 28, 2009: Applied for EU membership
Macedonia	A constitutive republic of the Second Yugoslavia; has inherited a more open attitude toward the West	As a newly independent country, needed to build institutions from scratch	Left the Ottoman Empire only in 1912: long-lasting Ottoman legacy	The most underdeveloped economy among the Yugoslav republics, yet with some freely developed economic sectors	Heterogeneous: Macedonians: 64.2% Albanians: 25.2% Turkish: 3.9% Roma: 2.7% Serbs: 1.8% Others: 2.2%	1) October 12, 1995: Joined OSCE 2) November 9, 1995: Joined the CoE 3) September 2001: signed the SAA 4) December 2005: Official EU candidate

and financial support for those reforms. The EU is expected to oppose a policy or reform if it goes against the prescribed policies designed by the EU; although such cases might be extremely rare, instances or elements of some reforms might face EU opposition. EU preferences can be plausibly assumed through the way the EU employs membership conditionality and allocates funds that support the EU accession. From a rational point of view, it is conceivable that the EU would enforce policies that allow EECs to achieve its *acquis* (preferences) and would only recommend, but not require, policies in areas in which it has weak or neutral preferences. But, of course, the best way to measure EU preference for a specific reform is to heed its annual progress report, wherein the European Commission assesses reform progress in the candidate or membership aspirant in question and outlines "homework" for the coming year. A careful scrutiny of the language of those reports can detect differences of emphasis across sectors and years.

I am aware that measuring the assumed EU and Eastern European leaders' preferences only as positive (+), negative (–) and neutral (0) represents an oversimplification of the value range that these preferences might cover. A consociational approach suggests that EU preferences in certain sectorial reforms in a EU membership–aspiring country is negatively correlated with the existing institutional capabilities of that country to absorb consociational practices of EU internal integration when it joins the EU ranks; namely, the less these institutions are able to absorb such consociational practices the stronger the conditions are. We should expect the conditions to be even stronger in the case when domestic institutions need to be receptive to consociational practices, both for establishing a stable democracy at home and for enabling the EU integration of the country. However, for the moment, I lack any other scale measure that would help in assessing intermediate preferences. I detect these intermediate preferences qualitatively, and employ the same methodology to trace preferences in the intermediate range. I admit that, due to the lack of indexes that accurately measure actors' political preferences in reforms, my categorization of interests might bear a certain level of subjectivity that is unavoidable in qualitative research.

Here I measure institutional reform outcomes, the presumed dependent variables, using both qualitative and quantitative evaluation methods. I use quantitative measurements wherever possible; this includes constitutional and judicial reforms where reform progress has been indexed by the American Bar Association. Moreover, for judicial reform and decentralization reform, Freedom House introduced an index in 2005. However, the only way to measure these reforms before the introduction of these indexes is qualitative. In order to fulfill this task, I use reports from the CoE and the EU. Reports of the Congress of Local and Regional Authorities (CLRA) of the CoE are also good sources to evaluate the reform progress in local decentralization.

Currently, we lack a quantitative indexation of asylum and immigration reforms in Eastern Europe; hence here I assess reform progress in this sector only qualitatively, mainly by relying on EU's annual progress reports. Before the introduction of the progress reports, UNHCR and the International Organization of Migration both commented about the quality of asylum and immigration protection systems in these countries.

Data

I rely on a large variety of both qualitative and quantitative data. One type of source is interviews, consultations and opinion exchange that I have developed with politicians and state administrators in countries in the region. My long-time experience within Albanian politics and my friendship with some Albanian and Macedonian politicians has facilitated the collection of such data. Usually, data collected through such interviews help to assess both leaders' political preferences and their perceptions about EU preferences. Other data come from research developed by domestic and foreign institutions and scholars. A major source of data is reports written by the EU and other international organizations about the reform process in the countries analyzed, as well as government statements on related topics. Also, domestic press in both countries provided invaluable data.

Conclusions

In this chapter, I argued that viewing the EU as a stable democracy brought about by consociational practices helps explain not only the internal integration of the Union but also its eastward expansion. Arguably, the EU has employed consociational practices to establish a stable democracy from the severely divided continental/regional society of states. Thenceforth, the EU has also expanded through demanding its aspirants to build institutions receptive to these practices. In the case of countries with unified societies, institutional receptiveness to consociational practices should rest only at the national level, that is, between the aspirant countries and the EU. In the cases of severely divided societies, these institutions should be receptive to consociational practices both at the domestic and international levels; at the domestic level, they help establish a stable democracy; at the international level, they help the process of integration of the country with the EU political system. Moreover, in socially divided countries aspiring to membership in the EU, consociational practices themselves are necessary to build such institutions, since their existence implies the existence of a stable democracy. I call this a consociationalist approach to studying EU membership conditionality.

EU policies meet varying reactions from domestic leaders; the combination of preferences communicated by the EU and domestic leaders for specific institutional reforms are key variables that explain reform results. Sometimes, some structural independent variables interfere, but actors' policy preferences mainly determine the outcomes. EU preferences are represented as conditions of membership. The question is not whether or not membership conditionality works, but under which circumstances it affects policy changes. EU membership conditionality is more intensive and consistent in cases where it encourages the establishment of institutions that are receptive to consociational practices through reforms affecting both domestic policies and sectors that are relevant in the EU integration. The latter affect every country that aspires to join the Union; the former affect only those EU aspirants with deeply divided societies. This explains why the EU does not require the same sectorial reforms in every country, hence my sectorial contextual approach. Afterward, the dynamics of the tug of war between the EU's and domestic leaders' political preferences in specific reforms helps to explain the outcome of these reforms.

The sectorial contextual approach and the consociational approach to the EU eastward expansion are intrinsically linked. While the latter explains why the EU instigates institutional reforms in countries aspiring to EU membership, the former explains why institutional reforms develop the way they do. Implicitly, the consociationalist approach to the EU's eastward enlargement explains the source of EU preferences in Eastern European institutional reforms, as well as the intensity of EU conditions in different sectorial reforms; the sectorial contextual approach helps to explain the outcome of the reforms when both domestic and foreign variables are taken into account. The consociationalist approach helps to explain the source of EU conditions and, by breaking down the rationale behind these requirements, also to evaluate their intensity; the sectorial contextual approach expands our understanding and explanation of specific Eastern European institutional reforms by adding to the consociationalist approach domestic leaders' political preferences about these specific reforms, as well as other independent structural variables that reflect the social context where a specific reform occurs.

Chapter 3

CONSTITUTIONAL REFORMS IN ALBANIA AND MACEDONIA: CONDITIONING CONSOCIATIONAL PRACTICES FOR EU AND DOMESTIC DEMOCRATIC STABILITY

Constitutional reforms in Albania and Macedonia represent a good opportunity to analyze EU–Eastern European Countries (EECs) negotiations as a process where the EU imposes on membership-aspiring countries consociational practices on two levels. The case regarding Albania is much simpler than that of Macedonia. Although Albanian elites were bitterly divided, the same was not true of the Albanian public. The almost half century of communist rule had played a major role in culturally unifying Albanian society. Shaped according to a Stalinist-type repression, communist rule in Albania combined Marxism with Albanian lore, and proletarian internationalism with local mythology, while dreams of industrialization and technological progress created a surrealist environment in which time stalled and everyone found themselves equally poor. Systematic purges within the Partia e Punës (PP) (Party of Labor), the Albanian communist party, stirred by a dictator growing increasingly paranoid with age, oppressed communists and dissenters alike. The strict system of *pashaportizim* (residence permit) thwarted any demographic movement outside the party's control and, as the pace of industrialization slowed after a rupture with China in 1978, population movement practically stalled.

Two to three generations of Albanians were born and died in the same residential site, and perhaps even in the same apartment. High mountains and a poor national highway system isolated the country's regions from each other, while the state-run internal transportation system was deplorable; movement of people within the country was very limited. In 1969, the communist regime managed to close all religious institutions without any resistance, for the population had never displayed any dedication to religion even in better days. Religious practices and institutions were declared illegal in the constitution of 1976, and the Albanian communists boasted of having created the first atheist state in history. Class division was abolished. Even though minority rights, which mostly benefited a tiny Greek minority in the south, were constitutionally promulgated, all minority members were equally oppressed as the rest of the population. The regime of Ramiz Alia, the new authoritarian leader after the death of Enver Hoxha in April 1985, continued faithfully on the same course. In sum, in the wake of the last decade of the twentieth century, Albanians found themselves equally impoverished and oppressed, incapable of revolt and confused about what should be done.

Political dynamics in Macedonia differed drastically from those in Albania. When, near the end of the 1980s, Yugoslavia first started to falter, Macedonian national conscience was not fully ripened; though, arguably, the Macedonian ethnic identity was the only one encouraged in communist Yugoslavia (Brunnbauer 2002; Palmer and King 1971).[1] The need to consolidate, once and for all, an uncertain ethnic identity led Macedonian elites to superimpose the notion of a potentially independent Macedonia onto the extant perception of a Macedonian nation subject to the state (Brunnbauer 2002). On the other hand, ethnic Albanians in Macedonia, a group that made up roughly one-quarter of the country's population, were experiencing a steady awakening. That process, however, remained painfully slow due to the fact that many of the Albanian elites had previously moved to the Albanian-dominated Kosovo, where ethnic Albanians had been enjoying political and cultural autonomy since 1968 (Lebamoff and Ilievski 2008). The two ethnicities, Macedonian and Albanian, lived side by side yet completely isolated from each other.[2] Most Macedonians worked in state jobs,[3] while ethnic discrimination kept Albanians out of such employment and pushed them to private business.[4] In fact, Albanians were generally discriminated against, including in areas like education, political participation, administrative employment and cultural life (Lebamoff and Ilievski 2008).

The deep political mistrust among the elites in both Albania and Macedonia led to a perception of constitutional reforms as little more than efforts to establish institutional settings that would allow the dominant group to wield maximum power and benefits. However, while in Albania the power struggle was between opposing political groups of the same ethnicity, in Macedonia much of the political struggle developed between the Macedonian majority and the Albanian minority; the former fighting for "the eternal rights of the Macedonians,"[5] the latter advocating the political rights of Albanians in Macedonia while silently dreaming for a unification with Albania. This may explain why, although in Albania political debates over constitutional reform were often heated, they did not lead to armed struggle as was the case in Macedonia. However, while Albanian constitutional reform was not the source of distrust and violent protest that it was in Macedonia, it did contribute to the simmering political climate of the country. Constitutional arrangements were thought to assist in establishing a system of checks and balances not only between the institutions but also the parties that would dominate such institutions. Thus, the EU's role in stabilizing Albania after the 1997 crisis consisted mainly of focusing intensely on the approval of a new constitution. The approval of the 1998 constitution shows how the political will of the dominating elites, combined with EU support for the process, can lead to successful reforms even under strong domestic opposition.

In Macedonia, constitutional reform involves concepts such as nationality, ethnicity, statehood, majority, minority, citizenship, state symbols and even literary metaphors. Several issues, such as to whom the country belongs, who should be considered local majority and under what circumstances, what the official language(s) of the country should be and what state, national and/or ethnic symbols should be used, needed to be addressed in constitutional arrangements. Since these issues often have had to do with or have been perceived as being related to the very existence of an ethnic group, and since fear of extinction has been a major element in formulating political responses to social processes in ethnically divided societies (Kaufman 2001), constitutional reform in Macedonia was only "won" through armed struggle and enormous diplomatic efforts of the EU, US and OSCE.

This chapter revisits constitutional reforms in Albania and Macedonia. The purpose is to highlight the effects of both domestic and international factors on those reforms, and to determine whether policy outcomes, that is, the sectorial reforms produced by their interplay, corroborate my argument. Since Albania was already a unified society, there was no need to require a constitution that would transform its society into a unified "segment" for its further negotiation with the Union; hence, the EU has had only peripheral involvement in the Albanian constitutional reform, and it is a stretch to speak of real conditionality. EU involvement was limited to the support of a process toward a constitution that would facilitate receptiveness to EU consociational practices during the accession process and continued progress toward further integration, subsequent to eventual membership to the Union. On the other hand, the omnipresence of the EU throughout the Macedonian constitutional reform process during the early 2000s, as well as its firm resolution to reach an agreement between the Macedonians and Albanians, shows the EU's need to impact the establishment of institutions that would be receptive to consociational practices at two levels: at the domestic level such institutions would produce a stable democracy; at the regional level they would facilitate negotiations and further Macedonian integration into the Union. Analysis of this process is especially important since, as we will see during the empirical discussion, constitutional reform was a key factor in the outcomes of other institutional reforms. After the successful completion of constitutional restructuring in Albania and Macedonia, these reforms became causal factors in sectorial reform.

The EU and Albanian Constitutional Reform[6]

The wave of democracy sweeping Eastern Europe during the late 1980s found Albania still subject to a communist constitution that propagated the unchallenged rule of the PP. The communist rule recognized neither separation of powers nor checks and balances. Hence, the Albanian constitution was intended to bolster and legitimize the communist rule, rather than establish a constitutionally republican political system. Self-isolation from the rest of the world and a widespread regime of terror associated with intensive propaganda helped Albania's communist clique to shield the country from the wind of change that has swept the rest of Eastern Europe since 1988.

By late 1990 however, the democratic wave had finally reached Albania, as evidenced by the Democratic Revolution of December 1990 and the ensuing first pluralist elections in early 1991. The most important issue that the first pluralist Kuvend (the Albanian legislative body) had to tackle was constitutional reform. In an attempt to reflect the changing Eastern European political context, the communist PP, which emerged as the victor of March 31, 1991 elections, had its own project for a new constitution. The PP's preference rested on the approval of a constitution that would allow communist control over democratization and liberalization processes. The opposing Partia Demokratike (PD) (Democratic Party) viewed this agenda not only as a communist effort to manipulate and ultimately benefit from democratization, but also as a way to block extensive reformation. The fierce political battle in Kuvend during April–June 1991 resulted in a political victory for the PD. This success owed much to paralyzing strikes throughout the country and massive demonstrations, which often ended up as violent clashes between security forces and angry anti-government demonstrators during most of May and early June 1991. The PP's reluctance to reform itself served well the PD's argument, and fueled popular protests in most of the major cities, crippling Premier Fatos Nano's capability of governing and led to its resignation on June 7. The failure of the PD to amass the necessary parliamentary votes to form its own government, however, as well as the lack of preparation by both parties to enter new elections, prompted them instead to enter into a broad base governing coalition known as the Qeveria e Stabilitetit (Government of Stability).

Establishing a new constitution represented one of the most important components of the June 1991 political agreement between the Albanian political parties. During its congress in June, 1991, immediately after the inauguration of the new government, the PP entered into a period of internal restructuring, beginning with its transformation into the Partia Socialiste (PS) (Socialist Party), which was associated with some cautious criticism of the past, and also stripping the communist old guard of all party functions. A new generation of opportunistic and flexible political leaders under the leadership of Fatos Nano decided to maintain a lower profile, consolidate the party and prepare to minimize any devastating political loss in the coming elections. The political vacuum left by the socialists' abandonment of the political initiative offered the PD the opportunity to go on the political offensive with the option of a mini-constitution, a temporary constitutional package named Dispozita Kryesore Kushtetuese (DKK) (Major Constitutional Provisions). The PS had no choice but to accept the PD's joint leadership in the country's constitutional reform for two reasons: first, its political power at the time was rapidly eroding; and second, the new generation of socialist reformers was becoming increasingly aware of the need for a new constitution built on a broader national consensus. The reform was ultimately successful both insofar as what the parties wanted to achieve and the ways they wanted to achieve their goals. While, on the one hand, all parties involved used the process of approving the DKK as a sign of good will to rise above their factional interests for the sake of national interest, on the other, the very content of the new legislation seemed to balance immediate needs with those expected to arise in the future. The DKK also provided the foundation for the Albanian transition toward democratic reforms in other sectors such as reforms of the parliament, the electoral system, the judiciary system and, to a lesser extent, local government. This process occurred without any interference by international actors, and consequently reflected only the domestic power struggle in Albania. The PD's proposal was aimed at taking the political initiative from the PS, as well as consolidating some of its recent political achievements, which included political pluralism, multiparty elections, institutionalization of private property, restitution of religious institutions and guaranties of fundamental human freedoms. This case supports my claim that domestic power games may still lead to successful reforms, even when international actors are not involved.

The PD's political victory with the 1991 Major Constitutional Provisions and its main role in the June–December 1991 coalition government switched the popular perceptions from fear and suspicion toward democratization to an overwhelming support for the PD. The revolutionary political atmosphere of the March 22, 1992 elections resulted in a landslide victory for the PD and its coalition of some small parties from all political wings. During the rest of 1992, the new PD-led governing coalition was quick to use its two-third majority in the Kuvend to pass constitutional amendments aimed at consolidating its increasingly authoritarian rule. The PD's leader, Sali Berisha, was elected president of Albania in April 1992, and swiftly engineered constitutional changes that would enable him to maintain control of the party, the judiciary and the newly established Shërbimi Informativ Kombëtar (ShIK) (National Intelligence Service).[7] However, when in 1994 the PD tried to gain popular support for a referendum for a new constitution, attempting to thus circumvent the Kuvend in which it had already lost its two-third majority due to party splits, its initiative met a surprisingly aggressive and successful resistance from the opposition. After a low-profile first year in the opposition, the PS had begun to increase its activity in spring 1993, and the arrest on corruption charges of its leader, Fatos Nano, in summer 1993 served as a turning point of the PS's political strategy. The growing authoritarianism of the PD government, the chaotic and inefficient privatizations and the cronyist nepotism that had plagued the PD since day one in office served the PS as powerful political tools to mobilize the discontented masses (Zogaj 1996). Already in the mid-term, the referendum became a means for both the ruling coalition and the opposition to settle scores. Therefore, rather than discussing the proposed constitutional draft, political debates were littered with accusations coming from the PD about the alleged criminal past of PS leaders; and, coming from the opposition, accusations of corruption, authoritarianism and treason to the national interest and the country's international commitments, referring thus to the government's already-uncovered secret agreement with Yugoslav president Slobodan Milošević, through then president of Montenegro Momir Bulatović to tolerate the violation of the UN embargo against Yugoslavia along the Albanian-Yugoslav border.[8]

The opposition had frequently asserted its willingness to compromise in the Kuvend for a new constitution. They claimed that, in order to consolidate a democratic future of the country, the current draft offered by the PD needed revisions, but more and foremost the entire process needed a larger political consensus that would include the growing opposition forces. Moreover, in a smart move to break its international isolation, the socialist dominated opposition also voiced the need to consult Albania's Western partners on any new constitution that the country would implement. Instead, bluntly overestimating his popular support, President Berisha made the success of the referendum his personal political battle, and an opportunity to give a major blow to opposition hopes for an electoral success in 1996. In turn, the opposition, driven by the same rationale, was interested in preventing a constitution that would significantly increase the president's prerogatives, as well as demonstrating that, during the last two years, the opposition had been capable of politically capitalizing on the Albanian chaotic transition and that it could rally supporters behind its causes. Ultimately, the opposition prevailed with a narrow negative vote on the referendum. The atmosphere of the entire narration surrounding the 1994 referendum on the constitution indicates that the Albanian elites were not genuinely interested in passing a constitution, but rather in having a mid-term test of the electoral weight of both sides that resulted in the failure of constitutional reform.

The referendum's outcome was a message to the Albanian ruling elites that any efforts to pass a new constitution would require compromises across the aisles, a political enterprise that President Berisha was not ready to undertake.[9] Moreover, the referendum's failure changed the PD's focus in its preparation for the national elections of May 1996 from efforts to motivate its voters toward a scheme to manipulate elections and fix their results. During the period 1995–96, a lack of interest in reform, in particular constitutional reform, removed the issue from Albanian political discourse; no attempts toward constitutional reforms were recorded during that period.

Albanian institutional weakness led to an utter failure of democracy during its first postcommunist transitory period, 1992–97, and a collapse of the state in February 1997. It first began with the May 26, 1996 rigged elections, which the opposition parties abandoned by early afternoon, hours before the closing of the voting process, as their activists were met with sheer violence from police, security forces and armed pro-government gangs. The election failure met initially with opposition protests, followed by an unprecedentedly violent government crackdown against them. However, after some initial endorsements and much confusion, most of the international observers joined the chorus of those who dismissed the elections as sham and the overwhelming PD majority as illegitimate. Pressures from the United States, a country with an overwhelming sway over Albanian politics, led the government to concede 40 out of 115 electoral constituencies for re-elections. That move did little to restore election legitimacy since the opposition, having asked for brand new elections, did not participate in this partial solution.

Thus, the PD's second term in government was undermined by legitimacy issues that would later help a downward spiral of violence to evolve and cause the collapse not only of its own government but of the entire state institutions. In late fall 1996, several Ponzi investment schemes that had been flourishing around the country since early years of the PD takeover lost solvency and began to collapse. In an effort to minimize what looked like a national financial crisis, the government intervened and froze the accounts of other schemes. However, it was too late for a government that not only tolerated the existence of these schemes but also took advantage of their existence by both spreading fear that its electoral defeat would mean their end and openly accepting their financial contributions. Therefore, it was easily conceivable to the public that the government was responsible for the existence of these schemes and should compensate the tens of thousands of families that had been affected. The government's refusal to compensate for those losses stirred public unrest, which, in turn, was masterfully exploited by the opposition. Massive demonstrations throughout the winter of 1996–97 paralyzed the country; the streets and squares of the Albania's major cities became scenes of violence as clashes between demonstrators and security forces erupted.

The events took an ugly turn in early February when angry protesters began to attack and loot military barracks and arsenals, expelled security forces from the cities and burned state and local government institutions. In a matter of few weeks, most of the country's territory found itself without any functioning institutions and public order sank in chaos and violence. The political crisis ended with a cross-spectrum agreement on March 9, 1997, and the establishment of the Qeveria e Pajtimit Kombëtar (Government of National Reconciliation), which was given the task of restoring order and preparing the country for the new elections in the summer of the same year. Subsequent efforts to restore order and public institutions included the establishment of a new constitution. The foreign actors who were interested in the country's stability believed that a newly invigorated constitutional reform process could serve as a means of creating cooperation between those parties already involved in the violent struggle that had contributed to the demise of the nation. Since the EU had spearheaded international assistance in reorganizing the Albanian state, it embraced the issue of a new constitution as one of the pillars on which the new state ought to be founded. At that point, Albanian constitutional reform became a matter of international, not just domestic, politics.

The June 29, 1997 elections brought to power a center-left coalition led by the PS and its leader, Fatos Nano, who was released from prison in early March only to return to public affairs as prime minister. One of the first tasks of the new government was the promulgation of a new constitution. Its drafting began with a special decision of the Kuvend in September 1997, but the work of the Commission for Drafting the Constitution only began in early 1998. It concluded in October of the same year. The commission was in fact an inter-party and inter-institutional committee co-chaired by the majority representative Arben Imami, the minister for legislative reforms, and a minor partner of the opposition coalition, Sabri Godo, chairman of the Partia Republikane (PR) (Republican Party). On November 28, 1998, Albania's Independence Day, a referendum was called to approve the new constitution. The PS-led governing coalition had a clear political interest in this process; it wanted to succeed where the PD had failed. Moreover, now the PS clearly viewed the process of constitution building as a way to gain political legitimacy from international actors distrustful of the country's communist legacy.[10] The PS, in turn, needed the support of the international community in order to institute the entire constitutional reform process. The latter had an embedded interest in such reform because, while deemed important both for forging constitutional order and cross-party cooperation, national stability would help regional stability in the already troubled Western Balkans. Thus, in January 1997, on the eve of the Albanian state collapse, the Parliamentary Assembly of the Council of Europe had called upon the government and the opposition parties to end the political crisis in the country and to prepare and adopt a new constitution through a process properly involving all parties represented in Kuvend.

The Albanian constitutional reform of 1997–98 occurred as a result of a well-orchestrated cooperation at a political and technical level between the European troika— the EU, the Organization for Security and Cooperation in Europe (OSCE) and the Council of Europe[11]—with the EU holding the political leverage needed to bring about constitutional reform, while the other two organizations assisted by lending technical expertise. Domestic actors were interested in a constitution that would fit the idiosyncratic domestic context. Their bitter experience with a powerful president compelled Albanian elites to envisage a constitution that concentrated most of the power in the hands of a more controllable prime minister. Additionally, the principles of a qualified majority underpinned several articles in order to secure a system of compromise between political actors in institutional matters that extended beyond everyday governance; hence, a constitutional provision was created that ensured the election of a president with three-fifths of the Kuvend's votes, but also stipulated that some appointments within the upper judiciary institutions and laws related to the judiciary also needed three-fifth majority. International actors were able and eager to offer assistance as long as these reforms were framed within the already well-developed Western constitutionalism. In January and July 1998, a Three Parliamentary Delegation (the OSCE Parliamentary Assembly, the Parliamentary Assembly of the Council of Europe and the European Parliament) visited the Albanian capital, Tirana. On both occasions, the delegation stressed the need of drafting and approving the constitution as a fundamental platform to build political stability.

Continental organizations funneled financial and technical assistance to the Albanian process of constitution drafting through two channels: first, the Commission for Democracy through Law (the Venice Commission) assisted with legal technicalities during the drafting process;[12] second, the OSCE established an infrastructure for communicating with the public and other domestic and foreign associations interested in the process. Such assistance was given by the OSCE-established Administrative Center for Assistance Coordination and Public Participation (ACACPP) in Tirana, which was financially supported by a US government fund granted to the OSCE for that specific purpose. The EU, as well as the German, Japanese and Norwegian governments, also gave direct financial and technical support (Imami 1998). From an institutional standpoint, EU influence on Albanian constitution drafting and approval cannot be considered a typical exercise of EU membership–conditionality policy, since formal conditions to Albania emerged only after the EU–Western Balkans Summit of Zagreb, November 2000, when the Stabilisation and Association Program for the Western Balkans was launched, and Albania accepted the invitation to join. However, knowing the persistent desire of the Albanian public and elites to join the EU, as well as the strong pro-American feelings among Albanians, it is easily perceivable that both the EU and the US could wield major influence on political developments in the country even without formal EU membership conditionality.

Arben Imami, former co-chair of the Commission for Drafting the Constitution and minister for legislative reform and the relationship with the Kuvend,[13] insists that the EU never applied any open or specific pressure on the Albanian government to approve the constitution. Indeed, EU concerns rested mainly on whether the constitution would meet the widely accepted democratic, EU-style criteria, now by and large known as the Copenhagen criteria. Interpreted according to my model, the EU was interested in having a partner segment/pillar that would be receptive to EU consociational practices. In case the EU and Albania ever decided to negotiate unification into a common "society," the EU needed to make sure that the negotiating pillar was playing by the same rules as the rest of the EU; that the Union was not importing problems from the newly partnered segments; and that the Union was exporting stability through its membership. Albanian willingness to abide by the rules of the game explains why there was never a need for the

EU to interfere politically in the process and why EU assistance consisted only of the tacit commissioning of the issue to the Council of Europe.

However, this is not to say that the domestic elites forgot their power-oriented preferences. The political will that led to the approval of the 1998 constitution occurred because the 1997 crisis produced an overwhelming anti-PD majority. However, after eight years of faltering center-left coalition rule characterized by continuous crisis within the leading PS, the coalition suffered an electoral defeat in the general elections of 2005 to the PD led by Sali Berisha, who also became the prime minister of the new ruling center-right coalition. Soon after assuming power, Berisha's egocentric personality led him into conflict with the country's president Alfred Moisiu, and later with Moisiu's successor and Berisha's former deputy in the party, indeed, his own presidential choice, Bamir Topi. Moisiu's mandate came to an end in spring 2008. Having failed to gather the constitutionally stipulated three-fifths majority for electing a new president, the PD had two options: compromise with the PS to find a candidate acceptable to both sides or dissolve the Kuvend and call for new elections. A new political crisis was in the sight.

Berisha's long-lasting enmity with Fatos Nano came to an end when Nano resigned from the leadership of the PS following its electoral defeat of 2005. With the mayor of the capital city Tirana, Edi Rama, at the helm, the PS began a restructuring process in order to become more appealing to younger voters. Despite his charisma, Rama had poor connections with the PS's structures, and his election as the chairman of the PS thrust him into a power struggle with segments of the party's establishment. In order to establish himself as the undisputed leader of the PS, Rama needed new elections. A parliamentary crisis over the election of the new president would have provided a golden opportunity. However, several PS representatives known to be supporters of Nano broke ranks and voted for the PD's candidate, Bamir Topi. The election of Topi killed chances for new elections, and Rama began preparations for the regular elections of 2009. In this uphill struggle, Rama needed institutional prerogatives that would consolidate his power within both the party and the leftist electorate, required the marginalization of Ilir Meta, a former prime minister from the PS, who split from the party in 2000 to form Lëvizja Socialiste për Integrim (LSI) (Socialist Movement for Integration), and was trying to carve his own political niche in the left by wooing PS voters.

The combination of Rama's and Berisha's preferences led to the last development in Albania's third constitutional reform. In the spring 2008 session, the Kuvend, with the united votes of parliamentarians from both PD and PS (115 votes out of 140), passed constitutional amendments that changed procedures for electing both the legislature and the president, as well as procedures for a confidence vote for the prime minister; shortened the mandate for the general prosecutor from seven to five years; and changed the electoral system from a corrected majoritarian system to a regional proportional one. These were obviously important changes since they affected some of the most powerful institutions of the country. These changes drew much criticism from some political parties, as well as from a loose movement of concerned citizens, intellectuals and semi-independent media. The entire procedure seemed fishy: the constitutional amendments had been proposed only few weeks earlier by a junior representative of the ruling PD who had no political muscle for such an action. The bill was immediately discussed in the parliamentary Commission of Laws, and presented for approval to the plenary session by both the Democratic Party in power and the main opposition party, the Socialist Party. The mysterious bill, which was debated neither in the Commission of Laws and parliamentary deliberation nor with relevant international actors, was swiftly approved, in spite of fierce opposition from the LSI and isolated representatives from the majority.

The constitutional change of the electoral system concerned a persisting problem of Albanian politics: its inability to hold free and fair elections. The constitution of 1998 laid out the principle of a mixed electoral system, a two-ballot contest, with one vote for the candidate and the other for the party. That system was abused by competing political parties, leading to distortions of the voter's will and producing voting inequality. As noted by the OCSE's Office for Democratic Institutions and Human Rights (OSCE/ODHIR) in its final report on Albania's national elections of 2005, the strategies conducted by some parties "undermined the constitutional objective of proportionality 'to the closest possible extent' of the electoral system, which remains open to abuse and should be reformed in an inclusive manner."[14] As the report went on, "the legal framework does not ensure that the Constitution's stated objective can be realized, i.e. to achieve a parliament composed of the principle of proportional representation."[15] Therefore, the report specifically recommended that the Electoral Code "should be amended to ensure that the objective of proportionality to the closest possible extent in Article 64.2 of the Constitution can be realized more effectively."[16] The constitutional amendment that introduced the regional proportional electoral system, Law Nr. 9904, April 21, 2008 was perceived to be helpful in indirectly reducing informal electoral donations and aggressive electoral campaigns.[17] A major negative ramification of the amendments was the practical expansion of the electivity threshold from 3 per cent to 25 per cent.

Reform of the Electoral Code became a constitutional topic and not simply a technical issue for two primary reasons. First, the PD, as the governing majority party, bore the brunt of the responsibility of working with the EU. The ruling party was therefore interested in reaching a consensus with the PS and other opposition parties for the approval of a new electoral code to show its fundamental commitment to improving election standards, thus likely ensuring a major leap towards EU membership. Second, the PS sought to eliminate or perhaps marginalize through institutional means its disobedient junior ally, the LSI. While Premier Berisha remained neutral about the clashes between the PS and the LSI, his eagerness to institute the reform is evidenced by his public declaration that the majority party would agree with any proposals submitted by the opposition parties, especially those coming from the PS, the largest opposition party. Moreover, Berisha was feeling threatened by the growth of the Partia Demokristiane (PDK) Christian Democratic Party, an insignificant electoral force, but a growing parliamentary faction seen as a refuge for renegade representatives from both sides. The same electoral system that would have benefited Rama against the LSI would have benefited Berisha against the PDK or other small splinters from his political block as well.

Reducing the number of parliamentarian votes needed to elect the president from three-fifths to a simple majority was simply a decision of domestic elites, with no input from the EU or any other foreign actor. Rather, Albanian elites were interested in those changes. The PS leader Edi Rama pressed for the reform in order to achieve two objectives: first, Rama needed to strengthen his party's cohesion and extend his influence within the PS parliamentary faction (as the mayor of Tirana, Rama could not be a member of the Kuvend); and second, Rama hoped to further marginalize his smaller rival, the LSI. Both Berisha and Rama preferred a winner-takes-all political game, with the majority having all the power needed to rule during its term, while the opposition acted free from any institutional responsibility.

More important than specific amendments, however, was the fact that the opposing parties were inclined to pass reforms that would make cross-party cooperation either unnecessary or impossible. In the long run, such a solution carried the potential for deep divisions that would undermine the very cooperation that EU-conditioned consociational practices sought to forge.[18] However, in the short term, a bipartisan agreement on such fundamental issues as constitutional reform would create a fake consensual political climate, which seemed to serve each domestic and international political entity separately. It fulfilled continual EU demands for the normalization of government–opposition relations and undermined politically destabilizing reactions by the opposition, who were already on the political offensive against perceived corruption of Premier Berisha and his family, themselves allegedly involved in an ammunition demolition scandal after an accidental explosion at a demolition factory in Gërdec, near Tirana.[19] The massive blast claimed the lives of 26 people and caused enormous material damage in the surrounding villages.

One of the amendments defined the conditions under which a confidence vote could be undertaken. It stipulated that a confidence motion against the prime minister could be held only if those who proposed the motion offered in advance the name of a new candidate. The real intention of that amendment was to make impossible any parliamentary vote of confidence against Berisha since, in the 2005–2009 period, his political adversaries could easily unite *against* him; yet due to their ideological diversity, they could not remain united beyond him, and hence could not agree on a potential replacement. Apparently, this was a PS compensation for the PD's concessions, which in turn would serve the PS proper in case it won the 2013 elections.

The most important feature of this constitutional reform was the overcoming of an age-old enmity between Berisha and Rama. Indeed, Rama had always positioned himself with the radical anti-Berisha wing, as opposed to the former leader of the PS, Fatos Nano, who had been open to political deals with Berisha—such was, for instance, the PS–PD agreement of 2002, also known as the Nano–Berisha Agreement. The 2008 agreement regarding the constitutional amendments interested the EU, which was pleased at the level of cooperation between the Albanian political parties. However, caught off-guard, and often unacquainted with the bisantinisms of the Albanian politics, EU officials either could not foresee the potentials for irreconcilable division between parties that the new constitutional amendments carried, or simply held naïve hopes that the case for such divisions might never emerge. The rational interests of domestic leaders alone drove the constitutional reform of 2008. The next day, the OSCE representative in Tirana, Ambassador Robert Bosch, praised the reform as a visible step toward the OSCE/ODHIR recommendations of 2005 (Shkëmbi 2008). Helmut Lohan, the representative of the EC in Tirana, agreed that the EC would analyze the constitutional changes, but seemed more interested in the fact that the majority of the Albanian lawmakers stood united behind these changes (ibid.).

A consociational interpretation of Albanian constitutional reform

Albanian constitutional reform represents a first level conditioning of consociational practices from the EU, that is, the establishment of institutions receptive to consociational practices. While these institutions would help maintain domestic social cohesion, their main goal is to facilitate negotiation for country's accession, as well as its integration with EU institutions after accession. Requiring a constitution that would create domestic institutions receptive to EU consociational practices would ensure that any domestic power struggles would occur within the confines of these institutions, thus preventing elite divisions from spilling over into the rest of society. However, our empirical analysis showed that in the last round of the constitutional reform in 2008, Albanian elites had been willing to compromise. Moreover, the current state of Albanian society shows that deep political divisions at the elite level do not reflect the feelings of the public, which is actually unified around the idea of the nation state. Contemporary authors point to religious harmony in Albania, but sometimes overemphasize north–south divisions. Such views reflect their familiarity with Albanian society through old textbooks and travelers' memoires from before the Second World War rather than a knowledge of contemporary Albania. Expressions such as "Ghegs" for northern Albanians and "Tosks" for southern Albanians are almost alien to Albanian generations born during the communist era.[20]

The unified Albanian society already resembles a pillar within the European society of states; hence, EU conditions focus on addressing certain elites' political behavior in a manner whereby they institute reforms that conform to current EU consociational practices. This explanation was validated by the Copenhagen European Council of December 2002, the Thessaloniki Agenda for the Western Balkans on June 16, 2003 and the Declaration of the EU–Western Balkan Summit in Thessaloniki on June 21, 2003, all of which recognized Albania, Bosnia and Herzegovina, Croatia, the former Yugoslav Republic of Macedonia, and Serbia and Montenegro "as potential candidates."[21] Since Albanian elites are willing to compromise, there has been no need for the EU to require consociational practices, so they simply watch and endorse the process, though technically it has been assisted by the CoE's Venice Commission.

Although EU officials did not seem excited about the political style of the April 2008 constitutional reform,[22] the EU had no choice but to accept it. Perhaps EU officials were not able to perceive the damaging potentials against consociational practices carried by the amendments, or maybe they had hoped that their damage to the receptiveness of Albanian institutions to EU consociational practices was distant and malleable. Though constitutional amendments reflected and served the power struggle, they neither directly contributed to nor undermined the processes of good governance or the better functioning of institutions. They simply created a set of rules by which to conduct the power struggle.

Since the EU had no vested interest in the reform, it supported the amendment with evasive, yet meaningful, rhetoric.

A sectorial contextual interpretation of Albanian constitutional reform

The case of the constitutional reform process in Albania leads to the conclusion that its positive results during 1991–92 and 1992–94 stem from joint positive preferences of domestic actors, albeit in the absence of any condition imposed by foreign actors. From 1991 to 1998, all of the Albanian governments had been interested in crafting a new constitution, since many reforms had been stalled because of a lack of an overarching constitutional framework. The PD's failure to pass a constitution through a referendum does not reflect a rejection of the idea of a constitution by opposition parties or the majority of voters, but rather a rejection of the PD's rule. Hence, because of deep divisions between the two main political parties, the preferences of the main opposing actors regarding a new constitution did not converge. In 1997, for the socialist–centrist coalition, drafting and passing a constitution became a political issue: where PD-ists failed during their five-year rule, they could succeed in their second year in government. Additionally, the EU, having introduced the principle of membership conditionality in June 1997 for Central and Eastern European countries, heavily supported the process of constitution approval. In this case, both EU and Albanian ruling elites had positive preferences. A revival of the preferences of the new majority that emerged from the June 1997 elections, combined with the increasing role of some international actors, facilitated the process of constitutional reform, in spite of deep divisions between opposition groups in government. And finally, from April 2008 domestic elites undertook constitutional changes based solely on power-oriented considerations, without any regard for EU opinions, and perhaps with sufficient information that EU representatives would not object to such changes.[23]

The empirical case of Albanian constitutional reform helps to confirm the hypothesis that the best scenario for instituting such reforms is that in which either the preferences of both domestic elites and the EU coincide or the preferences of domestic elites meet indifference from the EU. While it might seem a self-evident hypothesis, careful analysis of this case holds two major implications for the future of this research: first, it might help, at least, diminish or, at best, partially devaluate claims that EECs do not possess enough expertise and human capital to conduct reforms. As a wry anonymous observer who asked to remain anonymous told me, the April 2008 constitutional changes were agreed upon and passed during only two days' worth of cell-phone text exchanges between majority leaders and the opposition. However, the constitutional amendments were sufficient to alter some of the major principles of the 1998 constitution, such as the electoral system and the presidential selection system. The first one aimed at correcting representation issues while still allowing constituencies the chance to address their respective representative; and the second aimed at forcing agreement among parties by selecting a president with a broader support. Table 3.1 charts Albanian constitutional reform as affected by both the EU's and domestic leaders' political preferences toward the reform.

Table 3.1. Developments in Albanian constitutional reform

Period	Situation	EU Interests	Domestic Leaders' Interests	Reform Results
1991	Period of "extraordinary politics"	0	+	**Good results** and positive spillovers on other reforms. The approval of the DKK happened through a pact of domestic elites who were interested in some transitory constitutional arrangement, yet without any input from any international actors.
1992	The beginning of "ordinary politics"	0	+	**Good results.** The elites were divided since the opposition did not want only amendments of the DKK but a new constitution. However, the PD controlled the sufficient two-third of the vote in the *Kuvend* for the amendments. No international presence or assistance in the process.
1994	The constitution referendum	0	–	**No reform.** The elites were divided. On the one hand, the ruling elites were interested in passing the constitution in a referendum, and the opposition asking for its passing in the *Kuvend* as stipulated by the Major Constitutional Provisions. No international presence and/or assistance in the process.
1995–97	Period of political instability	0	0	**No reform.** As both the government and opposition realized the impossibility of passing a new constitution, they lost interest in a constitutional reform and focused on other political priorities. No international presence or assistance in the process.
1998	Restoration of state and order	+	+	**Excellent results** and positive spillovers on other reforms. The new constitution was passed since the majority of the elites, namely the ruling elites, managed to gain popular support on the process. Strong international/EU support for the reform.
2008	Constitution amendments	0	+	**Swift reform,** but fierce critiques from some elites. However, since an overwhelming majority of the elites supported the reform, it garnered legitimacy, and was rhetorically accepted by the EU officials. While it undermined some consociational practices (e.g. qualified majority as a form of mutual veto), it strengthened some others (e.g. established a proportional electoral system).

Imposing Two-Level Consociational Practices: The EU and Macedonian Constitutional Reform

While Albanian constitutional reform focused on the transition from Stalinism to pluralism, the constitutional reform in Macedonia undertook the massive task of building a nation state centered on Macedonian ethnicity. We can understand better that phase of the Macedonian constitutional reform as being propelled by constitutional nationalism. This concept refers to "a constitutional and legal structure that privileges the members of one ethnically defined nation over other residents in a particular state," which envisions a state where sovereignty resides with a particular ethnic group and where only the members of that privileged ethnic group "can decide fundamental questions of state form and identity."[24] Moreover, the struggle for constitutional arrangements in Macedonia was plagued not simply by hostility between two contending ethnic groups, the Macedonians and the Albanians, but also with mutual racist feelings aimed at questioning the very legitimacy of their opponent as a real ethnic group or autochthonous population on that land. Interethnic discussions in Macedonia center on political, demographic, historic and mythological topics. Thus, the view of the Albanians was (and continues to be) that the very concept of Macedonia as a political entity is a Titoist invention of the Second Yugoslavia emerging after the Second World War, intended to weaken Serbia within Yugoslavia, yet to prevent the society of the newly established Yugoslav Socialist Republic of Macedonia to develop any Bulgarian, Greek or, to a lesser extent, Albanian identity. According to the ideologists of Albanian nationalism in Macedonia, the Macedonian ethnicity was invented to justify the existence of the Republic of Macedonia within Yugoslavia. Consequently, while all the other nationalisms were oppressed in the Titoist Yugoslavia, Macedonian nationalism was tolerated and even encouraged.[25] Macedonians, in turn, argue against a solid historical presence of the Albanians in that territory, thus attributing the current presence either to waves of migration from Kosovo during the Yugoslav era or to Albanian high birth rates (Daskalovski 2006).

The entire constitutional discourse in Macedonia develops around ethnicity, and constitutional developments in Macedonia mainly concern interethnic relations. Thus, studying Macedonia's constitutional reform is tantamount to studying the Albano–Macedonian ethnic conflict that have haunted Macedonia since its conception. Debates over the national anthem, national flag, official language, local decentralization and state "ownership" that have been either non-existent or very low profile in most of the rest of Eastern Europe are part of the daily lexicon in Macedonian politics. Some of these issues have been resolved only through armed conflict and multifold international diplomacy.[26] Therefore, the constitutional reform process in Macedonia is probably the best case study of the effects of EU membership conditionality as a set of consociational practices. First, the interests of both domestic and international leaders are clearly observed and assessed; Albanians could expand their political influence through constitutional change; Macedonians preferred the status quo; and EU leaders sought to prevent war, learning a lesson from Bosnia and Kosovo (Ragaru 2007). Second, both the EU's proverbial sticks and carrots were transparent and easily distinguished.

Moreover, studying the Macedonian crisis is tantamount to studying the dynamics of the affairs of political elites within each of the major ethnic groups. The cohesion of

Macedonian elites has ranged from being united around the Sojuz na Komunistite na Makedonija (KPM) (Communist League of Macedonia), perceived as caring of and affirming Macedonian national interests in the wake of independence, to deep disagreements regarding the country's ethnic identity in the late 2000s, to confusion on how to tackle the domestic Albanian-centered crisis, as well as the international crisis with Greece. The Albanian elites moved from a peripheral role granted by the Macedonian majority during the process of independence,[27] to a mostly unified elite during the heydays of the Partia Demokratike e Shqiptarëve (PDSh) (Democratic Party of the Albanians), 1998–2001, to an increasingly fragmented elite ever since (Lili 2009; Sejdiaj 1998).

Macedonian constitutional reform in paper and practice: Dodging the bullet or baiting it?

The Macedonian crisis reemerged as the Yugoslav altercations unfolded. Parallel to their efforts to keep the Yugoslav federation together, the Macedonian elites prepared for a potentially independent Macedonia, making sure that the new state would belong to Macedonians.[28] Immediately after their power takeover in early spring 1945, communist elites negotiated for and shaped Titoist Yugoslavia using arrangements and structures that, arguably, offered symbolic satisfaction to the various ethnic groups in the newly constituted state (Schöpflin 1993, 188). However, in 1989 the Macedonian communist elite changed the Titoist nature of the Yugoslav Socialist Republic of Macedonia, claiming the new state for the "Macedonian people" instead of "a state of the Macedonian people and Albanian and Turkish minorities" as referred to in the 1974 constitution (Lebamoff and Ilievski 2008, 37; Daskalovski 2006). However, while contributing to the foundation of a Macedonian-dominated, ethnic nation, that act served as a red flag to Macedonia's main minority group, the Albanians, who saw the declaration as an ominous sign that their very existence might be at stake. As the very nature of the Balkan ethnic conflict would suggest, the Macedonian 1989 constitution enticed Albanians into the cultural battlefield of nation building, namely rejecting everything considered by Macedonians to be a cornerstone of their new nation state: the country's history, language, flag and autochthony. The only element of the emerging Macedonian identity that was not openly challenged by the Albanians was its name. Obviously, Albanians did not want to share a common cause with Greece, a long-time political rival of the Republic of Albania proper, a country held sacrosanct as the motherland of all Albanians in the Balkans and perceived to be the kernel of the tomorrow's Greater Albania.

During the 1989–91 period, both the Macedonian public and its leaders were too busy to heed Albanian grievances. While a collective nationalist hysteria swept the Macedonian public, Macedonian elites simultaneously prepared the institutional framework of the new country and scrambled to shore up Yugoslavia (Daskalovski 2006; Zimmermann 1999). We can easily detect the effect of this nationalistic tide in the radicalization of the rhetoric. Thus, in October 1990, the Executive Council of the Republican Assembly issued a statement on state and legal relations within Yugoslavia that referred to Macedonia contradictorily both as "the national state of the Macedonian nation founded on the sovereignty of the nation," and a democratic state of its citizens.[29]

The Macedonian elites' turn to constitutional nationalism began in the summer of 1989. On July 19, the Sobranie (the Assembly) passed several constitutional amendments. Amendment LVI clearly stated,

> The Socialist Republic of Macedonia is the state of the Macedonian people, based on the sovereignty of people as well as the working class, of workingmen and the self-administering democratic community of workers and citizens, of the Macedonian people as well as other members of nations and nationalities who live in it.

This amendment, significantly, removed the phrase "as well as its Albanian and Turkish nationalities," which had appeared in the version approved in 1974. This change was aimed at defining state "ownership" (to whom the state belongs) and succeeded in downgrading the status of Albanian and Turkish minorities from constitutive nationalities to unnamed minorities. KPM ideologist Svetomir Shkarić clarifies matters: "Macedonia is to be defined as a state, and the only bearer of this statehood should be the Macedonian nation. That is why the new definition excludes the sovereignty of the nationalities in Macedonia" (cf. Daskalovski 2006, 37). Daskalovski (2006, 37) notes that by amending the constitution, and thus preserving Macedonian interests against any potential manipulations by minorities, Macedonian communist elites intended to show that they cared about the interests of the Macedonian people.

The new constitution of Macedonia launched by the Sobranie on November 1, 1991 took one step further in consolidating the Macedonian constitutional nationalism. The preamble of the new constitution stated, "Macedonia is established as a national state of the Macedonian people providing full citizens' equality and permanent cohabitation of the Macedonian people with […] [the] nationalities living in the republic of Macedonia" (Hayden 1992, 659). Aside from dropping citizens' sovereignty, the implementation of the Yugoslav notions of "nation" for Macedonians and "nationality" for the others implicitly assigned country's ownership to ethnic Macedonians. Moreover, Article 7 of the new constitution declared the Macedonian language in the Cyrillic script as the official language of the Republic of Macedonia. Article 19 mentioned specifically the Macedonian Orthodox Church, while referring to no other religious community. Other provisions such as Article 8 (the use of languages by nationalities), Article 48 (the right of nationalities to establish cultural associations and public education in their mother language at certain levels of education) and Article 45 (the right for private education at all levels except the primary one) ensured that the constitution would apply the concept of nation state for Macedonians, and relegate to minority status any other ethnic groups.

Albanians interpreted these changes to mean they were no longer constituent elements in the state formation process, and hence not equal citizens of the country. The new constitution substantially reduced their rights, in contrast to the 1974 constitution; it introduced the concept of "majority requirement" regarding the official use of language, limiting application of the Albanian language only to municipalities where Albanians represented the majority, therefore practically abolishing it at a national level and in many municipalities where Albanians were a minority population. The constitution abolished group rights and ethnic political representation for any group other than people of Macedonian ethnicity, thus abolishing some political features originating from and specifically protected under the 1974 Yugoslav constitution.

The Albanians of Macedonia complained that the legislative process for the new constitution both in commissions and on the floor of the Sobranie was characterized by unproductive debates.[30] The constitution finally passed on November 17, 1991; yet, rather than clearing the way for a stable, functioning society and resolving accumulated problems, the constitution itself generated some of the very problems that would thrust the country into a violent ethnic conflict a decade later. None of the proposals offered by Albanian parliamentarians were approved, thus marginalizing the Albanian political factor, but also opening opportunities for its radicalization. Unsurprisingly, Albanian parliamentarians did not vote for the constitution.

Daskalovski (2006) has given a very detailed picture of Macedonian elite behavior throughout that process. By the late 1980s, various pro-Macedonian groups and associations pressured those who held political and intellectual monopoly over the Communist League of Macedonia, the local communist organization. Such groups pointed out that the political and human rights of the ethnic Macedonian minorities in Albania, Greece and Bulgaria were allegedly being systematic violated. The role of the Orthodox Church in political affairs surfaced for the first time, and the building of a colossal Orthodox cathedral in the center of Skopje became the symbol of a national renaissance and ethnic pride for both the population at large and the communist elite that endorsed the project. Aegean Macedonians and their descendants who had lived as a minority in Greece, but fled their villages during the Greek civil war in 1949, became vocal, demanding the Greek government to allow them to return to their properties. The International Reunion of Child Refugees of Aegean Macedonians staged massive demonstrations in and outside the country. The Macedonian communist elite also managed to persuade the Yugoslav government to pressure Greece into recognizing its Macedonian minority (Danforth 1995, 134–7).

As the political and social life of the country embraced pluralism, the newly founded political parties and citizen associations became increasingly radical. First, the Movement for Pan-Macedonian Action that emerged from the Macedonian Writers Union, and then the Vnatrešna Makedonska Revolucionerna Organizacija–Demokratska Partija za Makedonsko Nacionalno Edinstvo (VMRO–DPMNE) (Internal Macedonian Revolutionary Organization–Democratic Macedonian Party for Macedonian Unity) sought to capitalize on both the rights of Macedonians in Bulgaria and Greece and the status of Macedonia within Yugoslavia. The communist elites responded sympathetically, trying to ensure their political survival on the republican political stage and secure the position of Macedonia in an uncertain federal future. Thus, while, on the one hand, the Macedonian elites molded the citizen movement unleashed by political liberalization to their political needs, "tolerating critique as long as it did not directly threaten party interests," on the other hand, they "made use of the growing Macedonian pluralistic society to legitimize and magnify the Macedonian public support for their position in the federal level debates" (Daskalovski 2006, 28). As Maleska (1998, 159) notes, "the Macedonian party elite estimated that it would inevitably carry victory in [*sic*] multiparty elections" (cf. Daskalovski 2006, 28).

The entire process of Macedonian transition from the Socialist Republic of Macedonia within the Socialist Federal Republic of Yugoslavia to the independent Republic of Macedonia was conducted without any input from the large Albanian minority in the country.[31] During the Yugoslav period, the Albanians of Macedonia felt severely oppressed and isolated. While the Albanians of Kosovo were enjoying extended political and cultural autonomy in 1970s and 1980s as guaranteed by the 1974 Yugoslav constitution, the Albanians of Macedonia were confined only to minimal ethnic rights. Any political dissent was suppressed ruthlessly and, during the 1980s, many Albanian activists in Macedonia suffered long periods of imprisonment under charges of irredentism and separatism. Many members of the young elite moved to Kosovo where they could better develop their intellectual and professional interests; intellectual life amid Albanians in Macedonia died. Practicing Islam became the only intellectual outlet for a large portion of Albanian youth.

Thus, the underdevelopment of political structures among the Albanians in Macedonia left their elites unprepared, unorganized, inexperienced and slow to respond to the constitutional transformation of Macedonia. Albanian resistance to the establishment of a Macedonian nation state at the expense of Albanian political rights consisted of boycotts of several legislative actions, such as the referendum for independence on September 8, 1991, a parliamentary vote for the new constitution on November 17, 1991, and the promulgation of the new constitution in the Sobranie, January 6, 1992. In turn, the Albanians decided to unilaterally declare their own political entity in the Albanian-dominated western regions of Macedonia, namely, the Albanian Autonomous Republic of Illyrida. However, except for the formal act, none of these tactics influenced any further political action, and the impetus for further escalation diminished as Albanian political efforts focused on issues of smaller scope, e.g. domestic reforms in education and public administration. However, when in spring 1991 then president of Macedonia Kiro Gligorov succeeded in his efforts to build a "government of experts" representing all parliamentary parties, the Albanians participated. As it has been noted, the exit options in the early 1990s looked dreadful for the Albanians of Macedonia; Milošević ruled Kosovo, while Albania was preoccupied with recovery from its debilitating communist experience (Lebamoff and Ilievski 2008, 13).[32] Arguably, with the costs of repression too high for Macedonians, and the price of exit too great for Albanians, "peace was maintained by Macedonian and Albanian elites mutually adjusting the terms of their partnerships" (Hislope 2005).

Hence, the early years of the new Macedonia witnessed a paradoxical experience in which the elites became somewhat unified by fears of a foreign power, even though they disagreed on almost all domestic issues. During that period, all the major international actors had been reluctant to heed the rancor of the Albanians in Macedonia. In 1991, the US foreign policy was being reconstructed along with the dwindling preoccupation with its previous archrival, the USSR, only to end up with the isolationism of the early Clinton administration caused by the events of October 1992 in Mogadishu. As for the EU, its member countries were divided: German interests favored independent Croatia and Slovenia, as well as the need to show consistency with the already recognized newly independent former Soviet republics; whereas French and British caution reflected their historic alliance with Yugoslavia and Serbia. However, in an attempt to unify its policies regarding the faltering Yugoslavia, in August 1991 the EU created the Arbitration Commission on the Peace Conference on Yugoslavia, also known as the Badinter Commission headed by the French lawyer Robert Badinter. A respected constitutionalist, Badinter nevertheless had little knowledge of international law, ethnic conflict or the Balkans. In Opinion No. 6 (on Macedonia), the Commission recommended "the European Community accept the request of the Republic of Macedonia for recognition, holding that the Republic had given the necessary guarantees to respect human rights and international peace and security." However, the opinion met with EC skepticism and initial reluctance to accept its recommendations due to the Macedonia naming dispute (Lauterpacht and Greenwood 1993).

Under the given circumstances, "working within the system" remained the most viable option for Albanian elites,[33] and the Albanian political struggle focused on carving out an Albanian presence in Macedonian institutions in which their influence had been traditionally denied, such as the police, army, public administration and local government; and strengthening its role in institutions in which it had been weak. As a result, Albanians increased their participation in the judiciary system, education and armed forces,[34] visibility in the parliamentary struggle and assertiveness of their political representatives. Indeed, the latter became the real focus of their larger political battle that fiercely challenged the 1991 constitution.

That challenge began in December 1994 when the Albanian-dominated municipal councils of Tetovo, Gostivar and Debar established the Albanian-language Universiteti i Tetovës (UT) (University of Tetovo). However, it soon became obvious that ethnic rivalries would overshadow and trivialize the original purpose of the university, and would bring Macedonian police and protesting Albanians face to face. As police destroyed one of the UT makeshift facilities in the village of Reçica outside Tetovo, they were confronted by crowds of angry Albanian demonstrators. The resulting fire left one demonstrator dead and dozens wounded; the rector of the UT Fadil Sulejmani was arrested and later sentenced to jail time. The political struggle on the issue continued throughout the year 1995 as Albanian politicians continued to claim that Albanians had the constitutional rights to a private university in their own language (Article 45) and Macedonian officials who considered the university to be illegal. Moreover, following the "parallel system" model of their brethren in the occupied Kosovo, the Albanians decided to conduct lectures at the UT, although all acknowledged that, as it was, the university did not meet any academic standards (Sejdiaj 1998). Finally, the UT reopened in November 1995, tolerated by the obviously weary Macedonian authorities who saw no political benefits in prolonging that struggle (Daskalovski 2006; Marko 2004).

Other major showdowns happened in Gostivar and Tetovo. Candidates from the newly formed Partia Demokratike e Shqiptarëve (PDSh) (Democratic Party of the Albanians) won votes from some of the most important Albanian-dominated regions in Macedonia. PDSh was formed by the unification of a former radical faction of the mainstream Partia për Prosperitet Demokratik (PPD) (Party for Democratic Prosperity), which had splintered, with another splinter from a minor ethnic Albanian party, Partia Demokratike Popullore (PDP) (Democratic People Party), in 1994. Soon, the more radical stances and rhetoric of PDSh attracted Albanian voters and, bolstered by its success in the 1996 local elections, its newly elected officials began to challenge government authority. Albanian-dominated city councils of Gostivar and Tetovo decided to put the Albanian and Turkish flags on their city halls' facades. After two months, the Constitutional Court declared the action unconstitutional and demanded their immediate removal. A May 1997 ruling of the Constitutional Court allowing for the use of such symbols only in private preceded a law adopted by the Sobranie on July 7, 1997 regarding the use of national symbols. Parliamentary debates in the Sobranie lasted late into the day, revealing the irreconcilable divisions between Albanians and Macedonians on the issue.

On July 9, 1997, around 3AM, only a few hours after the new law was passed, police forces entered the city of Gostivar and removed the Albanian and Turkish flags from the city hall. In the morning, an angry Albanian crowd protested the removal of their flag. Responding to the appeal by the Albanian mayor of the city, Rufi Osmani, "to protect their flag with their blood," they confronted the Macedonian-dominated police forces (Daskalovski 2006, 73). The ensuing riot resulted in 2 fatalities, 30 people injured, including 9 police personnel, and 320 people detained (Sejdiaj 1998, 271). Police took control of city entrances and reinforced their presence on city streets and squares. Mayor Osmani and the president of the city council were detained and, later, arrested. Charges were also brought against the mayor of Tetovo, Alajdin Demiri and the president of the Tetovo City Council, Bedri Rexhepi.

In sum, the strategy of Albanian elites in Macedonia worked. During 1990–2000, their participation in public administration increased fivefold (Lebamoff and Ilievski 2008, 15). Emboldened, Albanians continued to contest all the pillars upon which the Macedonian nation state was built: the constitution, education laws, local self-government, public displays of national minority symbols and the ethnic make-up of the police, army and administration (Daskalovski 2006, 58). On the political stage, they continued to boycott parliamentary activities, national referendums and population censuses.[35] Now the Albanian community in Macedonia had gained a new level of political consciousness and organization; several Albanian–Macedonian professionals who developed their careers in Kosovo during the 1970s and 1980s returned to their towns of origin in Macedonia only to find "themselves locked up in an uneasy face-to-face with the Macedonians" (Ragaru 2007, 6). They brought with them a stronger national conscience, political will and intellectual credibility. Their increasing influence among the Albanian masses helped them to keep the Albanians mobilized through major popular demonstrations, projects of political autonomy and outright threats to resort to violence if necessary in order to achieve their goals.[36]

The confused and indecisive Macedonian response to the Albanian demands, as well as radicalization of the Albanian political elite, increased confidence among the Albanians that a strong response would force the Macedonian elites to compromise. Indeed, as the events of the UT and Gostivar demonstrated, Macedonian elites reluctantly acknowledged the need to negotiate, but unfortunately only after the situation was already radicalized (Marko 2004). The disjointed and belated Macedonian elites' response to the emerging crises, the reshaping of Albanian elites' rational calculations and changes in the regional political environment led to the violent conflict of the early 2000s.

As a United Nations Development Program (UNDP) survey held on the eve of the Macedonia's interethnic violence in 2001 indicated, 60 per cent of Albanian male respondents (aged 18–24) and 16.4 per cent of Macedonian males of the same age group found violence an acceptable political approach (cf. Lebamoff and Ilievski 2008, 13).

While "working within the system" remained the practiced policy, Albanian politicians always retained the option of working "outside the system." Following the violent reaction of the Macedonian government against the Albanians' unilateral decision to open the UT, many Albanian parliamentarians in the Sobranie walked out of the plenary. However, while PPD members returned later, others refused to return. Its leader, Arbën Xhaferi, threatened: "if Skopje does not heed our demands, we will build our own institutions" (Sejdiaj 1998, 62). Already signs existed that many Albanians in Macedonia were no longer willing to accept the status quo, and Albanian elites warned both Macedonian leaders and officials of European organizations of the simmering situation.[37] One of the most worrisome events was the so-called Weapons Affair; however, also violent clashes between Albanians and Macedonian security forces in Debar, Ladorishta, Ljuboten, Radolishta and Bit-Pazar, as well as bombs in Priljep, Kumanovo and Skopje, could also have served as alarm bells.[38] Yet, both Macedonian elites and officials of European organizations ignored the warnings and continued to see Macedonia as the "oasis of peace" in the otherwise troublesome Balkans.

The results of the October–November 1998 national elections brought to the fore the most radical fractions among both Macedonians and Albanians. The nationalistic Macedonian VMRO–DPMNE of Ljubčo Georgievski and the radical Albanian PDSh of Arbën Xhaferi forged an unlikely governing coalition that began to show surprising courage in its attempts to improve the plight of Albanians. The coalition functioned tacitly as if it was operating in a federal state, with the highest official in each of the ministries (ministers or vice ministers) practically serving as the senior official for the specific policy area in the respective ethnic territories (see also Brunnbauer 2002, n16). The VMRO–PDSh coalition tried to resolve many of the country's lingering problems, while initiating some economic reforms that would affect all citizens. However, the coalition frequently ruptured as both sides slipped into nationalistic rhetoric to maintain political legitimacy with their respective voters. Perhaps the gravest crisis between VMRO–DPMNE and PDSh occurred when waves of Albanian Kosovar refugees tried to enter Macedonia in the spring of 1999, in an attempt to escape the ethnic genocide that Milosevic unleashed on the eve of the NATO bombardment of Yugoslav military units and facilities. While the coalition survived the crisis due to the short duration of the Kosovo War and the return of Kosovar refugees, the real threats to the coalition emerged from the mountains separating Macedonia and Kosovo during the second half of 1999 through the end of summer 2001.

In the fall of 2000, small groups of ethnic Albanian guerrillas began engaging Macedonian special police troops in the outskirts of Tetovo, the capital of Albanian territories in Macedonia. Rusi (2004), who more than anyone else has probed into the history of Ushtria Çlirimtare Kombëtare (UÇK/NLA) (National Liberation Army), notes that its early origins remain unknown. Initially the guerrilla movement was simply a number of small, largely uncoordinated gangs composed mainly of former fighters of Kosovo's

UÇK/KLA from both Kosovo and Macedonia.[39] Yet, by the spring of 2001, these groups became unified under the military command of Gëzim Ostreni and political leadership of Ali Ahmeti. Soon, the UÇK/NLA found large support among the disgruntled Albanian youth in Macedonia and a vast military arsenal in Kosovo and Albania at loose.[40] The public began to learn more about the UÇK/NLA after they attacked on January 23, 2001 a police station in Tearce, Tetovo region (Rusi 2004).

Many commentators overlook the domestic factors that caused the Macedonian conflict and tend to see it as imported from abroad. Some consider it as an aggression from Kosovo, and others view it more as a spillover from battles fought by ethnic Albanians in Southern Serbia. However, Ilievski (2007, 6), a Macedonian author, gives this more complex and accurate explanation:

Without weapons smuggled from Albania in 1997 and from Kosovo in 1999, without organizational and logistical support from Kosovo, and without unrestricted crossing of the Macedonia-Kosovo border, the armed conflict of 2001 could not have occurred. Nevertheless, once the conflict began, organizational and logistical support from Kosovo alone would not have achieved the effect it did if ethnic Albanians within Macedonia had not joined the insurgency as well.

Initially, the group's goals and organizational structure were vague, but later they became consolidated along with their military might. In one of its first political statements, the UÇK/NLA committed itself to targeting "the uniform of the Macedonian occupier until the Albanian people are freed." However, a few months later, contradictory messages began to air.[41] Perhaps Communiqué No. 4, which followed an attack in Tearce, showed that the UÇK/NLA was becoming unified and its political goals streamlined. The communiqué pointed out that, "so far, the Albanians in Macedonia have sought our rights through dialogue in a constitutional and peaceful way" but "our demands have been ignored." Outlining the UÇK/NLA's ultimate goal, the communiqué stated that the UÇK/NLA "will fight until Macedonia constitutionally becomes a Macedonian–Albanian, or Albanian–Macedonian, state," and concluded: "we are in favour of preserving Macedonia's sovereignty and territorial integrity. We respect NATO's interests in Macedonia and especially those of the USA."

Although by the end of winter, 2000–2001, Macedonian authorities announced the defeat of the rebels (Daskalovski 2006), in the spring of 2001 guerrillas swept the western part of the country. By mid-summer, they took control of most of the Albanian territories, including Aračinovo (Haraçinë), putting most of the Macedonian central institutions and industries around the capital within range of their mortars and surrounding Skopje. At that point, the Albanian guerrillas had already established a permanent military presence in almost all the relevant sites with a majority Albanian population.

Not surprisingly, the Albanian elites' strategy of combining "working within the system" with threats to opt out of the system altogether sent mixed signals to the public. On the one hand, the process of the expansion of Albanian rights during the VMRO–PDSh coalition rule had demonstrated that the Macedonian elites were not unified (rather they were confused about how to advance their idea of ethnic rights and the multi-ethnic state), and that they could conceivably compromise under certain conditions. On the other hand, the nationalistic and often radical rhetoric of the Albanian representatives in government signaled that the Albanians of Macedonia were not really interested in a unified state (Ragaru 2007). The same cannot be claimed for Macedonian elites: the need for social peace during harsh periods of economic austerity, a long-lasting standoff with Greece about the country's official name, and the country's bid for EU membership compelled the nationalistic VMRO–DPMNE to pacify the Albanians with some concessions. While certainly the VMRO–DPMNE had not shirked in its commitment to promoting Macedonia as the nation state of the Macedonian people, its concessions toward the Albanians were read by both Albanians and Macedonian political opposition as signs of weakness.

International reaction to the Macedonian crisis was remarkably swift, determined and well coordinated. Initially, the sudden appearance and growth of the UÇK/ NLA came as an embarrassment for Macedonia's international partners, who had believed that the country had already established sustainable interethnic relations and, consequentially, political stability (Mincheva 2009). What is now commonly known as international community, was indeed a politico-diplomatic concert of the EU, US, NATO and OSCE, with each of the actors performing various parts of a strategy that combined consociational practices and "carrot-and-stick" approach to different actors. Thus, the EU's effectiveness rested on the seductive offer of EU membership that concerned Macedonians more than Albanians. However, US and NATO effectiveness was based mainly on their capacity to credibly bash Albanians; indeed, the US's pivotal political and military role in NATO attacks against Serbian forces during the Kosovo conflict has ensured obedience to the US and NATO from the Albanian-dominated government of Kosovo, the government of Albania proper and the Albanian guerrillas in Macedonia.[42] Both the EU and NATO seduced Macedonian elites with membership as a "carrot" and the refusal of membership as a "stick." And finally, the OSCE, trying to carve a role for itself, offered diplomatic and logistic assistance through its office in Skopje.

Specifically, the EU offered "carrots" to Macedonians when on April 9, 2001, as the crisis was exacerbating, the Union invited Macedonia to sign the Association and Stabilization Agreement, even though the country was far from fulfilling any criteria in both stability and associative capabilities. The US rattled "sticks" against Albanian fighters. Executive Order 13219, issued June 26, 2001, ordered "the blocking of property and interests in property," and "the prohibition of the making or receiving by a United States person of any contribution or provision of funds, goods, or services" for a list of names with the UÇK/NLA's most prominent political leaders and military commanders, as well as some well-known Albanian Kosovar political and public figures.[43] As Garton Ash (2001) reveals from his November 2001 interview with UÇK/NLA leader Ali Ahmeti, the latter was mindful of the existence of the Geneva Convention and the Tribunal of Hague.

The EU took over a leading role in resolving the conflict. As PDSh leader Arbën Xhaferi stated, troops and weapons did not stop violence; yet violence was stopped by "the hope provided by the EU that it would intervene in starting political negotiations" (cf. Daskalovski 2006, 107). On March 19, 2001, the EU foreign ministers agreed on a package of measures that would provide assistance to Macedonia, including assistance on border control and the promotion of interethnic relations. At the European Council of Stockholm, March 23–24, 2001, the EU sent supportive messages to Macedonian leaders and warning notes to Albanian leaders both in Macedonia and in Kosovo. To President Trajkovski and the Macedonian government, the EU affirmed its "solidarity" and urged them "to continue to respond with restraint." The EU asserted its support for "the sovereignty and territorial integrity of FYROM and the inviolability of borders in conformity with OSCE principles."[44] EU member countries also stated their determination to pursue collective and individual efforts in close cooperation with NATO to help the authorities cope with the present situation. Most importantly, the EU noted that "effective internal political reforms and *consolidation of a true multi-ethnic society are indispensable*" (emphasis added).

Wagging "the stick," the Union reaffirmed strongly that "there is no future in our Europe for those who follow the path of intolerance, nationalism and violence," that "the Union will not give assistance to those who take this course," and that it "will only support those who choose clearly peace, democracy reconciliation and regional cooperation." Offering "the carrot," the Council iterated that, as previously agreed during the EU–Western Balkan Summit of Zagreb, November 24, 2004, Macedonia would be "the first state of the region to be linked to the European Union through the Stabilisation and Association Agreement [to] be signed on April 9."

Financial pledges ensued to ensure the sweetness of the "carrots": the EU pledged to Macedonia a financial package of 40 million Euros through its Community Assistance for Reconstruction, Development and Stabilization (CARDS) program for the Western Balkans; and the IMF promised some 50 million Euros in macro-financial grants and loans, conditional to a standby agreement between the International Monetary Fund (IMF) and Macedonia. On April 5, the Union granted the country the status of most favored nation; and on April 9, Macedonia became the first country included in the so-called Stabilization and Association zone to sign the Stabilization and Association Agreement with the EU (Daskalovski 2006, 108). Meanwhile, EU employed "sticks" as well, both during negotiations to reach an agreement for a political solution and during political debates over the implementation of the Ohrid Agreement. While at the beginning of the conflict Western governments firmly criticized the UÇK/NLA, they also recognized the need for a political solution to the problematic status of Albanians in Macedonia.

The EU "carrot-and-stick" approach continued even after the signing of the Ohrid Agreement. To assist Macedonia in the implementation of the Ohrid Agreement, the Union opened in 2001 the Office of the EU High Representative.[45] Since then implementation of the EU directives has met fierce resistance by both the Macedonian public and segments of its elite; every legal and institutional change required a mixture of international pressure and "carrots" (Ragaru 2007). Thus, in the fall of 2001, the EU used an especially strong "stick" against Macedonian authorities, which refused to pass required constitutional amendments. Then EU high representative Alain Le Roy succeeded postponing a donor conference initially scheduled for October 2001 until

March 2002, in the hopes that Macedonians would pass the constitutional amendments and the belated Law on Local Self-Government. The constitutional package finally passed on November 16, 2001 amid fierce parliamentary debates over many topics that were previously agreed upon in the Ohrid Agreement. The Law on Local Self-Government passed in January 2002.[46]

NATO's role stemmed from its military presence in the neighboring Kosovo. The alliance sought to prevent the destabilization of Kosovo. NATO secretary general George Robertson was often criticized by the Macedonian government, believing the NATO forces under the KFOR mission in Kosovo were not doing enough to control the border between the two countries. The alliance strengthened its involvement in the crisis by appointing German ambassador Hans-Joerg Eiff as a special representative in the country and Pieter Feith as a political envoy. It also sent military assistance to the Macedonian government. NATO's US general Joseph Ralson asked the US Congress for additional troops for the KFOR mission in Kosovo as an extension of the NATO mission in Macedonia. Even though NATO member countries wanted to avoid further open-ended, expensive peacekeeping missions like those in Kosovo and Bosnia, the alliance responded positively to President Tajkovski's request to demilitarize the UÇK/NLA under the condition that political factions in the Sobranie signed a peace agreement. It took more than two months for all the NATO conditions to be fulfilled, and the alliance decided on August 21 to deploy some 3,100 troops in order to observe the UÇK/NLA's disarmament (McNeil 2001).

Concurring with the EU and NATO positions, the US emphasized the need to address "the legitimate concerns of minorities." On March 23, President George W. Bush released a statement, asserting that "[t]he United States joins its allies and the United Nations in strongly condemning the violence perpetrated by a small group of extremists determined to destabilize the democratic, multi-ethnic Government of Macedonia," and that "[t]he United States and its allies have a longstanding commitment to the sovereignty and territorial integrity of Macedonia" (Bush 2003). President Bush expressed support for "NATO's effort to assess Macedonia's immediate security needs," and pledged military and technical assistance to the Macedonian government. Later, in a meeting in the White House with President Trajkovski, President Bush also pledged $10 million for the newly established multilingual Southeast European University in Tetovo. On April 12, the US secretary of state Colin Powell visited Skopje to express the US's support for the country's territorial integrity and the need to find a political solution to the crisis. Moreover, even though in his June tour to Europe President Bush had dismissed the possibility of US personnel participating in a NATO force that would observe the disarmament of the UÇK/NLA, 500 US troops eventually joined the NATO Essential Harvest mission.

Compared to the EU and NATO, OSCE had a logistic "advantage" in dealing with the Macedonian crisis. Since September 1992, OSCE had the Spillover Monitor Mission to Skopje, and OCSE High Commissioner on National Minorities Max van der Stoel had been very active in negotiating solutions to Albanian grievances with Macedonian authorities. The mission followed the crisis closely on the ground and reporting human rights abuses by both sides. On March 21, 2001, OCSE chairman-in-office Romanian foreign minister Mircea Geoana appointed US diplomat Robert Frowick as his personal representative. Ambassador Frowick became very active in his efforts to hold direct talks between the government and the UÇK/NLA. As the Macedonian partners in government rejected his invitations, Frowick organized talks between Albanian mainstream parties, including the PDSh, an already government partner, and the UÇK/NLA, hence applying a strategy that has worked in the southern Serbian conflict (Daskalovski 2006, 113). His attempts resulted in the Prizren Declaration, May 22, between the PDSh, PPD and UÇK/NLA, which, notwithstanding its denunciation and prophecy of doom, opened the way to the political solution of the crisis.

The peaceful withdrawal of the UÇK/NLA from Aračinovo was a clear signal that its leaders had accepted a negotiation of the crisis. The UÇK/NLA agreed to a settlement that would satisfy the Prizren Declaration. After intense negotiation, the four main Macedonian and Albanian political parties, the VMRO–DPMNE, Socijaldemokratski Sojuz na Makedonija (SDSM) (Social-Democratic Union of Macedonia), PDSh and PPD met in Ohrid, a lakeshore town less than 10 miles from the Albanian border, to agree to a political end to the ethnic hostilities. On August 8, 2001, after eleven hours of intense negotiations under the mediation of EU special envoy François Léotard and the special US envoy to Macedonia James Pardew, Albanian and Macedonian leaders reached an agreement for constitutional changes that would improve the status of Albanians in the country, known as the Ohrid Framework Agreement (hereafter Ohrid Agreement). It was signed by the Macedonian president Boris Trajkovski, prime minister Ljubčo Georgievski, Sobranie member and PDSh chairman Arbën Xhaferi and Sobranie member and PPD chairman Imer Imeri.

It is clear that an agreement between the Macedonian majority and Albanian minority would have been very difficult without the presence of international actors. Arguably, the Ohrid Agreement, achieved under the strong pressure and carrot-and-stick approach of an international concert of the EU, NATO, OSCE and the US, saved Macedonia from the brink of a full-scale civil war (Marko 2004/5; Daskalovski 2006; Schneckener 2002). In this case, the "carrot" appeared in the shape of the EU-supported Stabilization and Association Agreement with Macedonia, whereas the "stick" represented the potential threat of international indictments for both rebels and government officials in the Hague Tribunal. The difficulties in reaching and signing the agreement were clear indicators of the difficult road in the implementation phase.

The Ohrid Agreement consists of eight topics. Under Topic 1, basic principles include the prohibition of the use of violence in pursuit of political aims; the preservation of territorial integrity and the unitary character of the state; the preservation of the multi-ethnic character of Macedonia's society; a constitutionally guaranteed democratic accountability; and the development of local self-government to encourage participation and the promotion of the respect for the identity of communities. Topic 2 regulates the cessation of hostilities. Topic 3 specifies the development of a decentralized government, including a revised Law on Local Self-Government in order to devolve power in the areas of public services, urban and rural planning, environmental protection, local economic development, culture, local finances, education, social welfare and health care; a provision for revising the boundaries of municipalities after completion of a new census; and a provision that foresees the selection of the local heads of police by municipal councils. Topic 4 regulates non-discrimination and equitable representation of communities in all central and local public bodies with the affirmative duty to correct present imbalances, in particular within the police. It provides a double majority vote for the election of one-third of the constitutional court judges, the ombudsman and three members of the Judicial Council. The double majority vote (the Badinter principle) means that while members of parliament represent a majority of voters, they must also represent a majority of the minority populations not typically represented.

Topic 5 stipulates the double majority voting system for certain constitutional amendments, for the proposed Law on Local Self-Government and for laws which affect culture, specifically the use of language, education, personal documentation, symbols, local finances, local elections, the city of Skopje and the boundaries of municipalities. Topic 6 regulates the use of languages in education and public bodies. The most important elements are further guarantees for mother-tongue instruction in primary and secondary education and at university-level education in languages spoken by at least 20 per cent of the population of Macedonia, that is, in fact, only Albanian. Affirmative action continues in state universities until equitable representation can be achieved. Topic 7 provides for the use of emblems of communities along with that of Macedonia in front of local public buildings if the community has population majority in the municipality. Topic 8 provides guidelines for timely implementation of the agreement.

The implementation of the Ohrid Agreement represented a major challenge for all signatories. First, it was a challenge for Macedonian politicians who had to operate in a climate of open public hostility toward the agreement. A 2003 UNDP–Kapital Center for Developmental Research survey revealed strong resistance to the implementation of the Ohrid Agreement from the Macedonian public, satisfactory support by Albanians and only lukewarm acceptance by other minorities (Table 3. 2).

Second, the agreement's implementation presented major legitimacy challenges for Albanian parties in the governing coalition, the PDSh and PPD. Although their leaders were signatories to the agreement, it was already well known that only the military pressure wielded by the UÇK/NLA could manage to shake the status quo politics in Macedonia (Garton Ash 2001). The PDSh and PPD were left to fight a difficult political venue in which every slide backwards would be easily perceived as incompetence at best and treason at worst. Under the unbearable weight of such a challenge, Arbën Xhaferi and Menduh Thaçi of the PDSh and former prime minister Georgievski (VMRO–DPMNE) launched a direct assault on the Ohrid Agreement, declaring it "dead" and calling for the country to be partitioned. At its annual congress in July 2003, the PDSh demanded further constitutional changes which would eliminate the Ohrid compromise, including a bicameral parliament, an Albanian vice-president, "consensual democracy" to allow a fuller veto power and the right to self-determination.[47] As for the international community, their challenge consisted of maintaining coherence in the face of Balkan political tricks, lack of commitment by the signatories to the agreements and the absence of reliable domestic partners.

Table 3.2. Results from the 2003 UNPD and Kapital survey

Question: Do you support/not support the Ohrid Agreement?

	Ethnic Background			Total
	Macedonian	Albanian	Other	
	Col %	Col%	Col%	Col%
1 Strongly support	5.7	68.1		20.5
2 Support somewhat	32.3	23.5	28.3	30.1
3 Somewhat not support	17.2	1.6	20.8	13.8
4 Do not support all	37.9	1.2	22.6	28.9
5 Refuse	0.4		1.9	0.4
6 Don't know	6.5	5.6	7.5	6.3

Source: United Nations Development Programme (UNDP) and Kapital Center for Development Research (2003).

Marko (2004) recognizes that the Ohrid Agreement has led to considerable improvements in equitable representation of Albanian Macedonians in public bodies as well as increased enrollment of minority students. Reportedly,

the number of Albanian Macedonians paid from the state budget increased from 11.65% in 2002 to 14.54% in December 2004. In the health organizations, not paid by the state budget, the increase was from 5.72% to 7.34%. Much more impressive are the results in the security forces where the numbers of Albanian Macedonians between 2001 and 2004 increased in the Ministry of the Interior from 3.6% to 13.31%, the Criminal Police from 3.9% to 10.37% and in the armed forces from 2.25% to 10.18%. (Marko 2004/5, 11)

However, while Marko (2004, n50) praises these advances and credits the improvement on the introduction of community policing and a system of mixed police patrols in Albanian territories of Macedonia, other authors have pointed out the increasing ethnic clientelism in public administration appointments (Lili 2009; Lebamoff and Ilievski 2008; ESI Macedonia Security Project 2002).[48]

Marko (2004) reports better success in implementing the agreement in education:

For pupils who are part of the Albanian and Turkish communities, the education process in kindergarten groups and primary schools is carried out in their mother tongue. In secondary education the education process is performed in Macedonian, Albanian and Turkish, whereby Macedonian Albanian pupils can receive instruction in Albanian in six municipalities and the City of Skopje. Now, 18.57% of Albanian pupils receive secondary education in their mother tongue. As far as university enrolment is concerned, due to the establishment of two new universities, the figures show a tremendous increase. The number of Albanian Macedonian undergraduate and graduate students in 1992 was 2.23%, and this jumped to 15.5% in 2004–5. The number of Turkish students, however, increased only slightly from 0.65% to 1.34%, but the share of Serbs actually dropped from 3.19% to 1.52%.

When the already delayed constitutional changes entered into the parliamentary agenda in the fall of 2001, it became clear that constitutional reform in Macedonia had become a zero-sum game (Brunnbauer 2002; Loomis, Davis and Broughton 2001, 17). Macedonian leaders perceived Albanian gains as detrimental to the status of Macedonians and therefore maneuvered to limit those gains. Two major issues emerged: the new preamble of the constitution and the relationship of the religious communities with the state and each other. The drafted preamble referred to "the citizens of the Republic of Macedonia," thus avoiding any specific reference to distinct ethnic groups.[49] However, when the draft preamble was leaked to the public, it unleashed anger among the Macedonian masses, intellectuals, politicians and the media, who strongly opposed the fact that the preamble did not nominally mention the Macedonian people. Macedonians have always quarreled with Albanians over the point that Macedonia was the only motherland they had, while the Albanians already had a motherland, Albania proper. Now Macedonians saw the deletion of their name from the preamble as a sign that they were losing their country, the only country that recognized them as a people. Albanian political parties avoided negotiation, fearing that it would lead to an unraveling of the original agreement, but two Macedonian opposition parties, the Democratic Alternative and the Real VMRO, as well as politicians from the VMRO–DPMNE, opposed the new preamble, which according to them extinguished the historic development of the Macedonian state (cf. Brunnbauer 2002, 11).

International actors became involved once again. The EU's special representative in Macedonia François Léotard asked for help from the Venice Commission in an attempt to bolster the constitutional reform.[50] President Trajkovski, in turn, asked the US president George W. Bush to facilitate a compromise. Yet, the NATO secretary general Lord Robertson and EU high representative for common foreign and security policy Javier Solana negotiated the preamble that later was passed by the Sobranie. The new preamble states:

> The citizens of the Republic of Macedonia, the Macedonian people, as well as those citizens who live within the borders of the Republic of Macedonia and are members of the Albanian people, the Turkish people, the Vlach people, the Serbian people, the Roma people and of other peoples, take on themselves the responsibility for the present and the future of their fatherland. (cf. Brunnbauer 2002, 11)

The second contested issue arising from the 1991 constitution concerned the special relationship that it created between the Macedonian Orthodox Church and the Macedonian state. A new Article 19 was therefore drafted as a result of the Ohrid

Agreement.[51] Although the problem seemed to be resolved by simply mentioning the Islamic religious community in Macedonia and the Catholic Church, the very fact that these religious groups gained an equal status with the hitherto privileged Macedonian Orthodox Church provoked criticism by the latter. Instead, the church argued that "it should be granted special status at least in Macedonia, since it was not recognized by other Orthodox Churches" (Brunnbauer 2002, 11). Consequentially, an amendment was made with the words "as well as between the Macedonian Orthodox Church and the other religious institutions," so the former would stand out and address its concerns and those of the ethnic Macedonian Orthodox majority (Ilievski 2007, 22).

The implementation of the Ohrid Agreement, especially the projected constitutional amendments, showed how deeply Macedonians and Albanians still distrusted each other. The process also revealed that for Macedonia to be a stable democracy it would require assistance from its international sponsors, either to force negotiation and compromise or enforce consociational practices.

A consociational interpretation of the Macedonian crisis and its aftermath

A consociational explanatory model would suggest that the Macedonian ethnic conflict erupted because both Albanian and Macedonian elites lost cohesion.[52] The fact that among Albanians public support for the UÇK/NLA was not taken for granted (Ragaru 2007, 8) and that Bashkimi Demokratik për Integrim (BDI) (Democratic Union for Integration), which was founded from its legacy after the Ohrid Agreement, never managed to incorporate the entire Albanian electorate shows the division that existed among Albanians. As Rusi (2004) reveals, interviewed UÇK/NLA members remained consistently critical of Albanian politicians in Macedonia. As Rusi (2004, 7) notes, when talking to foreigners those days Ali Ahmeti bluntly described Albanian politicians as "looking after their own interests." Other members of the former UÇK/NLA were openly critical of the PDSh. When the Government of National Unity was established on May 8, 2001, the deputy speaker of the Sobranie, Ilijaz Halimi of the PDSh, was vilified by the PPD for insisting that the PPD must publicly distance itself from the UÇK/NLA as a condition for joining the new government coalition. On March 20, while still in opposition, the Partia Demokratike Popullore (PDP) (Democratic People Party) signed a joint statement with the PDSh, calling on the UÇK/NLA to lay down its arms (cf. Rusi 2004). Even now, twelve years after the conflict, the division remains deep and, occasionally, the political debate among Albanian politicians and their partisan supporters degenerates into violence (Lili 2009).

The Macedonian elites were divided as well. Premier Lubčo Georgievski and the minister of the interior, Ljube Boškovski, supported a military solution to the crisis, while President Boris Trajkovski and Branko Crvenkovski's SDSM called for compromise and negotiation. A major crisis occurred on May 22, 2001 when, under the brokerage of the OCSE envoy Robert Frowick, leaders of the PDSh and the PPD met with UÇK/NLA leaders in the Kosovo city of Prizren. Frowick had been involved in long and difficult negotiations with the UÇK/NLA following a request from President Trajkovski. With the VMRO–DPMNE and Premier Georgievski rejecting direct talks with the UÇK, the latter signed the plan only with the ethnic Albanian government partners.

Ali Ahmeti, the political representative of the UÇK/NLA, as well as Imer Imeri and Arbën Xhaferi, the leaders of the PPD and PDSh respectively, signed the document produced by the meeting, titled "Declaration of the Albanian Leaders from Macedonia Regarding the Peace and Reformation Process in the Republic of Macedonia." The document states that the various Albanian leaders, mindful of an historic juncture in Macedonia, agreed to act in the national interest toward a common goal: the reformation of the state to create a democracy for all citizens and national communities. The consensus among Albanian leaders was to be based upon a number of shared principles: support for the territorial integrity and multi-ethnic character of Macedonia; a rejection of "ethnic territorial" solutions to Macedonia's problems and a recognition that ethnically based separatism would damage the citizens of Macedonia, as well as threaten peace in the region; a recognition that there could be no military solution to the problems facing the Republic of Macedonia; a commitment to transforming the Republic of Macedonia by advancing its European and Atlantic integration; and finally, a willingness to accept the US and EU as facilitators to resolve internal problems (cf. Rusi 2004, 8). Moreover, the signatories also pledged to work together for a set of specific reforms. These included a review of amendments to the constitution of Macedonia; unrestricted use of the Albanian language as one of the country's official languages; proportional ethnic presence in the institutions of the state; enhancement of the authority of local government; complete secularization of the constitution and state; and the introduction of mechanisms to ensure a consensual resolution of issues of national interest involving ethnic rights (cf. Rusi 2004, 8).

However, Frowick's plan began to unravel when the Prizren Declaration was made public. Key representatives of the international community were also opposed, most notably Mark Dickinson, then British ambassador to Macedonia, who at the time also represented the EU high representative for common foreign and security policies, Javier Solana. Even though private EU sources considered the plan "very, very good, and in line with the international community" (Daskalovski 2006), bad timing and a lack of coordination doomed it. A storm of Macedonian and international criticism rose against Ambassador Frowick, OSCE, the US and the Albanian leaders. The daily paper *Nova Makedonija*, for example, ran a headline announcing, "Xhaferi and Imeri sign a document betraying Macedonia." President Trajkovski added: "These meetings are unacceptable and run against the government and their own [the PPD and PDSh] commitment not to negotiate with terrorists." The PDSh and PPD were urged by Macedonian political parties to renounce the signatures of their leaders. Robert Frowick was instructed to leave the country in disgrace. The rejection of the Prizren Declaration as a basis for talks obstructed the discussion process that President Trajkovski had overseen.

The Prizren negotiations caused a major crisis within the governing coalition, and it took long and tense negotiations between EU high representative Javier Solana, senior US diplomat James Swigert and President Trajkovski to persuade finally the Macedonian and Albanian government coalition partners to resume political dialogue on May 29. A June 2001 meeting with Solana and Swigert concluded with an agreement. EU diplomatic pressure grew since Macedonian party leaders were expected to report their political progress to the EU General Affairs Council, to be held on June 25 (Daskalovski 2006, 104). By that time, it appears that others reached the conclusion that nothing could be resolved if the UÇK/NLA were excluded from the negotiating process. Even the Macedonian government later acknowledged that some of the conditions set in Prizren would have to be met, when Premier Georgievski said in a television interview that "it is probable that we will have to drop the preamble to the Constitution, or announce a second constituent nation. It is likely that we will have to announce a second official language" (cf. Rusi 2004, 9).

By the very end of the 1990s and early 2000s, feelings of political and economic frustration combined with euphoria over the Albanian triumph in Kosovo resulted in an increasingly angry and impatient Albanian population in Macedonia. Despite their expanding role in the affairs of the country, Albanians in Macedonia found themselves the only disenfranchised Albanian entity in the Balkans. Radicalized Albanians returning from the Kosovo War found themselves alienated from a political system built on dual-ethnic, partisan criteria for participation (Ragaru 2007). The existing status quo allowed no room for other political actors to participate; yet these guerrilla fighters realized that there existed much grievance among the Albanians in Macedonia and they possessed enough guns as to enter the power game. By then, the Albanian political elites had lost much of their representative legitimacy, and large sections of the Albanian population were searching for other voices to represent them. As Ragaru (2007, 8) argues, an awareness of such a cleavage between the Albanian political elites and their voters is extremely important in understanding post-Ohrid political dynamics.

Macedonian elites lost legitimacy as well. Several times, Macedonian politicians were intimidated by the pressure of massive and violent Macedonian crowds, who viewed closed doors negotiations as secret deals to "sell out the country" (Daskalovski 2006). For instance, negotiations between the coalition partners that began on June 25 broke up the next day due to angry Macedonian demonstrations in Skopje. A month later, masses of angry Macedonian protesters demonstrated in Skopje against what they perceived as a "constant Western support to Albanian Militants" (Daskalovski 2006).

The Ohrid Agreement aimed to introduce consociational practices and restore such practices where there were disrupted. The agreement was designed in such a way that would ultimately result in a peaceful yet separate cohabitation among the different ethnic groups. While on the one hand the principle of equitable representation in state institutions would expose state employees to individuals of different ethnic backgrounds, local decentralization reforms and higher education reforms would likely result in increasing the distance between ethnicities (Ragaru 2007). However, democratic stability, not ethnic harmony, was EU's ultimate goal. The Ohrid Agreement was designed to ensure that the elites remained unified on the issues concerning EU–Macedonian negotiation. For example, the intention of the dual majority principle (the Badinter principle) was to enforce simultaneously consociational practices on each ethnic group so it could remain a cohesive pillar. With that principle, the EU could be confident that both Macedonians and Albanian elites would enter negotiations with the EU equipped with unified proposals.

Some modifications to the constitutional amendments that occurred during parliamentary debates strengthened the multi-ethnic emphasis of Macedonia, hence bringing to the process additional consociational practices. First, concerning the symbolism of the preamble, the Ohrid Agreement originally stipulated the replacement of concepts in the 1991 constitution, which Marko (2004) considers a mixture of nation state and state-nation concepts, in which a solely state-nation concept no longer refers to a "Macedonian nation" and "other ethnic groups," but only to "citizens." The agreed preamble now states: "Citizens of the Republic of Macedonia, the Macedonian people, as well as the citizens that live within its borders, who are part of the Albanian people, Turkish people, Vlach people, Serb people, Roma people, the Bosniak people, and others [...] have decided to establish the Republic of Macedonia as an independent, sovereign state" (Amendment IV of the constitution, cf. Marko 2004, 9).[53] The EU accepted this modification: the multi-ethnic constitutional design is a consociational practice.

The implementation of the Ohrid Agreement navigates between the Scylla of federalization and the Charybdis of centralization and therefore affects major intra-ethnic issues. However, it seems that the EU has found this tension compatible with its consociational practices. For instance, Italy has mitigated tensions between centralization and federalization through devolution. People close to Ali Ahmeti have affirmed what Garton Ash (2001) reveals in his article: generally, the Albanian elites were interested only in expanding Albanian rights within a unified Macedonia. As several Albanian politicians in Macedonia have told me time and again, in the case of a partition, Albanians would have been the ultimate losers and they therefore needed to be better consolidated, demographically and politically, in order to become better positioned for the politics of partition. Simply speaking, Albanian nationalists did not want to secede from Macedonia and leave behind two of their historical cities, namely Skopje (in Albanian, Shkup) and Bitola (in Albanian, Manastir). While this attitude of the Albanian leaders seems to avoid ethnic clashes until, arguably, Albanians might become a majority in Macedonia due to their high birth rate, it also gains some time for peace as emerging crosscutting cleavages might mitigate ethnic divisions.

The implementation of the Ohrid Agreement reflects this nationalistic platform. One of the most contested interethnic issues in Macedonia has been the use of other languages besides Macedonian in education and administration. The new regulations have enabled the use of more communities' languages; in local self-government the 50 per cent threshold was reduced to 20 per cent and the same threshold was introduced for state administration operating in both local and central level for municipalities with a 20 per cent share of an ethnic community. Although the Albanian language can now be used again in parliamentary sessions, this does not mean that the Albanian language has become an official national language like Macedonian. The Albanian leaders focused on consolidating their political authority over the territories where they maintain a significant presence. This makes political struggle necessary in order to redraw the municipal boundaries to include Albanian Macedonian villages so that the community could reach the 20 per cent threshold. Following such a policy, Albanians were able to reassert their historical presence in Skopje, which, as will be discussed in the next chapter, became bilingual by adding to its municipality neighboring Albanian-inhabited suburbs. Appendix B shows the demographic dynamics in Macedonia since the 1981 census.

With the practical loss of control over some of the most productive and economically active administrative-territorial units in the country, such as the Albanian-inhabited municipalities of the northwest, Macedonian elites viewed it futile to resist constitutional changes regarding language and the use of national symbols. Thus, constitutional amendments regarding education in the languages of communities and Article 48(3) and Article 48(1) regarding the use of the flags were passed with minor changes.

As Marko (2004, 10) points out, the most important elements of group rights according to the model of consociational democracy were embodied in provisions for equitable representation and the double majority voting system in parliament instead of a simple majority. Article 8 of the constitution guarantees equitable representation of citizens in public bodies at all levels and in all areas of public life as one of the fundamental values of the constitutional order; in Article 77(2) it is stipulated that the role of the public attorney is to safeguard this principle. Yet equal representation on the basis of the double majority voting system is also anticipated for the composition of the Security Council, the Judicial Council and the Constitutional Court. The Sobranie was entitled to establish a committee for intercommunity relations composed of seven Macedonian and Albanian members each and five other members each from the Turk, Vlach, Roma and two other communities. The double majority voting system is also anticipated according to Article 114(5) for laws regarding local self-government, i.e. laws on local self-government, local finances, local elections, boundaries of municipalities and the city of Skopje. Article 69(2) enumerates subject matters such as culture, use of languages, education, personal documentation and use of symbols which affect ethnic identities and for which again a double majority vote is foreseen (Marko 2004, 10). However,

> although (or because) representatives of the communities are regularly elected into parliament due to the ethnically split party system and interethnic government coalitions are formed on a regular basis in actual practice, the OFA and respective constitutional amendments did not include a system of constitutionally fixed seats for ethnic groups in parliament or posts in the government connected with a system of veto powers for specific groups. This is in marked contrast to the constitutions of Slovenia, Croatia and Bosnia-Herzegovina. (Marko 2004, 10)

Hence, the consociational arrangements foreseen by the Ohrid Agreement are much weaker and do not impose restrictions on individual rights, such as the right to stand as a candidate (as in the Bosnian constitution), which excludes from membership to certain high political positions in the country anyone who is not Serb, Croat or Bosniak (Marko 2004, 10). However, under the conditions discussed above, this poses no problem to Albanians since their claim rests only over the municipalities where they represent or aspire to represent a majority or substantial minority. Implicitly, Marko criticizes Daskalovski's take for missing the point when the latter considers the changes to the constitution as reflecting an ethnification of the Macedonian constitution and advancement of a political identity best described as "millet," and considering this ethnified Macedonia not able to "support just solutions to problems in multi-ethnic societies" insofar as only "liberal nation building guarantees a culture of protection of national minorities" (Marko 2004, 11). Instead, according to Marko (2004, 11):

> exactly this "liberal nation building with the protection of national minorities" ended up in the spiral of intensification of ethnic tensions [...] since the main political problem was and still is that Albanian Macedonians do not consider themselves a "national minority," but want to be an "equal partner" in the state and nation-building process.

An account of Albanian achievements as they are stated in the Ohrid Agreement, as well as the ensuing constitutional reform, shows that EU consociational practices and the compromises that forged them brought Macedonia as close as it could to a more stable democracy. First, the changes insist that all ethnic communities have formal equality as state and nation-building forces, as reflected in the language of the preamble, thus making Macedonia a multi-ethnic, not bi-national state of Slav and Albanian Macedonians.[54] Second, the changes result in equal representation for all groups in the civil service, particularly Albanian Macedonians, but not full veto power in parliamentary decisions. In this respect, Marko (2004, 12) notes, the double majority voting system is a much weaker mechanism than comparable provisions regarding veto powers in the constitutions of other former Yugoslav republics. However, as I have argued, as a consociational practice, the Badinter principle aims at forcing unity within social segments themselves. When the legitimacy of the elites erodes, the double majority principle would assure that different subgroups within the social segments unify around the decisions made by their elites. Third, the lowering threshold needed for using a certain language in public administration and the judiciary to 20 per cent reflected a European "best practice" established by the Advisory Committee under the Framework Convention for the Protection of National Minorities (Marko 2004). Even though the new language provisions did not give the Albanian language "full equality," it served the purpose of redrawing administrative borders in a way that would assert the Albanian presence. Fourth, while some authors (see Marko 2004, 12) deplore the rejection of the Albanian aspirations for territorial autonomy or federalization of the country and while the implementation of the Ohrid Agreement has ghettoized the country along ethnic lines, that ghettoization might have served the elites very well. Generally speaking, the Ohrid Agreement functions as a powerful tool for ethnic elites to strengthen their grip on respective social segments/pillars.

The application of EU membership conditionality to Macedonia represents the case of a country building institutions that would be compatible with consociational practices in two levels. The first level is the national level: the Ohrid Agreement and the ensuing constitutional reform intend to implement consociational practices needed to pacify ongoing ethnic conflict and transform Macedonia into a stable democracy. As the historical process tracing makes clear, not only is Macedonian society deeply divided, but each of the segments/pillars is further split within itself. First, analysis shows that the situation escalated to outright conflict because of the radicalization of the Albanian political elite. No clear evidence exists that Albanian leaders radicalized the masses; yet the shift of sympathy in the course of the 1990s from the PPD to the PDSh to the UÇK/NLA, as well as the electoral performance and resilience of the more moderate PDSh, show that the Albanian population in Macedonia is divided. Every time a more radical Albanian movement appears, the political support of the majority of the Albanians seems to shift to that movement. However, as long as Albanian leaders continued working within the system to carve an Albanian space within Macedonian institutions, their political discord and rivalries did not threaten the existence of the country. The only time this has occurred was when the UÇK/NLA struggle appeared to be developing toward a possible forceful division of Macedonia. As long as Albanian elites were unified, Macedonian democratic stability appeared to be sustainable; once rifts appeared among Albanians, however, they echoed dissent that was similar among Macedonians. By the same token, Macedonian elites are also divided; their disagreements concern not only how to tackle the Albanian minority, but also how to respond to the country's crisis with Greece (Taleski 2010). Constitutional reforms following some consociational practices would help to unify Macedonian elites as well.

Moreover, rifts among Albanian elites reflected the frustration among Albanians regarding their social status in Macedonian society. The division between elites from different ethnic backgrounds highlights deep ethnic divisions within Macedonian society. The rifts within each ethnic group would make agreement between ethnic groups impossible because political deals can be easily interpreted as treason by elite groups left out of the process. But unified ethnic elites operating under frameworks such as the Ohrid Agreement and institutional settings such as the amended constitution would give ethnic elites the opportunity to negotiate co-existence with other elites. The Ohrid Agreement and the constitution serve now as unifying grounds for the country's elites.

The second level is the international level, that is, the EU–Macedonia level. In order to facilitate the integration of Macedonia within the EU institutions, the Union needs to negotiate with a unified Macedonian segment (or pillar) that is receptive to the EU consociational practices. The need for such a unity would have not been an issue had Macedonia not aspired to EU membership. In the latter case, institutions receptive to consociational practices only would have sufficed for guaranteeing domestic stability. However, in the case of Macedonia, institutions receptive to consociational practices do not only serve domestic stability but also the convergence of the Macedonian stability with a unified segment or pillar. The amended Macedonian constitution offered a chance to satisfy both of these needs. The preservation of the unitary character of the Macedonian state, on the one hand, and the conversion of Macedonia from a nation state to a multi-ethnic country, on the other, represented a compromise that did not leave everyone totally satisfied, just as usually happens with compromises.

A sectorial contextual interpretation of Macedonian constitutional reform

The dynamics of the EU–Macedonian negotiations fit my proposed model. During 1989–91, the Macedonian communist elites were hoping for the best (i.e. the maintenance of Yugoslavia), but preparing for the worst (i.e. the collapse of Yugoslavia and the precarious situation of the country). Following such a strategy, they introduced constitutional arrangements that would help them to appear to care for the Macedonian people, enabling them to succeed politically. Albanian elites in Macedonia were weak, unprepared, institutionally debilitated and unwilling to go beyond threats. Meanwhile, the EU was pleased with Macedonian stability, and never pushed the Macedonian government for changes beyond slogans related to minority rights, while at the same time rebuking Albanians for threatening the stability of the country.[55] With the political will of Macedonian elites and the lack of interest from the EU, the former employed the majority-vote principle to perform constitutional arrangements perceived as paramount to establishing the Macedonian nation state. However, while the 2001 conflict persuaded the EU as to the need for constitutional reforms, the ruling Macedonian elites resisted. At that point, the EU became highly interested in constitutional reforms in Macedonia, but only after the Albanian and Macedonian elites compromised can we say that the ruling elites of Macedonia also became positively interested in reform itself. After difficult negotiations that involved the "carrots" of SAA and the "sticks" of potential dissolution of Macedonia, as well as "carrots" of constitutional changes and "sticks" of being placed on the US's ban list and facing a Hague Tribunal for Albanian fighters, an agreement was finally reached and constitutional reform proceeded successfully.[56]

The sectorial contextual interpretation of the Macedonian constitutional reform suggests that in ethnically divided societies a constitutional reform does not always imply progressive movement toward democratization unless it builds institutions receptive to consociational practices. Elites might swiftly pass a constitutional reform, yet might not necessarily be committed to progress. Only constitutional reforms that establish institutions compatible to consociational practices can be considered as a "good progress." In a divided society, swift constitutional reforms without the support of the most relevant societal pillars might lead to destabilization rather than democratic stability. Table 3.3 summarizes the dynamics of Macedonian constitutional reform.

Conclusions

The purpose of this chapter was to demonstrate empirically how the EU employs membership conditionality to help its aspirant countries from the Balkans to conduct institutional reforms that produce institutions receptive to the EU consociational

Table 3.3. Developments in Macedonian constitutional reform

Period	Situation	EU Leaders' Interests	Domestic Leaders' Interests	Reform Results
1989	Preparation for independence	0	+	**Swift reform** and spillovers on other reforms. The Constitution of the Yugoslav Socialist Republic of Macedonia was approved in order to strengthen the position of the Macedonians both within their Republic and within Yugoslavia. Yet, they did not concern the status of other ethnic groups. These changes happened without any input from international actors.
1991	Independence	0	+	**Swift reform** and spillovers on other institutional reforms. The goal of the 1991 Constitution was the creation of a state that would serve as a nation-state to the Macedonians and a state of the citizens to other minorities. The ruling (Macedonian) elites supported the reform, but the Albanian minority opposed it. There is no evidence about any international interests and/or involvement in that reform.
2001	Violent ethnic conflict	+	–	**No reform.** The country slipped into ethnic conflict and, obviously, the EU and other international actors became increasingly interested in a constitutional reform that would implement consociational practices to bring about democratic stability. Yet, the Macedonian ruling elites were reluctant to undertake such reforms. Finally, the reform was agreed with the Ohrid Agreement.
2003	Interethnic elite pact	+	+	**Good progress** and spillovers on other institutional reforms (local decentralization, judiciary, security forces, public administration, and education). This is the case when both the EU and domestic ruling elites converged to positive preferences for the reform.

practices. In a unified society such as Albania, the main goal is to establish institutions receptive to EU consociational practices during the process of internal integration with the EU institutions. In this case, the purpose is not to unify the social segment (or pillar) but to shape it and enable it to operate with consociational practices. In the case of Macedonia, the requirement of constitutional reforms implies the establishment of a constitution that would serve both the purpose of creating a unified segment and the enabling of this process. In this case, the consociational practices affect institutional behavior at two levels. At the national level, consociational practices guarantee democratic stability and social cohesion; at the international/EU level, these practices help the integration of Macedonia in the EU without threatening the EU democratic stability.

Chapter 4

LOCAL DECENTRALIZATION REFORM

The different mechanisms employed by the EU to transmit consociational practices to countries undergoing democratization can be better understood through a comparison of local decentralization reforms in Albania and Macedonia. In a mostly unified society such as Albania, the involvement of the EU in such sectorial reforms proved minor. Instead, other specialized regional organizations like the Council of Europe (CoE) and the Organization for Security and Cooperation in Europe (OSCE) stepped in to assist the Albanian government with the technicalities of reform. By contrast, local decentralization reform represented the core of the Ohrid Agreement and was one of the most important consociational practices designed to maintain social cohesion in Macedonia; yet despite the radical decentralization reform implemented in accordance with the Ohrid Agreement, the country still lags far behind Albania in that sector. Between 1992 and 2002, these countries' local government systems became remarkably similar, but they have since progressed at different rates.

A historical analysis of the reform process reveals that some of the problems relating to fiscal decentralization continue to linger both in Macedonia and Albania. This chapter shows that, while Albania follows a typical Eastern European path toward local decentralization, Macedonian decentralization reform involves more complex dynamics; policy choices and implementation in Macedonia reflect the peculiar social context, that is, the seemingly impossible task of decentralizing local government while consolidating a unitary nation state out of a society deeply divided along ethnic lines.

While the motivations of political actors involved in the Albanian and Macedonian decentralization processes vary and produce distinct policy outcomes, it is necessary to outline some similarities for the sake of context. The most important similarity between the Albanian and Macedonian decentralization reforms, one that they share with other EECs, is the debate between deconcentration and decentralization policies. According to Illner (1998, 1997), deconcentration is understood to be a process whereby government functions shift downward within the hierarchical system of state bureaucracy without weakening the vertical hierarchy of the system; deconcentration units remain vertically subordinate to central authorities. According to the same author, decentralization means the devolution of state functions into autonomous territorial governments that can act without consultation with central governments. Decentralization can be interpreted according to either of two competing philosophies of state: a communitarian, conservative approach would see local government as deriving from a central authority and enjoying as much autonomy as granted by the central government; or an individualist, liberal tradition that views local government as primary, and the central government as serving the purpose of resolving the dilemmas of collective action among local communities (Illner 1998).

Difficulties with Eastern European decentralization reforms rest on the incompatibility between the Eastern European communitarian view of the state and its aspiration to implement Western European individualist models of governance. According to the liberal model, local government promotes citizen participation in governance; such a government is more responsive to concerns and more able to find acceptable solutions to problems raised by citizens; offers a counterweight to an authoritarian state (Illner 1998; Baldersheim et al. 1996); and is effective in delivering services to meet local needs (Illner 1998; Goldsmith 1992). As for functions that might fall outside of a social space that belong strictly to the individual or reflect a communitarian approach to governance, decentralization provides opportunities for the development of a new elite (Illner 1998; Baldersheim et al. 1996); creates a sense of place or community (Illner 1998; Goldsmith 1992); and is an element of civil society or a bridge linking civil society to the central state (Illner 1998, 9). Thus a communitarian approach would consider local decentralization as a gift that central government offers to local communities at its own expense. Arguably,

> Political actors perceive the reform of regional-level administration as more relevant to the distribution of political power than was the local reform, and it became, therefore, intensely disputed—conflicts have led eventually to a political stalemate that blocked further progress (Illner 1998, 25).

Further elaborated, this type of reluctance by the central government to relinquish its grip on local issues satisfies several needs: the need to maintain control of economic and political development during the still volatile postsocialist transformation; to control the distribution of scarce resources during transition periods of recession or crisis; to control, and possibly level, social differences among territorial units in order to prevent the marginalization of some regions and the resulting social and political tensions that would endanger social cohesion and stability; and to formulate policies aimed at maintaining national integration in a general atmosphere of societal fragmentation, resulting from structural reforms (Illner 1998; Elander 1997).

As Illner (1998, 10) points out, three sets of socio-political contextual factors influence territorial reforms: (1) the political, administrative and psychological legacies of the communist era; (2) the prevailing expectations toward decentralization; and (3) the political context of the reforms. As I have already discussed in Chapter 2, Illner's first and third factors are elements of my argument, and Illner's second factor can be easily merged with either. While euphoric expectations concerning democratization prevailed in the early postsocialist Eastern Europe, Illner (ibid.) also points to "a popular distrust of institutions, of any political representation, and of formal procedures; as well as unwillingness of citizens to get involved in public matters and to hold public office." The source of such feelings can easily be traced to the political experiences of citizens in general and local government in particular under communist governments.[1] They are also embedded in the political context of reforms, since the latter can affect people's expectations of distinct reforms.[2]

The political, administrative and psychological legacies of the communist era include low expectations of local government and a general view that it is merely an extension of the central government (Bird, Ebel and Wallich 1996). Under the principles of democratic centralism and homogenous state authority, both secured under communist party hegemony, local officials were viewed as simply party officials who merely implemented local administrative functions of minor political and economic relevance. Some authors (Illner 1998, 1993; Coulson 1995; Elander 1997) have pointed to the differences between the official ideological model of territorial government in communist regimes and its practical application, highlighting the leverage wielded by major state-run economic enterprises. The enormous financial resources and employment capacities of these enterprises often made them the effective power center within the territories where they exercised their activity, mounting another challenge to local government besides the communist party's ideological centralism (Illner 1992). Moreover, referring mainly to the most developed and, ostensibly, most liberal communist regimes of Eastern Europe, some authors claim that local government was far from static, since attempts at reform had occurred in some of these countries as early as 1961 in Czechoslovakia, 1973–75 in Poland and 1984 in Hungary. These reforms helped centralize the territorial structure of public administration (Illner 1998). Other attempts to introduce modest elements of decentralization and democratization tackled the fundamentals of the system. Efforts to reform local government that had atrophied in these countries were under way by the late 1980s, when the collapse of communist regimes brought to an end the old local government system and cleared the path for radical local decentralization reforms. However, one should keep in mind that decentralization efforts during communist regimes were not equally spread throughout the region.

The legacies of communism in Albania and Macedonia present similarities and differences both in quantity and quality. Albania's local government was a typical Stalinist one: an elected assembly, called the Këshilli Popullor (People's Council); an executive committee elected by the *këshill* called the Komiteti Ekzekutiv (Executive Committee); a council chairman for the *këshill* called the *kryetari i këshillit* (chairman of the council); and an executive chairman for the komitet called the *kryetari i komitetit ekzekutiv* (chairman of the executive committee). Of course, the Albanian communist party, the Partia e Punës (PP) (Labor's Party), had its own officials in all of these territorial structures, but hardly anyone saw local government as being anything different from a party extension in local administrative affairs. Thus, whether it was *sekretari i partisë* (party secretary) or executive committee/executive council chairperson the person who ran local affairs, the authority often rested with the personality of that particular official rather than written codes. As for Macedonia, the Yugoslav constitution of 1974 practically turned that country into a federation of municipalities where local taxes generated resources for each level of political administration: federal, republican, regional and municipal. For instance, due to some special taxes, the municipality was able to pay salaries even for military personnel dislocated in its territory. Arguably, this was Tito's policy to affect the transformation of the Yugoslav republics into nation states.[3]

The primitive Albanian economy and PP's vigilance against any potential rival in exercising power left no room for economic enterprises to influence local government activity. In fact, in Albania's predominantly agrarian economy, few enterprises were large enough to affect local policies. Yet, in the Yugoslav Macedonia, where economic enterprises were the direct fiscal source of the entire administrative hierarchy, the intermingling of the economic sector and local administration was more obvious and effective. This explains differences between the expectations of Albanians in Albania and those in Macedonia of their local governments. In Albania, the voices in favor of local decentralization were relatively quiet until October 2000, when Edi Rama from the Partia Socialiste (PS) (Socialist Party) became the first socialist major of the capital city of Tirana since the introduction of pluralism. Rama vigorously opened up the debate over local decentralization. By contrast, Macedonian authorities feared that substantial local autonomy would serve Albanian demands for federalism.

As for pre-communist legacies, my interviews with politicians from Albania and Macedonia revealed that hardly any had any recollections of pre–Second World War local administration systems. During this era, Albanian society was organized into communes in which it was difficult to find any literate person, and officials were appointed from the Ministria e Brendëshme (MB) (Ministry of the Interior). The situation resembled that in Macedonia. Yet, since Macedonian territory was considered simply the southern region of Serbia, the communal official's main goal was to promote Serbian consciousness and nationalism. Since both countries housed two to three generations born after the pre-communist period, hardly anyone was able to assess whether such a system could work.

As for the political context of reform, a deeper elaboration is needed. Arguing that political considerations prevailed over principles such as efficiency, representation and promotion of local values, Illner (1998, 17) points out:

> Expediency was an important factor in the implementation of the reforms: the need to build a new system of territorial administration in the postcommunist countries of Central and Eastern Europe was viewed as a political task that could not be postponed—a delay would have had a negative impact on economic and political components of the transformation.

True, this was the case for the initial reforms in most of Eastern Europe; however, the momentum of territorial reform was lost as post-revolutionary enthusiasm was exhausted. By 1998, time was no longer on the side of decentralization. The local government system produced in Albania by the Law on the Organization and Functioning of the Local Government and the Law on the Elections of Local Government, July 1992, established local governments that, being structurally different from those of the communist era, provided fewer services than the communist councils.

Moreover, to make things worse, destitute as it was, the country entered into a difficult period of economic restructuring through a shock-therapy strategy that brought the entire economy to an immediate standstill. Land distribution turned out to be counterproductive in face of an impoverished and demoralized peasantry more interested in migrating than cultivating the land. In Macedonia, the elites' interests in decentralization seemed to be different from those of Eastern European countries with an established sovereignty and statehood. Rather than taking advantage of the already decentralized local government, Macedonians centralized the governance as an assertion of sovereignty and nation-state building (Selami and Risteska 2009). Until 2005, local government in Macedonia reflected the Macedonian concern that any kind of decentralization would nourish further demands by Albanians for autonomy, federalization and, ultimately, secession. Statehood issues and uncertainties that the new Macedonia faced in a hostile Balkan environment led to an emphasis on independence rather than democratization and government efficiency. The fervor of establishing the Macedonian-ness of the new country prevented any momentum for decentralization in the first place.

Thus, while local decentralization reforms should have taken into consideration principles of efficiency and good governance, the Eastern European decentralization reforms proved to serve symbolic politics. As a consequence, local government restructuring mirrored structural changes in Eastern European societies, but with little practical applicability. As Illner (1998) argues, political concerns were of primary importance, while administrative and economic concerns ranked second. Thus, we can look for answers about reform outcomes in the political context of the reforms. This context in Albania reflects the tug of war between central and local governments over the ability to design and implement policies related to local issues. Such a tug of war is almost non-existent when the same party controls the central government and the most economically productive local units, but becomes acute when power is divided. For Macedonia, that tug of war was an intrinsic part of ethnic clashes between the Macedonian-dominated central government and Albanian-dominated local governments in the western part of the country, a region with a large population and some of the wealthiest municipalities in the country.

The Politics of Local Decentralization in Albania: Denying Yourself What You Do Not Want Your Rival to Have

Albania inherited a Soviet-style local government established only to implement centralized government policies and control the population, with no input in or access to the decision-making process (Rhodio and Van Cauwenberghe 2006). Although during the first years of transition the focus was mainly on reforms related to building central institutions, a number of laws and by-laws defining the responsibilities of local government were approved (Hoxha 2002).

The first attempt to reform local government took place in July 1992 with the Law on the Organization and Functioning of the Local Government and the Law on the Elections of Local Government. Both laws assigned considerable political autonomy to local authorities, some services in favor of local communities, and greater administrative and financial autonomy. These laws enshrined the principle of local self-government as one of the basic goals and principles of local government in Albania (Rhodio and Van Cauwenberghe 2006, 2). Yet the process was frozen when the Partia Demokratike (PD) (Democratic Party), who held a parliamentary majority and controlled the government, lost ground to the PS in the local elections of July 26, 1992. Moreover, although the law asserted the autonomy of local governments, it did not provide the authority and necessary instruments for its exercise. A local authority, controlled by the opposition, that could develop policies, raise and use funds, and employ people independently of the central government, rejected the concept of strictly centralized government carried out that time by the PD.

The PD's overwhelming victory in the local elections of October 1996 might have been a golden opportunity for the Albanian decentralization reform. However, the crumbling of the financial Ponzi schemes that flourished during the PD's rule, 1992–96, as well as skewed political representation in the legislature and local governments generated by the rigged May 1996 parliamentary elections, stirred popular unrest, resulting in massive riots and armed conflict throughout the nation.

The socialist-centrist coalition that emerged after the elections of June 1997 had to work with PD-controlled local government; therefore, there was no pressure for the central government to undertake decentralization reforms. Yet, the Council of Europe began to pressure the Albanian government to ratify the European Charter of Local Self-Government (ECLSG) as an obligation for membership. The Albanian ratification of ECLSG in November 1999 was followed by incremental steps toward reforms related to financial decentralization undertaken during the same year. These reforms included the establishment of block-grants by the central government and permission to select sectors of administrative expenditures; the transference of revenues collected locally by property taxation to local government, as well as the responsibility of collecting and administering these tax proceeds; the lifting of public expenditure limits; and permission to transfer into future years unexpended revenues of local budgets and block-grants.

In November 1998, a new constitution was adopted by the parliament and later ratified by a referendum. Regarding local autonomy, Article 108 of the new constitution followed the 1994 model, thus adopting the principle of local self-government. In December 2000, the government adopted the Strategjia Kombëtare për Decentralizim dhe Autonomi Vendore (National Strategy for Decentralization and Local Autonomy),[4] a document that defines long-term reform of the local government decentralization process. The document includes a decentralization schedule, resources and specifications regarding the role and involvement of key actors. The strategy acted as a guideline for decentralization reform and served as a reference document for reforms in other sectors that affected the decentralization process. From this point of view, the strategy could stimulate a wider array of reforms involving the decentralization of health and education policies, public investments, police and the fiscal system. The document anticipated a process that would take several years to implement.[5] Moreover, in 2000, the Kuvend passed Law No. 8652 On the Organization and Functioning of Local Government (hereinafter the 2000 law) and a number of other laws that concluded the legislative process of establishing democratic local government in Albania (Rhodio and Van Cauwenberghe 2006).

Thus, December 1998–July 2000 witnessed intensive political and legislative activity toward local government and decentralization reform.[6] The approaching October 2000 elections affected this process, as well as expectations that the ruling PS-led government coalition would win these elections. Indeed, the socialists, as soon as they assumed power in the summer of 1997, restored public order in most regions of the country, maintained six to eight per cent annual economic growth rates, and reduced inflation to below four per cent annually. These successes, plus the weak opposition PD, strengthened the PS's confidence that they would achieve victory in the local elections. Amid high expectations stemming from the mayoral candidacy of then Minister of Culture Edi Rama, the PS passed in Kuvend a special law that would govern the Tirana municipality. Indeed, during

1999–2000, the PS-led coalition began preparing a decentralization framework that would serve its members once they assumed office.

The legislative framework that underpinned the 1999–2000 decentralization reform helped the country comply with 19 ECLSG articles, 11 of which were core articles. Yet, since the 2000 law was implemented in two phases, in January 2001 and January 2002, it took two years before the Albanian legislation became compatible with Paragraph 9.3 of the ECLSG related to local finances. Moreover, some have only partially fulfilled the ECLSG's standards;[7] the Albanian legislation has yet to align with the ECLSG on issues related to the control of the central government over local administration.[8]

Although the constitutional and legislative bases of Albanian local government largely conform to the norms established by the Council of Europe and to best practices in Western Europe, the actual practices of local administration remain beset with difficulties. A number of laws, passed before the constitutional guarantees of local autonomy and the 2000 law, are not in harmony with the principles of local self-government. Laws that have led to conflicts between central and local governments include a law establishing the construction police, a law on urban planning that sets up national planning agencies, as well as urban planning agencies, and a law on prefectures.

As in other Eastern European countries, a deconcentration process occurred in Albania, paralleling the country's decentralization process. A number of ministries established their offices, called directories, in many of the prefectures. These offices were directly subordinate to the central government. In a massive duplication of effort, municipalities created their own offices for the same public services. Regional councils, composed of municipality council delegates, also established departments that covered the same areas. And finally, prefects developed their own administrative units to cover public health, agriculture and education. Such a proliferation demonstrates the power competition between central and local governments. On the one hand, the central government distrusted local government's administrative capabilities, and sought to continue controlling the allocation of resources; on the other, local governments were becoming increasingly aware of their potential role in local administration. One explanation shared by both central and local governments was that power holders from all parties rewarded political supporters with public offices, hence the swallowing of local administration.

The key problem of Albanian decentralization reform was financial decentralization. Due to limited tax collection capabilities, most municipalities relied on national financial resources that, for example, between 1998 and 2000, covered 93–96 per cent of their total revenues. These figures remained unchanged during 2001, because the newly elected local authorities could not implement the new Law on Organization and Functioning of the Local Government.[9] During this period, local governments were unable to count on any federal grants, since the central government had implemented only ad hoc procedures. The central government steadily increased the ratio of unconditioned grants compared to the conditioned ones. However, the looming 1:3 to 2:3 ratio in favor of conditioned grants demonstrated the continuing mistrust of the central government toward the administrative capabilities of local government, as well as its inclination to control the orientation of government grants. The PS's efforts to decentralize local government that had peaked on the eve of the 2000 local elections came to a standstill in 2002 when the PS-dominated government sought to control the investments of local governments politically.

Financial decentralization was not the only reform that stalled; the transfer of utility companies from central government management to local administration, as well as the reassignment of property evaluation and registration responsibilities from central to local governments were also suspended. The result was that many PS-controlled municipalities in southern Albania received as much as 15 times more government grants than some PD-controlled municipalities in the northern part of the country. Upon taking office in August 2005, the PD government instituted a policy to balance that misdistribution by increasing financial support to the northern municipalities and distributing unconditioned grants directly to local authorities. Thus, by narrowing the gap of 15:1 ratio to a 10:6 ratio, the PD tried to satisfy its own constituents in northern Albania, but also to offer a chance for more public investments to the impoverished northern regions of the country.[10]

It is worth noting that the intensive project of the local decentralization reforms that was drafted between December 1998 and July 2000 occurred during a period when the parliamentary majority belonged to a socialist-centrist coalition led by the PS, while local power in the majority of municipalities belonged to the opposition PD. Yet that entire process was driven by strong expectations that the PS would emerge as the winner of the 2000 local elections On the other hand, although financial decentralization progressed during 2000–2002 when the PS controlled both the central government and most local municipalities, the overall reform outcome did not meet ECLSG standards. Sources within the Albanian government during that period have revealed that the slow pace of decentralization resulted from the power struggle within the ruling PS, between Prime Minister Meta and PS chairman Fatos Nano. In that struggle, the premier routinely rewarded PS mayors who supported him and punished those who backed Nano.[11] Decentralization reform therefore came to a virtual standstill in the last three years of PS government rule, 2002–2005.

Upon reclaiming power in 2005, the PD undertook efforts to increase the disbursement of unconditioned grants for civic work projects and pledged to transfer water utility management to local administrations. In implementing this policy, the PD wanted to show its commitment to decentralization, thus enhancing its prospects for winning the upcoming fall 2006 local elections. But, PD may have taken such a pro-decentralization position simply because it was in the rational interest of the government to unburden itself of the cumbersome and costly task of managing local utilities and services. As Premier Sali Berisha reiterated at the Conference for the Donors' Activity Coordination in Decentralization and Local Government held in Tirana in May 2006, the retention of centralized health and education services "would bring only the relentless decrease of the service quality, of teaching and health care" (Berisha 2006). The prime minister used the conference as an opportunity to lay out his government's plan for decentralization: to transfer the water utility services to local government; expand of local fiscal autonomy; increase government grants; and transfer state-owned properties, as well as health and education services, to local authorities (ibid.).

However, six years after that pledge, state-owned and centrally controlled companies continue to run water and sewer utilities, and local officials from the opposition PS still demanded their transfer to local government, as stated by law.[12] The 2009 Freedom

House's Report on Nations in Transit Rankings and Average Score notes that decentralization remains one of the main challenges facing local government in Albania. Introduced in 2005, the Freedom House's Nation in Transit Rating and Average Scores ranks, along other sectors, local government democracy for countries in transition.[13] Ranging from one to seven, the score reflects the nation's level of local decentralization, with one denoting the highest possible level of local democracy and seven denoting its total absence.[14] The report explains that the National Decentralization Strategy aims at completing the institutional framework for the transfer of responsibilities for local taxes, water pipes and sewers to municipalities, as well as loans to local government in order to facilitate the capital investments necessary for better services. Local authorities have opposed the way the government plans to transfer the water and sewer enterprises to local government, since it includes only the transfer of bonds but not the management of the companies who run these services. These companies were projected to remain under the authority of the central government (Bushati 2009).

In 2006, management of small-business tax was fully transferred to local government, and in one year, collections increased significantly. This achievement was reversed on January 1, 2008 when the government cut the fiscal burden of this tax in half, causing an immediate drop in the amount of taxes that local governments could collect. One interpretation of this setback might be that the government's policy of delegating collection of national-level taxes to local governments was not coordinated and there was no increase in capacities for achieving better fiscal administration at a local level (ibid.).

However, since the PD's victory in the June 2005 general elections, Albanian politics has been plagued by the conflict between the PD, whose chairman was Albania's prime minister, and the PS, whose chairman was the mayor of Tirana.[15] Thus, the PD's enthusiastic electoral promise in 2005 to reverse the ratio of conditioned versus unconditioned grants so it could favor the latter began to be implemented more slowly than was expected. The government feared that the major beneficiary of such a policy would be the PS-controlled municipality of Tirana. However, the PD–PS conflict peaked in the spring of 2006 as construction police, part of the executive branch, halted the construction of a traffic flyover that had begun in 2005, financed by the municipality. The country's central institutions, including the Tirana District Court who ruled in favor of the construction police, were divided in that debate. The Këshilli i Rregullimit të Territorit (Territorial Regulation Council) claimed that serious violations of urban planning rules had occurred during construction (Rhodio and Van Cauwenberghe 2006). Meanwhile, the ombudsman and the high state audit ruled that no consistent irregularities had been noted in municipality projects regarding public works. Giovanni Di Stasi, then president of the Congress of Local and Regional Authorities (CLRA), criticized central authorities during a visit to Albania in January 2006, and stated that "the powers of the Construction Police and the composition and functioning of the Territorial Regulation Councils do not conform to the provisions of the European Charter of Local Self-Government, and this creates a lot of misunderstanding and confusion."[16] In July 2006, the Zogu i Zi flyover was completely demolished by the construction police.

On February 18, 2007, Edi Rama was re-elected mayor of the capital city and the PS also gained control of other important municipalities around the country.

Perhaps because the electoral fervor was soon forgotten or because the government was focused on other political priorities (mainly the construction of the Tirana–Morina highway), the political climate following local elections shifted to cooperation. Jurisdiction over the Inspectorate of the Construction Police, whose office is responsible for verifying that projects go through proper licensing procedures, was transferred to local government. In addition, during the same year, legal and institutional measures were taken to transfer responsibilities related to the value-added tax (VAT), local taxation, water supply and sanitation from the central government to municipalities.[17]

However, such a détente came to an end with the approach of the summer 2009 parliamentary elections. In April 2009, the Kuvend established an investigative commission to look into building permissions issued by the municipality of Tirana. No parliamentarian from the opposition agreed to sit on the commission, and it continued to work only with parliamentarians from the ruling coalition. Also, during the same spring, the Kuvend approved a proposal to reduce local government's fiscal share of small business taxes from 30 per cent to 10 per cent. These changes in the fiscal system of the country also limited the ability of local government to impose tariffs on trade and services, thereby reducing local income from tariffs by 90 per cent. The central government has not yet undertaken measures to compensate local government budgets for these losses.[18]

Later that year, on November 15, local representatives initiated a round of protests regarding the subject of financial autonomy, accusing the government of cutting local budgets as a way to balance the impact of the global economic crisis on the state budget. They asked for concrete actions, warning that they would otherwise use all democratic forms of protest to force the government to find an appropriate solution. Additionally, local and central governments continued to clash over the transfer of water supply and sewage systems as evidenced by related judicial proceeding initiated by the municipalities of Tirana and Himara against the central government in 2008. In February 2009, the Constitutional Court declared an attempt by the central government to take over responsibilities from local authorities on issues involving administration of the territory to be unconstitutional.[19]

In early 2009, the Kuvend passed changes to the Law on Legalization, Urbanization and Integration of Unlicensed Buildings that would transfer responsibilities of local government to the state-run Agjensia për Legalizim, Urbanizim dhe Integrim të Zonave të Ndërtimeve Informale (ALUIZNI) (Agency for Legalization, Urbanization and Integration of Informal Buildings). The changes were brought before the Constitutional Court by PS parliamentarians, and the court declared the amendments unconstitutional. However, in May 2009, the government passed an executive decision claiming that local governments would not be able to execute their responsibilities on time, and thus mandated that these duties should be transferred to the ALUIZNI. The decision challenged the earlier court ruling, as well as constitutional principles that clearly emphasized that the distribution of power may not be altered by a simple majority law or by a subordinate legal act. The government was determined to overstep its responsibilities regarding local government.[20]

The conflict even became physical when, at the beginning of November 2009, a dispute took place in downtown Tirana between the construction inspectorate of the municipality and state police, ending in violent clashes. The conflict arose over a decision by the government to halt construction of the city center approved by the Territorial Regulation Council of Albania in 2004, and later approved by the Territorial Control Council of Tirana in October 2008, after an international bidding process. The government demolished the construction site, stating that it would build a public park on the area, which had been designated for private investment. One of the investors affected by the government's action was a stockholder of Vizion Plus, a TV media outlet known for its criticism against the government.[21]

Since becoming prime minister in 2005, a major concern of PD chairman Sali Berisha has been to regain control of the Tirana municipality. The PD had controlled the municipality of Tirana from July 1991 to October 2000, when they lost it to Edi Rama from the PS. Ever since, the PD lost two mayoral elections in the capital, even though Premier Berisha has endorsed as mayoral candidates some of the most popular politicians from his party.[22] The PD's failure to regain the Tirana municipality has had negative repercussions for the decentralization process in the country. Ever since it took the control of the central government, the PD has expanded the range of local government responsibilities, while continuing to control most of the local taxes and even narrowing opportunities for expansion of local fiscal capabilities.

Opposition complaints against the government's efforts to reduce the fiscal base of local governments received some international recognition when the Report of the OSCE Presence in Tirana claimed that "[t]he 2009 amendments to the Law on Local Taxes appear to conflict with the Law on the Organization and Functioning of Local Government that grants local government the right to establish fees in connection with the cost of service provision" (Grabbe 2001, 1,020). Another view maintains that the Law on Loans to Local Government, adopted by a unanimous vote of the Kuvend in February 2008 will eventually enable municipalities to increase long-term local investments. However, critics maintain that the Ministry of Finance has yet to complete the implementing legal acts (Bushati 2009). The outcome of the 2009 parliamentary election has also had a deleterious impact on the performance and reform of local government in Albania as a re-mandated PD has pursued since the very beginning a policy that has resulted in a number of diminished local responsibilities and budget cuts; while the PS's bitter opposition to the what it called rigged elections has polarization the country's political life to such an extent that a number of municipal councils have faced difficulties in approving their budgets for several months (Gjipali 2010).

On April 20, 2010, Bledar Çuçi, a former secretary general of the Ministry of Local Government and Decentralization and the current spokesperson for Shoqata për Autonomi Vendore (ShAV) (Association for Local Autonomy), an organization that represents elected local officials from the PS, appealed to the government to stop blocking foreign funding for development projects in municipalities administered by PS officials.[23] This statement was released after the representative for the World Bank in Albania, Camille Nuamah, complained that the Albanian Ministry of the Interior in charge of implementing one component of the Land Administration Project (LAMP) "has not awarded any civil works contracts, despite consistent efforts and support by the World Bank during its supervision of the project."[24] LAMP is the largest and perhaps most complex project the Bank has financed in Albania; a US$56 million (with US$35 million coming from the World Bank) venture involving three ministries—justice, public works and interior—and 10 municipalities—Berat, Durrës, Elbasan, Fier, Gjirokastër, Kamëz, Korçë, Lushnjë, Shkodër and Vlorë. The project has also been co-financed by the Swedish International Development and Cooperation Agency (SIDA) and the Japanese government. In its complaints against the government, the PS pointed to the fact that eight of the ten municipalities administered by PS mayors had not received the untapped LAMP awards.

By the end of 2010, the political struggle between PS mayors and the PD government erupted over two hotly contended issues. First, the PS appealed to the government to withdraw a bill from the Kuvend regarding changes in the current law on local taxes that, according to the mayor of Tirana, Edi Rama, sought "to shift on[to] the local government the burden of government corruption with the newly introduced cash registers."[25] In Rama's views, the government was trying to take municipalities administrated by mayors of the opposition party hostage, right on the eve of the spring 2011 local elections. In addition, the ShAV called upon the government to discuss items related to local government in the 2011 state budget before the parliamentary procedures for its approval.[26] Second, the government attacked the new urban plan of the capital city. The new plan was drawn by a French studio selected through an international competition organized and financed by the municipality of Tirana in 2008. Even though the Tirana Territorial Regulation Council had approved the new plan, in November 2010 the government threatened to reject it, claiming that the plan did not satisfy all the needs of the capital.[27]

The political struggle between the PD-dominated central government and PS-dominated local governments has also attracted criticism from international observers noting that "a less politicized dialogue is needed among central and local government in order to foster a clearer framework."[28] One of these observers, the head of the OSCE presence in Albania, Robert Bosch assesses the current state of local decentralization in Albania as follows:

> The process [of local decentralization] itself often appears disjointed and lacking in transparency as the government's approach currently lacks clarity regarding the desired structure of local and regional government. The provision of financial resources to local government has not kept pace with their expanded scope of responsibility and authorities for public service provision. New legislation in areas such as territorial planning, construction inspection and water supplies further challenged the principles of local decision making. The role of local government associations as advocates for common local interests also needs to be strengthened in order for them to achieve their considerable potential. The distributions of funds to the local authorities is also often less objective, meaning municipalities ruled by mayors of the opposition are less favoured especially with regard to the so-called competitive grants which are allocated in competition on top of the standard grants.[29]

Also, the European Commission's Albania 2011 Progress Report, while pointing to the amendments to the Law on Local Government Taxes as an effort to give local government units a mandate to reimburse small businesses for the cost of purchasing fiscal devices, emphasized that the increasingly difficult relationship between the

PD-led central government and the majority of PS-led local government units has continued to impact the process of decentralization reform, "which had previously been successful."[30]

Therefore, no positive developments have been recorded during the period of 2010–11 in the Albanian decentralization reform. However, in the political realm, tensions continued between the national government led by PD leader Sali Berisha and the municipality of Tirana led by PS leader Edi Rama to the point of reversing any previous progress in local decentralization reform, as noticed by both the EC's Albania 2011 Progress Report and an increase of the Freedom House's score of local democratic governance from 3.0 to 3.25.[31] The EC's Albania 2012 Progress Report was even harsher in assessing the country's lack of progress in the decentralization reform, noticing "no [...] progress [...] made on territorial administrative reform," thus continuing to allow the operation of small municipalities that are often economically unviable; "no improvement in revenue collection by local authorities during 2011"; a lack of transparency in local government decision making; and an over-politicized debate concerning the composition of local government bodies associated with the existence of two separate local government associations, split in membership along partisan lines.[32] As a consequence of the latter and the political disagreement between the associations, Albania has not been able to establish a unified delegation that would represent the country in the Council of Europe's Congress of Local and Regional Authorities of the Council of Europe since May 2011. Table 4.1 displays the scores assigned to Albanian local democratic governance.

The scores in Table 4.1 generally fit the observations of this empirical analysis for the period 2004–2009 (the years indicate the release of the score, and thus the developments of the previous year). As in other cases, the PD returned to power with the promise of reforms. The 2006 report, which indeed reflects progress during 2005, shows that the PD-led government's policy of increasing competences of local government, as well as its tax basis, significantly improved the level of decentralization in the country. However, my account reveals nothing that would cause the level of decentralization in Albania to move from 2.75 to 3.0. Therefore, I have interpreted the reform progress of that time simply as "reform halts" rather than "reform reverses." As for the reform reversal of the 2010–11, reported in the EC's Albania 2011 Progress Report and Albania 2012 Progress Report, the deteriorating score from 3.00 to 3.25 in the Nation in Transit's level of local democratic governance represents coherent evidence in favor of reversal of the local decentralization reform.

Table 4.1. The level of Albanian local democratic governance

1999–2000	2001	2002	2003	2004	2005	2006	2007	2008	2009	2010	2011	2012
n/a	n/a	n/a	n/a	n/a	3.25	2.75	2.75	2.75	2.75	3.00	3.25	3.25

Source: Freedom House, "Nations in Transit 2012." Online: http://www.freedomhouse.org/report/nations-transit/nations-transit-2012 (accessed February 10, 2010).
Note: The years reflect the period of the report, which is an assessment of the previous year's developments.

A consociational interpretation of EU motivations toward Albanian decentralization reform

Albania is a unified society. Thus, the country needs consociational practices only to build institutions receptive to EU consociational practices during the country's accession negotiations with the EU and its subsequent integration with EU institutions and processes. A local government built by consociational practices and receptive to them can be a powerful instrument for maintaining social cohesion in a deeply divided society. However, such local government might be unnecessary in a unified society. The case of the EU shows that it may be unnecessary even in a deeply divided society (in this case, the society of EU member states) if that society applies consociational practices to other institutions and policy areas. EU member countries utilize different local government systems and the EU has not included any local governance model in its Copenhagen criteria or Agenda 2000; nor does the EU usually assess in its annual progress reports a country's state of local decentralization or offer specific recommendations regarding the topic. Indeed, there exists no agreement among the EU countries and institutions about how much decentralization is about right for a country. Some scholars argue that a model of decentralization that may be appropriate for a federal state such as Russia, with its large territory and population diversity, may be inappropriate for small countries such as Albania (Sewell and Wallich 1996).

The 2010 Commission Opinion on Albania's application for EU membership does not refer to decentralization reforms in its rejection of the Albanian application.[33] Nor do the recommendations for mid-term development toward opening accession negotiations mention local decentralization.[34] Again, quoting OSCE's Robert Bosch, "the government's approach currently lacks clarity regarding the desired structure of local and regional government." Yet, the EU neither recommends one nor seems to possess a strategy for the rest of the EU; local government models and levels of decentralization of EU member countries widely vary. Thus, as Grabbe (2001, 1020) has pointed out, although the EU has advocated greater decentralization and regional development in Central and Eastern European countries, it has no clear model of regionalism to present. If we go back to Gabel's description of the EU as a "consociational democracy," we can easily see that neither the model of local governance nor the level of local decentralization play a role in establishing the EU as a stable democracy nor in its maintenance as such. Local decentralization seems not to be a consociational practice at the EU level, hence, in the case of Albania, this discussion is absent from EU membership conditionality.

A sectorial interpretation of Albanian decentralization reform

The Albanian local decentralization relies mainly on the political will of domestic leaders. The CoE can pressure governments to sign the ECLSG, but cannot do much to enforce its implementation. As a CLRA report notes, a very positive feature of Albanian politics is that every political party, whether ruling or opposition, and all key administration and civil society actors, unanimously agree that decentralization and the creation of an effective system of local government are to be given the highest priority

(Rhodio and Van Cauwenberghe 2006). However, the political parties do not always agree on how to tackle these problems or to what extent territorial structural reform needs to be enacted. One of the major difficulties in achieving the necessary consensus is the high level of distrust between the two main political parties, the PS and the PD. One of the byproducts of this mistrust has been a series of attempts by the ruling coalition to control local government. Yet, ostensibly, Albanian government's interests in controlling local government seem to have been undermined by the poor results these efforts have produced during the last 21 years, the growing pressure from local officials demanding more decentralization, and different NGOs focused on local development (Hoxha 2002).

From 1992 to the present, Albanian leaders' preferences with regard to decentralization have shifted from positive to neutral to negative. In 1992, the positive preference of the PD for decentralization resulted in the first local government reform after communism (Sewell and Wallich 1996). After local elections of July 1992, however, the reform stalled until 1996. The PD's interest in decentralization turned negative once it became clear that it would mean the increase of the autonomy for the predominantly PS local governments. The Albanian elites also dropped decentralization as a priority during the period of 1996–98, as the country was facing more acute problems. Decentralization reform advanced in 1998–2000. The PS-led ruling coalition wanted to prove to domestic and international audiences that its communist past was over, and that they had embraced the rules of democratic governance. However, the PS's internal power struggle brought decentralization reform to a halt. The reform revived in 2006 when the PD took control of the government following its electoral success in the summer of 2005. On the one hand, the PD wanted to demonstrate that it had abandoned its previously authoritarian style of rule; on the other, the PD was hoping that its candidates would win the fall 2006 local elections. The PS's electoral takeover of local governments in some of the most economically productive municipalities curbed the PD's interest in expanding local autonomy. Ever since, decentralization reform has either stalled or, in some areas, even reversed.

Developments in the country's local government reform during 2011–12 bring further evidence in favor of my model. First, obviously, is the fact that the EC did not include local decentralization in its 2010 Opinion's 12 key policy priorities that Albania should pursue in order to qualify for the EU candidate status. Rightly, one could consider it a methodological fallacy to infer motivations/interest from actions. However, in light of a previous lengthy discussion on this issue, and EC's persistence in not mentioning local decentralization even in such a detailed policy prescription such as its 2010 Opinion, clearly demonstrates its lack of preference in any specific outcome of local decentralization.

In turn, consistent with my model, 2010 represented the final year before new local elections. As I have argued before, there are no incentives for the ruling coalition to conduct reforms in the year before elections, especially when their outcomes seem uncertain. As for the second half of 2012, as Chapter 7 shows, the government remained overwhelmed by other policy priorities already highlighted in the EC's 2010 Opinion (hence the "0" rating for domestic leaders' interests in Table 4.2). The latter summarizes the findings of the reform efforts and compares EU preferences with domestic leaders' preferences.

Table 4.2. Developments in Albanian local decentralization reform

Period	Situation	EU Interests	Domestic Leaders' Interests	Reform Results
1992	Period of extraordinary politics	0	+	**Good progress.** The reform created a considerable degree of political autonomy to local authorities, some services in favor of local communities, and wider administrative and financial autonomy. These laws enshrined the principle of local self-government as one of the basic goals and principles of local government in Albania.
1992–96	The shift to ordinary politics	0	−	**No reform.** The PS's electoral success in the 1992 local elections doomed any deepening of decentralization reform by the PD-led central government.
1996–98	Political instability and state collapse	0	0	**No reform.** Political destabilization put local decentralization out of the political agenda.
1998–2000	PS assumes power	0	+	**Good progress.** The legislative framework underpinning decentralization reform helped the country to comply with 19 ECLSG articles, 11 of which are core articles. Yet, Albanian legislation still remains at odds with ECLSG on issues related to the administrative control of the central government over local administration.
2000–2005	PS's internal power struggle reflects in local governments	0	−	**Reform halts.** Some local decentralization legislation was passed, but most of the measures undertaken were follow-ups of 1998–99 policies rather than a sign of any positive political will.
2006	PD's first full year in power	0	+	**Good progress.** This represents the PD's first year in power during which time the party tried to implement some of its electoral promises and hoped to expand its electoral base for the upcoming local elections.
2007–2009	Second half of PD's first term	0	−	**Reform halts.** The PS's electoral success in the local elections of the fall of 2006 curbed the PD's interest in expanding local decentralization.
2010–12	Second half of PS-dominated local government mandate	0	−/0	**Reform halts/reverses.** Some changes in tax law can be interpreted as a setback for local decentralization reform. The difficult victory of the PD in the 2009 general election decreased PD officials' confidence in achieving victory in local elections of May 8, 2011. However, the highly disputable victory of the PD's candidate for mayor of Tirana did not contribute to improve local decentralization in the country. By then, both the EU and Albanian leaders were focused on the 12 key priorities outlined by the 2010 EC Opinion, and local decentralization was not among those priorities.

Conditioning Consociational Practices in Local Government: The Case of Macedonia

For Macedonia to become the multi-ethnic state it aims to be as laid out in Ohrid, reforms were required in at least three major areas: ethnic representation in state jobs, including the security forces and the army; the improvement of ethnic, and especially ethnic Albanian, public education; and a deep decentralization reform that guaranteed responsibilities to municipalities without devolving into a federal system. Therefore, an analysis of the local decentralization reform in Macedonia requires, first and foremost, an examination of the dynamics of ethnic politics in the country. However, since the problems of Eastern European democratic reform haunt Macedonia as well, one can easily imagine the challenges faced by the country's decentralization efforts. Macedonian leaders have oscillated from strong support for the reforms to dragging their feet, while ethnic Albanian political leaders have been eager to exploit such reluctance in their political rhetoric; meanwhile, all along the EU wanted to see the Ohrid Agreement fulfilled as a guarantee of peace and stability in the country. Thus, we can test both elements of my argument: first, by explaining how the EU continues to insist on exporting consociational practices to Macedonia in order to ensure its cohesion as a unified pillar in accession negotiations; and second, investigating how the combination of different preferences among the main actors, including domestic actors, leads to various policy outcomes.

Macedonian decentralization reform

Macedonia initially inherited 36 municipalities from the Yugoslav system, which consisted of the country's major cities and their surroundings. The 1996 Law on Territorial Organization[35] increased the number of these municipalities to 123, plus the large municipality of Skopje, the country's capital. Pre-existing municipalities in some local administrative units were thus split into smaller units "with no essential prerogatives and no intermediary level between them and the central government."[36] During this period, the Macedonian political process was sharply divided along both political and ethnic lines. The causes for the delays in Macedonia's local government reform rest on attempts by the central government to reduce the political influence of the Albanian minority. While the collective and individual rights of Albanians in Macedonia had been significantly expanded since independence, Albanians continued to consider such progress insufficient (Daskalovski 2006, 66). Macedonian leaders' interests in delaying major decentralization reform mirror the widespread fear among the Macedonian population that decentralization might lead to federalization and subsequently the autonomy of territories predominantly inhabited by ethnic Albanians (Marko 2004, 13). Arguably, for most Macedonians, local decentralization

is not a matter of territory or more abstract constitutional arrangements. The unitary state established after the break of the SFR of Yugoslavia is at the core of the very identity of the Macedonian nation and is perceived as a major guarantee for its survival. Namely, the fear for autonomy in Albanian-populated areas has prevented a deeper and meaningful decentralization throughout the entire period since the establishment of the republic.[37]

One must keep in mind that 1991–99 was a period of economic and political stagnation. The slow reformation of Macedonia has been affected by a complicated nation-building process as much as by the lack of will of leaders of the ruling, former communist Socijaldemokratski Sojuz na Makedonija (SDSM) (Social-Democratic Union of Macedonia) to institute such reforms. During much of the 1990s, the country marked little progress in any reform program. However, Macedonia signed the European Charter of Self-Government in 1996 and ratified it in 1997. Indeed, these milestones can be considered the initial steps necessary for a decentralized, local government system. Yet it took two more years for the VMRO–PDSh coalition to introduce measures for decentralizing the local government within the country's Strategy for Reforming the Public Administration. In order to implement these policies a working team was created within the Ministerstvo za Lokalna Samouprava (MLS) (Ministry of Local Self-Government) in March 1999. Meanwhile, a government report for LSG activity during 1996–2000 was deemed adequate to serve as a backup document for decentralization reform.[38]

Despite these minor developments, Macedonian ruling elites showed little interest in the decentralization process during 1991–2001. Meanwhile, the EU, trying to avoid another conflict in the Balkans, praised Macedonia as being an "oasis of peace," and remained committed to maintaining political stability in the country. Perceiving local decentralization as a risk to the country's stability, the EU preferred the latter rather than the former. Hence, the EU interests in local decentralization during 1991–2001 remained neutral.

The Ohrid Agreement did not relieve Macedonian fears related to what they perceived as the hidden agenda of Albanians. Macedonians, therefore, continued to see the agreement as a straitjacket that needed to be circumvented in order to maintain the pre-Ohrid Macedonia without somehow endangering Macedonia's prospect for EU membership. Fears that adhering to the Ohrid Agreement might threaten the existence of the Macedonia for Macedonian people, or even worse imperil the state's further existence, have had a major impact on discussions related to implementing local decentralization policies as foreseen by the Ohrid Agreement. Similar to constitutional reforms, both Macedonians and Albanians seemed to regard the devolution of power to local government as a zero-sum game, in which one gains control over communities at the expense of another (Brunnbauer 2002; Loomis, Davis and Broughton 2001). Macedonians fear the so-called Albanian hidden agenda in local decentralization, which implies that, once the Albanians take control of a decentralized local power and become the majority, they will develop centrifugal tendencies and eventually secede. Moreover, they also fear that the Macedonian identity will be threatened in Albanian-dominated areas (Brunnbauer 2002; Loomis, Davis and Broughton 2001).

A clear confirmation of these fears occurred in the fall of 2001 when the minister for local government in the National Unity Government, Faik Arslani, an ethnic Albanian from the PDSh, submitted to the Sobranie a bill outlining a new law on local self-government. Reportedly, the bill was drafted with the assistance of experts from the CoE. While the draft proposed wide-ranging responsibilities for local communities in education and health care, it alarmed the Macedonian parliamentarians, as its Article 61 provided an opportunity for communities to merge and create common administrations (Balalovska, Silj and Zucconi 2002; Brunnbauer 2002). In spite of the real intentions of its writers and proponents, the proposal could be easily interpreted as an attempt to merge Albanian-dominated municipalities in the northwestern and western part of the country. Macedonians were concerned that state authority in Albanian-dominated areas would be further weakened if devolution went too far. The opponents of Arslani's proposition pointed to the hostile attitudes of Albanians toward formal institutions in Albania and Kosovo, alluding that Albanians in Macedonia would display the same hostile behavior.

Both of the main Macedonian parties opposed the original version of the bill and suggested amendments, resulting in the postponement of an international donor conference. Albanian parties began to boycott parliamentary sessions and threatened to continue with such protests as long as Macedonian parties did not withdraw their amendments to the original draft. Only after intense and painstaking international mediation, mainly by then chief of EU common foreign and security policy Javier Solana, was it possible to reach a compromise. As Arslani explained in the parliamentary debate over the conciliatory bill, instead of common administration the bill now allowed for the establishment of common administrative bodies among the municipalities.[39]

The Law on Local Self-Government passed in January 2002 amid squabbles over who would have access to the lucrative state health fund. Although the law expanded municipal capacities, it gave little direction for implementation. The transfer of a dozen functions performed by the central government to local governments lacked both a mechanism and a schedule (Marko 2004).[40] According to the proposed amendments, the local administration director would be appointed by the mayor and not the municipality council.[41] In order to adopt three additional laws to regulate this sphere, as well as the needed changes to some 80 other laws, the deadline for implementation was postponed until the end of 2003. It was finally passed by an almost unanimous vote on January 25, 2002 (ibid.).[42] Reportedly, the US Department of State welcomed the agreement on the Law on Local Self-Government reached by the political leaders in Macedonia.[43]

Article 22 of the new law on Local Self-Government enumerated 12 activities transferred to local government,[44] but it did not include or schedule how and when to transfer these powers. In addition, two more laws were required according to the Ohrid Agreement: a law on local finance and a law on municipal boundaries. A meeting of the agreement signatories in December 2002 extended all the decentralization deadlines until the end of 2003, thus undermining the chances of a timely harmonization of laws that would make implementation of the new Law on Local Self-Government possible. Finally, the completion of the transfer of responsibilities was postponed until after local elections in late 2004 (Marko 2004).

The process for implementing local decentralization as stipulated by the Ohrid Agreement was met with objective and subjective hurdles. First, the slow pace of decentralization reflected the need to resolve all questions related to finances and boundaries before transferring responsibilities (Marko 2004).[45] Another source of delay was the IMF's insistence that municipalities be barred from assuming debt and that they should be consolidated into more economically viable units.[46] Criteria of good governance required that, as Minister of Local Self-Government Aleksandar

Gestakovski highlighted, virtually all questions of financing and boundaries needed to be resolved before any substantial transfer of responsibilities.[47] In contrast, Annex B of the Ohrid Agreement stipulated that the law on local finance should have been adopted by the middle of the 2002, the end of the parliamentary term, and the law on municipal boundaries by the end of 2002. Taking into account the much-delayed census results, the parties largely recognized that the law on municipal boundaries had priority over the law on local finance. However, arguably, the government could have transferred powers that require little money to select municipalities as it continued to work on the complexities of full decentralization.[48] Moreover, reportedly, some mayors expressed strong willingness to cooperate over projects such as water treatment plants. Keeping in mind that municipal cooperation is freely permitted in the Law on Local Self-Government, and with active international support this could help reduce tensions and stimulate further local activism, it can be concluded that, at that time, the governments continued to display centralizing tendencies (ibid.).

Obviously, such a clash of good governance principles and the political stipulations of the Ohrid Agreement allowed room for political maneuvering; Premier Crvenkovski tried to represent the process as a zero-sum game (Marko 2004).[49] The Albanian leaders had their own difficulties: reportedly, Ahmeti's "blasé attitude" toward the reform reflected his problems with the Albanian mayors elected in 2000 from the rival PDSh.[50] Criticized about the slow pace of reform, a frustrated Gestakovski predicted that decentralization would take "ten to fifteen years to complete" (ibid.). As for the international actors, a total of 23 foreign government agencies, international organizations and NGOs were working separately on Macedonian decentralization with little coordination among them (Marko 2004).

The operational program for decentralization that the government was to begin to implement in 2003 listed 38 laws needed to complete the transfer of power from central to local governments, in addition to 12 other laws related to matters of fiscal decentralization, territorial restructuring, local elections and citizen participation. A mixed group of officials and experts began working to reduce the number of municipalities from 123 to between 60 and 67. With the Council of Europe's assistance, the Ministry of Local Self-Government developed five main criteria for eliminating municipalities related to size, economic resources, adequate municipal property, infrastructure, and natural and geographic conditions. The minister cited a sixth criterion, which was not registered in the government document: specific historical and cultural features, a blatant attempt to preserve certain ethnically distinct municipalities (Marko 2004).[51]

Moreover, these criteria fueled political rivalries as each ethnic group tried to maximize its benefits. Reportedly, a BDI representative explained:

> We want to maximize the number of municipalities where Albanians make up 20% of the population (and thereby make Albanian an official language) and we want to bring Albanians into connection with the urban center. The Macedonians wanted the opposite, namely, to preserve Macedonian urban control, keeping Albanians in rural areas, and minimizing the number of 20% Albanian municipalities. (Marko 2004, 15)[52]

However, both Albanian and Macedonian locally elected officials from small municipalities feared consolidation since many stood no chance of being elected in larger territorial units.

In February 2004, the ruling coalition began to discuss municipal border revisions during closed-door meetings among the three partners of the ruling coalition: the SDSM, BDI and Liberalno-Demokratska Partija (LDP) (Liberal Democratic Party). Reports were regularly leaked to the press, revealing that key municipalities such as Struga, Skopje and Kičevo had become the topic of hot political debate (Marko 2004). The redistricting efforts sparked public protest, as they were perceived as an attempt to destroy the unitary character of the country and to disregard local interests and traditional regionalisms. Thus, the Skopje-based Center for Research and Policy Making (CRPM) criticized the process for being developed without incorporating broad public debate on the new territorial boundaries of the municipalities, without consulting local officials within the Zadniča na Ediničite na Lokalna Samouprava (ZELS) (Association of the Units of Self-Government of the Republic of Macedonia) or considering the concerns of foreign and domestic experts. The process was also criticized for not taking into account the will of the people, ignoring in particular the expressed objections of 41 municipalities for redrawing the district boundaries. Moreover, the process was considered in violation of Article 3, Section 2 of the Ohrid Agreement, which proclaims that "the revision of the municipal boundaries will be effectuated by the local and national authorities with international participation." Finally, CRPM stated that the process put Macedonia at odds with its international commitments since the country had signed and ratified the European Charter of Local Self-Government which states that "changes in local authority boundaries shall not be made without prior consultation of the local communities concerned, possibly by means of a referendum where this is permitted by statute" (Article 5) (Daskalovski 2006, 209).[53]

These objections came from the ethnic Macedonian public and organizations, which promoted Macedonian dominance. While their arguments publicly stressed technical matters and good governance, they rested on underlying fears of Macedonians that the new divisions would create an administrative territory, stretching uninterrupted throughout the western territories of the country, dominated by Albanian population.[54] Although the draft left about 55 per cent of the existing local units unchanged, the Macedonian public was concerned about two potential interconnected ramifications of the proposed bill. The first was related to good governance and fears that some ethnic categories, namely Macedonians, would be denied access to public resources in municipalities dominated by Albanians, a concern supported by events occurring in the Albanian-dominated cities of Tetovo and Gostivar where, after 1991, most Macedonians lost their jobs in the public sector due to the Albanian takeover of local government.[55] Some Albanian municipalities expressed fears that if large Albanian villages, such as Zajas and Velešta, join Kičevo and Struga respectively, they would remain underdeveloped and would lack access to public resources.[56] The second major ramification of the proposed bill, according to Macedonians, was the potential erosion of Macedonian-ness in the new Albanian-controlled municipalities, as well as in Skopje. Some argued that municipal services in the Albanian language would waste municipal resources. Others claimed that the bill jeopardized the symbolic meaning of Skopje, and the capital of the Macedonian nation would lose its Macedonian identity (Daskalovski 2006, 213).[57]

On July 15, 2004, the draft bill was presented in the Sobranie's floor; it was passed on August 11 with only the votes of the ruling coalition. However, before the law was passed, it met fierce resistance from the opposition party, the VMRO–DPMNE. The latter partnered with Svetski Makedonski Kongres (SMK) (World Congress of Macedonia), a diaspora organization that had organized a 20,000 participant protest in Skopje on July 27. From February of that year, the SMK had begun to collect signatures for a referendum, but managed to collect only 80,000 of the required 150,000 signatures during the first six months of the initiative (Daskalovski 2006, 213; Marko 2004). While there had been protests and a series of referenda in 41 municipalities across ethnic lines, these were ignored by the government coalition (Daskalovski 2006, 214; Marko 2004). However, after the VMRO–DPMNE allied with the SKM initiative, the grassroots campaign gained significant citizen participation. As a result, by the August 23 deadline, the movement had collected 180,454 signatures, more than what was needed, causing President Crvenkovski to declare a referendum vote on November 7, 2004 (Marko 2004).[58]

Although poll data showed support for the referendum across ethnic lines, the overwhelming ethnic gap in such support (73.9 per cent of Macedonians and only 7.8 per cent of Albanians), illustrated the gulf between Macedonian and Albanian perceptions of decentralization reform.[59] The entire referendum propaganda was built on the dichotomous fear that the Macedonians would either lose their country or their bid for EU membership. The opponents of the referendum argued that a vote "for" would jeopardize the country's membership in the EU and NATO. The proponents of the referendum claimed that Macedonia would not "lose" the EU since a vote "for" should not be considered against the Ohrid Agreement or the EU and NATO membership, but only against shady political maneuvers of self-serving groups during the reform drafting process.[60] Such rhetoric notwithstanding, the proponents of the referendum accused the government of treason, by bowing to ethnic Albanians' demands and gerrymandering, thus showing that their opposition was grounded not on concerns about good governance but on fears that ethnic Macedonians would further lose their dominant position in the life of the country.[61] Therefore, while their explicit claims seemed to concern mainly the "dirty" political tactics employed, their campaign language suggested simply a return to the law of 1996 with no alternative proposals for decentralization (Marko 2004). Local Macedonian officials, such as the mayor of Struga, rejected the law and proclaimed that the city would declare independence "following the example of Monaco, Andorra or San Marino" (ibid.).

Given the legal stipulation of the 50 per cent participation threshold for a referendum to be valid, the government decided to undermine the referendum by using a demobilization strategy, telling people that it was "not worth an answer" (Daskalovski 2006, 215). The ruling coalition defended the reform as an obligation to the Ohrid Agreement, and then-president Crvenkovski argued that decentralization was the most important part of the Ohrid Agreement (Marko 2004). Ali Ahmeti of BDI, the

Albanian partner of the ruling coalition stated in an open letter: "Shall we participate in the referendum, thus becoming a stumbling block for our country's integration into the European Union, or shall we vote for Europe by ignoring the referendum? Shall we vote for the future or the past?"[62] Support came also from the EU. The president of the European Commission Romano Prodi addressed the Sobranie, and waved the EU "carrot" by linking the referenda results with the country's future in the EU by stating: "Europe is here, at the reach of your hands [...] However, the decision depends on you [...] to say whether you want Europe" (ibid., 4).

Two events affected the outcome of the referendum: first, with only two weeks until the referendum day, rumors circulated regarding the presence of uniformed men in the Albanian-inhabited village of Kondovo on the hills northwest of Skopje. As public and media tensions concerning the group's origins and motives mounted, it became clear that the group was a ragtag mix of roughly 50 men from Kosovo's UÇK/KLA, Macedonia's UÇK/NLA, Albanian fighters from the Albanian-inhabited southern Serbian region of Preševo and local countrymen. They threatened violence if the referendum passed. Second, on November 4, 2004, the US announced that it would recognize Macedonia by its constitutional name the "Republic of Macedonia." This was a surprising decision, since international arbitration on the name issue still continues under UN auspices. The US explained that although it recognized the name "Macedonia," it still supported the UN process.[63] The EU reacted quietly in support of the US position, sparking Greece's outrage and threats to block Macedonia's accession unless the name issue was resolved. However, the very next day, Greek premier Kostas Karamanlis assured fellow members in the EU summit in Brussels that Greece would not block Macedonian membership negotiations over the issue, but emphasized that the issue must be resolved before Macedonia could actually join the EU. The US action was greeted with great enthusiasm in Macedonia and gave President Crvenkovski the chance to celebrate and reinforce the government's message in a speech at a "victory party" celebrated on the eve of the referendum on Skopje's main square (Marko 2004).[64]

To the surprise of even those who opposed the referendum, the 26.58 per cent voter turnout was lower than anyone expected, thus making invalid 94.01 per cent of votes "for." Scholarly efforts to find domestic reasons for the referendum's failure have emphasized the split in VMRO–DPMNE, the main opposition party (Marko 2004).[65] From the Albanian camp, keeping voters away from the polls was much easier, since the referendum itself was perceived as a Macedonian effort to stall the implementation of the Ohrid Agreement. Although the PDSh initially declared that it would ask its voters to vote "for" in the referendum as a protest against the slow implementation of the agreement, finally it boycotted the referendum. Arguably, Gruevski's VMRO–DPMNE saw the referendum as an opportunity to weaken the government's legitimacy and consolidate its image as more capable of defending the Macedonian-ness of the country. Even though Gruevski never spoke against the Ohrid Agreement, he picked the referendum as an opportunity to campaign against the government.

One interpretation is that the VMRO–DPMNE effort fell short in large part because the party failed to provide an attractive alternative vision, and that simply striking a contrarian pose, something of a hallmark of Gruevski's leadership, failed to motivate voters (Marko 2004).[66] This may not be a sufficient explanation, however, given the strong ethnic alignment of the country's electorate and the significant role that emotions play in people's political behavior in ethnically divided societies. It seems much more plausible to find the causes of the referendum's failure with international actors, namely the "carrot-and-stick" policy of the EU and overwhelming enthusiasm generated by the US's recognition of Macedonia by its constitutional name. As Marko (2004) reports, polls published by the International Republican Institute (IRI) revealed that, between June 2003 and April 2005, approximately 93–97 per cent of respondents showed overwhelming support for Macedonia becoming a member of the EU. On the other hand, US support for the constitutional name of the country, against the wishes of NATO ally Greece, helped soothe the Macedonian public's frustrations with US policies in the Balkans and Macedonia proper, as the US was perceived by Macedonians to be pro-Albanian. I discuss this issue in more detail in the next subsection.

The referendum led to the postponement of local elections previously stated for 2004. Those elections were eventually held in March 2005, and won by the parties of the governing coalition: the SDSM won 37 mayors, the BDI 21 mayors. From the opposition camp, the VMRO–DPMNE placed 21 mayors and the newly formed VMRO–NP only 3, whereas the PDSh–PDP coalition won 2 mayoral seats.

The referendum's failure and the initiation of Macedonian decentralization reform increased citizens' acceptance of local decentralization. In 2003, almost the same number of Macedonians and Albanian Macedonians found the decentralization process "acceptable," at 53 per cent and 58.9 per cent respectively. In 2004, just before the referendum, these figures increased slightly to 59.5 per cent and 63.7 per cent. In 2005, after the local elections, support for the decentralization process rose to 73.7 per cent and 81.2 per cent respectively (Marko 2004). Asked whether "the new law on territorial organization will improve the relations in your municipality," as many as 75.7 per cent of Macedonians responded that they would stay the same or improve in comparison to 78.4 per cent of the Albanians (ibid.). A major sign of a growing mutual trust between the Macedonians and Albanians was the appointment of an Albanian minister of self-government in June 2007, after successful negotiations between the ruling VMRO–DPMNE and PDP brought the latter into the ruling coalition.

The implementation of the new Law on Local Self-Government has allowed municipalities since 2006 to raise funds from their own revenue sources, government grants and loans. According to the new law, municipalities are responsible for setting tax rates and municipal fees on property. In addition to these revenues, the law on financing the local self-government units permits grants to municipalities from the central budget, and also allows municipalities to borrow from capital markets, if approved by the Ministry of Finance.

By 2007, only half of municipalities fulfilled the criteria for entering into the second phase of fiscal decentralization.[67] Another 17 of the 85 municipalities entered into this second phase in July 2008, bringing the total to 59. The 22 municipalities not permitted to enter the second phase of fiscal decentralization were those still burdened by sizable debts, whose activities were blocked by legal proceedings related to arrears (Daskalovski 2009). As a solution, the Ministry of Finance began to implement an EU-funded project to assist municipalities with public-finance management, especially those municipalities that had not met the financial criteria for entering the second phase of fiscal decentralization (Daskalovski 2010).

In 2008, internal audit units were established in 28 municipalities and an additional 10 put in place during 2009, but the local government units failed to introduce budgeting programs. In 2009, the ZELS demanded from the government that the three per cent of VAT allocated to municipalities be raised to six per cent, while the personal income tax allocated to municipalities be raised from three to 30 per cent. The government indicated willingness to gradually, until 2012, increase the percentage of VAT allocations to the municipalities from three to four per cent but refused to change the percentage allocation of personal income tax. Upon demands by ZELS, the government agreed to change the distribution of profits from mining concessions so that 78 per cent is allocated to municipalities. More importantly, the government agreed to transfer oversight of land to be used for construction of buildings and factories from the central to the local authorities, and is considering legal options for implementation (ibid.).

The first contact with any European Commission assessment of the decentralization in 2011 reads as follows: "Decentralisation of government—which is a basic principle of the Ohrid Framework Agreement—continued."[68] However, substantially, government measures during that period would bring only minor forward steps, involving mainly quantitative progress in the number of municipalities that have switched from the first phase of the fiscal decentralization to its second phase; the five municipalities that undertook that step brought the number of the municipalities to have entered the second phase to 79 out of a total 85 municipalities of the country. For a broader audience, this means a more substantial local management of financial resources. In quantitative terms, it means the application of the Law on Financing the Units of Local Self-Government with its requirement that the share of VAT transferred to municipalities increases to 3.7 per cent. Yet no significant reform progress has been achieved apart from adjustment to routine technical problems of local governance.[69]

Such a sluggish incremental development sets the tone for the 2011 Progress Report as well. With some sentences copy-and-pasted from the previous year's report, the latest report highlights that a program for implementing decentralization and local self-government for 2011–14 and the corresponding action plan has been adopted; and that all but one of the 85 municipalities has entered the second phase of fiscal decentralization, enabling a more substantial transfer of responsibilities and financial management to the local level. Finally, the 2011 Progress Report duly recommends that "[i]n the field of local government, progress on decentralization needs to be accelerated, in particular as regards the financial framework."[70] Table 4.3 displays the local democracy score of Macedonia according to the Freedom House's "Nation in Transit" annual reports.

Table 4.3. The level of Macedonian local democratic governance

1999–2000	2001	2002	2003	2004	2005	2006	2007	2008	2009	2010	2011	2012
n/a	n/a	n/a	n/a	n/a	4.00	3.75	3.75	3.75	3.75	3.75	3.75	3.75

Source: Freedom House, "Nations in Transit 2012." Online: http://www.freedomhouse.org/report/nations-transit/nations-transit-2012 (accessed February 10, 2010).
Note: The years reflect the period of the report, which is an assessment of the previous year's developments.

As the table shows, the failure of the 2004 referendum, which opened the way to the implementation of the 2004 Law on Local Self-Government, is reflected in the score improvement from 4.0 to 3.75. Ever since, the progress has been sluggish and insufficient to bring about any score improvement.

A consociational interpretation of Macedonian decentralization reform

What sets apart Macedonian decentralization reform from similar reforms in any other country in Eastern Europe is that in Macedonia local decentralization was seen not simply as a matter of good governance but as a political issue between two largest, contending ethnic communities, the Macedonians and the Albanians.[71] Therefore, the EU had to include this reform in its set of consociational practices. The most important of these practices is the designation of minority languages as official languages in local units where they are spoken by at least 20 per cent of the population. However, the rest of the Macedonian decentralization reform resembles other Eastern European decentralization reforms, with conflicts between local and central governments over responsibilities and taxes that crosscut partisan and ethnic lines. Moreover, praised as it continues to be, Macedonian decentralization reform has not managed to bring the country below the 3.75 score for local democratic governance as set by the Freedom House index, which is 0.5 worse than the much-criticized Albania in the same category. Obviously, local decentralization reform in a deeply divided society raises different expectations than a similar reform would in a more united society.

Local decentralization reform was seen as a key element of the Ohrid Agreement in three focus areas: decentralization of responsibilities in public services and fiscal policies (Paragraph 3.1); the redrawing of local unit borders (Paragraph 3.2); and the appointment of local police chiefs by local governments from a list proposed by the minister of the interior (Paragraph 3.3).[72] Even though Paragraph 3.3 remains a stipulation unique to the Macedonian case, its implementation seems to have been smooth (Daskalovski 2010).

Thus, the implementation of Paragraph 3.1 resembles decentralization reforms in other Eastern European countries. It is characterized by a struggle over responsibilities, a mutual distrust between the central and local governments, and limited human and financial resources within the local government (ibid.). This is a reform area beyond EU concerns for both Macedonia and other Eastern European countries that aspire to its membership. The implementation of Paragraph 3.2 typically calls for the application of consociational practices. As the paragraph is formulated, decentralization reform cannot be achieved through majority rule. Its implementation resulted with the creation of Albanian majorities in the towns of Kičevo and Struga, as well as a 20 per cent Albanian population in Skopje and other rural municipalities. On a larger scale, the latter implies that the language used by ethnic minorities in the municipality serves as an official language. Such a policy has been crucial for achieving peace and stability in Macedonia. It also entails proportional representation as a consociational practice, namely, the increase in the number of municipalities administered by ethnic minorities, reflecting these minorities' proportional share of local power. The redrawing of communal borders increased the number of Albanian mayors in the March 2005 elections to 23, 27 per cent of the 85 municipalities. Meanwhile, the 20 per cent requirement for implementing a second language as an official language at the local level replaced the majority requirement for the official status of minority languages at the local level.

Thus, the EU's strong support for Paragraph 3.2 of the Ohrid Agreement regarding Macedonian decentralization reform, as well as its near indifference to the issues stipulated in Paragraph 3.1, are understandable. The EU's recommendations to Macedonia in the conclusions of the "Communication from the Commission to the European Parliament and the Council: Enlargement Strategy and Main Challenges 2010–11" mention "constructive cooperation" between coalition members and emphasized the need for "more dialog [...] on issues concerning interethnic relations."[73]

These issues are interconnected: cooperation between coalition partners implies the cooperation of partners from different ethnic groups. The fact that the European Commission included recommendations for financial decentralization suggests that it connects the entire local decentralization process with a country's social cohesion. However, these conclusions came after the Commission recommended that the European Council should open accession negotiations with Macedonia in November 2009. Such soft language is quite different from Prodi's vigorous appeal to the Sobranie on October 1, 2004, to reject the referendum on the law on local self-government.

The following conclusions can be drawn: (1) the EU envisaged decentralization reform as an instrument to achieve democratic stability; (2) while the EU displayed interest in furthering Macedonian decentralization reform, it openly used the "carrot-and-stick" approach whenever the issue of referendum emerged. The redrawing of municipal borders and the implementation of minority languages as official languages at the local level are consociational practices, which have been applied during the Macedonian decentralization reform process and were required by the EU.

Macedonia is a deeply divided society and the EU is expected to demand consociational practices at two levels: domestic and EU. In the case of Macedonian decentralization reform, the requirement for consociational practices addressed only those policy aspects that were relevant to mitigating ethnic conflict. Lessening ethnic tensions will eventually help Macedonia to emerge as a single segment and allow it to negotiate consociational practices at the EU level. The EU is no longer advocating local decentralization in Macedonia because the practices that have already been implemented have managed to bring about a certain level of democratic stability. The remaining local decentralization reforms in Macedonia involve policies that do not directly affect democratic stability. Yet, the EU does not possess, nor provide guidance regarding a specific model and/or preferred level of decentralization. The very mention of local decentralization in the European Commission's recommendations to Macedonia may reflect the EU's looming concerns over potential ethnic conflict in Macedonia, but might also simply be a residue of previous language used to assess reform development in the country.

However, in the last two years political stability in Macedonia has been threatened more by intra-party than interethnic conflicts. Therefore, EU's consociational practices have aimed at the creation of elite cohesion as much as societal cohesion. As a result, fearful of the outcomes that elite fierce political struggle might cause, the EC and the Macedonian government launched the High Level Accession Dialogue (HLAD), on March 25, 2012. When the EC describes the purpose of the HLAD as to "inject new dynamism into the EU accession reform process, thereby strengthening confidence and boosting the country's European prospects," one can read it as an effort to keep elites unified around the already sluggish sectorial reform. While consociational theory assumes a social pillar's elites to be united, divisions among these elites would cripple their ability to reach out to elites of other pillars, a situation that would further undermine social cohesion rather than foster it.

The HLAD focuses on five key policy sectors, including protecting freedom of expression in the media; strengthening the rule of law; reforming public administration; improving the election process; and developing the market economy. Some of these sectors represent areas where tangible reforms have been taken and continue to be underway. However, I am not claiming that EU interest in Macedonian reforms has disappeared. Rather, its preferences have diverted to reforms that most likely would generate a broader intra- and inter-elite consensus, and avoid the inherent controversies of the local decentralization reform.

A sectorial contextual interpretation of Macedonian decentralization reform

We have thus mapped out the EU's interests in Macedonian decentralization reform. Earlier in this section we have analyzed the Macedonian ruling elites' preferences regarding decentralization. To reiterate, until 1996, Macedonian ruling elites were not interested in decentralization reform. As discussed in a previous chapter, the former communists who won the elections in 1990 and 1994 had little interest in showing any break with the past. Their main concern was the consolidation of independence and national sovereignty; a decentralized local government was perceived as threatening both to the unitary character of the Macedonian state and Macedonia's territorial unity. During the same period, the EU was interested in defusing any potential ethnic conflict in the Balkans, and Macedonian stability was perceived as more important than human rights and good governance. EU officials have often been either indifferent to or critical of Albanian complaints about their lack of ethnic/group rights.[74] A combination of the EU's neutral preferences and Macedonian ruling elites' negative preferences in local decentralization reform explains the absence of progress in that sector until 1995.

Two events improved the Macedonian elites' preferences in local decentralization reform in 1995: Greece's lifting of the embargo on the country; and the General Framework Agreement for Peace in Bosnia and Herzegovina, also known as the Dayton Accord. Both these events increased confidence among Macedonian elites that the country's independence was assured and that they could therefore focus on domestic reforms to increase government efficiency. The result was the 1996 law on territorial organization. Although the law was a major leap forward as it changed the local government system in the country substantially, it still reflected the central government's fear of a widely decentralized local government; therefore, local government's responsibilities on public services and fundraising capabilities remained extremely limited. Indeed, the 1996 law concerned deconcentration more so than decentralization. No evidence exists to support the idea that the EU displayed any special interest in Macedonian local decentralization reform during that period; rather, it appears that reform was guided solely by domestic leaders' interests.

The local decentralization reform stalled in 1998 when the VMRO–DPMNE won the elections and the PDSh emerged as the largest ethnic Albanian party. The new government decided to draft the strategy for reforming the public administration in 1999, including adding measures to improve local government's efficiency. But the exacerbation of ethnic tensions in the period 2000–2001 interrupted this project. While the government continued to progress slowly with local decentralization, its focus turned more toward public administration reform. Again, there is no indication of any EU preferences on this matter, and the issue continued to rest with domestic elites. During 2001, the EU's interest in Macedonian decentralization reform increased, while the ethnic Macedonian ruling elites remained adamant against deepening decentralization. However, increased military pressure from UÇK/NLA and an effective "carrot-and-stick" policy from the EU, NATO and the US brought about the Ohrid Agreement and the 2004 Law on Local Self-Government.

Subsequent policy measures have reflected the gradual implementation of the 2004 law, rather than a substantial deepening of local decentralization in Macedonia. However, while these efforts show the government's commitment to implementing the 2004 law, Freedom House's 3.75 score for local democratic governance in Macedonia (despite its possible inaccuracies) shows that the country has a long way to go in expanding and strengthening local decentralization. Currently, the EU's interest in Macedonian local decentralization has diminished, although the nation's central government remains committed to the process. Macedonian fears regarding the country's federalization continue to impact the local decentralization process negatively, but that is not the only cause. Another impediment to progress might be the lack of human capacity to implement the financial decentralization package in rural and underdeveloped municipalities, especially Albanian municipalities.

Indeed, the last four years have shown a slowdown in Macedonian decentralization reform, as well as in all other sectors along with the quality of democracy in the country.[75] Such an outcome is consistent with my model, as well as with what other authors have argued: since the perspective of Macedonia to open accession negotiations with the EU no longer hinges on reform progress but on the Greek veto, pursuing financially and politically expensive reforms as strategies to acquire and maintain power seems the least feasible alternative. Therefore, Macedonian leaders across all parties and ethnicities have been paying great attention to short-term political gains through politicking, political process disruptions, overemphasis on procedures and identity politics.

Entrenched as they are in identity politics, the leaders of the Albanian community in Macedonia have never shown any sincere concern for good governance. Historically, they have built their political struggle on group rights and have been fierce combatants in political and military battles over the use of the flag, education, language and the like, as if these were the magic tools that would improve the livelihood of an ethnic Albanian in Macedonia. When many of these demands were finally met, the Albanian politicians in Macedonia showed the same indifference, and sometimes disdain, for good governance topics. While local decentralization in Macedonia needs a further push not simply to improve the political situation of the Albanians in Macedonia or to fulfill any EU conditions, but to improve the efficiency of local institutions for the benefit of all the citizens of the country, the Albanian elites in Macedonia have cheerfully jumped on the bandwagon and contributed to the tense political climate of the country. Like the rest of the Macedonian elites, they have dropped all interest in reform, instead focusing on potential quick and cheap gains that might come from political instability in the country.

One can also read the HLAD as an effort to not allow the country to backslide on sectorial reforms deemed key to political stability and the country's interethnic dialogue and cooperation. Now, the EU assesses local decentralization reform with blank statements such as "Decentralisation of government—which is a basic principle of the Ohrid Framework Agreement—continued," and "Progress in meeting the objectives of decentralisation needs to be accelerated"; it seems to pay closer attention to political instability—such as that caused by the boycott of the SDSM during the spring of 2011; the ethnic clashes spurred by the construction of a church-shaped museum inside the Kala Fortress in Skopje inhabited by an ethnically mixed population; or the ethnic violence against Albanian pupils by Macedonian mobs—than to the already exhausted decentralization reform. Table 4.4 charts the reforms over time, as well as their outcomes.

Conclusions

In the case of decentralization reforms, the EU has exercised membership conditionality unevenly and inconsistently. EU membership conditionality aims at enforcing consociational practices in deeply divided societies such as Macedonia, but remains absent in united societies such as Albania. As my argument states, the EU recommends consociational practices in order to enable its membership aspirants to build institutions that lead to stable democracies. Thus, institutions in united societies that aspire to

Table 4.4. Developments in Macedonian local decentralization reform

Period	Situation	EU Interests	Domestic Leaders' Interests	Reform Results
1989–95	A period of state building at the national level	0	–	**No reform.** During this period, Macedonian ruling elites were interested in promoting country's independence and national sovereignty rather than democracy and good governance.
1996	Macedonia overcomes some of its existential fear	0	+	**Good progress.** The end of the Greek embargo and the Dayton Accord alleviated some Macedonian existential fears, and helped the government to focus on reforms promoting democracy and good governance.
1998–2000	VMRO-DPMNE assumes power on a nationalistic platform	0	–	**No reform.** Reform stalled as leaders of the VMRO-PDSh coalition focused more on deconcentration than decentralization.
January–July 2001	Armed ethnic conflict	+	–	**No reform.** The reluctance of Macedonian elites to expand Albanian political rights led to an Albanian armed rebellion and strong pressures from the EU and other international actors to undertake reforms that would improve Albanians' position in the life of the country.
August 2001–November 2004	Post-conflict national consensus on reforms	+	+	**Good progress.** Local decentralization reform succeeds albeit strong domestic opposition.
2005–2012	Disillusion over countries' denied accession negotiations	0	0	**Slow progress.** This segment of the Macedonian decentralization reform is characterized by the implementation of the 2004 reform; yet, country's elite has been more focus on other policy priorities. The sluggish progress in fiscal decentralization represents more enumerating municipalities who have switched from one phase to the other, without any substantial impact in local development.

EU membership are asked to adopt appropriate consociational practices that can improve democratic stability on only one level, that of the EU, while institutions in divided societies are encouraged to appropriate consociational practices that can improve democratic stability at both domestic and EU levels. The lack of a unified EU decentralization model suggests that such a model plays no real role in achieving and maintaining EU democratic stability; hence there is no reason why the EU should uniformly require it from EU membership–aspiring countries. In the case of Macedonia, the EU demands local decentralization specifically so that Macedonia can emerge as a unified segment—or pillar—in the society of European states. However, not all Macedonian decentralization reform requires consociational practices, and the EU has been very active only in mandating consociational practices within the framework of local decentralization.

Chapter 5

JUDICIAL REFORMS

Let us begin with two observations about the judicial reforms in Albania and Macedonia. As one author notes,

> Establishing the rule of law, for Macedonia is not just part of the process of successful transition. [...] [A]s a candidate for full membership in the European Union is a crucial requirement for the country to fulfill the political criteria. [...] However Macedonia badly failed on the assessment from the European Commission. Although the progress report in 2008 stated that the country has progressed in adopting new legislation and changes in the judicial system, yet it concluded that the judicial branch is not independent and efficient. (Taseski 2010)

Meanwhile, the European Commission's Communication on Albania 2010 Progress Report points out that

> [s]erious concerns remain on the overall functioning, the efficiency and independence of the judicial. There is a lack of transparency in the appointment, promotion, transfer and evaluation of judges and there are considerable weaknesses in the inspection system of the judiciary. The cases of nonrespect of Constitutional Court decisions by government in recent years and the politicization of the vote on the President's Constitutional and High Court appointments are of concern as they challenge fundamental principles such as the independence of the judicial and the respect for the rule of law.[1]

These two quotes bring us to one of the most contentious institutional reforms in Eastern Europe: judicial reform. Why do Eastern European countries (EECs) experience such difficulties in conducting judicial reforms although the latter represent vital components of the Copenhagen criteria and are the focus of direct and bold conditionality from the EU? Before answering this question, we must take a brief look at the very nature of judicial reform.

Carothers (2006, 7) outlines three types of reforms that together can be interpreted as integrated judicial reform. Type one reforms involve the strengthening of law-related institutions, usually to make them more competent, efficient and accountable. These reforms include increased training and salaries for judges and court staff, and improving the dissemination of judicial decisions. Targets of type one reforms include the police, prosecutors, public defenders and prison administrators. These reform packages include efforts to toughen ethics codes and professional standards for lawyers, revitalize legal education, broaden access to courts and establish alternative dispute resolution mechanisms. Type two reforms include strengthening legislatures, tax administrations and local governments. Type three reforms aim at the deeper goal of increasing government's compliance with the law. As Carothers states,

> A key step is achieving genuine judicial independence. Some of the above measures foster this goal, especially better salaries and revised selection procedures for judges. But the most crucial changes lie elsewhere. Above all, government officials must refrain from interfering with judicial decision making and accept the judicial as an independent authority. They must give up the habit of placing themselves above the law. […] The success of type three reform, however, depends less on technical or institutional measures than on enlightened leadership and sweeping changes in the values and attitudes of those in power. (Carothers 2006)

One can claim with confidence that EECs have successfully resolved problems with type two reforms. A number of regional and global IOs, foreign governmental agencies and actors, international and domestic nongovernmental organizations (NGOs) and even individual foreign and domestic experts have offered Eastern European governments abundant technical expertise to draft laws and build judicial institutions and practices compatible with the best models used by advanced democracies. Carothers (2006, 4) rightly points out that "the primary obstacles to [type three] reform are not technical or financial, but political and human," and that rule-of-law reform "will succeed only if it gets at the fundamental problem of leaders who refuse to be ruled by the law," Type one reforms appear to be more complex; their implementation and further maintenance of functioning judicial institutions imply the need for human capital. While my research concerns Carothers's type three reforms, we still need to eliminate alternative explanations inherent in type one reforms.

One particular question arises: if the judicial methods are not traditional consociational practices that have helped to establish the EU as a stable democracy, why does the EU so forcefully require its membership-aspiring countries to establish independent, impartial and efficient judiciaries? My argument has two elements: one concerns the reforms and the other the institutions that they generate. First, the reform process is often as important as the reform outcomes, if not more so, during the difficult metamorphoses judicial reforms prove to be. The complexity of the judicial system makes it impossible to have a successful reform without elite pacts. Those very pacts represent consociational practices. Thus, judicial reforms highly rely on consociational practices. Second, I argue that judicial systems represent some of the most powerful and efficient instruments for guaranteeing the maintenance of consociational practices by all pillars. First, there can be no democracy without the rule of law; second, contracts need to be enforced for a market economy to operate; and third, the communitarian *acquis* must be implemented and, if necessary, enforced by tribunals.[2] Since the EU lacks "federal" criminal and administrative courts, only separate national judicial systems functioning along similar judicial and administrative principles would make possible equal treatments of cases throughout the Union.[3] By guaranteeing stable democracies in their societies, these judicial systems allow each of the EU member countries to exist as a united pillar-state, entitled and able to negotiate consociational practices with other pillar-states.

The rule of law is a prerequisite of the Copenhagen criteria that EECs need to fulfill in order to join the Union. In turn, the fulfillment of all the three Copenhagen criteria requires the establishment of the rule of law and an independent, impartial, competent and efficient judicial system that guarantees such a rule of law. The European Commission's Agenda 2000 succinctly sets "independent judicial and constitutional authorities" as one of the components of the "stability of institutions guaranteeing democracy, the rule of law, human rights and respect for and protection of minorities" (European Commission 1997).

On the other hand, Eastern European ruling elites tend to view the judiciary as the government's backyard. Several factors explain this sentiment, but I argue that the need to employ the judiciary as an ally in power struggles is the most plausible explanation. In unified societies, the ruling elites tend to play the control of the judiciary against their political opposition, but in ethnically divided societies an ethnically controlled judiciary serves one ethnic group at the expense of others. Political circumstances in which domestic leaders' preferences favor reforms toward independent, impartial and efficient judicial systems do exist. Several factors impact such preference change, and EU membership conditionality is one of them.

Albanian Judicial Reform

The collapse of communism left Albania with a totally politicized judicial system, which primarily served as an instrument of the political control of the Partia e Punës (PP) (Labor Party) over the entire life of the country. There existed a complete lack of judicial independence and due process of law. Moreover, the abrogation of private property and state monopoly on economy and trade under the former system made trade and civil codes irrelevant. The communist criminal code was repressive and the entire judicial system was accusative, that is, both prosecutor and judge were only interested in protecting state interests, leaving the accused stripped of legal defense rights.

In 1990, under the influence of democratic revolutions throughout Eastern Europe, the Albanian communist regime undertook the first steps toward transforming its judicial system. Thus, for the first time in 25 years, the Ministry of Justice and the bar institution were reinstated. The first pluralist Kuvend that emerged from elections of March 1991 addressed primarily constitutional issues. Time constraints prevented a full-fledged constitution drafting and approval process, and domestic actors were unable to develop a compromise within a reasonable time limit; in April 1991, the Kuvend approved a package of 44 constitutional laws, the Dispozita Kryesore Kushtetuese (DKK) (Major Constitutional Provisions), which became a provisional constitution. While the DKK lacked constitutional arrangements for the judicial sphere, the retraction of the old communist constitution, which forbade freedom of speech, citizens' association, peaceful protest, religion, free movement and private property, brought about dramatic improvements in legal and judicial conditions of the country. Moreover, due to political compromise, the composition of the High Court became more balanced with appointments from major political groups, including former communists and anticommunists alike. As the Organization for Security and Co-operation in Europe (OSCE) Report on Legal Sector Reform 2004 points out, the creation, organization and activity of the courts and the judicial sector, in general, were left as they had been with the constitution of 1976, except for segments inconsistent with the new constitutional structure. Intensive work took place during 1991–92 to restructure this sector.[4]

In March 1992, Albania held its second multiparty elections, which resulted in a landslide victory for the Partia Demokratike (PD) (Democratic Party) and its allies. The new PD-led government used its two-thirds parliamentary majority to introduce judicial reforms. The process began with revising the existing DKK, and adding articles that would help shape a new judicial system. First, the Kuvend passed Law No. 7596, April 29, 1992, which defined the shape of the judicial system and introduced the Constitutional Court, as well as the High Council of Justice, a mixed judicial/executive body which supervises the lower courts through Law No. 7574, June 24, 1992, on the Organization of the Judiciary.[5] However, the new reform took off along with a growing authoritarianism of the PD and in its service. The European Commission for Democracy through Law (hereafter the Venice Commission), with its Opinion on the Albanian law on the Organization of the Judicial in December 2005, criticized in retrospective the negative effects of the 1992 Law on the Organization of the Judiciary, specifically the reform setbacks caused by the redaction of articles promulgating rights and duties of the magistrates stated in the prior Law on the Status of Magistrates.[6]

The 1992 judicial reform was driven by domestic preferences in establishing a functional judicial system in the new political and institutional context of postsocialist Albania. Moreover, while domestic elites' preferences in reforming the judiciary were positive, assistance from international actors was insignificant; their preferences in judiciary reform in that period can be considered neutral. Furthermore, no evidence exists to show any EU involvement either in providing technical assistance or in recommending policies. In spite of OSCE partial criticism, the overall progress of judicial reforms during this period can be considered satisfactory and was even recognized by the OSCE as such. As an OSCE report notes, many of the elements created at this time continue in a somewhat modified form under the 1998 constitution.[7]

Foreign assistance to the Albanian government regarding judicial reform began in 1992, soon after the amendments to the DKK, through the Council of Europe's (CoE) programs and jointly through the CoE and the European Commission's (EC) Poland and Hungary Assistance for Restructuring their Economies (PHARE) program. Since 1993, the EU has provided funding for judicial reform and cooperated with the Council of Europe (CoE) in their first joint program, completed in June 1995. This program concentrated on drafting the Criminal Code and the Criminal Procedure Code, and also included intensive training for magistrates and other legal staff. During that period we can distinguish a growing positive preference for judicial reform in Albania by both the EU and the CoE. Witnesses to Albanian political developments during this time explain that these positive preferences toward reforms of the judiciary rested with the need of the EU and CoE to encourage political stability in a country that inherited a thorough absence of legislative and institutional framework to support reforms.[8] By that time, political stability in Albania had become more significant internationally given the conditions on an unsettled Balkans and the ongoing Yugoslav wars.

However, as we saw with other reforms, the positive preferences in improving the judicial system by Albanian ruling elites during a period of "extraordinary politics" (1991–early 1992) soon reversed due to a shift to "ordinary politics" in 1992–94. The ruling PD was concerned primarily with consolidation of power through a combination of nepotism and intimidation.[9] Thus, the shelving of judicial reforms during this period parallels the progress of other reforms, which was caused by the rising authoritarianism of the PD in power and its inclination toward centralized rule. The Venice Commission delegation's opinion viewed the 1992 Law on Organization of the Judicial as a step backwards in efforts to establish judicial independence from politics. First, they pointed to the fact that "questions of judicial qualification, appointment, transfer and discipline be left unregulated by either the Constitution or an Act of Parliament."[10] Second, it criticized the fact that, in reality,

> only some legislative action has since been taken, with the result that there is at present only piecemeal provision in the ordinary laws in force in Albania for rights and duties of judges in the exercise of their judicial functions, or for their qualification for office, or the grounds and manner in which they may be appointed, transferred or dismissed.[11]

The commission reached its conclusion based on the most important piece of legislation of the Albanian judicial reform from 1992 to 1994, namely the 1992 Law on Organization of the Judiciary: "the Commission wishes to record that it has been unable to satisfy itself that judges in Albania feel themselves free to arrive at their decisions without fear of negative consequences for their professional life."[12] These remarks made clear that Albanian judicial reform in 1992–94 had stalled and, in some aspects, even suffered setbacks.

A reply to the Venice Commission by then Albania's minister of justice Hektor Frashëri unveiled the existing tensions between the CoE and the Albanian government. Minister Frashëri countered, arguing: "[I]t is incorrect to consider that to date no legislative action is in hand, or that no enactment of the Albanian parliament is in force in Albania for defining the rights and duties of judges, their training, etc." (Frashëri 1995). Furthermore, defending his government's position, Minister Frashëri considers "incorrect the conclusion drawn in the third paragraph of item 'e' that the relevant chapter of the Constitutional Law No. 7561 of 29 April 1992 does not specify the grounds for [the] removal of district and appeal court judges, and that there is no other applicable statutory provision in this regard" (ibid.).

The PD's failure to pass its constitution through a referendum in 1994, the persistent critiques from the CoE and the EU about the pace and direction of the country's institutional reforms, and the PD's need to overcome the referenda failure by securing Albania's membership in the CoE, thus finally scoring a foreign policy success, drove the government toward judicial reform. The year 1995 saw a period of intensive legislative activity related to the judicial reform as the Kuvend passed the Criminal Code, January 1995; the Criminal Procedure Code, March 1995; and the Military Criminal Code, September 1995. In 1996, under the auspice of the CoE, the School of Magistrates for training and retraining judges and prosecutors opened in Tirana while the government prepared the Law on the Office of the Judicial Budgeting.

In addition, in the spring of 1995, upon the request of the Albanian authorities, a second joint program for judicial system reform took root in the EU and the CoE. The program was comprised of a series of specific projects including: (1) assistance to the Ministry of Justice for drafting an organic law, as well as the by-laws needed for its implementation; (2) the establishment of the State Office for Publications; (3) the creation of the School of Magistrates for training and improving the professional capabilities of judges; (4) support for the Office of the Bailiff; (5) prison reform, including the establishment of a training academy for prison personnel; (6) reform of the police academy and improvement of administrative law, including assistance to make Albanian legislation compatible with the European standards; (7) assistance to draft a new constitution; and (8) the reorganization of the Office of the Public Prosecutor. The success of the codification reform of 1995 stems from positive preferences toward judicial reforms by both Albanian and international actors, namely the EU and CoE, in the reform process and outcomes. By and large, Albania continues to apply the legal codes adopted in 1995.

After acquiring CoE membership in May 1995, the zeal of the PD government for pursuing further judicial reform diminished. The government continued its highly criticized policy of replacing old judges inherited from communism with poorly trained PD militants who had acquired knowledge of judicial procedures through intensive six-month courses. While the replacement of many old judges and prosecutors might have been necessary, the politicized manner in which the PD conducted the process jeopardized judicial independence and spurred reactions from opposition groups.[13]

Meanwhile, the CoE–EU Second Joint Programme confronted difficulties in the full implementation of judicial reform. After the rigged election of May 1996, the pace of reforms slowed considerably, due especially to the reconfiguration of the country's political theater. Political instability distracted leaders' attention from reforms as the ruling elites shifted their attention and resources to other political priorities. Political unrest and armed civil conflict between February and July 1997 led to a freezing of all PHARE activities in Albania until August of same year.[14]

The Albanian crisis of 1997 demonstrates the catastrophic consequences stemming from the inability of the judiciary to resolve contractual and institutional conflicts in society. First, a successfully reformed judicial system would have helped to establish an independent, stable constitutional court, which could have resolved conflicts between institutions and would have been able to resolve the constitutional crisis generated by the rigged elections of May 1996. Second, an efficient judicial system would have prevented the genesis of financial pyramid schemes. Instead, the judiciary's inability to arbitrate between contending political fractions, to ensure the safety of financial transactions or to guarantee that contracts were respected was a major cause of the 1997 institutional and financial crisis. An analysis of this segment of judicial reforms demonstrates that reform, or the lack thereof, reflects different levels of Albanian ruling elites' preferences in controlling the judiciary. Those preferences focused on maintaining power by any means rather than concerns for democratic stability. The staggering development of the Albanian judicial reform during that period clearly shows that, without domestic willingness to develop reforms, such efforts are doomed.

After the general elections of June 1997 the socialist-centrist coalition led by the victorious Partia Socialiste (PS) (Socialist Party) initially demonstrated a willingness to work toward judicial reforms. After having fought a difficult political battle during its five years in opposition, the new ruling coalition wanted to garner international support. However, the PS's political struggle as an opposition group has always been hampered by its Stalinist legacy. Therefore, most of the country's international partners continued to view skeptically the PS's return to power. The PS decided to use its newly won majority in the Kuvend to demonstrate to domestic and international audiences that it had abandoned its Stalinist past and was ready to play according to the rules of a pluralist society. The PS's commitment to follow such a path, born of its immediate need to redeem its thoroughly tarnished image, created enormous opportunities to resume reforms that had stalled since 1992.

Initially, the determination of the coalition generated successful results. A report of the World Bank notes, "The situation did improve dramatically [...] during the course of 1998. Albania's brand new constitution of November 1998 provides a clear foundation for judicial independence and the new law on Judicial Organization gives further legislative basis of this independence."[15] During the summer of 1997, the government resumed its collaboration with the CoE and EU. In January 1998, Albania signed an agreement with the European Commission and the CoE and began to implement the action plan for legal and judicial reforms. The Joint Programme coordinated the European Commission's and CoE's assistance to Albania, and the Albanian government committed itself to cooperating with the program. Since 1998, annual conferences have been held to assess progress with the action plan.

Important milestones of the institutional, legal and judicial reforms in 1999–2001 included the establishment of the Office of Ombudsman, the Office for the Budgeting of the Judicial System and the State Office for Publications. The Kuvend also passed a number of laws related to judicial reform, such as the organic laws of the High Court, Constitutional Court, High Council of Justice, Ministry of Justice and the Office of the Bailiff. In the same wave, with the initiative of the Albanian government, the Kuvend made some significant improvements to the Criminal Code and Civil Code in order to combat some newly emerging criminal activities in the economic sector as well as cybercrime and organized crime. The Standing Rules of the Minister of Justice for the judicial administration marked the beginning of reforms in judicial administration.

The years 1998–2001 represent a period of successful and fruitful collaboration between domestic and foreign actors; the coalescence of these actors' preferences brought further progress. Judicial administration and judges' careers emerged as reform priorities. The government program for 2002 states that "the judicial reform would also consist in drafting and approving a precise system of recruitment, career, stipend and protection."[16] After 2001, however, especially after the PS-led coalition's victory in tarnished elections, the country began to slip into a deep political crisis. The PS, as well as other minor parties of the coalition, became trapped in internal power struggles, and the ruling coalition lost its political initiative and vision. This multifold political crisis led to collusion between the government with organized crime, including contraband, human smuggling and trafficking and galloping corruption (Hysi 2004). It seemed as if the ruling coalition had already exhausted its energy during its first governing term, and the second term was destined to be plagued by reform fatigue. Not only did the coalition government lack the political will to further reform the judiciary; it also hampered any effort in this area.[17] Consequently, corruption encapsulated the Albanian judiciary, and recruiting judges involved in organized crime became commonplace.[18] Moreover, higher courts, abusing the already-established judicial independence, played a negative role in the progress of judicial reform by blocking reforms in court administration and career of judicial employees, as well as the regulation of the distribution of legal cases.[19]

The EU became aware of the Albanian government's lack of political will to carry out reforms. As the European Commission's 2004 Stabilization and Association Report notes, although the Albanian government continues to state that the country's progress toward the Stabilization and Association Process is a top priority, "its actions have not always supported this." The report also points out that many of the reforms needed to guarantee the proper implementation of the SAP had not been carried out, including "the fight against organized crime and corruption and the functioning of the judicial system."[20]

Yet another indicator of the judiciary's condition in that period was the inability to adjudicate government officials. As Freedom House notes, "[s]tatutes and courts granted government officials unacceptable privileges and special protections."[21] In the same vein, Human Rights Watch's report compiled a list of cases of the judicial system's reluctance to indict police officers with records of human rights violations, and pointed out that the Albanian Human Rights Group's legal actions in defense of victims has met with stonewalling by judicial authorities.[22] The evaluation of the Council of Europe regarding Albanian judicial reform during this time notes that:

> [t]he judicial system, which should play the most critical role in the fight against corruption and organised crime, is weak and ineffective. Its personnel is poorly paid and trained and seems to be at least partially corrupt. This also affects the enforcement of new laws, in particular with regard to serious crime.[23]

These remarks show that, despite the interest of the EU and its continuous pressure throughout Stabilization and Association negotiations to position the Albanian judiciary on the path of thorough reform, its efforts clashed with preferences of the Albanian government.[24] That conflict brought to a halt many elements of the reform process, except for laws relating to the Office of the Serious Crimes Prosecutor and the Court of Serious Crimes, for which EU pressure was especially firm.

The power shift that followed the 2005 national elections caused the EU to replicate its requirements regarding short-term, key priorities for future judicial reform. The Council of the European Union demanded that the newly elected PD-led center-right coalition (1) increase the transparency of the criminal and civil justice process; (2) guarantee that judges and prosecutors be appointed through competitive examination; (3) foster the status, independence and constitutional protection of judges; and (4) establish a transparent and merit-based system for the evaluation of prosecutors.[25] However, in 2007, Resolution 1538 of the Parliamentary Assembly of the Council of Europe (PACE) implies that the progress of the new Albanian government toward judicial reform had not gone far beyond what was inherited from its predecessor.[26] This tone resembled the EC's Albania 2005 Progress Report, which had called for caution, noting that despite "some positive developments, the proper implementation of the existing legislative framework and the overall effective functioning of the judicial system remain a matter of concern."[27]

Fervent efforts from the government to depose the prosecutor general and some of the members of the High Council of Justice characterized the 2005–2007 PD rule. In both cases, the government considered the targeted officials to be linked with organized crime, while its opponents considered governments' efforts to remove them as an attempt to control the judiciary. In such a politicized atmosphere, the reform process stalled despite the intensive technical assistance offered by the European Assistance Mission to the Albanian Justice System (EURALIUS) to the Albanian Ministry of Justice, which started on June 13, 2005.[28] As a result of the ruling elites' lack of willingness to promote judicial reform, some presidential decrees relating to some aspects of the reform, namely the reduction of district courts from 29 to 19, remained pending. Another decree, namely Decision 200/1, October 18, 2006, was turned back from the High Council of Justice who commented that "it should have been accompanied by a presentation of methodology and principles taken into consideration in drawing it up, as well as by a study and analysis of more concrete data collection."[29] Meanwhile, the Albanian press had been swift to criticize the Ministry of Justice for not having adopted a strategy for its reorganization (Sokolaj 2007).

In spite of incremental progress in the quality and transparency of the judiciary in 2006, Albania's judicial system remained weak and corrupt. Citizens continued to not have full access to court decisions. The government sent to the Kuvend a new draft law on the judiciary, which provided for the creation of administrative courts, transparent assignment of cases and improvements in the career structure of judges. The new draft required that appointed judges be graduates of the School of Magistrates in order to increase professionalism in the judiciary.[30] However, the draft failed to address some other causes of judicial weaknesses, namely the poor education and training of the judges, problematic pretrial detention systems, erratic implementation of court decisions and corrupt incentives for each actor in the judiciary that would undermine the rights of the defendant. For instance, the draft law failed to address the division of duties between the two inspectorates of the High Council of Justice and the Ministry of Justice. However, regarding disciplinary proceedings and the discharge of judges, the draft law has been considered an improvement over existing legislation; it specified the criteria and procedures for appointing court chairpersons and provided a list of their duties.[31]

The year 2006 can be remembered for the efforts of the judiciary to fend off political interference in the judicial system. The Constitutional Court ruled the 2006 amendment to the Law on the High Court of Justice as unconstitutional, as it required judges in the High Council of Justice to give up their judgeships in order to eliminate conflicts of interest.[32] The European Commission's Albania 2006 Progress Report refers to increased transparency in judicial procedures through the publication of more judicial decisions, the results of checks on violation of the procedural code, as well as in the field of enforcement of final judicial decisions through the reorganization of the Bailiff Service and the upgrading of the level of its employees.[33] However, in spite of changes aimed at improving the independence and accountability of judges, the system continued to be rife with inefficient appointment procedures and performance evaluation, unclear division of competences, slow judicial proceedings and a general lack of transparency.[34] In addition, while the 2006 amendment to the Law on the High Council of Justice aimed at eliminating conflict of interest among members of the High Council of Justice, it failed to address other important issues facing the institution.[35]

Government policies of 2007 produced mixed results for Albanian judicial reforms. The amendment to the Law on Organization and Functioning of the Ministry of Justice in March 2007 reshuffled names and responsibilities among the departments but left several issues unaddressed. However, the most significant events during 2007 were the reorganization of district courts and the dismissal of Prosecutor General Theodhori Sollaku.[36]

The reorganization and reduction of district courts from a total of 29 to 21 represented an effort to increase court efficiency and transparency. According to the National Strategy for Development and Integration, the reorganization of the courts should have increased both efficiency and transparency of trials and provided the necessary space and infrastructure within the courts. However, 24 judges, along with most of the administrative staff, lost their jobs during the reorganization process, causing serious constitutional problems due to the constitutional guarantees regarding employment of judges (see Bushati 2009).[37] EURALIUS made recommendations concerning a three-step strategy for the organization of courts, but the Ministry of Justice ignored these guidelines.[38] Reportedly, in November 2007, just two months after the implementation of Albania's own reorganization project, workload increased in central courts, efficiency fell and administrative costs skyrocketed.[39]

In October 2007, at the request of 28 parliamentarians from the ruling PD, a parliamentary investigation commission was established with the intention of removing Prosecutor General Sollaku, who faced accusations of corruption and links with organized crime.[40] Then president Alfred Moisiu fended off an earlier attempt to dismiss Sollaku, claiming that the Kuvend's decision lacked constitutional support. Asked by the prosecutor general to judge the constitutionality of the parliamentary investigation, the Constitutional Court ruled that "[p]arliament has no competence to check and evaluate the decision of the prosecutors in concrete cases."[41] However, the PD's efforts to remove Sollaku resumed after Bamir Topi, the previous leader of the PD's parliamentary faction, was selected president in July 2007. Although the opposition boycotted the commission, on November 5 the Kuvend voted in favor of dismissing the prosecutor general. Spartak Ngjela, parliamentarian and former ally of Premier Berisha, stated that "[th]e dismissal of the prosecutor general is an attempt of the prime minister to control independent institutions."[42] On November 22, President Topi decreed that the Kuvend's decision to dismiss Sollaku was valid. Soon after, the Kuvend approved Ina Rama as the new prosecutor general at the request of the president.[43]

The 2008 American Bar Association's Judicial Reform Index (JRI) for Albania noted that the "pace of judicial reform, with the aim of encouraging the functioning of an independent, transparent, impartial, efficient and professional judicial, is slow."[44] The report continues: "[C]ertain actions by political and judicial bodies over the last two years [were] perceived as political interference in the independence of the judicial and a dogged perception by the majority of citizens that the judicial is corrupt."[45] Meanwhile the European Commission's Albania 2007 Progress Report notes that

[o]verall, there have been some steps to improve the efficiency of the judicial. However, it has continued to function poorly due to shortfalls in independence, transparency and efficiency. Legislation planned to address these issues is delayed.[46]

The approval by the Kuvend in February 2008 of the long pending revised Law on Organization and Functioning of the Judicial System, which created the foundation for an objective, merit-driven appointment and evaluation system for judges, renewed hopes for change. The Law on Organization and Functioning of the Judicial System and the Law on the Office of the General Prosecutor, as well as the establishment of the parliamentary Subcommittee on Judicial Reform and the parliamentary Committee of Laws, Public Administration and Human Rights, passed as the result of a surprising bipartisan consensus in the Kuvend at the beginning of the year (see Bushati 2009).[47] However, obviously, the Law on Organization and Functioning of the Judicial System opened a window for the executive branch to control some appointments in courts. Specifically, the law leaves the appointment of the court chancellor in the hands of the minister of justice. Moreover, the law gives the court chancellor an important role in the appointment and removal of the judicial administration. Six months after the Law on Organization and Functioning of the Judicial System came into force, Shoqata Kombëtare e Gjyqtarëve të Shqipërisë (ShKGj) (National Association of Judges of Albania) challenged the law in the Constitutional Court for violating the independence of the judiciary.[48] In 2009, the Constitutional Court pronounced the duty of the chancellor to appoint the judicial administration to be unconstitutional. However, the government's attempt to involve court chancellors in appointments and removals of judicial administration, as well as the draft Law on Judicial Administration that the government sent the same year to the Kuvend, strengthened executive control over the courts. Moreover, the Law on Organization and Functioning of the Judicial System failed to address the division of responsibilities between the two inspectorates of the High Council of Justice and the Ministry of Justice.[49] These efforts clearly show that, during that period, the preferences of the Albanian ruling elites toward an independent judiciary were negative, and the PD's interests were in controlling the judiciary system of the country.

A new directive on amendments to the Law on the Office of the General Prosecutor became another bone of contention between the Office of the General Prosecutor and the government. Draft amendments completed in September 2008 by the Ministry of Justice were contested by the Shoqata Kombëtare e Prokurorëve të Shqipërisë (ShPSh) (National Association of the Prosecutors of Albania) as well as the general prosecutor Ina Rama. They saw the amendments as a way to increase the executive's control over prosecutors and allow the suspension of the general prosecutor, as well as the reduction of prosecutors' salaries. The amendments were perceived as opportunities for interfering in judiciary independence. Criticism from international partners assisting the Albanian judicial reform compelled the Ministry of Justice to involve the Office of the General Prosecutor in consultations. As a result, a new Law on the Office of the General Prosecutor was adopted by the Kuvend on December 29, 2008.[50]

The government's efforts to encroach upon the independence of the judiciary continued to be the most distinct feature of Albanian judicial reform during 2007–10, providing clear evidence of government's negative preferences in judicial reform in the direction prescribed by the EU. This was, indeed, the second half of the PD's term in government, and this dip in interest in judicial reform is consistent with my argument. In 2009, the government tried again to target judges and prosecutors through a lustration law. Passed by the Kuvend in December 2008, the new Law on Lustration foresaw the removal of judges and prosecutors who served during the communist regime. Although the implementation of the Law on Lustration was suspended by the Constitutional Court, the debate around it affected the judicial proceedings against former minister of defense, and current minister of environment, Fatmir Mediu as well as other high officials implicated in the 2008 accident in the ammunition plant in Gërdec, 20 kilometers west of the capital, in which 26 people died after a series of explosions caused by operation malfunction. The head of the team of state prosecutors building the case against Minister Mediu, Zamir Shtylla, was personally attacked in the media by Premier Berisha for alleged criminal involvement in the political persecution of citizens during the former communist regime. Shtylla resigned soon after the Law on Lustration was adopted. The case against Mediu, whose parliamentary immunity was revoked in order to allow investigations around him, was later dismissed by the High Court in September 2009 on grounds that his immunity had been reinstated with his re-election to the Kuvend (Gjipali 2010). In another instance of judicial malfunctioning due to intrusions from politics, Minister of the Interior Lulëzim Basha was accused by the Office of the General Prosecutor of abuse of office during his previous service as minister of public transportation and communication. The trial against Basha involved courts at three levels and was adjudicated in two parallel lines before the District Court of Tirana. Both cases ended up before the High Court, which issued two distinct decisions by separate criminal panels. According to the constitution, criminal proceedings against persons with immunity must be dealt with by the High Court, but the latter finally dismissed the case as a result of the contradictory decisions (ibid.). In both cases, the government openly took stances in favor of its officials, with the prime minister personally attacking the prosecutors of the cases.

As the European Commission's Albania 2008 Progress Report concludes,

[T]here has been limited progress in judicial reform, mainly on the legal framework. However, the justice system continues to function poorly due to shortcomings in independence, accountability and transparency.[51]

One major problem inherent in the Albanian judicial system is the gap between court decisions and their implementation. Although the number of implemented decisions increased in 2009, the number of unimplemented decisions was much higher (5,806 to 8,057, respectively, according to the Annual Statistics Report of the Ministry of Justice). State institutions continue to fail to enforce court rulings. In many cases, state institutions blame their failure to execute court decisions on budget shortfalls. The Constitutional Court decided in January 2009 that the failure of the Bailiff's Office to enforce decisions was a violation of the constitution. The new Law on Private Bailiffs adopted in 2009 aims to liberalize the enforcement services and thereby increase competitiveness while reducing corruption, but implementation has been slow. Other secondary legislation for the implementation of the law has yet to be adopted and enforcement fees are still under negotiation. In the meantime, an increasing number of complaints (up to 200 in 2009) about the state's failure to execute court decisions have been submitted to the European Court of Human Rights. These unexecuted decisions are often related to property issues and illegal discharges from the civil service.[52]

After more than two decades of persistent problems with the judicial sector, also reflected in continuous lamentation from the EU and explicitly listed as a top policy priority in the EC's 2010 Opinion on Albania's Application for Membership of the European Union, the government adopted the Judicial Intersectorial Strategy and Action Plan only in July 2011.[53] The deep political divisions, along with uncertainties over EU preference priorities on Albanian reforms, prevented the Kuvend from adopting the bill on the establishment of administrative courts. Proposed by the government in the end of 2008, the law aimed at establishing specialized administrative courts and faster judicial procedures for adjudication. The administrative court system foresaw the creation of seven courts that would arbitrate the disputes of citizens and businesses on matters such as employment, tax, customs, pensions, property registration and compensation of property, as well as other important issues. These courts would align further Albania's judicial system with required EU integration standards.[54] The business community supported the adoption of the law, considering it an important step toward shortening judicial administrative procedures. By the same token, another bill introduced in April 2009 on judicial administration was strongly opposed by judicial representatives as an attempt by the executive to exercise judicial power (Gjipali 2010). The adoption of both laws required a reinforced majority of three-fifths, something that the ruling coalition lacked while the opposition was not willing to assist. Nobody could foresee the role that the adoption of these laws would have later in the process of EU negotiations with Albania, representing explicit conditions for the country to receive its EU candidate status. At that time, the EC's Albania 2009 Progress Report considered the Albanian judicial reform to be "at an early stage" and that it "continue[d] to function poorly due to shortcomings in independence, transparency and efficiency."[55] However, further developments would make the judicial reform a cornerstone of Albania's progress toward the Union, acquiring tremendous commitment from Albanian elites but also attracting the active interests of other international players.

In a press release on September 27, 2010, the Embassy of the United States urged the approval of the bill on Adjudication of Administrative Disputes and the Organization of Administrative Justice, known as the Administrative Courts bill. The Administrative Courts bill is one of the six components of the Millennium Challenge Corporation

Threshold Program II, Albania, signed in September 2008. The press release warned that, "[i]n order to complete planned activities with US funding, the law must be passed by September 30, 2010."[56] The adoption of the Administrative Courts bill required a qualified majority of three-fifths, and the PS had conditioned its vote for the bill with the opening of an investigation on the 2009 general elections.[57] In addition, the PS leader, Edi Rama, declared that Albania's international partners objected to one-third of the draft.[58] Rama's position did not change even when the director of Threshold Programs for the Millennium Challenge Corporation, Bruce Kay, revealed that Albania could still qualify for funds to assist with the establishment of the administrative courts if the Kuvend passed the Administrative Courts bill before January 2011.[59] The conclusions of the European Commission's 2010 Progress Report recognize the lack of substantial progress in judicial reforms and emphasize the need for a comprehensive reform strategy for the judiciary, reiterating that "[a]ttempts by the executive to limit the independence of the judicial remain a serious concern."[60]

Similar to other sectors, 2011 was a very bad year for the Albanian judicial reform; indeed, considering the Freedom House score on the Judicial Framework and Independence of 4.75 (the worst grade Albania received in this sector since 2000), Albania's judicial reform had reversed. During 2011, the political attention of both elites and society were captured by two events: first, the tragic ending of a PS-led rally in front of the prime minister's office where four anti-government demonstrators were killed by gunfire apparently from the security forces who were trying to prevent a violent attempt to take over the building; and the May 8 local elections, which ended in the seizure of the municipality of Tirana by the PD candidate Lulëzim Basha after a lengthy institutional debate over procedures. Both battles could be considered Pyrrhic victories for the Premier Berisha and his ruling coalition. These events deprived the government from both the necessary energy needed for crucial reforms and the necessary consensus of the opposition to adopt legislation that require reinforced majority. Understandably, the opposition was no longer willing to offer any consensus that would be translated into one more victory for the majority.

That explains why there was only "some limited progress in completing the legal framework for judicial reform" during 2011 in Albania.[61] Even though the Judicial Intersectorial Strategy and Action Plan was adopted on July 20, 2011, and it was considered to "form a good basis for reform efforts," its implementation remained in an initial phase.[62] Few low-profile laws and by-laws had been already passed in February 2011, but none of them represented any major breakthrough in the judicial reform. Such a breakthrough could only have been achieved with the adoption of relevant legislation that attained three-fifths reinforced majority vote in the Kuvend, including the Law on Administrative Courts, amendments to the Criminal Code, the Law on Judicial Administration and the law on the National Judicial Conference. The majority had failed to persuade the opposition to join in creating the three-fifth majority in order to pass the Law on Administrative Courts, and by the end of 2011 it still needed to prepare the latter two laws.

The polarized political climate of the year 2011 put heavy pressure on the independence of the judiciary. In order to keep morale high among its supporters, the government did not conceal its efforts to interfere in or hinder independent investigations of security personnel involved in allegedly criminal offences during and following the events of January 21. The tense political climate was reflected in the parliamentary appointments of judges to the High Court and the Constitutional Court, since it was deemed that the political equilibriums in those instances of the judiciary would determine the ongoing political struggle. As a consequence it was not difficult to reach the conclusion that neutrality and independence in these institutions were far from being fully guaranteed.[63]

However, while breakthroughs in judicial reform did not occur in 2011, on November 14 both sides decided to begin a process of joint cooperation in order to perform reforms that required broader consensus. The Kuvend's conference of faction leaders drew the roadmap of that cooperation: the establishment of a parliamentary commission to design the electoral reform, and of a working group for the revision of Kuvend's rules; as well as the agreement over a timetable for adopting legislation that required three-fifths majority. First, the parliamentary commission on the electoral reform took over addressing loopholes in the electoral system, following forceful recommendations by the OSCE and explicit stipulation in the EC's 2010 Opinion. The ten-member commission shared five members among the ruling coalition and five members among the opposition, with two co-chairpersons. Second, there was bipartisan agreement in principle that the working group would adapt the rules of the Kuvend to those of the European Parliament, following thus a PD offer as a compromise locus. Third, while the Kuvend's speaker sought to discipline the process of adopting reinforced majority laws until April 2012, the opposition preferred to funnel this process through the regular three-week schedules implemented by the Kuvend according to its existing rules. In accordance with the agreement, the Kuvend began right away with the adoption of some of those laws on which there were no disputes between the parties, including some amendments of the Traffic Code and Air Traffic Code.[64]

The year 2012 was characterized by "moderate progress in judicial reform."[65] During that time, the government began the implementation of the 2011 Judicial Intersectorial Strategy and Action Plan, which was also revised in March 2012. However, the EC had expressed concerns over interim sectorial cooperation, budget allocations, budget planning and the level of human resources in this sector.[66] The Ministria e Drejtësisë (MD) (Ministry of Justice) established several working groups to review key legislation in the sector. On May 3, 2012, the Kuvend passed, with 122 votes out of 140 members, the Law on Administrative Courts right after the EU commissioner for enlargement, Štefan Füle, gave a speech on the Kuvend's floor, encouraging parliamentarians to follow through with the November 2011 roadmap that Füle had personally brokered. The Law on Administrative Courts, set to be implemented in 2013, allowed for the establishment of five first-level administrative courts, one administrative court of appeal and one administrative high court.[67] On July 26, the Kuvend passed the Law on Organization and Functioning of the National Judicial Conference, with the support of the 128 parliamentarians present.[68]

However, obviously, the Albanian leaders underestimated the progress that they needed with regard to the independence and impartiality of the judiciary. A set of new rules governing transfers of judges on the basis of their merits and other objective criteria adopted in September 2012 brought about only limited progress. The real progress that the EU wanted to see was in the reform of the High Court and the Constitutional Court. The EU showed concern over the highly politicized process of appointing judges to these courts. In October 2012, Albanian elites could not imagine that the adoption of the Law on the Organization and Functioning of the High Court would be one of the three laws that the European Council would stipulate two months later for the country to receive EU candidate status. However, these divided elites failed to generate the three-fifth majority needed for its adoption, thus missing, for the third year in a row, the opportunity to receive the EU candidate status for their country.

Table 5.1 consists of the Freedom House score on the Albanian Judicial Framework and Independence, and Table 5.2 comprises the American Bar Association's Central and East European Law Initiative (ABA–CEELI) Judicial Reform Index. Ranging from 1 to 7, the Freedom House score reflects the nation's level of Judicial Framework and Independence with 1 denoting the highest possible level of independence and 7 denoting its absence.

Table 5.1. Albanian judicial framework and independence

2001	2002	2003	2004	2005	2006	2007	2008	2009	2010	2011	2012
4.50	4.50	4.25	4.25	4.50	4.25	4.00	4.00	4.25	4.25	4.25	4.74

Source: Freedom House, "Nations in Transit 2012." Online: http://www.freedomhouse.org/report/nations-transit/nations-transit-2012 (accessed February 10, 2010).
Note: The years reflect the period of the report, which is an assessment of the previous year's developments.

The scores provided by Freedom House reports in Table 5.1 are consistent with my account. They show both the improvement of the score with the return of the PD to power and the reform reversal of the last years and the dramatic drop from 4.25 to 4.75 in the year 2011 (reflected in the column 2012).

The interpretation of Table 5.2 offers a more detailed view of the Albanian judicial reform, at least until 2008. Mapping out the trend from 2001 to 2008 reveals that nine of the factors have experienced an increase, three factors have gone down and eighteen factors have remained about the same. These results can be interpreted as a slight improvement in the state of the judiciary in the country for that period. However, both reports reveal incompatibilities with each other and my account. Therefore, I think that reaching conclusions based on EC progress reports, at least for the most recent years, brings a complementary evaluation of the reforms progress, which, arguably, is highly influenced by EU membership conditionality. The following subsections give a more detailed account of EU and Albanian leaders' preferences in the judicial reform.

A consociationalist interpretation of Albanian judicial reform

When it comes to EEC's judicial reforms, we expect that EU carrot-and-stick policies will be more powerful and enjoy greater success than in other policy sectors.

Table 5.2. Albanian judicial reform index: Table of factor correlation

		2001	Trend	2004	Trend	2006	Trend	2008	Trend
I. Quality, Education, and Diversity									
Factor 1	Judicial qualification and preparation	Neutral	↑	Neutral	↔	Positive	↑	Positive	↔
Factor 2	Selection/appointment process	Positive	→	Positive	↔	Neutral	→	Neutral	↔
Factor 3	Continuing legal education	Negative	↑	Neutral	↑	Positive	↑	Positive	↔
Factor 4	Minority and gender representation	Neutral	↔	Neutral	↔	Neutral	↔	Neutral	↔
II. Judicial Powers									
Factor 5	Judicial review of legislation	Positive	→	Neutral	↔	Neutral	↔	Neutral	↔
Factor 6	Judicial oversight of administrative practices	Neutral	↔	Neutral	↔	Neutral	↔	Neutral	↔
Factor 7	Judicial jurisdiction over civil liberties	Positive	↔	Positive	↔	Positive	↔	Positive	↔
Factor 8	System of appellate review	Positive	↔	Positive	↔	Positive	↔	Positive	↔
Factor 9	Contempt/subpoena/enforcement	Negative	↔	Negative	↔	Negative	↔	Negative	↔
III. Financial Resources									
Factor 10	Budgetary input	Positive	↔	Positive	↔	Positive	↔	Positive	↔
Factor 11	Adequacy of judicial salaries	Negative	↑	Neutral	↔	Neutral	↔	Neutral	↔
Factor 12	Judicial buildings	Neutral	→	Neutral	↔	Neutral	↔	Neutral	↔
Factor 13	Judicial security	Negative	↔	Negative	↔	Neutral	↑	Neutral	↔
IV. Structural Safeguard									
Factor 14	Guaranteed tenure	Positive	↔	Positive	↔	Positive	↔	Neutral	→
Factor 15	Objective judicial advancement criteria	Negative	↔	Negative	↔	Negative	↔	Neutral	↑
Factor 16	Judicial immunity for official actions	Positive	→	Neutral	↑	Positive	↑	Positive	↔
Factor 17	Removal and discipline of judges	Neutral	↔	Neutral	↔	Neutral	↔	Neutral	↔
Factor 18	Case assignment	Neutral	↔	Neutral	↔	Neutral	↔	Neutral	↔
Factor 19	Judicial associations	Neutral	→	Negative	↑	Neutral	↑	Positive	↔

Table 5.2. Continued

	2001	Trend	2004	Trend	2006	Trend	2008	Trend
V. Accountability and Transparency								
Factor 20 Judicial decisions and improper influence	Negative	↔	Negative	↔	Negative	↔	Negative	↔
Factor 21 Code of ethics	Negative	↔	Negative	↔	Neutral	↑	Neutral	↔
Factor 22 Judicial conduct complaint process	Neutral	↔	Neutral	↔	Neutral	↔	Neutral	↔
Factor 23 Public and media access to proceedings	Negative	↔	Negative	↔	Negative	↔	Negative	↔
Factor 24 Publication of judicial decisions	Negative	↑	Negative	↔	Neutral	↑	Negative	↔
Factor 25 Maintenance of trial records	Negative	↔	Neutral	↔	Neutral	↔	Neutral	↔
VI. Efficiency								
Factor 26 Court support staff	Negative	↑	Neutral	↔	Neutral	↔	Neutral	↔
Factor 27 Judicial positions	Neutral	↔	Neutral	↔	Neutral	↔	Neutral	↔
Factor 28 Case filling and tracking systems	Neutral	↔	Neutral	↔	Neutral	↔	Neutral	↔
Factor 29 Computers and office equipment	Negative	↑	Neutral	↔	Neutral	↔	Neutral	↔
Factor 30 Distribution and indexing of current law	Neutral	↔	Neutral	↔	Neutral	↔	Neutral	↔

Source: *American Bar Association–Central European and Eurasian Law Initiative, Albanian Judicial Reform Index*, vol. 1 (2001), vol. 2 (2004), vol. 3 (2006), vol. 4 (2008).

In the case of Albania, "carrots" included €21 million from the Community Assistance for Reconstruction, Development and Stabilization (CARDS) program for judicial reform during the 2002–2004 period as well as the establishment of EURALIUS, June 13, 2005–June 30, 2010.[69] In the European Commission's progress report, the judicial reform rubric within the democracy and the rule of law subsection, political criteria section, meticulously described recent developments in judicial reform, assessed progress and provided recommendations on the expected direction of reform for the near future. The establishment of a judicial system in Albania that is compatible with the EU member countries' systems remained a goal and, hence, a guarantee for the consociational practices that have created and ensured that the EU remains a stable democracy.

However, the "stick" is the most visible aspect of recent EU policy toward the Albanian government related to judicial reform. While the dramatic deterioration of the country's Freedom House Judicial Framework and Independence score might reflect governmental attempts to interfere with the judicial process by resisting inquiries of its ministers and by influencing prosecutors and courts, the language of the EC's 2012 Progress Report points mostly to the lack of political cooperation in adopting key legislation and improving judicial independence. While criticism against the politicization of electing judges for the High Court and Constitutional Court only indirectly points to the need for cross-aisles cooperation in that direction, the outright denial of the EU candidate status for not applying consociational practices in the policy process, including judicial reform, points to the EU emphasis of consociational practices as its preferred framework in conducting reforms. At this point, it seems as though the EU's preferences for the reform process conducted according to consociational practices trump its preferences for the actual outcomes of reforms.

A sectorial contextual interpretation of Albanian judicial reform

The previous section clarifies that throughout the period 1991–2010, the EU paid close attention to the Albanian judicial reform. First, the consociationalist interpretation of the Albanian judicial reform revealed the EU's positive preferences in helping Albania to establish a stable democracy that would emerge as a unified pillar in negotiations and absorb EU consociational practices during the nation's accession process and after the potential EU membership. Second, short of EU membership, the EU has seen the establishment and consolidation of independent, impartial, competent and efficient judicial systems in its neighboring countries from a security perspective. An independent and efficient judiciary is able to fight organized crime even if such illegal activity has political support, as often is the case in the Balkans. Fighting organized crime, illegal immigration, gun and drugs smuggling and human trafficking from the Balkans into EU member countries represents effort to increase security and democratic stability within the existing EU. These issues affect other areas beyond enlargement policies such as justice and home affairs and EU common foreign and security policy.[70] Third, a strong, independent and efficient judicial system would help resolve domestic human rights issues, especially those related to economic and minority rights, thus reducing the potential of EU membership–aspiring countries to become both economically and politically unstable. Indeed, the EU shares the latter perspective with the CoE, which also explains the willingness of the EU to heed the CoE's comments and recommendation about judicial reform progress in the Balkans, and to cooperate with CoE in joint programs.

During the period of "extraordinary politics" in 1991–92, Albanian leaders' supported judicial reform. The judiciary proved utterly unfit to deal with the new political and economic conditions of the country and was unable to guarantee or enforce trade contracts or settle disputes between individuals or between the latter and the state. Presumably, any reform in other institutional and policy areas, including economic reform, would have been impossible without some substantial changes in judicial practices. However, Albanian leaders' interests in instituting judicial reform were soon tempered as "ordinary politics." During that period, judicial reform stalled, reflecting the PD's growing authoritarianism. The failure of the referendum on the constitution in November 1994, the growing international pressure on the government and the government's need to score international achievements (mainly membership in the Council of Europe) switched its preferences toward the judicial reform to the positive during 1995. After the country gained membership in the CoE in June 1995, the PD lost interest in reforms that would erode its control of the judiciary. Moreover, due to the rigged elections of May 1996 and the ensuing political crisis of 1996–97, Albanian leaders lost any immediate interest in judicial reform and turned to other emerging priorities.

With the victory of the PS-led center-left coalition in July 1997, the new leaders showed positive interest in reforms in general and judicial reform in particular, in order to show domestic and international audiences that they were different from their predecessors. Such a political spirit was reflected in decisive, fast and comprehensive changes, including judicial reform, during the period of 1997–2001. However, after the PS sunk into a deep political crisis in 2002–2005, due to an internal power struggle, and entire segments of the PS leadership became allegedly embedded in alliances with domestic and international organized crime, these same leaders eventually abandoned their positive interests in judicial reform, thus once again causing a reform stalemate.

In 2005, the PD returned to power with a partially rehabilitated image. Such a spirit of change led the government toward improvements in the judicial sector as reflected by the improvement of the Freedom House Judicial Framework and Independence score from 4.5 to 4.25 in 2005 (shown in column 2006 of Table 5.3). As the Freedom House's Nations in the Transit Report notes, the further drop of the score from 4.25 to 4.0 in 2006 (also reflected in the Freedom House Report of 2007) represents the already-built institutional capacity to enable the judiciary to resist interference by the ruling majority.[71] The American Bar Association's Judicial Reform Index for Albania 2006, can also be interpreted as indicative of small progress in judicial reform.[72]

The continuous PD struggle against the Office of the General Prosecutor shows the PD's return to its original ruling style: control of the judicial to serve its political agenda. A small improvement in the Freedom House score in 2006 and 2007 (shown as 4.0 in the columns 2007 and 2008 of Table 5.3, respectively) mainly shows the judiciary's efforts to resist politics, not the progress of reform itself. Indeed, the very struggle of the judiciary to resist politics shows that, by then, the Albanian judiciary had built some independence, as well as institutional tools with which to defend it. In 2008–10, the government's preferences toward judicial reform reversed once more as the PD continued to perceive its control over the judicial system as a means to acquire and retain power.

The dramatic drop of the country's Freedom House Judicial Framework and Independence score, indeed the lowest score ever since its introduction in 2001, carried important theoretical significance. The persistent government intrusion into judiciary affairs to employ judicial procedures to save Fatmir Mediu from prosecution over the tragic events in Gërdec, along with the persistent attacks of the prime minister and speaker of the Kuvend against the Prosecutor General Ina Rama and the extreme politicization of the process of the appointment of the judges in the High Court and the Constitutional Court, had no precedent in the last twelve years, and might have reflected the ruling coalition's dwindling preference for reforms in the second part of the mandate. It might have also reflected the shifting political preference from using the progress toward the EU as an asset for re-election toward efforts to win elections by controlling institutions and manipulating institutional procedures. The PD's victory in the Tirana municipal elections, by exploiting procedural controls and controlling key electoral institutions and courts, was an indication of how rewarding such a strategy could be in the short run. Confronted with strong EU preferences for progress in the judicial sector, the actions of Albanian leaders would only reluctantly lead to some partial progress in that sector, yet they could not reap an overall positive assessment from the EC. While a consociational approach to EU preferences toward judicial reform will help us to assume a strong EU focus on the process, a sectorial contextual approach suggests that, throughout 2012 and early 2013, the Albanian ruling coalition was more interested in reform outcomes that would allow it to win the June 2013 elections, or at least to minimize its electoral defeat. I will return in detail to this discussion in Chapter 7. Table 5.3 tabulates the reform results as correlated with EU's and Albanian ruling elites' preferences over the last two decades.

Macedonian Judicial Reform

During the early years of its independence, Macedonia did not make any effort to reform its judicial system. By the same token, no evidence of any serious attempt by international partners to assist Macedonia in reforming its judicial system was recorded in the early 1990s. Some efforts were made by the OSCE and the ABA–CEELI in 1995 to invite lawyers to form a local NGO to represent criminal defendants pro bono, a responsibility the Macedonian state itself had failed to fulfill. However, these efforts failed owing to skepticism and a lack of a volunteer culture in the country.[73] Overall, during the period of 1991–95, Macedonian elites' interest in reforming the judicial system remained neutral.

The Dayton Accord of November 1995 alleviated much of Macedonia's existential fears and offered the government an opportunity to focus on reforms that would deepen democratization and improve government efficiency. As in the case of local decentralization, the Macedonian ruling elites developed positive preferences toward judicial reform. Thus, in 1995 Macedonia undertook its first steps toward reforming its judicial system with the Law on Courts, essentially eliminating specialized courts.

Table 5.3. Developments in Albanian judicial reform

Reform	Situation	EU Interests	Domestic Leaders' Interests	Reform Results
1991–92	Period of extraordinary politics	0	+	**Good progress.** The amendments to the DKK created an opportunity for successful continuation of the judicial reform.
1993–94	The shift to ordinary politics	+	–	**No reform.** Government's interests shifted toward the control of the judicial. The most important "policy" of that period became the replacement of the judges who have served during the communist era with PD activists, who have been trained for the judiciary in 6-month courses.
1995–97	Albania enters the Council of Europe	+	0	**Slow progress.** The implementation of the new Penal Code and Penal Procedure Code were good signs of progress. However, these successes were tarnished by government's attempts to control the courts, especially the High Court. The political instability of the 1996–97 period brought the judicial reform to a total halt.
1998–2001	PS assumes power	+	+	**Excellent progress.** The implementation of the constitution and the establishment and/or reformation of several services represented a major breakthrough for Albanian judicial reform.
2002–2005	PS internal crisis	+	0	**No reform.** The crisis within the PS and ruling coalition shifted policy interest to other priorities. The only notable (rather political) judicial act of this period is the abolition of the death penalty by the Constitutional Court in 2002.
2006	PD assumes power	+	+	**Good progress.** The progress in judicial reform following the PD's return to power came as a combination of the EU's positive interests and the PD's need to show that it had abandoned it authoritarian style.
2007–10	PD's second half of the first term and re-election	+	–	**Reform halts/reverses.** The PD's increasing interest in winning a second term and controlling the Office of the Prosecutor, as well as the High Council of Justice brought the reforms to a standstill, and even reversed it in some aspects.
2011–12	PD's second half of its second term; clear conditions with the EC's 2010 Opinion	+	–	**Insignificant progress/reform halts/reverses.** PD's interest to shield its ministers from judicial prosecution, but also its need to keep a grip at the judiciary with the hope of exploiting procedures to ensure a third mandate clashed with EU clear preference for judicial reforms achieved through political cooperation/consociational practices.

Prior to 1996, courts in Bitola, Skopje and Štip handled commercial cases, labor cases and cases of less serious criminal offenses, but the new law brought those cases into district courts.[74] In 1996, the Sobranie passed a brand new Criminal Code, thus replacing the old Yugoslav code, which had remained in use even after the country's independence in 1991. The Sobranie also passed a brand new Code of Criminal Procedure in 1997.[75]

Some analyses of the Macedonian judiciary's current status overestimate the role of the Ohrid Agreement in the country's judicial reform.[76] Indeed, the agreement's signatories were concerned mainly with ethnic ratios as criteria for selecting the Constitutional Court, ombudsman and the Judicial Council (Paragraph 4.3) and the right to translation at the state's expense of all proceedings and documents for accused persons at any level in criminal and civil judicial proceedings (Paragraph 6.7). By and large, Albanian elites perceived the Macedonian judicial system to be an instrument of the Macedonians, not of a state that stayed above and beyond ethnicity. In turn, Macedonian elites took advantage of the lack of Albanians' attention to judicial reform and tried to retain as much power as possible over the judiciary. It is no coincidence, then, that domestic and international attention focused mostly on restoring stability through representative formulae rather than institutional capacity and efficiency. Judicial reform remained entrapped in the representative logic of the Ohrid Agreement, thereby only focusing on issues contested by the Albanians; but it paid little attention to judiciary efficiency, impartiality, independence and transparence, which would benefit citizens beyond ethnicity.

The period from the signing of the Ohrid Agreement until the September 2002 elections was a difficult era for most reforms in Macedonia, including judicial reform, thus reflecting the resistance of the Vnatrešna Makedonska Revolucionerna Organizacija– Demokratska Partija za Makedonsko Nacionalno Edinstvo (VMRO–DPMNE) (Internal Macedonian Revolutionary Organization–Democratic Party for Macedonian National Unity) to the implementation of the Ohrid Agreement. The entire pre-electoral and electoral rhetoric of its leader and the country's premier, Ljubčo Georgievski, was rife with dissent and revulsion against "Albanian terrorists" and the international actors who had brokered the agreement. The VMRO–DPMNE decided to cling to its image of being tough on issues of national security and protection of the Macedonian-ness of the state.

From September 2001 to September 2002, Macedonia's rule of law and its guarantor, the judicial system, continued to be sabotaged by politics and its preferred instrument, the police. The Macedonian Helsinki Committee reported the unprofessional behavior of the police force. Moreover, its elite units of Lions and Tigers were recorded assailing workers, opposition journalists and media personnel, political activists and random civilians, as well as threatening opposition politicians.[77] Police trespassing often went unpunished, and so went in the criminal activities of the minister of the interior, Ljube Boškovski.[78] In fact, in spite of the fact Boškovski personally injured four spectators at a Lions' military exercise in May 2002, Premier Georgievski pronounced that the minister would be amnestied on the grounds of "past merit in service of the state." As summarized by the Macedonian Helsinki Committee, police behavior, especially during the pre-election period, undermined the reputation and role of the

Ministry of the Interior and the professional cadre of the police, making it "difficult to distinguish whether undertaken actions are part of legally defined functions of the police or are party orders."[79]

The situation changed after Crvenkovski's Socijaldemokratski Sojuz na Makedonija (SDSM) (Social-Democratic Union of Macedonia) victory in the September 2002 elections. The Socijaldemokratski Sojuz na Makedonija–Bashkimi Demokratik për Integrim (SDSM–BDI) (Social-Democratic Union of Macedonia–Democratic Union for Integration) coalition had strong incentives to institute reforms. First, the SDSM returned to power with ambitions to be a leading force for Macedonian democratization and a credible partner for international actors. The task of the Bashkimi Demokratik për Integrim (BDI) (Democratic Union for Integration), the Albanian partner of the government, was also complex. While it was founded by people mainly related to the UÇK/NLA, and led by UÇK/NLA's political leader Ali Ahmeti, in spring 2002, it needed to demonstrate its commitment to the stability of Macedonia. Moreover, its leader needed to demonstrate that the party was comprised of politicians and statespersons and not simply guerrilla fighters. And finally, the party needed to pay off many of its fighters, who felt that, personally, they did not gain anything from the rebellion, but also to protect them from harassment and persecution from the predominantly Macedonian security forces and law enforcement. In sum, in the aftermath of the Ohrid Agreement, due to positive preferences of both domestic elites and the EU, improvements occurred beyond those stipulated in Ohrid. Reportedly, 2002–2004 introduced a new political system at both national and local levels; provided for an equitable legal representation of ethnic minorities; provided for the use of minority languages; and introduced the institution of the ombudsman.[80]

International influences on decision making have helped Macedonia overcome its political fragmentation. In certain cases, Macedonian politicians have demonstrated a willingness to surmount partisan and ethnic divisions by adopting key laws. Many legislative reforms regarding money laundering, drug enforcement, wiretapping and citizenship have been mandated through Macedonia's commitment to the Stabilization and Association Agreement process with the EU. Additionally, national security pressures and a need to implement the Ohrid Agreement have dictated the smooth adoption of changes in the criminal code, including the voluntary disarmament of the UÇK/NLA. Likewise, parliamentarians almost unanimously have ratified a number of international human rights agreements, such as the Convention for Elimination of all Forms of Discrimination of Women, the Convention on Children's Rights and agreements banning child prostitution and pornography.[81]

However, the SDSM–BDI coalition had its own preferences related to judicial reform, as illustrated by the 2003 power struggle among the ruling SDSM, the opposition VMRO–DPMNE and President Trajkovski. The SDSM's lack of a qualified majority during that period hampered its efforts to build consensus for policies and reforms. In 2003, the SDSM failed in its first attempt to garner support for amendments to the Law of Executive Procedure and the Law on Courts. In addition, the SDSM appointee to the chair of the Republican Judicial Council, Lenče Sofronievska, was rejected by the VMRO–DPMNE parliamentarians who claimed that she represented a SDSM partisan appointment. At the same time, the parliamentary majority firmly rejected the two nominations to the Judicial Council of President Trajkovski.[82]

When in 2004, Minister of Justice Ixhet Memeti acknowledged publicly that the judicial system required thorough restructuring, it reflected the government's growing awareness that patchwork legislation might never result in thorough judicial reform. In April, Memeti announced that his team was working on a package of constitutional and legislative amendments. Those amendments aimed at redefining the position of judicial power within the country's political system, establishing a system for judicial appointments and reinforcing the independence of the judiciary by setting up a separate judicial budget. Legislative changes aimed at increasing adjudication speed, defining certain provisions of the criminal code and amending the entire judicial process.[83] Memeti also announced plans to abandon the practice of appointing judges through judicial exams and strengthening the administrative capacity of the judiciary by introducing a new system of recruiting, training, evaluating and promoting judges.[84]

In November 2004, the government adopted a strategy and action plan on judicial reform, outlining key changes to the country's legislation and constitution. The main principles of the reform were approved in the Sobranie on May 18, 2005, by a broad majority. The government presented draft amendments in June and, in August, the Sobranie adopted 15 of them. Meanwhile, the Law on Enforcement of Civil Judgments was adopted in May 2005, to abolish the separate motion required for the execution of court decisions, as well as to create a privatized bailiff system under the Ministry of Justice. The Law on Civil Procedure was later adopted in September 2005, to introduce changes that would make court procedures more efficient.[85] Also during the same year, the government discussed reforms to the Judicial Council's system for electing members in order to limit political interference. An expert committee had already been hired and later dismissed during that process.[86]

In a flurry of activity, on December 7, 2005, the Sobranie passed 10 constitutional amendments related to judicial reform. Among other amendments, those concerning the judicial reform included changes in the office of the public prosecutor (Amendment 30), the election of 15 members of the Judicial Council (Amendment 38) and the equitable and just representation of citizens of all ethnicities as judges, lay judges and presidents of the courts (Amendment 29). The Sobranie also passed legislation on the enforcement of the amendments, specifying that, by July 30, 2006, new laws on the judicial council, the courts, misdemeanors, the council of public prosecutors and the public prosecutor should be passed.[87]

In February 2006, a law was adopted establishing the Academy for Training of Judges and Prosecutors, and in November the EU announced a €1.1 million project to support the academy to enhance the professional skills of the country's judiciary. Candidates for the basic courts would have to complete a training course at the new academy. Also, the Law on Mediation was adopted in May with hopes that it would reduce the backlog of unsolved cases. Sixty mediators were appointed, and the law came into force in November 2006. May also saw the Sobranie pass new legislation on the courts, the Judicial Council, misdemeanors and administrative disputes, although the Law on the Judicial Council was the only one to go into effect in 2006.

Despite these reform efforts, inefficiency problems persisted as hundreds of thousands of cases remained untried. The courts grew burdened with administrative work, high numbers of misdemeanor cases and decisions requiring execution. Out of five judgments against Macedonia by the European Court of Human Rights in 2006, four noted violations related to the length of judicial proceedings. While in March 2005 the total number of pending cases was 730,700, in 2006 the number grew to 937,756.[34] In the Bitola Basic Court, 69,000 cases remained in limbo with only 40,000 cases resolved in 2006. During the same period, 44,000 unresolved cases remained in the Tetovo Basic Court and 43,649 in the Ohrid Basic Court. The Kičevo Basic Court had no air conditioning, and work during the summer months was difficult. This court also lacked computers and a meeting space, and had only five courtrooms for a total of 17 judges. The court in Kavadarci, heavily in debt, owed 1.2 million denars (€200,000) to the newspaper *Makedonski Poshti*. The Gostivar Basic Court had an accumulated debt of approximately 1.5 million denars, while the Ohrid Basic Court lacked an archive.[88]

The elections of July 2006 resulted in a return of the Vnatrešna Makedonska Revolucionerna Organizacija–Partia Demokratike e Shqiptarëve (VMRO–PDSh) (Internal Macedonian Revolutionary Organization–Albanian Democratic Party) coalition to power. This time around, the coalition was interested in actively portraying its governing style in a positive manner. With the former leader and premier Lubčo Georgievski gone, the new coalition renewed commitment to judicial reforms under the leadership of Nikola Gruevski. The process began in October 2006 when the government abruptly dismissed former public prosecutor Aleksandar Prčevski two years before his mandate ended, criticizing him for inefficiency and unprofessional behavior. With this move, the coalition exploited an institutional gap. The 2005 constitutional changes had placed the decision to dismiss prosecutors in the hands of a newly designed independent body, the Council of Public Prosecutors. However, by fall 2006, the council had not yet been set up owing to delays, and the government sacked Prčevski using the old laws. Yet, the legality of the dismissal was questioned, prompting experts to speculate that his removal was politically motivated and inconsistent with due process.[89]

An enthusiastic European Commission's Progress Report 2006 notes that "[t]he legal framework for strengthening the independence and the efficiency of the judicial is largely in place," supported by "a broad political consensus."[90] The EC's report assesses Macedonia's progress:

> [o]verall, the constitutional and legal framework for an independent and efficient judicial is now largely in place. However, most of the reforms in the judicial have not yet entered into force. There are important challenges in this field, which require a sustained programme of reforms.[91]

Progress in judicial reform continued in 2007 resulting with the adoption of 55 laws related to the judicial system in accord with recommendations of the Council of Europe and the EU. However, a loud public debate erupted among domestic experts over the interference of political parties in the composition of the Judicial Council, as well as the nomination of judges. The new Judicial Council started operating in January

2007, and it began to recruit judges to the new Administrative Court and Court of Appeals in Gostivar. However, the new Administrative Court, which became legally able to adjudicate administrative cases in May 2007, was still not functional, since its judges were not yet appointed. Other steps forward in the Macedonian judicial reform during 2007 were the adoption in December of the Law on Public Prosecution and the Law on the Council of Public Prosecutors, the two final laws needed to complete the legislative framework set out in the constitutional amendments of December 2005. In this year, the Academy of Judges and Prosecutors was also established and became operational. Further, the 2006 Law on Mediation, which aimed to lower court workloads via alternative dispute resolution, was enacted.

The year 2007 marked the end of the Socijaldemokratski Sojuz na Makedonija–Partia Demokratike e Shqiptarëve (SDSM–PDSh) (Social-Democratic Union of Macedonia–Albanian Democratic Party) coalition. Apparently, the approaching general elections drove all parties to a politics of identity strategy. The rising tide of ethnic tensions during that year affected the judicial system as well. In October, the Constitutional Court ruled on the constitutionality of the 2005 Law on the Use of Cultural Symbols by Ethnic Communities. The ruling found unconstitutional articles that regulated the public display of flags by ethnic communities. The ruling was strongly condemned by ethnic Albanian parties, with the governing Partia Demokratike e Shqiptarëve (PDSh) (Albanian Democratic Party) accusing the opposition BDI of influencing members of the court. The BDI made similar accusations. Three days later, the president of the Constitutional Court and another ethnic Albanian judge resigned in protest over the decision.[92] This shift of strategy from conducting reforms to promoting identity politics caused a reversal of the judicial reform process and was reflected by a worsening Freedom House Judicial Framework and Independence score, from 3.75 to 4.0. However, the EC's 2007 Progress Report neither praises any progress nor criticizes the setback.[93]

Political and ethnic tensions rose again in the aftermath of the July 2008 elections, when VMRO–DPMNE was hesitant to invite the BDI to serve as a governing partner, preferring its rival PDSh. However, the VMRO–DPMNE finally agreed to sit at the table in the spring of 2008, and negotiate an agreement with the BDI on several issues that Albanian party leadership claimed to pertain to the implementation of the Ohrid Agreement (Trajkov 2008). The negotiations led to a government coalition between the VMRO–DPMNE and the BDI. As Ragaru (2007) notes, Macedonia had once again lost several precious months in implementing much needed judicial reforms, as well as those pertaining to state administration, education and the economy.

Once in power, Premier Gruevski's image changed from a technocrat to a Macedonian nationalist. Gruevski tried to build his political success on a discourse that aptly combined promises to make Macedonia a prosperous country and boosting ethnic Macedonian self-confidence. It worked among Macedonians as they felt themselves to be major losers in the Ohrid process (Ragaru 2008). However, Gruevski's identity politics has entrenched the Macedonian public and elites into a Nash equilibrium position with Greece from which neither party could walk away without finding itself worse off. Yet, while EU membership provided Greece with an upper hand in this issue, both Macedonia and the EU found themselves stuck in the unprecedented and unlikely position in which

Macedonia should maintain its reform momentum even in the absence of a reasonable hope to open accession negotiations with the EU. I will return to this discussion in Chapter 7.

Ethnic tensions continued to simmer for the rest of the VMRO–BDI rule, as Gruevski focused on ethnic politics as a means of boosting political support. The small steps that had been taken to advance judicial reform proved insufficient to improve the country's judiciary significantly. However, the courts did strengthen gradually, thanks to earlier reforms undertaken in 2005 and because the Constitutional Court, with members appointed by the Sobranie using the double majority rule, had the power to annul legislation and decrees that were found to violate the constitution. The Judicial Council, also appointed through a parliamentary double majority, took over the task of overseeing the court system and judges. In 2008, the new Administrative Court and the new Court of Appeals of Gostivar began operating. The Law on Courts was amended to provide for just one, instead of five, specialized court departments to deal with cases of organized crime and corruption. The Judicial Council maintained its efforts to combat corruption in the judiciary (see Daskalovski 2009).

In 2009, critics levied allegations that, by blacklisting judges, the government was meddling in judiciary affairs. In April, the VMRO–DPMNE questioned the legitimacy of the Constitutional Court, which had ruled against the introduction of religious education in state schools. The party described the decision of the court as politically motivated, claiming that the leader of the SDSM controlled the court's work (see Daskalovski 2010). The Constitutional Court responded with a press release denouncing "unprecedented pressure" and "attempts to harm its reputation";[94] however, finally, the speaker of the Sobranie, Trajko Veljanovski, from the VMRO–DPMNE, announced that the decisions of the Constitutional Court were final and that the Sobranie should respect them. The Constitutional Court responded that Veljanovski simply sought to discredit and apply pressure to the court. In addition, Sterjo Zikov, a discharged Skopje public prosecutor, claimed that his dismissal was a political decision. Similar complaints were voiced by two other prosecutors, Dragan Gaždov and Mitko Mitrevski, who were not reappointed (see Daskalovski 2010).

A survey conducted in 2009 by the OSCE Spillover Monitor Mission reflects those concerns regarding the independence of the judiciary. As the conclusions of the report notes:

> The results show that attempts to influence the decisions of judges are a common practice and occur frequently. Common violations of the law and of the principle of independence of the judicial remain to a large extent unnoticed and unpunished. A considerable portion of the judges think that these attempts do have an influence on the administration of justice.
>
> The mechanisms and instruments to protect their independence are perceived by judges as ineffective and therefore are very rarely used. The conducted survey reveals a large degree of distrust in judicial institutions and mechanisms of the judicial system on the part of the judges. An overwhelming majority of judges views

the Judicial Council, probably the most important body for the independence of the judicial, as biased and the procedures it conducts as nontransparent and politically influenced.

Many judges are dissatisfied with their working conditions, their salaries and their possibilities for professional development. The high response rate to the questionnaire demonstrates that judges believe it is time to engage into discussion of this issue and initiate improvements.[95]

On the other hand, the EC's Communication on Macedonia Progress Report 2009 refers to the country's progress on judicial reform in almost neutral language. The report notes that "further progress was made on reform of the judicial, which is a key priority of the Accession Partnership" and that "[c]ontinued efforts are needed to ensure the independence and impartiality of the judicial, in particular through the implementation of the provisions regarding appointments and promotions."[96]

However, in another document, the EC recognized the limited progress in Macedonian judicial reform. In its "Communication on Enlargement Strategy and Main Challenges 2010–11," the Commission points to an improvement of the courts' efficiency, but displays concerns "about the independence and impartiality of the judicial." According to the document, "no further progress was made in ensuring that existing legal provisions were implemented in practice."[97] The language of the communication clearly shows that, after the reform reversal of 2007, no major steps forward had been taken. The slow progress of Macedonian judicial reform has been noticed by foreign and domestic observers alike.[98]

The EC's 2011 Progress Report takes a very ambiguous stance on Macedonian judicial reform progress during 2011. While the report lists several laws adopted by the Sobranie, as well as other policy measures, in its overall assessment it does not qualitatively classify the level of judicial reform progress.[99] Instead, the report points out only that "further amendments were made to the legal framework as regards independence, efficiency and transparency of justice." At this point, problems with Macedonia's judicial reform were no longer quantitative but qualitative as the report highlights the need of considerable efforts "to strengthen the quality of justice, in particular through continuous training and merit-based recruitment procedures, and to safeguard the independence of judges in the context of evaluation and dismissal procedures."[100]

By claiming that "[t]he main bodies tasked with ensuring the independence, *impartiality*, *accountability* and *professionalism* of the judiciary continued to carry out their functions" the EC's 2012 Progress Report reflects the state of judicial reform in Macedonia. While the country had already succeeded with the reform framework to some extent, it seemed that incremental procedural improvement remained to achieve the next step toward the improvement of judicial quality in the country.[101] The rest of the report shows concerns with nomination, transfer and assessment of judges and prosecutors, court backlog cases, budgetary issues and the functioning of the Academy of Judges and Prosecutors. Even though the country had yet to adopt a comprehensive judicial reform strategy or action plan, the lack thereof seemed to had not impeded what the 2012 Progress Report considers "significant reforms of the justice sector between 2004 and 2010." Table 5.4 provides the Freedom House Judicial Framework and Independence score for the period 2000–10, while Table 5.5 shows the more nuanced ABA–CEELI Judicial Reform Index for 2002 and 2003.

Table 5.4. Macedonian judicial framework and independence

2000	2001	2002	2003	2004	2005	2006	2007	2008	2009	2010	2011	2012
4.25	4.25	4.75	4.50	4.00	3.75	3.75	3.75	4.00	4.00	4.00	4.00	4.00

Source: Freedom House, "Nations in Transit 2012." Online: http://www.freedomhouse.org/report/nations-transit/nations-transit-2012 (accessed February 10, 2010).
Note: The years reflect the period of the report, which is an assessment of the previous year's developments.

Freedom House's score matches my historical account. During 2001, as reported in 2002, the index worsened from 4.25 to 4.75, but steadily improved up to 3.75 until 2007 (as reported in 2008). Then it reversed to 4.0. Such a reversal occurred in several Macedonian sectorial reforms, and reflects the disillusionment felt by Macedonian ruling elites and public caused by the EU's refusal to open accession negotiations even two years after the country became an EU candidate, due mainly to the potential Greek veto (see Karajkov 2010). However, the score has remained stable at 4.0 ever since, evidence that when there is persistent interest of the EU in judicial reform and waning interest from domestic elites in that particular reform an equilibrium point will be reached. Table 5.5 confirms a slow improvement in the judiciary from 2002 to 2003, with seven factors that determine the state of the judiciary improved, two worsened and twenty-one remaining about the same. I develop a further interpretation of the results in the following subsections.

A consociational interpretation of Macedonian judicial reform

Albanian elites in Macedonia perceived the Macedonian judicial system as an instrument of the Macedonian people against Albanians. In turn, Macedonian elites have tried to retain as much control as possible over the judiciary in order to improve their position in both political and ethnic rivalries. It is easily conceivable that the preferences of both elites have remained entrenched in resolving such conflicts through political arrangements rather than legal instruments. In the conditions of a weak and ethnically biased judiciary system, it is no coincidence that the focus of domestic and international actors has lain in restoring the country's stability through a political arrangement, the Ohrid Agreement, rather than judicial practices. The EU and other international partners that negotiated the agreement sought to reach an accord by emphasizing only issues contended by Albanians, hence focusing only on consociational practices needed to establish a stable democracy rather than the entire gamut of reforms needed for good governance. The judiciary does not represent a consociational practice per se, even though the organization of Macedonia's judicial system embodies some consociational practices

Table 5.5. Macedonian judicial reform index: Table of factor correlation

		2002	2003	Trend
I. Quality, Education, and Diversity				
Factor 1	Judicial qualification and preparation	Negative	Negative	↔
Factor 2	Selection/appointment process	Neutral	Neutral	↔
Factor 3	Continuing legal education	Positive	Neutral	↓
Factor 4	Minority and gender representation	Negative	Negative	↔
II. Judicial Powers				
Factor 5	Judicial review of legislation	Positive	Positive	↔
Factor 6	Judicial oversight of administrative practices	Neutral	Neutral	↔
Factor 7	Judicial jurisdiction over civil liberties	Neutral	Neutral	↔
Factor 8	System of appellate review	Positive	Positive	↔
Factor 9	Contempt/subpoena/enforcement	Negative	Negative	↔
III. Financial Resources				
Factor 10	Budgetary input	Positive	Neutral	↑
Factor 11	Adequacy of judicial salaries	Negative	Negative	↔
Factor 12	Judicial buildings	Negative	Neutral	↑
Factor 13	Judicial security	Positive	Neutral	↓
IV. Structural Safeguard				
Factor 14	Guaranteed tenure	Positive	Positive	↔
Factor 15	Objective judicial advancement criteria	Neutral	Neutral	↔
Factor 16	Judicial immunity for official actions	Neutral	Neutral	↔
Factor 17	Removal and discipline of judges	Neutral	Neutral	↔
Factor 18	Case assignment	Negative	Neutral	↑
Factor 19	Judicial associations	Positive	Positive	↔
V. Accountability and Transparency				
Factor 20	Judicial decisions and improper influence	Negative	Negative	↔
Factor 21	Code of ethics	Negative	Negative	↔
Factor 22	Judicial conduct complaint process	Neutral	Neutral	↔
Factor 23	Public and media access to proceedings	Neutral	Neutral	↔
Factor 24	Publication of judicial decisions	Negative	Neutral	↑
Factor 25	Maintenance of trial records	Negative	Neutral	↑
VI. Efficiency				
Factor 26	Court support staff	Neutral	Neutral	↔
Factor 27	Judicial positions	Neutral	Neutral	↔
Factor 28	Case filling and tracking systems	Negative	Negative	↔
Factor 29	Computers and office equipment	Negative	Neutral	↑
Factor 30	Distribution and indexing of current law	Negative	Neutral	↑

Source: *American Bar Association–Central European and Eurasian Law Initiative, Macedonia Judicial Reform Index 2003* and *Macedonia Judicial Reform Index*, vol. 2, 2004.

such as ethnic ratios for the composition of courts and the use of the languages of other major ethnicities in the legal process. However, when it comes to delivering justice, the process does not occur through consociational practices but through judicial ones. Thus, the theoretical relevance of judicial reform rests not in establishing a democracy through consociational practices, but in building a national consensus over reforms in such a key sector for maintaining a stable democracy through the rule of law.

It is evident that the EU needs an independent, impartial, functional and professional judicial system in its member countries. The rule of law not only reinforces a stable democracy but also builds the consensual framework for its functioning. It assures the functioning of institutions established through elite pacts and may also serve as a reference for citizens' overarching loyalties. Such a stable democracy emerges as a unified pillar in negotiations for further EU integration. Moreover, although judicial systems of EU member countries are national systems, their independence from and impartiality toward domestic politics may help establish a supranational network of the judiciary. A number of likeminded judicial systems could assist with EU internal cohesion more than any national legislative, executive or political party. A network of judicial systems that would provide the same justice from Iceland to Cyprus, and from Ireland to Turkey might be useful to address transnational issues such as transnational crime, migration, human rights and environment. It can ultimately serve as a reference for overarching loyalties toward the Union of member countries' citizens.

However, even if the judicial system does not function on consociational practices, its extensive size and intersectorial character calls for a national consensus on the judiciary in its reformation. It took one of such moments of elite consensus on July 1, 2007 to end a stalemate in Macedonia's judicial reform and reach a wider consensus on the prosecution office. As some media put it, the agreement can be hailed as a breakthrough in the judicial reform process for a topic that has been plagued with differences in opinion.[102] Yet consensus is a consociational practice and, as I will develop further in Chapter 7, a reform process based on such practices might sometimes be more important than reform outcomes, especially in such difficult areas such as judicial reforms.

A sectorial contextual interpretation of Macedonian judicial reform

The previous subsection assesses the EU's preferences in Macedonian judicial reform, which were mainly neutral in 1991–2001. This interlude coincided with the EU's fear that pressure for reforms might destabilize the fragile country.[103] The EU's interests in judicial reform turned positive after the Zagreb Summit in November 2000, and were reinforced after the Copenhagen European Council in December 2002, along with the confirmation that countries in the Western Balkans were potential EU candidates. Ever since, the EU's interest in Macedonia's judicial reform has been always positive. Since the early 2000s, the EU has used "carrots" in the form of financial assistance for judicial reform (€4 million from the CARDS Programme for the period of 2002–2004, for example), as well as its signature on the Stabilization and Association Agreement of April 9, 2001, right in the midst of violent ethnic clashes.[104] Meanwhile, "sticks" for the unsteady performance of judicial reform have been overshadowed by the great emphasis the EU has placed on the implementation of the Ohrid Agreement. As the historic process traced here demonstrates, the domestic ruling elites' preferences have varied from negative to positive to neutral. The combination on these different preferences explains the variation in the results and pace of judicial reform.

From 1991 to 1995 both the Macedonian ruling elites and the EU displayed no interest in Macedonian judicial reform, which in turn explains the lack of progress. The Law of Courts represented an initial step forward, but it dealt mainly with adaptations rather than deep structural and legislative improvements of the existing judicial system. The Dayton Accord in November 1995 relieved some of Macedonia's existential fears and, in 1996, the first steps toward reforming the judicial system were undertaken with the revision of the Criminal Code followed by a new Criminal Procedures Code in 1997.

The VMRO–PDSh coalition that seized power after the October 1998 elections did almost nothing to reform the judiciary. The coalition suffered no image problem, and their priorities lay in sharing power rather than conducting reforms. The neutral preferences on judicial reform from both the EU and the Macedonian ruling elites during 1998–2000 caused the reform process to stall. The EU's preferences in judicial reform throughout the region increased after the Stabilization and Association Programme was launched, but the ethnic conflict in 2001 brought to the fore more pressing issues. Nonetheless, after the 2002 elections, both partners of the coalition, the Macedonian SDSM and the Albanian BDI, harbored strong incentives for reform; the SDSM needed to clean up its tarnished image from its ruling period, 1990–98, while the BDI wanted to show that it was not just a ragtag group of former guerillas but a constructive political force. The combination of EU support and the coalition's interest led to a major breakthrough in the country's judicial reform during 2002–2006. However, one year before the July 2008 elections, all parties returned to the question of politics of identity, thus abandoning the path to reform.

The return to power of the VMRO–DPMNE and its unlikely coalition with the BDI, the former guerrilla group that fought against the government in 2001, brought with it new dynamics. None of the parties bore political image problems; the VMRO–DPMNE returned to power without some of its most discredited politicians; its former leader and Premier Ljubčo Georgievski had left the party along with the majority of its parliamentary fraction to found the Vnatrešna Makedonska Revolucionerna Organizacija–Narodna Partija (VMRO–NP) (Internal Macedonian Revolutionary Organization–People's Party). In July 2004, the BDI emerged as a victorious force among the Albanians of Macedonia; it had already established itself as a political force oriented toward political compromise. The coalition felt little incentive to commit itself to judicial reform, hence reform significantly slowed.

The victory in the June 2011 elections provided the VMRO–BDI coalition with a second government mandate. With the EU perspective on hold and possessing the clear support of the majority of voters, the slow pace of reform in 2008–10 brought reform to a halt. The continuing involvement of the EU through the High Level Accession Dialogue might have helped prevent any reform reversal, but it was not enough to encourage any significant reform progress. However, by not being able to offer any tangible accession schedule, the EU has lost its leverage with the Macedonia's elites. At this point, the interplay of EU positive preferences and neutral Macedonian preferences on the judicial reform produced only insignificant progress in the country's judicial reform. However, since Macedonia has managed thus far to establish a credible judicial system, the EU's efforts to maintain democratic stability in Macedonia seem to be redeemed for as long as there is no reform reversal. Table 5.6 summarizes these findings.

The Role of Human Capital: Eliminating Alternative Explanations

Several accounts of the Albanian and Macedonian judicial reform process point to the lack of human capital as a causal factor in these countries' slow progress in institutional reform. For instance, the European Commission's Communication on Albania 2010 Progress Report points out that "[h]uman and financial resources, as well as infrastructure conditions, are not adequate and need to be improved to ensure the efficient functioning of courts." By the same token, the 2011 and the 2012 Reports highlight "concerns over [...] human resources in this sector."[105] In the case of Macedonia, the European Commission's Communication on Macedonia 2010 Progress Report highlights that

the absence of a human resource management system has slowed down the recruitment of graduates from the academy for training judges and prosecutors into the judicial. The judicial continues to face budgetary constraints. The Skopje 2 basic court, which is the court with the largest number of cases, and the four courts of appeal along with the administrative court were unable to reduce their backlogs. The administrative court, the court of appeal in Gostivar and most of the public prosecutor's offices remained understaffed, which affected their performance.[106]

In 2012, the lack of human resources in the Macedonia's administrative courts and Supreme Court was considered to be the main cause of a backlog of cases.[107]

These are only few of the most recent observations related to the negative role that limited human resources have played in the reformation of the Albanian and Macedonian judicial systems. The question is: how much do they count in our assessment of progress toward these reforms? Carothers summarizes the issue as follows:

A key step is achieving genuine judicial independence. Some of the above measures foster this goal, especially better salaries and revised selection procedures for judges. But the most crucial changes lie elsewhere. Above all, government officials must refrain from interfering with judicial decision making and accept the judicial as an independent authority. They must give up the habit of placing themselves above the law. (Carothers 2006, 8)

A careful observation of the historical process tracing and the Freedom House Judicial Framework and Independence score reveals that obstacles to judicial reform, as well as breakthroughs, are caused by top government actors. They ultimately reflect political actors' preferences related to the judicial reform. An examination of the historical

Table 5.6. Developments in Macedonian judicial reform

Period	Situation	EU Interests	Domestic Leaders' Interests	Reform Results
1991–95	Consolidation of independence	0	0	**No reform.** Both the EU and Macedonian ruling elites were interested in maintaining Macedonia's stability, not instituting reform.
1996–97	New international situation for the country	0	+	**Good progress.** The Dayton Accord alleviated some existential fears of Macedonian elites, and turned their attention to reforms. The EU had yet to decide their strategy for the region.
1998–2001	Nationalistic VMRO-DPMNE assumes power	0	0	**No reform.** With the EU being engaged in helping to solve the Albanian and Kosovo crises and the VMRO-PDSh coalition involved on a silent power sharing deal, Macedonian judicial reform stalled.
2001–2002	Violent ethnic conflict	+	0	**No reform.** Armed conflict in the nation forced all parties to focus on forging a political deal rather than sectorial reforms.
2002–2006	The implementation of Ohrid Agreement	+	+	**Good progress.** The SDSM-BDI coalition was interested in sectorial reforms out of concerns for its image.
2007	Pre-election politics	+	0	**Slow pace of reform.** During the last year of its mandate, the SDSM-BDI coalition was interested in re-election and thus shifted to politics of identity. The slow pace of reform might represents inertia of the past or bureaucratic contribution to it.
2008–10	VMRO-DPMNE and BDI assume power	+	0	**Slow pace of reform.** The VMRO-BDI still hoped for the opening of the accession negotiations, thus maintained certain reform momentum. The slow pace of reform might represents inertia of the past or bureaucratic contribution to it.
2011–12	VMRO-BDI win a second mandate	+	0	**No reform.** In the conditions of no EU accession perspective, the ruling coalition abandoned judicial reforms to focus on power-oriented and identity politics.

process tracing of the judicial reforms in Albania and Macedonia, as well as the Freedom House's Judicial Framework and Independence score, shows that all the breakthroughs in judicial reforms in both countries have resulted from the will of political leaders to institute such reforms. Only once, in the case of Albania in 2006–2007, has the score improved due to the resistance of the judiciary to governmental encroachments.

The lack of human resources cannot be an alternative explanation. While purges in the Albanian judicial system during most of the 1990s and vacancies in the Macedonian judicial system during the 2000s may have slowed down the pace of reforms, both problems have been caused by political agents in pursuit of their power-driven preferences. In the case of Albania, the ruling PD sought to control the judicial by replacing judicial personnel inherited from the past, hence deemed loyal to the PS, with its hurriedly trained partisans. In Macedonia, most of the vacancies were caused by prolonging difficult negotiations between political actors from different ethnic groups, while other vacancies were caused by the cumbersome process of securing a double majority.

If human capital were an important factor, we would have observed incremental improvements in the judiciary as new graduates enter the system. While the latter might explain some incremental improvements in the judicial sector, and they might also be credited for shielding political interference in judicial business, we can observe reforms bouncing back as a result of political agents' meddling with judicial matters. The latter rather than the former seems to explain better the judicial reform's uneven record. Evidence abounds to show that human capital, or the lack thereof, is not a key explanatory variable of the Albanian and Macedonian progress in judicial reforms.

Conclusions

Although the judicial system does not fall within the traditional concept of consociational practices that help to establish and maintain a stable democracy, it remains a key player in assuring that the political and institutional arrangements of these practices survive amid centrifugal forces. Some consociational practices such as ethnic and linguistic representation in judicial administration have been important elements of the Macedonian judicial reform; yet, the reform has elements that go far beyond these consociational practices. However, there is an important consociational practice that counts in the overall establishment of the judicial independence, impartiality and efficiency: the elites' consensus on reforms. Evidence show that every time such a consensus has been achieved, countries have managed to perform successful judicial reform. Therefore, even though the judicial system does not usually function through consociational practices, it is important in the organization of the judiciary of a divided society and, at least one of them, elite consensus, emerges as a key consociational practice to undertake successful judicial reforms in both united and divided societies. Historical process tracing has provided solid evidence to support my sectorial contextual model. The combination of EU and domestic leaders' political preferences produces the policy outcomes theorized in Chapter 2.

However, EU interest in Eastern European judicial reforms stems from the need to equip EU membership–aspiring countries from the region with judicial systems and practices that will assure equal enforcement of the agreed consociational practices throughout the EU space. If the EU evolved as a stable, democratic entity due to consociational practices, a social contract would exist among pillar states. Of course, most cases related to breaches of such a contract go to the European Court of Justice, but the procedures and practices of this court cannot be detached from those procedures and practices of EU member countries. Indeed, they represent a European legal tradition reinforced by EU member countries' judicial systems. In the end, as guarantors of the enforcement of consociational agreements among EU member countries, Eastern European independent, impartial, professional and efficient judicial systems become important components of consociational arrangements necessary for the establishment and maintenance of the EU as a stable democratic entity.

Chapter 6

ASYLUM REFORMS

The establishment of asylum systems in Eastern European countries (EECs) aspiring to European Union (EU) membership represents a process guided by EU conditionality (Byrne 2003, 343). Until the 2005 Hague Programme Action Plan and the 2007 Green Paper on the Future of the European Asylum System (hereafter 2007 Green Paper), EU membership conditionality aimed at assisting EECs to establish asylum systems compatible with the 1951 Geneva Convention Relating to the Status of Refugees and the 1967 New York Protocol Relating to the Status of Refugees (hereafter 1951 Geneva Convention). However, with the 2007 Green Paper and its fundamental principle of solidarity and burden sharing, it became clearer that the EU expects its aspirants to establish asylum systems that would also contribute to the effectiveness and efficiency of the existing member countries' asylum systems. In order to fulfill such a task, Eastern European countries need asylum systems compatible with those of the EU countries, as well as policies consistent with the common European asylum policy. However, in some of the Eastern European countries, these institutions still do not serve any domestic need.

The EU's interest in Balkan asylum systems has shifted from initial concerns with regional peace and stability and preventing masses of refugees from seeking shelter in EU member countries to establishing asylum systems that will prevent migration through the region into EU member countries (Feijen 2007). Such policies have been associated with the conflicting dichotomy between principles of human rights and EU internal security (Peshkopia 2005a, 2005c). Apparently, the EU has tried to resolve this contradiction by establishing a common European asylum system (Thielemann 2008). It is easily conceivable that the countries aspiring to EU membership need to establish asylum systems according to international standards. This would make their asylum systems easily adjustable to the EU's after their accession.

Thus, the EU has increasingly linked the establishment of asylum systems in the Western Balkans to its accession strategies (Feijen 2007; Byrne 2003). In setting the criteria that EU aspirants should fulfill in its Agenda 2000, the European Commission (EC) foresaw a recurrent opinion on the progress of candidate countries, including asylum and migration as part of justice and home affairs. For the Western Balkans, developing asylum systems became part of the Stabilization and Association Agreements (SAA) from the launch of the Stabilization and Association Programme (SAP), May 1999, and included in the chapter on justice and home affairs. The annual progress reports assess each countries' progress in asylum and migration, and the EC releases recommendations on asylum and migration issues that national governments need to address.

The 1997 Treaty of Amsterdam envisions the EU as an area of freedom and security. As such, the EU views its enlargement as a social good, and requires the countries aspiring to EU membership to develop laws, institutions and rules compatible with those that underpin and promote EU freedom and security. Although the EU *acquis communautaire*, as a cornerstone of the Treaty of Amsterdam, is only legally binding to EU member states, the 1995 European Council in Madrid stipulated that candidate countries should transpose the *acquis* into their national legislations. Such a requirement represents a shift from the initial requirement that potential candidate countries harmonize and align their legislation with the *acquis* simply to a system of copying the "minimum standards" of the emerging common European asylum system.[1]

Postsocialist Balkan countries are located on the Balkan route, the transit route of illegal immigrants from the Middle East and Central and Eastern Asia into the EU territory (Peshkopia 2008b; Peshkopia and Voss 2011). The economic hardship of postsocialist reforms and the Yugoslav ethnic wars of the 1990s caused massive fluxes of refugees and economic migrants. In addition, the atrocities of the Yugoslav wars and the carefully crafted policies of ethnic cleansing produced large numbers of internally displaced persons (IDP), many of whom continue to be potential refugees to the EU in attempts to escape poor living conditions in refugee camps and improvised shelters in Bosnia and Herzegovina, Croatia, Kosovo and Serbia. Thus, the very same socioeconomic conditions made the Balkans both the countries of origin for refugees and illegal migrants seeking to flee the region and one of the primary transit routes for refugees and illegal migrants of other origins seeking to get into EU territory. Countless illegal economic migrants, mainly from Bangladesh, Eastern Turkey, India, Iraq, Iran, Pakistan and China, have traveled through the Balkans on their journey into EU countries during the last two decades (Morrison and Crosland 2001).

Since few of these illegal migrants and refugees are interested in actually staying in the Balkans, the governments in the region did not put serious efforts in thwarting this influx. As such, arguably, for the newly emerging democracies in Eastern Europe, institutional reforms in the area of asylum only succeed in adding unnecessary strain to their already weak economies and social welfare systems (Peshkopia 2005a, 2005b, 2005c; Byrne 2003; Nyiri, Toth and Fullerton 2001; Anagnost 2000; Lavenex 1998, 1999). Some authors have argued that EEC resistance to building asylum systems has been provoked by fears that EU asylum policies will turn these countries on the outskirts of EU territory into "buffer" zones for illegal migration (Byrne 2003; 2002; Byrne, Noll and Vedsted-Hansen 2002a, 2002b; Wallace and Stola 2001); however, I continue to argue, as before, that indifference rather than rational opposition has prevented Balkan leaders from conducting asylum-related reforms (Peshkopia 2005a, 2005b, 2005c). Regardless, EECs have yielded to the EU's demands to establish asylum systems that serve no domestic needs. The Albanian asylum system has undergone dramatic developments. Over the course of three years, it went from making great efforts to manage the massive refugee influx of Kosovars during the 1999 Kosovo War to a complete collapse of the system in 2002, due to mismanagement and curbing of government interest in asylum policies. The Macedonian case shows a similar reluctance by domestic leaders to advance asylum reform while the country faced more pressing issues.

However, most postcommunist Balkan countries have now established formal asylum systems (Feijen 2007). This chapter shows how EU membership conditionality has affected such outcomes; I describe the developments in the Albanian and Macedonian asylum systems and analyze how changes in the interests of domestic leaders and EU policies have impacted asylum reforms in both countries.

Asylum in Albania: The Politics of Oblivion and Obedience

Communist Albania never signed the 1951 Geneva Convention, thus refusing to become part of the international system of refugee protection. Indeed, as the country was growing increasingly introverted, it did not even need an asylum system. The last wave of refugees occurred in 1949, when defeated Greek communist guerrillas entered Albania, only to be transferred quickly to other countries of the Soviet Bloc. For the rest of the communist reign, the only refugees to enter the country were Albanians from the former Yugoslavia seeking to escape Yugoslavian anti-Albanian policies. The deeply suspicious regime in Tirana routinely relocated these refugees to remote communities under the permanent control of local authorities. Fearing refugee influxes from Kosovo, especially during the violent riots in the Kosovo capital, Prishtina, in March–April 1981, the Albanian communist regime sought to make Albania an unattractive country for refuge.

With the opening of the country in 1991, one of the obvious signs of Albanian eagerness to break free from communist isolationism was its adherence to international institutions and organizations. That popular mood was reflected in the rush of the newly elected Albanian authorities to acquire membership in many international organizations. As a result, in December 1991, Albania signed the 1951 Geneva Convention. The signature was simply a political gesture, since it did not trigger immediate policy change in refugee protection.

Albania of 1991–2001 was a chaotic hub of all types of trafficking and smuggling, which flowed in from the geopolitical East (Eastern Europe, former Soviet Union, Turkey, the Middle East and Central and Far Asia) and out to the geopolitical West. Streams of illegal immigrants entered every day over the Albanian–Greek and Albanian–Macedonian borders, heading toward the Albanian coasts. From there, Albanian gangs smuggled them across the Adriatic Sea to Italy on powerful speedboats. Immigrants included Turkish and Iraqi Kurds, trafficked girls from Moldova and Ukraine, Pakistani countrymen, Iranian from all social classes, young Chinese and a mixture of rural Albanians. The Albanian authorities remained silent, obviously supportive of human smuggling as a means of diminishing political pressures from rising unemployment; whereas the efforts of the Italian coastguard during the 1990s proved to be insufficient to quell the Balkan route (Peshkopia 2008b; Peshkopia and Voss 2011).

The idea that foreign citizens could seek asylum in Albania while Albania's own citizens were seeking asylum in other countries seemed strange to the Albanian authorities and public alike.[2] Consequently, efforts of the United Nations High Commissioner for Refugees (UNHCR) to persuade the Albanian government to establish an asylum system failed to produce any results before the country entered into the process of drafting a new constitution in 1997–98. After the rocky years of the Partia Demokratike (PD)

(Democratic Party) rule and the Partia Socialiste's (PS) (Socialist Party) subsequent victory in July 1997, the new ruling elites wanted to demonstrate to the country's international partners that they had abandoned their Leninist legacy and were committed to integrating the country fully into international rules and norms. Thus, for the first time, Albania recognized the right of foreign citizens to be granted asylum in its territory via its new constitution that came into force on November 28, 1998. Article 40 of the constitution states that "foreigners have the right [to] asylum in the Republic of Albania according to law."[3] On December 14, 1998, the Kuvend approved the Law on Asylum. On April 19, 2001, the Kuvend approved the Law on the Guard and Control of the State Border; and on May 27, 2001, it approved the Law on Foreigners, completing the legal foundations for a modern asylum and immigration system.

The Law on Asylum was drafted with the close cooperation of UNHCR Bureau of Tirana (BoT). The law generally met the 1951 Geneva Convention's criteria of refugee definition, refugee status determination (RSD) and refugee protection. It recognized the 1951 Geneva Convention's definition of a refugee (Article 4) and affirmed the concept of temporary protection for humanitarian reasons (Article 5). The law also reflected the 1951 Geneva Convention's principle of *non-refoulement* (Article 7 and Article 15/2/a). Articles 12/3 and 15/2/b recognize the right of those who have been granted asylum status to acquire labor and residence permission and social rights equal to those of Albanian citizens.

The law designated the Zyra për Refugjatë (ZpR) (Office for Refugees) as the institution that would process asylum seekers' applications and interviews. The ZpR, composed of five civil servants, also served as a collegial decision-making body (Article 17). The rejected asylum seekers had the right to appeal to the Komisioni Kombëtar për Refugjatë (KKR) (National Commission for Refugees), an eight-member committee that worked closely with government agencies related to asylum issues and two NGOs, Dhoma e Avokatëve (Albanian Bar Association) and Komiteti Shqiptar i Helsinkit (Albanian Helsinki Committee) (Article 19). The Komisioneri Kombëtar për Refugjatë (National Commissioner for Refugees) was the head of the entire asylum system. The commissioner chaired both the ZpR and the KKR, but could not vote in the KKR on cases of refugee appeals against the ZpR's decisions (Article 19/8).

Although the Law on Asylum had been considered to fit international criteria, loopholes still existed. For instance, Article 23/3 stipulated the obligation of the ZpR to appoint a state-paid lawyer to asylum seekers, in itself a major development compared to asylum laws of other Balkan countries. Yet it was unclear which state organization would pay for lawyers, as the ZpR itself had no resources for such expenditures, especially during 1999–2002 when it was financed by annual UNHCR programs.[4]

Even before the Law on Asylum was approved in June 1998, the ZpR was established as a small unit within the Ministria e Pushtetit Vendor dhe Decentralizimit (MPVD) (Ministry of Local Government and Decentralization) and commissioned with tackling an initially minor refugee crisis triggered by ongoing skirmishes in Kosovo. The establishment of the ZpR represented a quick fix without any legal underpinning and with an undefined status. In March 1999, soon after the Law on Asylum was approved, roughly 450,000 Albanian Kosovars fled to Albania and Macedonia, forced by a brutal policy of ethnic cleansing conducted by Serbian paramilitaries, government security forces and military units. The Serbian campaign of terror over civilian populations included raping women, executing civilians of all ages, looting houses and properties and forcing citizens to leave the country. The North Atlantic Treaty Organization (NATO) dispatched military air strikes to stop the Serbian massacres, and a large international effort began to help both Albania and Macedonia deal with the humanitarian crisis. The Albanian government granted temporary protection to fleeing Kosovars, the first legal Albanian move to protect refugees. As the majority of Kosovars returned to their homes after NATO troops entered Kosovo in June 1999, those that remained in Albania became the major preoccupation of the ZpR throughout the rest of 1999 and most of 2000. In 2000, the ZpR began to proceed with individual applications, and some rudimentary procedures of refugee status determination have since been developed. However, in the spring of 2001, another minor refugee crisis was caused by military clashes in Macedonia between the ethnic Albanian Ushtria Çlirimtare Kombëtare (UÇK/NLA) (National Liberation Army) and the ethnic Macedonian-dominated security forces, once again disrupting the normal function of the ZpR.

During the year 2000, the activity of the ZpR declined, and government interest switched to more pressing issues. Two subsequent elections, the October 2000 local elections and June 2001 general elections, turned the focus to domestic problems. The PS victory in the general elections was followed by a power struggle within the socialists themselves and the country only began to implement reforms in the summer of 2002. Asylum reform ranked low in the ruling elites' priorities. After his consolidation of power within the PS, the newly re-elected prime minister Fatos Nano seized the cause of the EU membership for the country, and returned to pursuing reforms that would facilitate Albania's road toward that goal. His policies were followed by the PD, who succeeded him after the summer 2005 elections. In November 2006, Albania and the EU signed an agreement for readmission; this agreement included not just Albanian citizens, but illegal migrants from third countries who had been denied asylum or refugee status in the EU countries, and who had been proven to have entered the EU through Albania.[5]

From October 2001 to April 2002, the ZpR struggled both for its survival and to recover from administrative blunders of the past.[6] The work focused on drafting and promoting legislation that would make the Albanian asylum system compatible with the requirements of the 1951 Geneva Convention; and undertook initiatives such as pre-screening procedures, a process of interviewing illegal migrants detained by police to determine whether they were refugees or economic migrants.[7] The ZpR also participated in Albania–EU task force committees to assess Albania's policy progress toward the Stabilization and Association Agreement. The ZpR's efforts to reach the refugee protection standards recommended by the EU were guided by UNHCR, not the Albanian government. Finally, the ZpR's awkward administrative situation ended on 30 April 2002 when the MPVD ordered the suspension of the ZpR's activity. The UNHCR BoT took over some of ZpR's functions, including receiving of new applications for asylum and assisting of those few individuals and families who were either under the RSD process or leftover from the Kosovar influx of 1998–99.

In October 2001, both domestic and international players established the long-delayed Albanian Task Force on Asylum. The task force was charged with drafting by-laws to fill the remaining legal gaps in policies for refugee integration. Three by-laws on education, health care and employment drafted in the spring of 2002 were incorporated into laws mandating integration and family reunion for persons granted asylum status in the Republic of Albania; they were approved by the Kuvend in June 2003 and went into effect on August 19, 2003. Similarly, the National Commission for Refugees was constituted in its first meeting in early November 2001, almost two years after the Law on Asylum stipulated its activity. RSD procedures were established according to the law, and their implementation began as a joint project between UNHCR, the ZpR, and Paqe Përmes Drejtësisë (PPD) (Peace through Justice), a local NGO which specialized in making legal assistance available for refugees and asylum seekers.

The ZpR enjoyed a wide range of autonomy, since most of its decisions did not require any endorsement by the minister of the line, which led to abuses by irresponsible or corrupted public servants. In an attempt to address administrative shortcuts, the minister of local government released a guideline for an internal reform of the ZpR, which resulted in its suspension on April 30, 2002. But the reform went beyond the guideline, changing the location and the name of the institution as well. By April 2003, the ZpR was transferred to the Ministria e Rendit Publik (MRP) (Ministry of Public Order), now Ministria e Brendëshme (MB) (Ministry of the Interior). Indeed, that was a necessary step, since the RSD processes aligned more closely with the police than with local governments. Finally, in October 2003, a decision of the Council of Ministers renamed the ZpR. Now known as the Drejtoria për Refugjatë dhe Nacionalitete (DRN) (Directorate for Refugees and Nationalities), the new name reflected the status of the institution within the MRP.

Before the summer of 2003, Albania did not have any official refugee reception center. NGOs accommodated asylum seekers in private mansions financed by the UNHCR protection program. The implementation of a project to establish the Qëndra Kombëtare për Azilkërkues (QKA) (National Center for Asylum Seekers), the country's first reception center for asylum seekers, began in October 2001. The issue of refugee and asylum-seeker accommodation had been a concern for both Albanian authorities and UNHCR. Usually, detained people caught traveling illegally through Albania by the police were kept in police stations without any legal case; even the police were confused about their legal status. Although Albanian law punishes illegal border crossing, the fact that tens of thousands of Albanian citizens were doing it on a daily basis continued to perplex Albanian authorities regarding the real meaning and application of such a law. The MRP provided no food or hygiene supplies; thus detained people often remained at the mercy of the police. Because of the sluggish cooperation between the ZpR and UNHCR with police, detained people were frequently obliged to live in terrible conditions for several days at a stretch.

In order to relieve detainee conditions, the UNHCR provided some local NGOs with funds to arrange accommodation for asylum seekers in privately owned houses. However, the UNHCR felt the final solution of the problem was to be found in the establishment of a dedicated refugee reception center that would shelter asylum seekers from the moment that an asylum request was received until its final decision. The Albanian government offered an old military building in Babrru, outside of Tirana. The UNHCR supervised the construction of the reception center, and the European Commission financed the entire project through the implementation of the EU High Level Working Group's (HLWG) Action Plan on Asylum in Albania and the Neighboring Region. Of the total 49,616,203 Albanian lek (roughly €350,000) the project cost, the Albanian government covered only a small portion, for telephone and utilities. The QKA opened in July 2003. In February 2010, there were 69 recognized refugees and 29 asylum applicants.[8] Most of the recognized refugees were remnants of the Kosovar refugee wave of the spring 1999, indeed, the same who enjoyed ZpR protection in 2002.[9]

However, the DRN remained volatile. It underwent another restructuring in 2006, which left it with three officials instead of five, undermining its capacity to implement the action plan for asylum and to process properly asylum applications.[10] On November 10, 2010, the European Commission (EC) noted that the institutional and legal framework that had been put in place through the new law on asylum adopted in 2009 was considered "generally in line with EU standards." However, the Commission warned that consistency needed to be ensured between the Law on Asylum, the Law on Integration and the Law on Foreigners. As the Commission acknowledged, "[t]he asylum system has sufficient human resources and capacity to deal with its current low caseload. However, in case of a higher influx of asylum seekers, the DShR would need additional and more specialized staff."[11] One can easily conclude that the asylum institution in Albania stands formally as an institution that can handle asylum seekers and refugees, but that there are very few asylum cases to manage.

Another example of the Albanian government's reluctance to implement asylum policies is the way it conducted the so-called "pre-screening process" from its inception in 2001. The concept of pre-screening was offered by UNHCR as a compromise between the international obligations of EU member countries and their need to prevent migration influxes (see, for example, Lubbers 2002, 2003). Pre-screening aims at identifying asylum seekers, trafficked human beings and illegal migrants among undocumented people detained by border police. The implementation of the pre-screening policy attempts to keep EU member countries regularly processing asylum seekers while trying to identify and reject cases that seem openly abusive. Originally, pre-screening was perceived as only an EU policy, implemented only by EU member countries.[12] However, both the EU and UNHCR agreed to implement such a policy also in Albania.[13]

The process of pre-screening began when the border police contacted the asylum institution in the country and informed about foreigners that had been detained. In such cases, a joint team of ZpR/DRN, UNHCR and International Organization of Migration (IOM) departed immediately to the detention site. After the interview, those who sought asylum or refugee status were sent to the QKA Babrru; those who qualified as trafficked women were sent in the Qëndra Kombëtare për Pritjen e Viktimave të Trafikuara (QKPVT) (National Reception Center of Victims of Trafficking In) in Linzë; while those who did not qualify and/or were not interested in seeking asylum were sent back to the country through which they entered Albania. Until 2004, detained undocumented foreigners were kept in police stations. Later, five reception centers were built at border-crossing stations, at the Rinas airport; Bllatë, on the border with Macedonia; the port of

Shëngjin; and Tre Urat, Përmet and Qafë Botë, Sarandë, on the Albanian–Greek border. Although those centers were intended to shelter detained persons, the police adopted most of these facilities for uses unrelated to detention.[14]

The funding for the pre-screening project came from the EU Community Assistance for Restructuration, Development and Stability (CARDS) Program. Originally, the process was implemented by the ZpR/DRN, UNHCR and IOM. However, in May 2005, the process was transferred to the Drejtoria e Policisë Kufitare (DPK) (Directory of the Border Police). From this moment, DRN lost access to people detained at border crossing points. With that change, the DRN also lost its responsibility for transporting detained people to Babrru or Linza. Police were neither able nor sufficiently trained to conduct pre-screening interviews with undocumented foreigners. Nor were police interested in committing personnel and vehicles to transport asylum seekers and/or trafficked human beings to the reception centers in mainland Albania. Allegedly, most of the people detained in the border were sent back to the country from where they entered Albanian territory. Ever since, the number of detained people sent to the QKA, Babrru and QKPVT, has dropped significantly.

The PD electoral victories of 2005 and 2009 did not contribute to changing the pace of the Albanian asylum reform. In its 2007 Progress Report, the European Commission emphasizes that "[t]here has been limited progress on asylum issues," that "no coherent single asylum strategy is yet in place" and that "progress on the planned review and amendment of the legal framework for asylum has been slow."[15] In May 2008, the EU Commission handed the Albanian government the roadmap on visa liberalization. The document contained four chapters: documents security; illegal migration; public order and security; and issues of foreign relations and fundamental rights.[16] The plan links the establishment of appropriate asylum procedures with visa liberalization. It asks the Albanian government to adopt and implement asylum legislation in line with international standards and the EU legal framework. But given the short time period between it and the release of the 2008 Progress Report, one could not expect much.[17] However, the revision of the Law on Asylum in January 2009, in order to incorporate European and international standards, marked a major breakthrough in the Albanian asylum system. Although the European Commission notes in its 2009 Progress Report a range of measures that still needed to be adopted to complete the legal framework, particularly in terms of health care, family reunion, social protection, education and housing, Albania was commended for having made good progress with regard to asylum. Albania's asylum system continued to meet its policy objectives only partially.

In November 2009, Albania was excluded from the first round of EU visa liberalization negotiations with the Western Balkans precisely because it had met its objectives only partially. That failure brought heavy criticism from the opposition PS, since visa liberalization and EU candidate status had been central promises of both the PD and the PS during their campaigns for the summer 2009 general elections. Under growing pressure from the opposition, the government undertook vigorous efforts to fulfill the EU's conditions. Those efforts were recognized by the Commission, which, in a November 2010 report on Albania's application for membership in the European Union, ruled that Albania had made progress in a number of key areas of this chapter in the framework.

The progress in the Albanian asylum system continued slowly during 2011. Even though the institutional framework was in place, the EC complained that the related legislation was not fully in line with the EU *acquis*. Specifically, the EC cited the fact that no ID documents had been provided so far to refugees and persons granted complementary protection. Reportedly, during September of that year, ethnic Albanian recognized 78 refugees and 30 asylum seekers.[18] The same sluggish progress continued in 2012 as refugees and persons who had been granted complementary protection were still awaiting ID documents. The number of people granted asylum system by August 2012 was as low as 80 (with 20 more applications pending).[19] Table 6.1 traces the developments in the Albanian asylum system.

Asylum in Macedonia: How Many Sticks and Carrots Count?

During the 1990s, the asylum system in Macedonia followed the practices set in place during the Yugoslav period. However, similar to the Albanian case, Macedonia remained both a country of origin for refugees and part of the Balkan route for refugees and illegal migrants of other origins seeking to enter EU territory. During that period, the Macedonian governments' main concerns were to consolidate the country as the homeland of the Macedonian people, to acquire international recognition and to escape the Yugoslav wars. These goals seemed to overlap with the EU desire to see a stable Macedonia. Thus, in the aftermath of the 2001 conflict, establishing asylum capacities was not a high priority, although the country had sheltered refugees from the Ashkali, Egyptian and Roma communities from Kosovo since March 1999.

Macedonia signed the Stabilization and Association (SAP) Agreement with the EU in the spring of 2001, when an armed ethnic conflict swept the western part of the country. Some authors have commented that the agreement seemed to be a reward for Macedonia's constructive role during the Kosovo crisis. However, it can also be interpreted as a guarantee by the EU to the Macedonian government, and a warning to the Albanian guerrillas, that EU interest rested in a united, democratically stable Macedonia. On the other hand, the EU seemed to understand initially the difficulty of prioritizing an infrastructure for dealing with asylum during the country's reconstruction period, and asked for only minimum standards to be set in place such as a new asylum law, the adoption of secondary legislation and improvement of institutional capacity to process asylum applications.[20] However, the EU remained firm in standing behind its preferences and, similar to Albania, Macedonia was required to sign a readmission agreement with the EU for both its citizens and third country citizens smuggled in the EU through the country.[21] The combination of such a lack of interest by Macedonian elites to engage in asylum capacity building and growing EU preferences for a functioning asylum system in Macedonia produced a stalemate in asylum reform during the period from 2002 to early 2003, as demonstrated by the EC's Stabilization and Association Report released in March 2003.[22]

Table 6.1. Developments in Albanian asylum reform

Period	Situation	EU Interests	Domestic Leaders' Interests	Reform Results
1991–97	Issues of asylum and immigration were outside government's scope	0	0	**No reform.** The EU was interested in thwarting waves of undocumented people crossing its border and Albania was a main gateway for people from the Middle East, and Central and Eastern Asia being smuggled into the EU territory. Albania was not interested in building any asylum system since no one from the undocumented people travelling through Albania toward the EU territories sought refuge in the country.
1998	New constitution	0	+	**Good progress.** With the drafting of the new constitution, the Socialist-Centrist coalition wanted to demonstrate to international partners its commitment to the country's international obligations. The real interest in the asylum reform was not a literal establishment of an asylum system, but only the establishment of a basic legislative framework that would be considered a progress in country's asylum policy. Meanwhile, EU policy continued to focus on Albania protecting its border.
1999	Kosovo crisis	+	+	**Good progress.** This period represents the only time when both the EU and Albanian government were interested in establishing asylum system. The EU interest came from its project to build a common European asylum, system with Albania as part of that system. The Albanian interest came from the need to handle the Kosovar refugee influx and potential refugee influx from Macedonia.

Year	Event			Description
2000	Government crisis	+	0	**No reforms.** Although EU interests on the Albanian asylum system was as high as in the previous period, the local elections of October 2000 and general elections of July 2001 made the government focus on major reforms, thus leaving the asylum reform outside its attention.
2001–2002	Continues government crisis	+	0	**Slow progress/system fails.** The crisis within the main partner of the ruling coalition, the PS, reduced the interest of the government in some reforms peripheral to both that domestic struggle and the containment of an increasingly aggressive opposition such as the PD. Ultimately, the government closed the ZpR.
2003–2008	EU pressure	+	0	**Insufficient/slow progress.** The prevalence of Fatos Nano in the internal struggle of the PS renewed government interest in reforms. The EU–Western Balkans Summit in Zagreb, November 2000 and the European Council of Thessaloniki, June 2003 renewed the Albanian hopes to join the Union, and the government began to follow the EU blueprint. The PD-led coalition that took over in 2005 followed the same path of reform, but the lack of a domestic need for the asylum reform reduced government's attention to asylum related policies, and the Albanian asylum system remains weak.
2009–10	Visa liberalization agreement	+	+	**Good progress.** Only when the EU linked asylum reform to the more tangible issue of visa liberalization policy, rather than EU membership, did the Albanian government become interested in fully implementing asylum policies.
2011–12	Political crisis strikes	+	0	**No progress.** The political crisis of the 2011–12 required excessive energies to foster cooperation in several more pressing reforms.

The first major development in the Macedonian asylum system was undertaken in July 2003 when the Sobranie passed a new Law on Asylum and Temporary Protection (LATP), and the law went into effect that August. The European Commission considered the law to be largely in line with EU standards, but secondary legislation was required for its proper implementation.[23] LATP puts the asylum system within the authority of the Ministerstvo za Vnatresni Raboti (MVR) (Ministry of the Interior), where the Oddelenie za Azil (OA) (Unit for Asylum) was established. During the second half of 2003, the Macedonian authorities began to work with UNHCR and other implementing partners in a series of joint meetings, information campaigns, detailed technical review and training programs on the EU *acquis*, the status determination procedures and the drafting of regulations and procedures. However, as always, the main goal was to find long-term solutions for existing refugees. By the end of 2003, 93 per cent of people in temporary protection, mostly leftovers from the mass influx of 1999 from Kosovo, had applied for asylum, a right conferred on them by the new law.

However, the RSD process was slow, thus leading us to the conclusion that simply establishing the Unit for Asylum and some asylum capacities in Macedonia could not ensure an effectively functioning asylum system.[24] As the EC's 2005 Analytical Report notes, the Governmental Commission, the competent body for hearing appeals against first instance decisions on refugee status, "remains untransparent [*sic*] and lacks independence."[25] Mainly, in that time, the commission emphasized the lack of asylum-seeker reception centers and the lack of resources from the Ministerstvo za Trud i Socijalna Politika (MTSP) (Ministry of Labor and Social Policy), which is in charge of providing advice to refugees and ensuring inter-ministerial and inter-agency coordination on the implementation of the LATP. Indeed, after the huge influx of refugees from Kosovo in 1999, the number of asylum seekers from 2000 to 2005 decreased. In the first six months of 2005, only 11 persons applied for asylum.

In 2004, the Macedonian government established the national CARDS Steering Committee that would supervise and coordinate the national CARDS project. The committee is chaired by the state secretary of the MTSP and consists of members from Ministry of the Interior, Ministerstvo za Pravda (MP) (Ministry of Justice), Vladiniot Sekretarijat za Evropski Prasanja (VSEP) (Government's Secretariat for European Affairs) and Ministerstvo za Nadvoersni Raboti (MNR) (Ministry of Foreign Affairs). The European Agency for Reconstruction (EAR), the UNHCR, International Organization of Migration (IOM) and International Centre for Migration Policy Development (ICMPD) maintain observer status. The policy implementation went through two projects. The goal of the first project was the establishment of institutional asylum capacities. The first phase of this project was completed in May 2004, and represented the legislative and procedural foundations of the asylum system, including a review of the existing legislation and a proposal for upgrading the National Action Plan to meet standards of the European Union *acquis* (Feijen 2007). The second phase was funded by the EU agency EurAsylum and had three objectives: the implementation of the National Action Plan through continuous reviews; recommendations and the efficient implementation of the agreed policies and procedures; and the revision of existing legislation, the identification of gaps and recommendations for the adoption of primary and secondary legislation. The second project aimed at completing the Macedonian asylum system with a reception center for asylum seekers (ibid.).

The implementation of asylum procedures in Macedonia is administered by the Ministry of the Interior's Unit for Asylum, which processes claims as the first stage of RSD. The Governmental Commission makes decisions on the second stage in the policy areas of the interior, judiciary, state administration, local self-government and issues of religious character. The commission was composed of seven members, one from the Ministry of Justice, four from the Ministry of the Interior, one from the Commission on Religious Communities and a high-ranking official from the General Secretariat of the Government, who becomes the commission's president. However, in 2008, the Administrative Court replaced the Supreme Court as the final word on asylum cases. Eight new asylum applications were registered in 2006 and no case was recognized under the 1951 Geneva Convention. Until late 2000s, the Macedonian asylum system has almost exclusively dealt with claims from Kosovo minorities and, cumulatively, less than 2 per cent of these claims have been recognized under the 1951 Convention (ibid.). That changed dramatically in the turn of the decade.

The European Commission's November 2005 Analytical Report for the Opinion on the Application from the Former Yugoslav Republic of Macedonia for EU Membership reviewed the issue of asylum reform, as did its November 2005 Commission Opinion on the Application from the Former Yugoslav Republic of Macedonia for Membership of the European Union.[26] However, the EU returned to the issue of asylum reform in 2006, when, in its Decision on the Principles, Priorities and Conditions Contained in the European Partnership with the former Yugoslav Republic of Macedonia and Repealing Decision, the European Council set as a mid-term priority "the operation of asylum procedures which are fully in line with international and European standards, including a reformed appeals system."[27]

The Commission's 2006 Progress Report on Macedonia explicitly mentioned the lack of significant progress in the area of asylum, yet considers the state of asylum in Macedonia as "moderately advanced."[28] Earlier that year, in March 2006, the Government issued its National Programme for the Adoption of the *Acquis Communautaire*, and has revised it several time ever since. For its short-term priorities on asylum, it undertook to earmark funds from the national budget to address the needs of asylum seekers in education, health, employment, juvenile reform and professional training (Feijen 2007, 507). By the same token, the EC's 2007 Progress Report continued to be critical of both the institutional functioning and the asylum policy implementation, concluding that Macedonia was "not yet sufficiently prepared."[29]

As in the case of other Western Balkans countries, the EU linked visa liberalization with Macedonia's performance in asylum reform. The roadmap on EU visa liberalization for citizens of Macedonia, which was handed out to Macedonia in May 2008, stipulates that Macedonia should "implement the legislation in the area of asylum in line with international standards [...] and the EU legal framework and standards"; and "provide adequate infrastructure and strengthen responsible bodies, in particular in the area of asylum procedures and reception of asylum seekers."[30] The opening of a new reception center for asylum seekers and the replacement of the Supreme Court by the Administrative Court as the site of the last opportunity to appeal asylum cases served the country an overall positive assessment in the EC's 2008 Progress Report.[31] Furthermore, in the 2009 Progress Report, the Commission reports "good progress in the area of asylum", even seeing Macedonia as "advanced" in the area of asylum. As steps that were undertaken over the last years, the report mentions that the new Law on Asylum and Temporary Protection "brought national standards even closer to European ones." The EC also praised the fact that the Government Commission hearing appeals against first-instance decisions on refugee status was abolished, and the administrative court became the final-instance body on refugee status.[32] The same evaluation Macedonia received from the 2010 Progress Report.[33] Along with the progress in the other three policy areas stipulated for visa liberalization agreements with the EU, progress in asylum reform rewarded Macedonia with a visa liberalization agreement in November 2009.

The tracing of Macedonian developments in the area of asylum shows that, similar to Albania, the lack of tangible incentives created by the more distant EU membership played a less important role than the more tangible and immediate promise of visa liberalization. The country did make good progress in 2005, the year when an EU decision about the country's candidate status was expected. Yet the asylum reform stalled again, along with the country's progress toward the candidate status, until the introduction of the roadmap in 2008. Macedonia scored good progress in the very important year 2009, when both the visa liberalization agreement and a European Commission recommendation for opening accession negotiations with Macedonia were expected.

However, both the failure of the EU to open accession negotiations with Macedonia due to the expected Greek opposition on the issue of the country's name, and the growing number of illegal immigrants entering the country from their southern neighbor, Greece, heading north toward the northern neighbor, Serbia, curbed incentives for Macedonian leaders to dedicate energy and resources to a problem that seemed to be not theirs during the period of 2010–12. Therefore, during that period, as the EC 2011 Progress Report on Macedonia states, there was only limited progress on asylum. Reportedly, some minor steps were taken, especially regarding rules establishing the role of each institution in the integration of refugees and foreigners, and providing for the appointment of legal guardians for unaccompanied minors and mentally disabled persons. Also, in 2011, the government adopted a program for the social integration of persons granted asylum but, due to delays in its implementation, a number of concerned families were in practice left without housing support for several months. And finally, from the beginning of 2011, the Macedonian government took over some of the funding for the Center for Integration of Refugees and Foreigners, later transformed into the National Center for Integration of Foreigners and Refugees and Reintegration of the Returnees, an institution in charge of preparing family integration plans for recognized refugees and persons under subsidiary protection and recently also for the domestic returnees who have been denied asylum or refugee status in EU member countries or who have escaped human trafficking nets.[34] However, Macedonia remained slow to adopt legislation that would improve social conditions of its asylum seekers, as the latter continued to face difficulties accessing information about procedures and social rights. Among those absent social conditions have been the lack of ID documents, free legal aid provided by the state and access to public health insurance for persons granted asylum.[35]

Some of the problems related to refugee social services and social standing were overcome in 2012. First, the amendment of the Law on Free Legal Assistance enabled asylum seekers to benefit from the provision of legal aid. Second, an amendment to the Law on Health Insurance addressed the issue of public health care access for persons who are granted asylum. Third, the adoption of an integration program promised state funding for housing support to persons granted asylum. Such efforts to improve social services and the social status of people who have been granted asylum rights were enshrined in the government's program for integration, which aimed to support refugee families and individuals who have submitted a written request for local integration in Macedonia. The government pledged 20 million denars (€330,000) for the program's implementation.

Fourth, there were some improvements in access to information about RSD. A major step related to RSD was the enforcement in July 2011 of the Law Amending the Law on Administrative Disputes.[36] The amendment provided the establishment of the Higher Administrative Court as having the power of final decisions for the appeal of an asylum-related decision adopted by the Administrative Court.[37] However, asylum procedures in Macedonia, especially for initial asylum decisions, remained slow and unsatisfactory and decisions continued to be released on procedural rather than substantive grounds. Furthermore, there was no progress in the process for providing asylum seekers with ID papers. Overall, even though the legislative and institutional framework was satisfactory, its implementation needed improvements.[38]

A key element of the Macedonian asylum system is the Reception Center for Asylum Seekers in Vizbegovo, which was inaugurated in March 2009 with the goal of accommodating asylum seekers during their RSD process. The initial accommodation capacity of the reception center was 150 persons and the EC's 2011 Progress Report claims that, until September 2011, the center had accommodated a total of 418 asylum seekers. However, located north of Skopje and near the Serbian border, the place seems to be a haven for those who seek to migrate northward toward Serbia with the goal of entering EU territory.[39]

The latest developments in Macedonian asylum reform took place on December 24, 2012 when the Sobranie adopted the Law Amending the Law on Asylum and Temporary Protection. In line with its reform priorities outlined in the 2012 revisions of its National Program for Adoption of the *Acquis Communautaire*, the country took some steps toward improving its asylum system, focusing mainly on the RSD. The amendments were a response to three EU directives, namely 83/2004, 9/2003 and 85/2005. The draft law was prepared by a working group established with the participation of the Ministry of the Interior, Ministry of Labor and Social Policy, the Secretariat for European Affairs, the Ministry of Education and the UNHCR Office in Skopje. It was submitted before to the European Commission in Brussels, which gave a positive opinion.[40] The amendments aimed both at RSD and refugee social assistance and integration. Changes related to the RSD included provisions to terminate the asylum procedure for applicants who did not respect the house order in the reception center; the free legal aid for the asylum seekers, although it was not clear who would provide the legal aid; and changes in expulsion criteria. A major change with the amendments concerned the timing of asylum decisions: the Unit for Asylum had to make a first decision within six months from the day of application, a significant extension from the two-month limit that it was previously. Amendments concerning refugee social assistance and integration addressed education, protection of minors and refugee health care. If Macedonia follows through with its National Programme for Adoption of *Acquis Communautaire*, then the country should be ready to adopt a new law on asylum in 2014.

A Consociational Interpretation of Albanian and Macedonian Asylum Reforms

A consociational interpretation of Albanian and Macedonian asylum reforms is a tricky enterprise, since the EU guidelines and principles relating to refugee status determination are clear, but decisions made at the national level tend to reflect domestic leaders' preferences on those reforms. While the European Asylum Support Office (EASO), established in 2010, is the first institution at the EU level working to strengthen and develop cooperation in the realm of asylum provision among the member countries, it is set to have no direct or indirect power on refugee status determination.[41] Of course, the EU's common European asylum system is being promoted by Council decisions and European Parliament regulations in an institutional setting, established by and functioning through consociational practices. However, breaches of compliance by member countries purporting to harmonize asylum legislation and procedures show the relevance of securing asylum policies at the national level.

With the Treaty of Amsterdam, asylum policies of member countries, along with immigration and external border control, are becoming communitarized. These policies along with the Schengen *acquis* have been transferred to the Justice and Home Affairs pillar. However, it seems difficult to persuade member states to give up refugee protection prerogatives, which, as part of population control, have been argued to be the very *raison d'être* of the state (see, for instance, Foucault 1994, 201–22). Finally, it was agreed that the five-year transition would occur under the condition of unanimous decisions among the member states, and only after that period would co-decisions and qualified majority voting be practiced. The agreement came under the provision that the EC would previously adopt legislation defining the common rules and basic principles governing the asylum field. Denmark decided to opt out of this policy, while Great Britain and Ireland chose to participate only partially in the new EU asylum policy.

The shift from a national asylum system to a common European asylum policy shows the EU's intention to implement consociational practices in managing this policy sector. Through the new policy, the EU scrambles to resolve the contradiction between, on the one hand, the need of its member countries to curb uncontrolled refugee and migrant influxes in their territories and, on the other, the need for its member countries to continue to respect their international commitments. The European Commission's 2007 Green Paper almost exclusively put the principle of solidarity and burden sharing at the

Table 6.2. Developments in Macedonian asylum reform

Period	Situation	EU Interests	Domestic Leaders' Interests	Reform Results
1991–2003	Consolidation of statehood	0	0	**No reform.** The main EU interest during the 1990s and early 2000s was the political stability of the country that would turn Macedonia from a predominantly country of transit to a refugee country of origin. By the same token, Macedonia's elites were focused in dealing with simmering—and later erupting—ethnic tensions.
2004–2005	EU candidate country	0	+	**Good progress.** After Macedonia returned to normality, the EU grew interested in expanding its concept of the common European asylum system to include this country. On the other hand, the Macedonian government was interested in undertaking some steps toward asylum reform in order to boost country's chances for EU candidacy status.
2006–2008	Cervenkovski's second term	+	0	**Insufficient/slow progress.** The EU hesitation to open accession negotiations with Macedonia curbed the Macedonian interest to implement reforms that did not interest the country. Hence, the European Commission 2006, 2007 and 2008 Reports for Macedonia's progress in asylum sector reforms were "insufficient."
2009	Visa liberalization agreement	+	+	**Good progress.** The stipulation of progress in asylum reform and the hopes that the EU would decide to open accession negotiations with Macedonia seemed to have shifted its leaders' interests toward progressing with the asylum reform, thus the European Commission's assertion that the country had made "good progress."
2010	The quest for accession negotiations	+	+	**Good progress.** The process of accession negotiations helped to maintain the interest of the Macedonian ruling elites in the asylum reform, which led to a report that the country had made "good progress."
2011	New national elections	+	0	**No progress.** Disappointment with not opening accession negotiation shifted policy preferences of the ruling elites toward more pressing domestic problems.
2012	The establishment of the High Level Accession Dialogue	+	+	**Some progress.** The establishment of the HLAD managed to shift Macedonian elites' policy preferences back to positive. The HLAD focused on keeping up Macedonian reforms through invigorating hopes that progress in reforms would strengthen support among EU member countries for opening accession negotiations.

center of that system. However, since previous EU burden sharing efforts have failed, the Green Paper shows that a shift to policies that would emphasize proportional distribution of asylum seekers throughout the EU sphere would be impossible without emphasizing the principle of solidarity and burden sharing.

Solidarity is a founding norm of the European Union; all its member countries have promulgated in one way or another such a principle in their national constitutions. From Schuman and Adenauer to Blair and Merkel, EU politics have been characterized by a combination of a pursuit of national interests and a commitment to push forward a more politically integrated Union. Schieffer suggests that solidarity should be seen as one of EU's most accepted norms, since it is shared by the domestic constitutions of its member countries (c.f. Thielemann 2003). Burden sharing is a form of solidarity and, in the case of the common European asylum system, it is considered intrinsic to solidarity.

The core document of the common European asylum policy is the Council Regulation (EC) No. 343/2003 (OJ 050/2003) (hereafter Dublin II), which amended the 1990 Dublin Convention. Along with the European Refugee Fund (ERF) and the EASO as the first and second pillars, respectively, the Dublin II constitutes the third pillar of asylum policy.[42] All these pillars emphasize solidarity, albeit in different ways. Thus, while EFR is more unambiguously dedicated to solidarity by tending to allocate funds proportionally to countries facing a greater influx of refugees relative to other EU member countries, the Dublin Convention and Dublin II emphasize the fact that the member state in which asylum is first sought ought to be responsible for that asylum claim; and that asylum seekers who have attempted to seek asylum in another EU country should be sent back to the country through which they entered the EU. Other EU documents have emphasized solidarity and burden sharing of asylum seekers even more explicitly.[43] As the common statement by Belgium, Hungary, Poland, Denmark and Cyprus on immigration and asylum of November 30, 2010 states, "[i]t is vital to ensure a common area of protection that is based on mutual trust between Member States."[44]

However, major compliance problems exist, as EU member countries seem inclined toward refugee deflection policies (Byrne 2003; Noll 2003; Thielemann). As the European Economic and Social Committee (EESC) notes, "The CEAS (common European asylum system) is being undermined by the tendency of Member States to limit the harmonization of legislation and national practices."[45] Indeed, the document points out that such a "[h]armonization is not a problem of asylum policy but it is the main instrument through which the benefits of the CEAS will be made tangible."[46] It has been hoped that harmonization will decrease the administrative and financial pressure on some member states and guarantee a higher level of protection for asylum seekers, at least in the initial phase. The so-called Qualification Directive—which is one of the four legal instruments of the EU *acquis* in the asylum field, along with European Dactyloscopy (Eurodac), Dublin Regulations and the Long-Term Residents Directive—laid the ground for standardizing asylum procedures throughout the member states.[47]

Noll (2000) has considered the efforts for a common European asylum policy as a strategy to minimize protection and maximize deflection of asylum seekers when control over migration and an effective regional refugee burden-sharing to be lacking. Further criticism has come from within the EU. For instance, the 2011 Opinion of EESC maintains that "[i]f harmonisation is to yield the expected results, it must not be based on the lowest common denominator of protection."[48] In addition, it has been argued that some provisions in the April 2004 Qualification Directive could be used by the member states as a way of lowering their existing standards. Other observers have pointed out that, in some areas, the Qualification Directive provides less in terms of protection than the 1951 Geneva Convention or the European Convention on Human Rights (Lambert 2006).

The EU *acquis* on asylum and migration represents the standardization of the asylum legislations and procedures throughout the EU member countries, while the EU conditionality on asylum and immigration consists of shaping EU accession to those countries that meet that particular *acquis*. The purpose of such an *acquis* transfer is to increase "the pool of states who meet common criteria to act as potential recipients for asylum applicants."[49] Thus, the EU encourages potential candidate countries to establish asylum institutions compatible with the emerging common European asylum system. Not only would the new entrants be able to adjust quickly to the solidarity and burden-sharing tasks once they joined the Union, but they would also be able to participate in advance in such burden-sharing efforts, especially after signings readmission agreements of their own and third country nationals. In sum, Byrne (2003, 340) considers the *acquis* to be "a composite of piecemeal instruments which aim to establish minimum standards below which state practice should not fall."

It is clear that the EU has strong interests in Albanian and Macedonian asylum reforms as extensions of the EU asylum reform.[50] Establishing asylum institutions in Albania and Macedonia would help the EU in several aspects. First, the readmission agreements allow the acceptance "upon application by a Member State and without further formalities" of their citizens and third country nationals who have failed to be recognized as refugees in any of the EU country.[51] Second, this strategy can be reinforced by declaring these countries as "safe," thus making Albanian and Macedonian citizens ineligible for asylum in EU member countries. Third, if these countries develop modern asylum systems, they can serve to buffer criticisms related to the violations of the *non-refoulement* principle (Bertotto 2003). With a modern asylum system in Albania and Macedonia, the EU would justify the return of third country asylum applicants who entered the EU through Albania or walked parts of their way toward the EU territory through Macedonia, on the grounds that these countries are safe for asylum seekers and their governments can provide now refugee protection.

A Sectorial Interpretation of Albanian and Macedonian Asylum Reforms

Albanian and Macedonian asylum reforms represent a unique case for which the EU has had to confront not the opposition but the indifference of its applicants to conduct that reform. It has been argued that those migrants seeking refuge in states that are more geographically proximate to their countries of origin are more likely to succeed in starting with the RSD in those countries (Byrne 2003). Moreover, it has also been noticed that while asylum applications in Western Europe declined by 40 per cent between 1995 and

1999, in some Eastern European countries at the edges of the EU (Poland, Hungary), with extensive green borders, asylum application tripled by the end of the decade (ibid.). Latvia and Lithuania have recently reported that trend as well. Moreover, data shows a dramatic increase in asylum applications in the Western Balkans, especially in countries lying along the Balkan route associated with human smuggling, namely Croatia, Kosovo, Macedonia, Montenegro, Serbia and Slovenia, but surprisingly no so much in Bosnia and Herzegovina and Albania. This data suggests that postcommunist Europe continues to carry the potential of being inundated by waves of refugees and asylum seekers. In addition, arguably, the implementation of the asylum *acquis* in EU aspirants in Eastern Europe would serve the deflection policies of EU member states, and unevenly transfer burden to the eastern countries.

The data in Table 6.3 shows an unruly pattern that reflects the unsettled meandering of the refugee influx in Central and Eastern Europe. Thus, until the end of 2009, except for Poland, none of the Eastern European countries that joined the EU in 2004 had experienced any increase in the number of asylum seekers. On the contrary, some of them like the Czech Republic and Romania have managed to curb their numbers to the rates of 1994. Slovenia and Slovakia experienced similar decreases in the number of asylum seekers. The number of asylum seekers in Estonia and Latvia remains insignificant, but even the hike in asylum applications in Lithuania still leaves it with a small number overall. Even Bulgaria and Hungary have recently received fewer applications than in pre-accession years. As for Albania and Macedonia, the number of asylum applications in these countries, especially in Albania, is insignificant.

However, with the revival of the Balkan route of human smuggling into EU member countries in 2010, caused by the collapse of the Greek asylum system, the asylum-seeking pattern in Central and Eastern European countries (CEECs) changed. Therefore, some of the Balkan countries that border Greece and other countries that border the Balkans experienced an increase in asylum seekers. For instance, Bulgaria experienced a spike in asylum seekers in 2010, and the next year the same spike was transferred to Romania. Albania has resisted illegal influxes dues to its stiff border control policy, but other Western Balkans countries such as Croatia, Kosovo, Macedonia, Montenegro, Serbia and Slovenia have seen rises in asylum applications since 2010. However, this increase in refugee numbers in these countries does not necessarily show the effectiveness of their systems but rather a refugee jam in the conditions of a general increase of asylum applications even in other refugee countries of destination such as Austria and Italy.

This data shows that simply having established asylum systems in accordance with international refugee protection standards does not immediately turn EECs into destination countries for refugees. Compared with data from refugee destination countries from Western Europe, one can argue that the high number of asylum applicants in the Balkans simply reflects a growing number of asylum seekers across Europe, triggered mainly by the Arab Spring, but also the collapse of the Greek asylum system. The improvement of refugee protection standards in Eastern European EU aspirant countries has not made their asylum systems more attractive to refugees or asylum seekers. Rather, they continue to prefer Western European countries with more developed social programs and job opportunities. In the light of such data, we can conclude that there is no reason to

Table 6.3. Asylum applications in postcommunist European countries, 1994–2011

COUNTRY/YEAR	1994	1995	1996	1997	1998	1999	2000	2001	2002	2003	2004	2005	2006	2007	2008	2009	2010	2011
Albania	-	-	-	-	-	-	-	-	-	-	36	30	20	30	10	-	12	17
Bosnia and Herzegovina	-	-	-	-	-	-	-	-	-	-	454	150	70	570	100	50	38	44
Bulgaria	561	517	302	429	833	1,331	1,755	2,428	2,888	1,549	920	820	640	980*	750*	850*	1,025*	705*
Croatia	-	-	-	-	-	-	-	-	-	-	33	190	90	200	160	150	290	807
Czech Rep.	1,187	1,417	2,211	2,109	4,085	7,220	8,788	18,094	8,484	11,396	1,119*	4,160*	3,020*	1,880*	1,710*	1,260*	485*	492*
Estonia	-	-	-	-	23	21	3	12	9	14	6*	10*	10*	10*	10*	40*	33*	67*
Hungary	207	130	152	209	7,097	11,499	7,801	9,554	6,412	2,401	354	1,620*	2,120*	3,430*	3,130*	4,670*	2,464*	1,693*
Kosovo	-	-	-	-	-	-	-	-	-	-	-	-	-	10	-	80	100	188
Latvia	-	-	-	-	58	19	4	14	30	5	1	20*	10*	30*	50*	50*	61*	335*
Lithuania	-	-	-	320	163	133	199	256	294	183	28	120*	140*	130*	220*	210*	372*	406*
Macedonia	-	-	-	-	-	-	-	-	-	-	1,232	70	60	30	50	90	174	740
Montenegro	-	-	-	-	-	-	-	-	-	-	-	-	20	-	10	20	9	235
Poland	598	843	3,211	3,533	3,373	2,955	4,589	4,506	5,153	6,921	3,743*	6,860*	4,430*	7,210*	7,200*	10,590*	6,540*	5,260*
Romania	647	634	588	1,425	1,236	1,670	1,366	2,431	1,151	1,077	210	590	460	660*	1,170*	830*	859*	1,720*
Serbia	-	-	-	-	-	-	-	-	-	-	-	90	20	50	80	230	693	3,132
Serbia and Montenegro	-	-	-	-	-	-	-	-	-	-	40	-	-	-	-	-	-	-
Slovakia	140	359	415	645	506	1,320	1,556	8,151	9,700	10,358	2,916*	3,550*	2,870*	2,640*	910*	820*	541*	319*
Slovenia	-	-	38	72	499	867	9,244	1,511	702	1,100	323*	1,600*	520*	430*	240*	180*	211*	327*

Source: UNHCR. *Number of asylum seekers in years when the country was an EU member

fear large numbers of long-term or permanent refugees in Albania and Macedonia. The delays in complying with the EU asylum *acquis* reflects Albanian and Macedonian leaders' low interest in conducting reforms in policy areas that do not directly affect their citizens. Refugee crises such as the Kosovar refugee floods of early 1999 might have sparked interest in introducing refugee protection policies and institutions, but now that most of the Balkans are pacified, any violent ethnic conflict seems unlikely. The EU perspective of the Balkans has compelled the acceleration of reforms, yet some sectors that have a greater impact on people's lives acquire more attention. Additionally, the reluctance of the EU to open accession negotiations with Macedonia, even eight years after the latter acquired EU candidate status, has pushed the EU perspective of the country toward an unknown future and made both country's leaders and its public anxious over whether or not they have been treated fairly (Karajkov 2010). As for Albania, the country's government submitted the application for the candidate status in April 2009 under skepticism from both domestic and EU actors; some EU member countries viewed the move as an electoral strategy in the eve of the 2009 summer elections with little chance of success, while the opposition considered it an electoral theatre (Waterfield 2009; Bogdani 2008).[52]

Therefore, only those policies that would shift the immediate interests of Albanian and Macedonian leaders toward asylum reform would encourage progress in establishing efficient asylum institutions and procedures. The EU found such an opportunity with agreements on visa liberalization. As many citizens of the Western Balkans connect the abstract idea of the EU as an area of justice, freedom and wellbeing with the more tangible idea of visa-free movement throughout the continent, conditioning the latter would be more efficient than conditioning the former. Ultimately, the EU made asylum reforms a condition of the visa liberalization agreements with both countries, and its progress reports for both 2009 and 2010 show that it worked. Both countries have been reported to have made good headway in their asylum reforms.

However, right after the visa liberalization agreements, both countries, especially Albania, abandoned asylum-related reform. Albania remained reluctant to fund the pre-screening program after the EU and UNHCR terminated their financial contribution to the program and handed it over to the Albanian government at the end of 2006. Alarmed by the growing number of asylum seekers entering EU countries through the Balkans, the EU later decided to re-invigorate pressures to revival pre-screening programs in Albania. For the first time after so many years, pre-screening returned as a topic in the EC's Albanian 2012 Progress Report, which states that an "effective pre-screening process needs to be ensured at the border in view of potential new migration trends and the possible rise in illegal transits by third country nationals."[53]

Comparing the developments of asylum policies in Albania and Macedonia, one can easily detect the role of the EU in those developments. Until early 2000s, the EU focused mainly on the Albanian asylum system, while paying little heed to the Macedonian asylum system. During the 1990s and early 2000s, Albania was the main gateway into EU territory, namely Italy, and EU policies sought to cut off the Balkan route by forcing the Albanian government to seal its border and monitor maritime smuggling traffic across the Adriatic Sea. Whereas much of that policy concerned border control, the establishment of a functional Albanian asylum system would accommodate those third country refugees before they could be smuggled in Italy, but also accommodate the returned third country nationals who had entered the Union via Albania and had been rejected the refugee status within the EU. The success of the Albanian border control policy resulted in a dramatic decline of the number of illegal migrants landing on Italian shores from Albania and, consequentially, the pressure on Albania regarding asylum policies.

Conversely, Macedonia saw no EU suggestions to establish an asylum system until the end of the 2001 conflict. During the rest of the 2000s, the EU exercised moderate pressure on Macedonia, but that increased when a growing number of asylum seekers entered Macedonia in 2011. The dramatic rise of asylum applications in 2011 (in the first half of 2011 there were 349 requests for asylum compared to 147 for the whole of 2010, while the entire year ended with 740 asylum applications compared to 180 in the previous year) spurred the EU's emphasis on asylum-related policies in Macedonia. Such an increase reflected the consequences of the collapse of the Greek asylum system under the combined weight of large numbers of asylum seekers and funding shortages for the asylum system due to the severe financial crisis that plagued the country. As a result, when both Bulgaria and Albania sealed their entry borders with Greece, and Albania sealed its exit maritime borders with Italy, illegal immigrants and refugees stuck in Greece found Macedonia (with its borders to Serbia, which in turn borders the EU member Hungary) a viable alternative.

Therefore, one can easily distinguish the difference between the asylum-related paragraphs of EC's progress reports for Albania and Macedonia. Whereas during the second half of the 2000s these reports were balanced in both length and intensity, the EC's 2011 and 2012 reports on Macedonia show a significant increase in the EU's concerns about the progress of the country's asylum system. Together with stronger calls for border control, we can easily perceive that the EU is asking for a Macedonian asylum system that would be instrumental in thwarting illegal migration into the EU, rather than simply a system that would be compatible with the common European asylum policy. In turn, these large numbers of illegal migrants and refugees who simply seek to move through Macedonia as fast as they can, and then exit toward Serbia, has dissuaded Macedonian elites to undertake policies that would encourage them to stay instead of leave. Moreover, since the lack of employment opportunities or sufficient social policies that attract illegal immigrants and asylum seekers makes Macedonia only useful for illegal migrants as a transit country, the Macedonian elites could reasonably consider any policy effort and financial commitment in this regard a waste. As all the Balkan transit countries demonstrate, seeking asylum in those countries acts only as a waypoint in illegal migration toward the EU member countries (Peshkopia 2005a, 2005b, 2005c, 2005d).[54]

Aware of this situation, in its 2011 Progress Report, the EC pointed to the lack of efficiency of and needs for improvement in the Macedonia's asylum authorities in issuing first-instance asylum decisions, and those capacities remained insufficient in 2012. In a rare occurrence, the EC turned its focus on the RSD process, pointing to the need to prevent potential abuses of the asylum system. The EC pointed to persistent problems with providing interpreters. Some of these problems are related to procedural rather than substantive appeal decisions by the Administrative Court, which could be addressed with the recent establishment of the High Administrative Court.

Conclusion

The case of asylum reforms in Albania and Macedonia brings evidence in support of the claim that if an EU-aspiring country is not interested in conducting a certain reform, even when the EU requires that reform as a condition for admission, the progress in that policy area will be slow and the institutions established as a result of it will be weak and ineffective. Visa liberalization agreements imply that the beneficiary countries become safe third countries. Moreover, EU officials have explicitly explained to both the governments and public of these countries that, with the signing of the agreement, the chances for asylum recognition for their citizens will no longer exist. Indeed, during 2010 authorities in several EU and other non-EU western European countries faced waves of asylum seekers from Macedonia, Montenegro and Serbia, all of whom were met with a negative response and expulsion.[55] Thus, combined with improved domestic asylum systems, visa liberalization agreements allow EU member countries to reject prima facie asylum applications from Western Balkans countries.

While it is clear that Albania's and Macedonia's progress in asylum reform is only one of the ways that visa liberalization conditionality helped these countries to conclude their visa liberalization agreements, I question whether it is enough for these countries to acquire EU candidate status. As a UNHCR protection officer writes, the EU *acquis* on asylum is the outcome of a compromise regarding minimum standards reached by states that already had national asylum systems (Feijen 2007). For countries with embryonic asylum systems, the adoption of such complex structures seems unnecessary. A simpler asylum system would be preferable. Basic asylum systems in line with international standards could occur in accordance with the EU *acquis*, and be less staff intensive and more manageable for countries with limited resources (Feijen 2007). Therefore, it is expected that the current status of the asylum system, especially considering the low number of applications in both Albania and Macedonia, is not a policy sector likely to determine the outcome of these countries' accession negotiations.

Chapter 7

BEYOND REFORMS

On December 11, 2012, after rejecting the European Commission's (EC) recommendation that Albania should receive conditional EU candidate status, the European Council pledged to grant that status only if Albania demonstrated progress in the areas of judicial, public administration and parliamentary reforms. The Council called for particular focus on conducting the June 2013 national elections in accordance with European and international standards; strengthening the independence, efficiency and accountability of judicial institutions; continuing to make determined efforts in the fight against corruption and organized crime, including pro-active investigations and prosecution in view of developing a solid track record; and instituting effective measures to reinforce the protection of human rights and anti-discrimination policies, especially in the area of equal treatment of minorities and implementation of property rights.[1] The Council's rejection came under staunch opposition from the Netherlands against Albania's candidacy, even though on October 10, the EU commissioner for enlargement Štefan Füle had communicated that the EC already recommended granting Albania the status of EU candidate country, subject to key judicial and public administration reforms and the revision of parliamentary rules of procedures.[2]

Thus, as of the fall of 2012, for the third straight year, Albania was denied EU candidate status. In his visit to Tirana in early February 2013, Füle reiterated the free election theme, emphasizing that "[t]he successful conduct of parliamentary elections in 2013 will be a crucial test for the smooth functioning of the country's democratic institutions."[3] Moreover, in the fall of 2012, the European Council rejected for the fourth straight year the opening of accession negotiations with Macedonia, in spite of a four years straight positive recommendation from the European Commission. The Council rejection of the EC's recommendation reflected EU concerns over internal cohesion, advising Macedonia to consider "maintaining good neighbourly relations, including a negotiated and mutually accepted solution to the name issue" to be essential.[4] Implicitly, the expression "good neighborly relations" concerned the country's name dispute with Greece, and reflected both the unwillingness of the EU to import such feuds and the procedural impossibility of advancing Macedonia's status in the face of Greek and, more recently, Bulgarian opposition. In order to navigate through such a unique situation without risking a Macedonian decline in interest in reform, the EU invented the High-Level Accession Dialogue (HLAD), which was launched on March 15, 2012. However, whereas Commissioner Füle considered HLAD as "a bridge which will lead [...] to the accession negotiations" (Füle 2012), there were absolutely no hints on how the HLAD, a reform-oriented initiative, could avoid the country's name dispute with Greece, which had no links with reform whatsoever. Clearly, the HLAD aimed at keeping up Macedonia's institutional reforms and cooperation with the EU, and avoiding any setbacks that would degenerate into political instability and ethnic conflict. Thus, Macedonia, in spite of having "sufficiently met" the political criteria to begin accession negotiations, was denied conditional candidacy.

To return to Albania, whereas the European Commission recognized that four of its twelve October 2010 conditions had been fulfilled, it pointed to three other reinforced majority laws that would fully satisfy three additional conditions. However, while the Law on the Civil Servant Status, the Law on the Organization and Functioning of the High Court and the Rules of Procedure of the Kuvend are important pieces of legislation and institutional regulation, respectively, it is hard to argue that they are such key factors of Albanian institutional reforms that failing to adopt them would jeopardize its EU candidate status. Hence the question: what lies beyond reform? I argue that both Albania and Macedonia are being held accountable for not abiding by or applying consociational practices at international and domestic levels, respectively. This chapter outlines the last two years' political trajectories of both countries and will interpret from a consociational approach their current failure to progress toward the EU.

Albania: In the Trap of the Politics of Obtaining and Maintaining Power

The EC 2010 Opinion, which was the first in a series of annual rejections of Albania's application for EU candidate status, was perceived in Albania as a setback for the Berisha government and was lauded by the Partia Socialiste (PS) (Socialist Party) led opposition as a victory. The report offered Albanian elites twelve recommendations related to policies needed for the country to qualify for EU candidate status (see table in Annex C).[5] With local elections scarcely six months away and an opposition who had refused to accept the results of the 2009 parliamentary elections, the Partia Demokratike (PD) (Democratic Party) needed a victory to reassert its power legitimacy. On the other hand, by embarking on populist methods, the opposition PS sought to undermine PD efforts to restore legitimacy, peaking with a prolonged hunger strike of its parliamentarians and other high-ranking members in front of the prime minister's office in May 2010.

On January 21, 2011, the PS organized a massive demonstration in the hopes of giving blowout damage to the PD-led ruling coalition, and as a PD confidence test. TV coverage showed violent demonstrators attacking a fence of police forces standing beside, not in front of, the people's march, and persistently attacking the gates of the building and the police forces surrounding it. Police responded with tear gas and water cannons, and gunfire from the defenders of the building erupted mostly into the air but also against the demonstrators, leaving four dead. In a fierce exchange of accusations, the government considered the entire event as a botched coup, while the PS called it a massacre against citizens expressing their indignation against the violation of their vote, as well as perceptions of government mismanagement and corruption.

The dramatic change in the country's political landscape that came with the May 8, 2011 local elections only exacerbated the political divisions. After a three-month-long administrative and legal process, the PD mayoral candidate, and former minister, Lulëzim Basha won the electoral contest for the city of Tirana with a difference of around 100 votes, thus ending the eleven-year administration of the capital by the PS leader, Edi Rama. The severely disputed contest and ensuing debated legal process did not help to mitigate the already polarized Albanian political stage. The simmering political climate of the summer of 2011 undermined the reform process, and the EC's subsequent 2011 Progress Report emphasized the lack of progress in almost all areas of reform prescribed by the 2010 Opinion. That rocky political period seemed to be an unfavorable period for any policy development, and the entire public space was captured by the politics of obtaining and maintaining power.

The second failure of Albania to receive its EU candidate status served as a wake-up call to the Albanian politics, but also to the European Commission. In an attempt to overcome such an unprecedented situation, Füle entered into an energetic mediation of both sides of the aisle. They finally agreed to speed up the adoption of reform-related laws on November 14, 2011. The agreement foresaw the establishment of a commission to design the electoral reform, a group tasked with revising the Kuvend rules, and the adoption of the laws that required a three-fifths majority. Electoral reform had been persistently required by Albania's international partners as a stepping stone toward a free and fair electoral process, and reflected concerns regarding the Albanians' inability to hold elections that would conform to international standards. The agreement for a parliamentary reform reflected a consensus over an earlier demand of socialists who had found themselves increasingly frustrated by their dwindling role in the Kuvend and the unwise and unruly practices of the PD speaker. An agreement between PD and PS parliamentary leaders foresaw the adoption of the European Parliament rules by the Kuvend. However, the parties did not reach a clear agreement on how to adopt laws that required reinforced majority; the PD proposed inserting its procedures into the regular calendar, while the PS sought the gradual adoption of these procedures until April 2012. In a breach of the spirit of the agreement, the PD used its majority vote in the conference of the parliamentary leaders to decide the adoption of those laws in regular sessions, while the PS remained ambiguous on that specific matter by neither offering consensus nor denying it.[6]

That ambiguity later crystalized into a policy of delaying and bargaining as the PS finally saw an opportunity to exert some leverage in decision making, but also a chance to capitalize on the ongoing power struggle. On January 12, 2012, Gramoz Ruçi, the leader of the PS parliamentary faction, demanded the removal of laws requiring a qualified majority from the parliamentary schedule, since the opposition needed more time to work on them.[7] Indeed, this policy shift seemed to reflect the PS's growing awareness of the relevance that its veto power on the reforms might play during the pre-electoral year 2012.

Indeed, as it was expected, 2012 turned out to be a heated political year. There were a series of defections of local councilpersons, mainly from PS to its minor left-wing rival and ruling coalition partner Lëvizja Socialiste për Integrim (LSI) (Socialist Movement for Integration) and vice versa, but also from the PS to the PD and vice versa. This movement unveiled both sides' willingness to put all their efforts into undermining each other's electoral chances. However, while much of it affected marginal municipalities, one of them carried tangible potentials to affect the 2013 parliamentary elections: the case of the Region of Fier. The latter is the second largest region of the country and the second most productive one. Its growing electoral relevance reflects its growing population, with the second largest number of parliamentarians. With few exceptions, the region has mostly supported the PS, a source of frustration for the PD.

On September 21, 2011, the 96-councilperson-strong Council of the Fier Region that emerged from the May 2011 local elections was constituted in its first meeting; the PS councilpersons and their political allies used their majority to elect a chairman from their ranks. Meanwhile, PD power structures engaged in a process of converting opposition councilpersons, succeeding in at least 14 cases, and began a legal battle to remove the council's newly elected chairman. On September 29, the Court of Fier ruled in favor of the prefect of Fier, a representative in the region of the central government, and suspended the chairman of the regional council along with all the administrative acts that the chairman had adopted during his one week in office, a decision that was later overturned by the Vlora Court of Appeals on November 17. Meanwhile, on November 16, the prefect of Fier invoked another constitutive meeting, although the Court of Fier and the Vlora Court of Appeals considered it illegal. However, the meeting went on and it revoked the mandates for several opposition councilpersons, all of whom later regained the mandate with court decisions. The PS claimed, and the court supported its claim, that the revocation of mandates of regional councilpersons was a violation of the constitution because the mandate of regional councilpersons is a term mandate defined by constitution and cannot be revoked after it is granted. However, the Premier Berisha maintained that the revocation of an opponent councilperson's mandate had been applied in several instances by the PS such as in the cases of municipalities of Dremenas, Divjakë, Bubullimë and Fier-Shegan.[8]

Even though the PS claimed that its focus was not on the control of the Fier regional council but on the defense of the constitution, there is much evidence to support the claim that PS local and central politicians perceived the political battle over the council of the Fier Region as a platform whereupon the embattled PS could show its supporters and opponents that it knew how to stand its ground.[9] After having lost a series of political battles since it took over the helm of the PS in 2005, including his seat as the mayor of the capital city, the PS leader Edi Rama embarked on a stand-your-ground policy with a focus on the June 2013 election, but with no concerns for the institutional reforms needed for the country to achieve the EU candidate status. However, on its journey to the much-yearned-for electoral success, the PS had to navigate among the Scylla of using its blocking veto for laws requiring reinforced majority in order to enforce political concessions from the government and the Charybdis of being perceived as a destructive force that prioritized its power calculations over the country's major interests.[10]

On the other hand, the embattled PD-led majority was perceived to carry most of the responsibility for the country's failure to receive the EU candidate status. The government tried to progress in reforms as much as it could; at that point, the PD wanted to show its willingness toward certain reform progress and shift the blame for its failures to the PS. As shown in Appendix C, the EC's 2012 Albania Progress Report concluded with "progress was made" or "moderate progress" in nine out of twelve priorities that were laid down by the 2010 Opinion. That was a remarkable success compared to the previous year when the EC reported "progress was made" only in one of its twelve 2010 Opinion priorities (see Annex C). However, most of this progress was made in areas where the PD could perform without opposition votes, with the exception of the limitation of the immunity of high-ranking officials, including judges, which needed a reinforced majority to amend the constitution. This was eventually achieved with cross-the-aisle consensus.

The political battle to limit immunity for high-ranking officials took months of tense exchanges and difficult negotiations not so much over what the law would bring about, but because the PS wanted to use its veto power to both sabotage the PD's reform efforts and to reassure its supporters that the party was still in the game. Indeed, the difficulties to reach an agreement reflected the PS's growing frustration of its dwindling role in the political life of the country, its electoral/procedural/political setback in the municipality of Tirana and its willingness to utilize its veto power to maximize its political clout. Thus, while the PS had the co-authorship of the draft-amendments and the chairman had promised the PS vote in its favor, on September 9, 2012, Representative Fatmir Xhafa was pessimist about meeting the September 20 deadline set by the minister of European integration to perform the constitutional changes needed for a positive EC 2012 Progress Report. That assertion flew in the face of a statement of the PS chairman only three days earlier, when the PS was ready to vote unconditionally for the immunity-limiting amendments. However, Representative Xhafa tried shrewdly to transfer the blame to the PD, hence the PS's request for more time to scrutinize the draft amendments.[11] Finally, the constitutional amendments needed to limit the immunity of the high-ranking officials were passed on September 18, 2012.

There was still hope in November 2012 that the European Council would respond well to the somewhat positive recommendation from the European Commission over Albania's EU candidate status. During 2012, mainly as a response to PS veto threats over constitutional amendments, the government undertook, on its own, several measures to further reform the judiciary.[12] The EC, however, made clear to the majority that there were three laws that needed to be adopted, namely the Law on the Civil Servant Status, the Law on the Organization and Functioning of the High Court and the Rules of Procedure of the Kuvend, for the country to overcome the growing opposition within the European Council. With an eye on the 2013 election, the PD desperately needed a positive response from the EU to boost its chances for reelection. Such desperation was best reflected with an atypical address of the speaker of the Kuvend to the opposition parliamentarians literally begging them to vote the constitutional laws that needed a reinforced majority, while the PS continued its policy of blocking the process as a bargaining chip for the political battle over the council of the Fier Region.[13]

On April 1, 2013, the junior member of the ruling coalition, LSI decided to abandon the government and join the opposition pre-electoral coalition led by the PS (Marena 2013). However, the coalition managed to survive due to parliamentary realignments that saw some socialist parliamentarians switching sides. Meanwhile, the LSI tried to manipulate its new role in favor of a compromise that would allow the adoption of the three laws stipulated by the European Council in December 2012. On May 2, 2013, the leader of the LSI Ilir Meta called on the prime minister and the leader of the opposition to adopt the three laws and avoid any failure of the current legislative term that would go down in history.[14] The opposition leader publicly agreed to join socialist votes with the ruling coalition, contingent upon the adopted laws coming into force after the June 23, elections.[15]

In the trap of power politics, both sides of the Albanian elites, ruling coalition and political opposition, continued to undermine the country's progress toward the EU. Thus the Albanian case indicates the need to further expand the theoretical focus to include the country's political structure in the theoretical argument. While this research builds on the assumption of divided domestic elites, most reform cases reflect decisions taken or not taken by a ruling coalition. However, the empirical analysis reveals instances where reforms have stalled because the opposition used its veto power to block reforms, not out of its objections against them but as leverage in the domestic power struggle. True, I have not paid adequate attention to this aspect out of fear that, by losing parsimony, the theory might become too complex and unmanageable. Besides that, constitutional reforms or other sectorial reforms that require constitutional changes always represent a minority among other institutional reforms; but the lingering problem cannot be overlooked indefinitely.

In order to gain further sustainable accuracy without losing too much parsimony, we need to lower the level of analysis by focusing on a single reform in several countries; at least two different reforms in a single country; or, even lower, a single reform in one country. However, in the first case, we should be careful to pick a reform that needs bipartisan cooperation and select both countries with conflictive domestic politics and cooperative domestic politics; in the second case, we need to pick at least two reforms with at least one of them being something that requires cross-the-aisle cooperation so that the other can progress even without such a cooperation. Even though my discussion reflects much of the domestic power struggle in the course of reforms, I have not included domestic power struggles as an explanatory variable. In the complex interaction of domestic leaders' preferences with EU institutional preferences, adding domestic power struggles—that, in fact, affect only constitutional reforms and aspects of other reforms that seek constitutional amendments—an additional independent variable seemed inefficient, and the model would have acquired little benefits for huge costs. For these reasons, this chapter discusses the contextual background of reforms in order to add more plausibility to the already assumed reform preferences of domestic elites in EU membership–aspiring countries.

Finally, the June 23, 2013, national elections produced a landslide victory for the PS-led Aleanca për Shqipërinë Europiane (ASE) (Alliance for the European Albania) coalition, which gained 82 seats out of the 150 seats of the Kuvend, while the PD-led Aleanca për Punësim, Mirëqënie e Integrim (APMI) (Alliance for Employment, Wellbeing and Integration) gained 57 seats. One seat went to the Partia Bashkimi për të Drejtat e Njeriut (PBDNj) (Party Union for Human Rights) of the Greek minority in Albania.

Macedonia: In the Trap of Identity Politics

The electoral defeat of the Vnatrešna Makedonska Revolucionerna Organizacija–Demokratska Partija za Makedonsko Nacionalno Edinstvo (VMRO–DPMNE) (Internal

Macedonian Revolutionary Organization–Democratic Party for Macedonian National Unity) in the 2002 parliamentary elections led to an internal power struggle that resulted with the resignation of its founding leader and former prime minister Ljubčo Georgievski, and his split with the party that he had co-founded and led for more than a decade. Ultimately, Georgievski created another party, the Vnatrešna Makedonska Revolucionerna Organizacija–Narodna Partija (VMRO–NP). With the image of a pro-European leader and a technocratic penchant, Nikola Gruevski, the former minister of finance in the Ljubčo Georgievski government emerged as the new leader of the VMRO–DPMNE. While at the helm of his party, Gruevski won the parliamentary elections of 2006 and became prime minister on August 25. Ever since, Gruevski has won five more parliamentary and local elections, including winning more than half of the seats in the Sobranie in 2008, and emerging from the 2011 parliamentary elections as victor with 56 out of the 123 seats.

The politics of antiquisation

A dominant force in the Macedonian politics since 2006, Gruevski decided to play identity politics to overcome the effects of the global economic crisis on Macedonia.[16] In the early 1990s, the newly molding Macedonian identity started off as a Slavic sub-identity, as clearly stated to the journalists by the first president of the independent Macedonia, Kiro Gligorov.[17] Arguably, for generations, Macedonians held onto a Slavic identity that was separate, but related to that of the Slavs of neighboring Serbia and Bulgaria, an identity feature reinforced especially while Macedonia was part of Yugoslavia (Georgievski 2009).

Yet Gruevski took matters in a different direction with his highly criticized Skopje 2014 project. Since he came to power in 2006, and especially since the country failed to receive an invitation to NATO in the April 2008 Summit of Bucharest, the VMRO–DPMNE government has pursued a policy of *antikvizatzija* (antiquisation) with the dual purpose of putting pressure on Greece and building an ethnic Macedonian identity clearly distinguishable from other Slavic neighbors, namely Bulgarians and Serbs, but which could also stand against their ethnic archrival, the sizeable ethnic Albanian minority. The *antikvizatzija* aimed at shaping a new Macedonian identity that could go back in history to the classical antiquity where the Albanians claim their ancestors, the ancient Illyrians, belonged. Launched in 2010, the Skopje 2014 project was first introduced as an effort to return some of the Skopje's urban flavor that was razed with the 1963 earthquake. Many historic buildings were lost or seriously damaged. Communist Yugoslavia reconstructed Skopje with arid, cheap and colorless socialist architecture. The supporters of the Skopje 2014 project claim that its goal rests with the transformation the grey-looking city into a contemporary European capital and tourist attraction. The project aims at building and renovating around 20 buildings and erecting the same number of statues and monuments from the Macedonian history. The government declared that the cost of the project would not exceed €80 million (Davies 2011; Marusic 2012a; Ilijevski et al. 2012).

As part of this policy, statues of Alexander the Great and Philip II of Macedon have been erected in several cities across the country. In 2011, the massive 22-meter-tall statue, *Warrior on a Horse*, purporting subtly to be Alexander the Great, was inaugurated in Macedonia Square in Skopje. An even larger statue of Philip II is under construction at the other end of the square. Statues of Alexander also adorn the town squares of Priljep and Štip, while a statue to Philip II of Macedon was erected in Bitola. A triumphal arch named Porta Macedonia, constructed in the same square, features images of historical figures including Alexander the Great, causing the Greek Ministry of Foreign Affairs to lodge an official complaint to authorities in the Republic of Macedonia. Additionally, many pieces of public infrastructure, such as airports, highways and stadiums have been named after Alexander the Great and Philip II. Skopje's airport was renamed Alexander the Great Airport and was adorned with antique objects from Skopje's archeological museum. Other antique sculptures have been placed in front of the Sobranie. One of Skopje's main squares has been renamed Pella Square, after Pella, the capital of the ancient kingdom of Macedon, which falls within modern Greece. The main highway to Greece has been renamed Alexander of Macedon, and Skopje's largest stadium has been renamed Philip II Arena (Georgievski 2009).

While the project has attracted criticism from Greece, it has also been subject to severe domestic criticism. It has opponents in the opposition Socijaldemokratski Sojuz na Makedonija (SDSM) (Social Democratic Union of Macedonia), as well as from independent intellectuals who claim that the project is politically motivated, megalomaniac and aesthetically distasteful. Other domestic critics point to the fact that *antikvizatzija* demonstrates feebleness of archaeology and of other history disciplines in public discourse (Lozny 2011, 427). Yet other critics point out that, in reality, the project could cost around €500 million and a poor country like Macedonia with an unemployment rate above 30 per cent should use that money to focus on other, mainly developmental, priorities. Some other critics consider the neoclassic style of the buildings to be a poor architectural choice and that the project should have embraced a more contemporary style (Davies 2011). Moreover, the project's emphasis on classical antiquity is dividing ethnic Macedonians, separating those who back *antikvizatzija* from others who think of themselves as Slav (Georgievski 2009). And finally, the project exposes the fragile interethnic relations in Macedonia, including the growing dissatisfaction of the large ethnic Albanian minority (ibid.). Initially, the Skopje 2014 project was bitterly opposed by Albanians of Macedonia who saw their cultural and historic legacy overlooked and even denied. However, the Albanian complaints were addressed by the erection of a monument to their national hero in the city square that holds his name, Skënderbeg, in the Albanian dominated Çairi municipality of Skopje. The project included three other monuments of Albanian patriots who lived in territories of the contemporary Macedonia.

However, it is not difficult to observe that the Skopje 2014 project goes far beyond an urban facelift to the Macedonia's capital city. Critics consider it to be a historical facelift of the Macedonian ethnicity and national identity (Davies 2011). Macedonian attempts to establish a new national identity encroach upon neighbors' histories, a problem to which the Balkan countries are not unacquainted. Arguably, *antikvizatzija* provokes first and foremost Greece, thus further exacerbating the dispute, and further stalling Macedonia's EU and NATO applications (Marusic 2012a). Even though the statue *Warrior on a Horse*, erected on September 8, 2012, has not been named officially, most Macedonians venerate it now as the statue of Alexander the Great (ibid.). By the same token, the Macedonians provoke Albanians over the ethnic heritage of Mother Theresa, the Skopje-born Albanian nun who won a Nobel Peace Prize in 1979 for humanitarian work in her adopted country, India, and around the world. The Skopje 2014 project includes the construction of a monumental complex composed of a statue of Mother Theresa and a water fountain. The Mother Theresa's monument will stand around 30 meters in height, even taller than the *Warrior on a Horse* monument. Earlier, the city honored the late nun with the Memorial House of Mother Theresa and a plaque marking the spot of her birth.[18] Another monument, the statue of Damjan Gruev, was erected in May 2010 in the Macedonia Square, at end of Stone Bridge. Bulgarians consider Gruev, often known by his short name Dame Gruev, a Bulgarian revolutionary and insurgent leader in Ottoman Macedonia and Thrace, while for Macedonians Gruev was a Macedonian insurgent fighting for the autonomy and independence of Macedonia. As a result of the ensuing complaints, *antikvizatzija* has not been well received by the EU. The EU's 2012 Macedonia Progress Report referred implicitly to *antikvizatzija*, and recommended that "[a]ctions and statements which could adversely affect good neighbourly relations should be avoided."[19]

Some argue that *antikvizatzija* is an inwardly oriented policy. In a June 2009 interview, Sam Vaknin, a former advisor to and co-author with Prime Minister Gruevski, described *antikvizatzija* as a nation-building project that was essentially anti-Albanian, rather than anti-Greek or anti-Bulgarian. According to him, *antikvizatzija* has a double goal, "which is to marginalize the Albanians and create an identity that will not allow Albanians to become Macedonians."[20] True, some Albanians feel the same. For instance, Abdurrahman Aliti, former leader of the ethnic Albanian Partia për Prosperitet Demokratik (PPD) (Party for Democratic Prosperity) agrees that the campaign is directed against them. Reportedly, Aliti argues that *antikvizatzija* "sends a message to Albanians that they are newcomers in this country and have nothing to do here."[21]

However, not all Albanians feel the same as Aliti. Except for the early stage of the project when they felt excluded, the Albanians have watched the Skopje 2014 with amusement, detecting in these grotesque efforts to forge a new identity signs of insecurity in contemporary Macedonian identity.[22] In turn, safe in their own unchallenged identity, Albanians rely on the plausible theories of nineteenth-century Austrian and German albanologists who argued that Albanians were descendants of the ancient Illyrian tribes who inhabited most of the Balkans before the arrival of the Slavs in the sixth century CE (see Hahn 2005). However, during the height of their nation-state formation, in the interwar period, the Albanians also had flirted with the idea of Alexander the Great being an Illyrian either from his mother, Olympia, or from his alleged illegal father, an Illyrian commander—hence the Albanian currency lek. However, the post–Second World War communist regime showed no interest in using ancient myths as tools of national identity formation, and so did not pursue that identity politics any further.

Yet strong evidence show that *antikvizatzija* might be more directed against Greeks than Albanians. The policy took off right after the NATO Bucharest Summit of April 2008 rejected Macedonia's membership application under the Greek veto caused by the name dispute between the two countries.[23] Rather than focusing on negotiations, the Gruevski government decided to counterattack by claiming not only the name but also the history of the ancient kingdom. The government began to finance archaeological projects in order to show that today's Macedonians descend from the Macedonians of classical antiquity, not from the Slavs. Says archeologist Pasko Kuzman, director of the

Bureau for Protection of Cultural Heritage: "Macedonia can only defend its name if it proves that the Macedonian nation has Classical Antique and not Slavic roots."[24] The external outlook of the *antikvizatzija* was best illuminated when President Gjorge Ivanov explained its roots with "the frustration and depression felt after the NATO Summit in Bucharest."[25]

On neighbors' toes

However, Macedonia's neighbors seem not to buy the argument that *antikvizatzija* is an inward-looking project. It is obvious that the populist hysteria that characterizes *antikvizatzija* is alienating key foreign allies and provoking Macedonia's neighbors. Arguably, both Bulgaria and Greece could exercise their veto power as EU members to delay Macedonia's accession to the Union.[26] Once they were the Four Wolves—now, with Kosovo independent, apparently, they seem to be five. Over decades, Bulgaria has been relatively restrained over the frequent identity change in the tiny republic, yet aware of it. They insist that a Macedonian identity was imposed on ethnic Bulgarians in Macedonia after 1944, when Tito's partisan army drove the Bulgarian army from Macedonia and re-attached the territory to Yugoslavia, which was newly reconstituted as a federation. Says Kassimir Karakachanov, the leader of the Bulgarian VMRO party: "An artificial identity was invented in Macedonia. There is no Macedonian language— it's just a dialect of Bulgarian with a few different words."[27] Also, Bulgarians are restive against the *antikvizatzija's* encroachment upon Bulgarian history, claiming figures such as Dame Gruev and Gotse Delchev, who are considered national heroes in Bulgaria, as ethnic Macedonians.[28]

It seems that official Bulgaria remained committed to pulling its strings. With its EU membership in 2007, a Bulgarian citizenship seemed seductive to many isolated Macedonians. Therefore, Bulgaria offered its citizenship to any citizen of Macedonia of Bulgarian origin; since then, more than 50,000 Macedonians have obtained Bulgarian passports. Thus, when the Macedonian authorities sentenced a female Macedonian citizen to three months imprisonment in August 2009 for denying her ex-husband visitation rights to their child, because she held a Bulgarian passport Sofia put pressure on Skopje to release their citizen. Again, threats to block Macedonia's EU accession were heard.[29]

By late 2012, it became obvious that Bulgaria was prepared to play the veto card jointly with Greece or independently in the case of Greece lifting its own for opening accession negotiations between the EU and Macedonia. In early November 2012, Bulgarian president Rossen Plevneliev told Füle that Macedonia was "not ready" to start accession negotiations.[30] As the Commission intended to support the proposal for starting negotiations with Macedonia at the December EU Summit, Füle rushed two weeks later to visit Bulgaria in an effort to clarify the government's position with respect to Macedonia, only to learn that Bulgarians carried deep concerns against Skopje and that they were committed to vetoing the EC proposal.[31] Bulgarian officials at various levels have accused Skopje of stealing from Bulgaria's history, manipulating historical facts, discriminating against Macedonians with Bulgarian citizenship and badmouthing their country. Boyko Borisov, Bulgaria's prime minister, argued: "An EU and NATO member should accept everything in real terms and respect others' history and opinions. The government in Skopje should solve their problems in a European manner so they can gain our support" (Trajkovski 2012). It seems that the "firm position" toward Skopje appears to have the support of the majority of the Bulgarians (ibid.).

Albania and Kosovo, the two harmonious Albanian states in the Balkans, do not openly provoke Macedonia. However they both hold the keys to its stability due to the large Albanian minority in the country. As we have seen in Chapters 3 and 4, while the roots of the Macedonia's 2001 ethnic conflict were domestic, its enabling factors were related to Albania and Kosovo, with the former being a haven of weapon supply and the latter providing both weapons and trained guerilla fighters. In their difficult journeys toward Euro-Atlantic alliances, both countries have been submitted to intense EU membership conditionality and US leverage, which have limited Albania's and Kosovo's potential impact on Macedonia's politics. Moreover, both countries have open claims and hidden dreams with very clear geopolitical boundaries in mind that range from the wellbeing of co-ethnic Albanians living within clearly defined territories in Macedonia to possible secession of Albanians in Macedonia and the unification of all Albanian-inhabited territories in the Balkans in a single Albanian state. Therefore, both Albania and Kosovo remain by and large indifferent toward Macedonian identity politics, and are more focused in helping to maintain the stability of the country for the sake of Macedonian Albanians, so long as they are expanding their population size, their role in the life of the country and their control over local administration of the territories where they reside.

Macedonia's relationship with Serbia is not without controversies. Although the former Serbian region was transformed in 1946 into a Yugoslav republic with the right to secession, one common institution between the two countries persisted: the Srpska Pravoslavna Crkva (SPC) (Serbian Orthodox Church). In an attempt to boost Macedonian ethnicity, in 1967 the communist government supported the Macedonian church in its declaration of autocephaly, or ecclesiastic independence, from the SPC. Other Orthodox churches rallied with the SPC, and Macedonian autocephaly has not been recognized by Orthodox leaders elsewhere. In an attempt at compromise, in 2002 the SPC suggested its Macedonian counterpart accept a semi-autonomous status under the SPC. Under public pressure, Macedonia's religious leaders rejected the offer (Bojarovski 2005). However, previously overlooked renegade clergies and monks within the Makedonska Pravoslavna Crkva (MPC) (Macedonian Orthodox Church) steadily gained ground until, in 2005, it became clear that they already represented one-third of the church. Zoran Vraniskovski, or Bishop Jovan to use his church name, was proclaimed the SPS's Archbishop of Ohrid in May 2004. He was joined by some high profile Macedonian monks in his revolt against the MPC. The movement managed to establish parallel church structures in the country, risking dealing both the Macedonian Church and the ethnic Macedonian identity a serious blow. On January 11, 2005, in a move that provoked international outcry from human rights organizations and Orthodox churches, the Macedonian police arrested Bishop Jovan and some of his followers in his apartment in Bitola, southern Macedonia, while holding a private religious sermon (ibid.).[32] Indeed, Bishop Jovan, was sentenced in October 2003 to a year in jail for conducting unauthorized baptism, but suspended for two years on condition that the bishop did not commit any further offences. The charge against him was "self-elevation," justified by the fact that the MPC does not recognize Bishop Jovan's ordination as a bishop of the SPC.[33]

Then prime minister Branko Crvenkovski was reluctantly dragged into the debate, mainly forced by a vote in the Sobranie on January 23, 2004. In an attempt to consolidate the position of the MPC, the Sobranie adopted a declaration of support for the church.[34] While in the past Macedonian authorities have stayed away from the church debate, the growing domestic pressure over fears of the MPC disintegration thrust Crvenkovski into political action. He vowed that his administration would back the independent church in "response to interference in the internal affairs of Macedonia coming from abroad."[35] A source from his ruling SDSM stated that the government took the threat to the church seriously, and that questioning the independence of the MPC was not simply an ecclesiastical matter but touched sensitive political issues, such as the dispute with Greece over the country's name: "We had to step in as the church seems incapable of sorting out its own problems [...] If this split were to escalate, it would reopen the whole debate on Macedonia's identity."[36]

However, during the second half of 2012, the SPC lessened its pressure on the topic and seemed ready to accept the MPC. Reportedly, in October, Bishop Lavrentije of the SPC said that the Macedonian Church should be given autocephalous status. Bishop Lavrentije added, to the Belgrade-based tabloid *Bloc*, that the long-standing dispute between the two churches should be solved without the assistance of the state organs. According to him, a debate about the "normalization of relations" with the canonically unrecognized Macedonian Orthodox Church could be discussed when the SPC Assembly met in May 2013; yet the SPC Holy Synod would first have to launch such an initiative. Reportedly, Bishop Lavrentije expressed his belief that "such an initiative would be welcomed with open arms in Macedonia." As he questioned, while almost all Orthodox churches are autocephalous, "why wouldn't the same be true of the Macedonia Church [*sic*]?"[37]

Lavrentije also considered Serbian president Tomislav Nikolić's suggestion that both Serbian and Macedonian states help their churches in overcoming their problems as "honorable and sincere," but insisted that their conflict should be solved by church authorities themselves.[38] Obviously, the governments of Macedonia and Serbia have been experiencing far better relationships than their respective churches. On January 29, 2013, during his official visit to Skopje, the Serbian prime minister Ivica Dačić stated that Serbia has no territorial claims on Macedonia. Dačić expressed the interest of his country to maintain good neighboring relations with Skopje and added that Serbians will remain the best friends of Macedonians and of Macedonia.[39]

The name dispute with Greece

Finally, there is the dispute with Greece over the name of the country and beyond. The dispute emerged with the break up of Yugoslavia and the emergence of a new geopolitical situation in the Balkans. Formerly a federal unit of the Socialist Federal Republic of Yugoslavia, the Socialist Republic of Macedonia appropriated its official name as the Republic of Macedonia under its 1991 Constitution. That prompted an unprecedented, energetic reaction from its southern neighbor, Greece, the home of roughly 2.5 million of ethnic Greeks who call themselves Macedonians, according to the northern Greek region where they live. Moreover, Greeks accuse the Republic of Macedonia of stealing symbols and figures that they consider to be part of Greek culture, including the symbol of the ancient kingdom of Macedon, the Vergina Sun and its kings, Philip II and Alexander the Great. Indeed, the territory of the Republic of Macedonia encompasses little of the ancient kingdom of Macedon which, in most part, overlaps with the current region of the contemporary Greece, but the name Macedonia "flowed" northward with the creation of Roman region of Macedonia, after the Romans occupied Greece in 168 BCE. Besides the former kingdom of Macedon, the Roman region included the territories of Paeonia where the contemporary Republic of Macedonia rests. The Roman region of Macedonia was maintained throughout the Byzantine Empire until the Ottoman Empire took over its territories, and included them in the Elayet of Rumelia, organized by Sultan Bayesid I in 1395. With the 1864 administrative reform, most of the territories of the present-day Macedonia fell between the Vilayet of Kosovo and the Vilayet of Monastery. In 1893, the Vnatrešna Makedonska Revolucionerna Organizacija (VMRO) (Internal Macedonian Revolutionary Organization), a revolutionary movement that rose against the Ottoman rule, began its struggle for secession of these territories from the Ottoman Empire, culminating on August 2, 1903 with the Ilinden Uprising. With the failure of the uprising, the movement split in two wings: one was led by Yane Sandanski and argued for an autonomous Macedonia inside the Ottoman Empire or inside a Balkan Federation; the other supported the inclusion of Macedonia in Bulgaria.

The Treaty of London 1913 assigned to Serbia the territories of the contemporary Macedonia and the 1919 Paris Peace Treaties returned them to the newly established Kingdom of Serbs, Croats and Slovenes under the sovereignty of Serbia. The province was known as the *Vardarska banovina* (the Vardar province), or Southern Serbia. The Kingdom of Yugoslavia, 1929–41, collapsed with its military defeat at the hands of Germans, and Southern Serbia was divided between Bulgaria, an Axis ally, and Albania as part of the newly created Italian Empire. After the Second World War, the People's Republic of Macedonia was established in 1946 as a federal part of the newly proclaimed Federal People's Republic of Yugoslavia, sparking protests from Greece and sowing the seeds of the contemporary dispute. In 1963, the republic was renamed the Socialist Republic of Macedonia, when the Federal People's Republic of Yugoslavia was renamed the Socialist Federal Republic of Yugoslavia; the "Socialist" prefix was dropped slightly before its independence from Yugoslavia in September 1991.

The weakness of Greek protests in 1946 over the name of the republic reflected the weakness of Greece's position on the international stage. When the debate reopened in 1991, it was during a season of an empowered Greece, by now an EU and NATO member country. Consequentially, Greece managed efficiently to mobilize to thwart Macedonia's efforts for international recognition unless some compromise over the name could be found. Thus, even though the Arbitration Commission of the Peace Conference on the former Yugoslavia concluded that Republic of Macedonia met the conditions set by the EC for international recognition, Greece effectively managed to condition the international recognition of the country with the need to change the country's name, flag and constitution. Greece's efforts to block the European Community's recognition of Macedonia culminated in the Community's adoption of a declaration on recognition of the countries emerging from former Yugoslavia, delineating conditions for recognition, including a ban on "territorial claims towards a neighboring Community state, hostile propaganda and the use of a denomination that implies territorial claims" (Koliopoulos and Veremis 2002, 315).[40]

The cross-border identity feud took to the streets, fueling populism and mass rallies in both countries. In Greece, about one million people participated in the 1992 Rally for Macedonia in Thessaloniki, objecting to the word "Macedonia" as part of the name of the newly established republic (Roudometof 2002, 32). In an example of what Anderson (1993) calls "long-distance" nationalism, both Greek and Macedonian diasporas took the dispute to the streets of their countries of emigration. In Canada and Australia, where large Greek and Macedonian populations live—many originating from the Greek region named Macedonia—the controversial issue brought these communities into conflict with each other. The conflict turned especially nasty in Melbourne, where, by then, 113,000 Greek-speaking and 21,000 Macedonian-speaking immigrants resided (Danforth 1995). Reportedly, about 100,000 people protested in a major rally in Melbourne organized by the Macedonians of Greek diaspora under the slogan "Macedonia is Greek."[41] In the US, a Greek-American group, Americans for the Just Resolution of the Macedonian Issue, placed a full-page advertisement in the April 26 and May 10, 1992 editions of the *New York Times*, urging President George H. W. Bush "not to discount the concerns of the Greek people" by recognizing the "Republic of Skopje" as Macedonia.

On April 13, 1992 Greece's major political parties agreed that the word "Macedonia" was not acceptable in any way as part of the new republic's name, thus making this position the cornerstone of the Greek position on the issue (Bellou, Couloumbis and Kariotis 2003, 146). The Macedonian name issue became the dominant theme of the 1992–93 Greek political climate, eventually taking down the Constantine Mitsotakis government. Then foreign minister Antonis Samaras adopted a rigid position that denied the existence of a Macedonian nation and the recognition of the new Macedonian state. On April 4, 1992 Mitsotakis forced Samaras out of the Ministry of Foreign Affairs, but the latter continued to voice his independent views on the matter until Samaras was compelled to retire from both his seat in parliament and from the Nea Dhimokratia (ND) (New Democracy) party. The radicalization of the Greek position, caused by a combination of the presence of right-wing criticism within the ND and the employment of the Macedonian issue as a political weapon by the socialist opposition Panelinio Sosialistiko Kinima (PASOK) (Panhellenic Socialist Movement), mounted important obstacles in preventing the adoption of a more flexible attitude toward the Macedonian question In the spring of 1993, Samaras and his supporters left the ND to found their own party, the Politiki Anixi (PA) (Political Spring), thus causing the collapse of the Mitsotakis government. Finally, the ND lost the October 10, 1993 elections and, under the leadership and premiership of the veteran politician Andreas Papandreou, PASOK returned to power. The new Papandreou government appropriated a more radical stance toward the issue when it claimed that no negotiations could take place between the former Yugoslav republic and Greece. Unsurprisingly, this led to the termination of any dialogue between the two sides (Roudometof 1996, 261).

Greek efforts paid off. First, the EC Council of Lisbon, June 26–27, 1992, issued a declaration expressing a willingness "to recognize that republic within its existing borders [...] under a name which does not include the term Macedonia."[42] Greece was also successful in blocking Macedonia's United Nation (UN) membership for nearly a year following the country's application on July 30, 1992. A few states, including Albania, Bulgaria, Turkey, Slovenia, Croatia, Belarus and Lithuania recognized the republic under its constitutional name before its admission to the UN (Koliopoulos and Veremis 2002, 315). However, most countries waited for the UN decision. The delay caused serious effect on the republic, as it led to a worsening of its already precarious economic and political conditions (Petkovski, Petreski and Slaveski 1992). The Greek opposition to the Republic of Macedonia's constitutional name placed the international community in the paradoxical situation of delaying its UN membership, while fearing the spread of a Bosnia and Herzegovina and Croatia–type conflict to Macedonia (Allison and Nicolàeidis 1997, 120). The deteriorating security situation in Yugoslavia and the rising tensions in the Balkans led to the UN's first ever preventative peacekeeping deployment in December 1992, when units of the United Nations Protection Force (UNPROFOR) were deployed to Macedonia to monitor possible border violations from Serbia.[43]

During 1992, some international organizations including the International Monetary Fund, World Bank and the International Conference on the Former Yugoslavia began to adopt the term "the former Yugoslav Republic of Macedonia" (FYROM) in their practices and relationships with the country. In January 1993, France, Spain and the United Kingdom, the three EC members of the United Nations Security Council, proposed the same terminology to enable the country to join the United Nations (Lewis 1993). On January 22, 1993, the United Nations Secretary General Boutros Boutros-Ghali launched "the former Yugoslav Republic of Macedonia" as a compromise solution, which was initially rejected by both sides in the dispute. In a letter to the secretary general dated January 25, 1993, opposing the proposal, the Greek foreign minister, Michalis Papaconstantinou argued that admitting the country,

> prior to meeting the necessary prerequisites, and in particular abandoning the use of the denomination "'Republic of Macedonia," would perpetuate and increase friction and tension and would not be conducive to peace and stability in an already troubled region.[44]

Uncomfortable with any naming that would associate it with former Yugoslavia, which might be seen as an endorsement of possible Serbian territorial claims, the Republic of Macedonia rejected the terms offered by the UN secretary general. In a letter of March 24, 1993, the Macedonian president Kiro Gligorov informed the president of the United Nations Security Council that "the Republic of Macedonia will in no circumstances be prepared to accept 'the former Yugoslav Republic of Macedonia' as the name of the country." Gligorov stated that the country refuses "to be associated in any way with the present connotation of the term 'Yugoslavia.'"[45]

While both sides were pressured by their international partners to compromise, the pressure began mounting more on Greece. Gradually, the support that it initially garnered from its NATO and EC allies began to fade as a result of both its recalcitrant position on the issue and allegations that Greece was flouting UN and EC sanctions against Slobodan Milošević's Federal Republic of Yugoslavia. The intra-Community tensions were publicly exposed on January 20, 1993 when the Danish foreign minister, Uffe Ellemann-Jensen, described the Greek position as "ridiculous" and expressed the hope that "the Security Council will very quickly recognise Macedonia and that many of the member states of the Community will support this" (Gallagher 2005, 7).

In an effort toward compromise, the Greek prime minister, Constantine Mitsotakis, took a much more moderate approach to the issue than many of his hardline colleagues in the governing ND (Koliopoulos and Veremis 2002, 315), and endorsed the UN secretary general's proposal in March 1993 (Bethlehem and Weller 1997, xiv). Reluctantly, Macedonia also responded by accepting the temporary compromise amid deep political divisions between moderates and hardliners on the issue. On April 7, 1993, Resolution 817 of the UN Security Council endorsed the admission of the republic into United Nations. It recommended to the United Nations General Assembly "that the State whose application is contained in document S/25147 be admitted to membership in the United Nations, this State being provisionally referred to for all purposes within the United Nations as 'the former Yugoslav Republic of Macedonia' pending settlement of the difference that has arisen over the name of the State."[46] The following day, April 8, adopting the same language as the Security Council, the General Assembly supported the recommendation and passed Resolution 225.[47] The former Yugoslav Republic of Macedonia thus became the 181st member of the United Nations.

The careful wording of the two resolutions reflects diplomatic efforts to meet the objections and concerns of both sides. The content of the resolutions reflects four key principles: first, the appellation "former Yugoslav Republic of Macedonia" was purely a provisional term to be used only until the dispute was resolved (Frowein and Rüdiger 1998, 239). Second, the term was simply a reference and not a name; the UN has facilitated the way toward a compromise but has not sought to determine the name of the state. In the words of the president of the Security Council, "the term merely reflected the historic fact that it had been in the past a republic of the former Socialist Federal Republic of Yugoslavia."[48] The agreement included the word "the former" with a low case letter "f" to show that the word acts as a descriptive term, rather than in the case of "the Former," where the capitalized "F" would turn "Former" into a proper noun. However, the fact that the appellation "the former Yugoslav Republic of Macedonia" was conceived as a reference rather than a name did not dispel Greek position that the term "Macedonia" should not be used in the republic's internationally recognized name. Third, the use of the term was for mere usage "for all purposes within the United Nations" and was not mandated for any other party. Fourth, the term intended to emphasize the historical rupture between the current Republic of Macedonia and the existing Federal Republic of Yugoslavia, as opposed to its membership to the defunct Socialist Federal Republic of Yugoslavia.[49] And finally, the diplomatic battle of symbolism continued with the issue of Macedonia's seating in the UN General Assembly. Greece rejected seating the fYROM's representative under M (as in "Macedonia (former Yugoslav Republic of)") and the fYROM rejected sitting under F (as in "Former Yugoslav Republic of Macedonia"). Instead, it was seated under T as "the former Yugoslav Republic of Macedonia" and placed next to Thailand (ibid.).

Gradually, the appellation was adopted by other international organizations and states, but each of them decided to do so independently, neither instructed nor required to by the UN. However, Greece did not adopt the compromised appellation at this stage, and refused to recognize the country under any name. The compromised appellation did not bring an immediate recognition by the international community either; but the number of states who recognized the new country grew significantly by the end of 1993 and early 1994. On October 13, 1993, the People's Republic of China became the first major power to recognize the country under its constitutional name, the Republic of Macedonia. On December 16, 1993, two weeks before Greece was due to take up European Community presidency, six key EC countries—Denmark, France, Germany, Italy, the Netherlands and the United Kingdom—recognized the republic under its UN designation. Other EC countries followed suit in quick succession and by the end of December, all EC member states except Greece had recognized the republic (Bethlehem and Weller 1997, xiv). Japan's, Russia's and the United States' recognitions came on December 21, 1993, February 3, 1994 and February 9, 1994, respectively (Jeffries 2003, 54). On November 4, 2004, in the eve of referendum on local decentralization in Macedonia, the US announced that it would recognize Macedonia by its constitutional name, Republic of Macedonia (see Chapter 4).

In spite of the diplomatic progress toward a compromise, the agreement led to an upsurge in nationalist feelings in both countries. The popular perception that its EC and NATO allies had betrayed them fueled anti-Western and anti-American feelings among Greeks (Gallagher 2005). The March 1993 compromise on the reference appellation and, consequentially, Macedonia's membership in the UN caused the defection of Greek former foreign minister Antonis Samaras and his supporters from the ruling ND, ultimately causing the fall of the Mitsotakis government. This was followed by a landslide defeat of the ND in the general election of October 1993. However, the new PASOK government under the premiership of Andreas Papandreou introduced an even more hardline policy on Macedonia and withdrew from UN-sponsored negotiations on the naming issue in late October (Bideleux and Taylor 1996, 136; Gallagher 2005). By the same token, the agreement was contested in Macedonia as well. Then opposition VMRO–DPMNE sponsored rallies against the reference appellation in Skopje, Kočani and Resen. The Sobranie ratified the agreement by a slim margin, with 30 representatives voting in favor, 28 voting against and 13 abstaining. The VMRO–DPMNE called a vote of no confidence over the naming issue, but the government survived it with 62 representatives voting in its favor (Phillips 2004, 55).

As usual in the case of this dispute, long-distance nationalism of both diasporas took to the streets of their adopted countries, voicing their opposition to the agreement by organizing large protest rallies in major European, North American and Australian cities. After Australia recognized the "former Yugoslav Republic of Macedonia" in early 1994, tensions between the two communities reached a climax; in Melbourne, churches and properties on both sides were hit by a series of bomb and arson attacks (Ager 1997, 63).

However, the governments of both countries seemed committed to respecting the agreement on the appellation reference, and moved toward the normalization of relationships, leading to the Interim Accord signed on September 13, 1995 in New York in the presence of Cyrus Vance as special envoy of the secretary general of the United Nations.[50] Under the agreement, Macedonia undertook constitutional changes, including the removal of the Vergina Sun from its flag, and dropping from its constitution what Greece perceived as irredentist clauses. In addition, both countries committed to continuing negotiations to resolve the naming issue under UN auspices. In turn, Greece agreed not to object to any application by Macedonia as long as such an application was submitted under reference appellation promulgated in Paragraph 2 of the Resolution 817 of UN Security Council. As a result, Macedonia joined a variety of international organizations and initiatives, including the Council of Europe (CoE), the Organization for Security and Co-operation in Europe (OSCE) and NATO's Partnership for Peace (Osmanczyk 2002, 1355). Although the Interim Accord was not a conventional international treaty, as it can be superseded or revoked, its provisions are legally binding in terms of international law. In order to avoid using the UN-agreed reference appellation, which contains the word "Macedonia," the accord refers to none of the names of the signatory parties. Rather than names, both countries were referred to as "the Party of the First Part," with Athens as its capital, and "the Party of the Second Part," with Skopje as its capital (Frowein and Wolfrum 1997; Koliopoulos and Veremis 2002). Subsequent declarations have continued this practice of referring to the parties without naming them.[51]

The naming issue continues to linger in bilateral and multilateral international politics. Over the years, various proposals such as "New Macedonia," "Upper Macedonia," "Slavo-Macedonia," "Nova Makedonija" and "Macedonia (Skopje)" have failed due to Greece's recalcitrance over accepting any permanent solution that would include the name "Macedonia" (Kentrotis 1996, 100; Bellou, Couloumbis and Kariotis 2003). Instead, Athens has proposed names such as "Vardar Republic" or "Republic of Skopje," but the government and opposition parties in Skopje had consistently rejected any solution that eliminates the term "Macedonia" from the country's name (Turncock 2003, 33). However, Greece gradually began to revise its position and to demonstrate more understanding of the need for a composite appellation, with a geographical qualifier, *erga omnes*, that is, the incorporation of the term "Macedonia" in the name, but with the use of a disambiguating qualifier, for international and intergovernmental use (see, for instance, Nikolovski 2013).[52]

Nonetheless, a number of states recognize the Republic of Macedonia by its constitutional name; a few countries did from the start, while most others have since switched from recognizing it under its UN reference. Against expectations of some observers who had suggested that the gradual revision of the Greek position means that "the question appears destined to die," there seem to be no indication that Greece will drop the issue altogether (Perry 1997, 270). Macedonia's attempts to persuade international organizations to drop the provisional reference have not been successful thus far. A recent example was the rejection by the Parliamentary Assembly of the Council of Europe of a draft proposal to replace the provisional reference with the constitutional name in CoE documents (Roussis 2008). The UN reference continues to be used in the presence of states that do not recognize the constitutional name.

Most Greeks reject the use of the word "Macedonia" to describe the Republic of Macedonia, instead calling it *Proin Giougkoslaviki Dhimokratia tis Makedhonia*, the Greek translation of the former Yugoslav Republic of Macedonia or, occasionally, Skopje, and its inhabitants *Skopiani* (Skopians) after the country's capital. However, the latter metonymic name is not used by non-Greeks, and many inhabitants of the Republic of Macedonia regard it as insulting. Greek official sources sometimes also use the term "Slavomacedonian" to refer to its inhabitants, while the US Department of State has used the term side by side with "Macedonian," taking care, however, to put both terms within quotation marks.[53] The name "Macedonian Slavs" is another term used to refer to the ethnic Macedonians, also use by a number of news agencies, although the BBC recently discontinued its use on the grounds that people had alleged it was offensive. This name has been occasionally used in a different historical context in early ethnic Macedonian literary sources such as in Krste Misirkov's (1903) work *Za Makedonckite Raboti* [On Macedonian Matters] published in Sofia.

Political frictions in the international arena notwithstanding, in practice, both countries deal pragmatically with each other. Economic relations and cooperation have resumed to such an extent that Greece is now considered one of the Macedonia's most important foreign economic partners and investors.[54] Paradoxically, it was Nikola Gruevski who, as minister of finance, sold the Macedonian OKTA oil refinery to ELPET, a member of the Greek Hellenic Petroleum. The biggest Macedonian bank, a leading supermarket chain and a mobile-phone operator are also all controlled by Greek investors.[55]

The diplomacy of the name dispute

In 2005, the UN Special Representative assigned to mediate bilateral negotiations, Matthew Nimetz, suggested using "Republika Makedonija–Skopje" for official purposes. Greece did not accept the proposal outright, but characterized it as "a basis for constructive negotiations." Macedonia's government rejected the proposal and Prime Minister Bučkovski counter-proposed a "double name formula," where the international community uses "Republic of Macedonia" and Greece uses "former Yugoslav Republic of Macedonia."[56] Reportedly, in October 2005, Nimetz proposed that the name "Republika Makedonija" should be used by those countries that have recognized the new country under that name, and that Greece should use the formula "Republic of Macedonia–Skopje," while the international institutions and organizations should use the name "Republika Makedonija" in Latin letters. Although the government of the Republic of Macedonia accepted the proposal as a good basis for solving the dispute, Greece rejected it.[57] Negotiations reached a dead end in December 2006 when the government of Macedonia announced its intent to rename the Petrovec Skopje Airport Aleksandar Veliki (Alexander the Great).[58] In January 2007, the Greek government invited Matthew Nimetz to Athens where he commented that the efforts to mediate in the issue over the name were "affected and not in a positive way."[59]

The name dispute and Macedonia's NATO and EU perspective

Macedonia's quest to join the EU and NATO without initially resolving its pending disputes with its neighbors, especially Greece, has been the source of unprecedented international controversy. With the Interim Accord of September 1995, Greece agreed not to obstruct the republic's applications for membership in international institutions, as long as it did so under its provisional UN appellation. However, leading Greek officials had repeatedly stated that Athens would veto the country's accession in the EU and NATO without a prior resolution to the dispute.[60] The Greek foreign minister, Dora Bakoyannis, expressed her belief in the unity of Greek politics on the matter when she stated that "the Hellenic Parliament, under any composition, will not ratify the accession of the neighboring country to the EU and NATO if the name issue is not resolved beforehand."[61] Greek premier Kostas Karamanlis initially denied ever committing himself unequivocally to exercising Greece's right of veto, stating instead that Greece would only block the neighboring country's application for EU and NATO membership if it sought to be admitted as the "Republic of Macedonia," but on February 25, 2008 he emphasized that without a mutually acceptable solution to the name issue, the country could not join either NATO or the EU (Vasilis 2007).

By the end of 2007, the name dispute negotiations acquired a new momentum with two consecutive bilateral meetings on November 1 and December 1, 2007, as well as another bilateral meeting in January 2008. On February 19, 2008 Matthew Nimetz invited both countries' delegations to Athens, and presented them with a new framework, which they both accepted as a basis for further negotiations. In spite of efforts to keep secret the new framework, it was leaked early to the press. The full text in Greek was published initially by the Greek daily *To Vima* and was quickly circulated by all major media. The platform contained eight points surrounding the general idea that was a "composite name solution" for all international purposes.[62] It also contained five proposed names, namely Constitutional Republic of Macedonia; Democratic Republic of Macedonia; Independent Republic of Macedonia; New Republic of Macedonia; and Republic of Upper Macedonia.[63] However, on March 2, 2008, Matthew Nimetz announced from New York that the talks had failed, and that the "gap" in the positions of the two countries could not be overcome unless there was some sort of compromise, which Nimetz characterized as "valuable" for both sides.[64] After Greek premier Karamanlis's no-solution-equals-no-invitation warning, it was already clear that Greece would veto the coming NATO accession talks for the country at the Summit of Foreign Ministers on March 6, 2008 in Brussels. As a result, Macedonia was not invited to join NATO in the Summit of Bucharest, April 3–4, 2008.[65]

However, the Greek political and public opinion's position on the topic had slowly begun to change. Until 2004, some groups in Greece continued to mount street protests against the northern neighbor.[66] However, recently, the mood has shifted toward a compromise. In a 2011 poll in Greece, the "composite name that includes the name Macedonia for the country" seems, for the first time, to be marginally more popular than the previous more hard-lined stance of "no Macedonia in the title" (43 per cent vs. 42 per cent). In the same poll, 84 per cent of the respondents were pro-veto in the country's NATO accession talks, if the issue had not been resolved beforehand.[67] By then, all Greek political parties except the small nationalist party Laikós Orthódoxos Synagermós (LAOS) (People's Orthodox Rally) had begun to support the solution for a composite name for all uses, and remained vehemently opposed to the "double name" formula proposed by Macedonia.[68] This shift in the official and public position was described by Prime Minister Kostas Karamanlis as "the maximum recoil possible."[69] In an attempt to persuade the Greek government not to veto Macedonia's membership, the NATO general secretary Jaap de Hoop Scheffer implied that, at that point, the onus to compromise rested on Macedonia.[70] By the same token, then EU Enlargement Commissioner, Olli Rehn, expressed his fear that the lack of a solution on the name issue might have negative consequences on Macedonia's EU bid because, "although it is a bilateral question, Greece—as any other EU member—has the right to veto."[71] On March 5, 2008, Nimetz visited Skopje to try to find common ground on his proposal, but left announcing that "the gap remains."[72] On March 7, 2008, the US assistant secretary of state for European and Eurasian affairs, Daniel Fried, made an unscheduled visit to Skopje, urging the two sides to cooperate with Matthew Nimetz to find a mutually acceptable solution to the naming dispute.[73]

At the same time, disputes within the government of the predominantly ethnic Macedonian VMRO–DPMNE and the predominantly ethnic Albanian Partia Demokratike e Shqiptarëve (PDSh) (Democratic Party of the Albanians) precipitated concerns about the stability of the ruling coalition, thus questioning the negotiating power of prime minister Nikola Gruevski with regards to the naming dispute.[74] However, Greek media considered the crisis as an allegedly diplomatic way of increasing pressure on the Greek government.[75] In Macedonia, the four major political parties, two predominantly ethnic Macedonian and two predominantly ethnic Albanian, responded positively to calls for cooperation by President Crvenkovski to support Gruevski's government until NATO's Summit in Bucharest in early April 2008.[76] This unusual ethnic Albanian rally with Macedonians reflected the fact that the Albanians of Macedonia were placing significant importance on the country's EU and NATO membership while remained indifferent on its name issue (Stojanovska 2009).

The declaration of Athens of a veto prompted increased intervention from the United States and the EU to solve the dispute through Victoria Nuland, the US ambassador to NATO and the EU commissioner for enlargement, Olli Rehn. Macedonia's minister of foreign affairs, Antonio Milošoski, announced that Nimetz's proposal remains unchanged. The Bulgarian daily *Dnevnik* reported diplomatic sources' claims that this was to be the last attempt from Americans to help in finding a solution. The report continued that the target of this effort was for the country to retreat from its position as regards a double name formula and for Greece to accept something along the lines proposed by Nimetz. Nuland continued to state that the US would exercise pressure on both sides to find a solution before NATO's Summit, so that the alliance could be expanded, while Rehn urged Macedonia to show the correct political will by seizing the opportunity to find an acceptable solution for both parts.[77]

Under the mediation of Nimetz, both parties met again on March 17, 2008 in Vienna, in the office of the former UN special envoy to Kosovo and former president of Finland, Martti Ahtisaari.[78] Nimetz did not present any new proposals, but remained optimistic that help from the US and other countries would contribute to a solution of the dispute.[79] By that point, Nimetz had limited his proposal to three of the five names that he had proposed in his original framework: Republic of Upper Macedonia; New Republic of Macedonia or Republic of New Macedonia; and Republic of Macedonia–Skopje.[80] Reportedly, the only serious contender remained the "New Macedonia," also a name favored by the US, which regarded it as the "most neutral" option (Athanasopoulos 2008). However, all three proposals were rejected by the Macedonian government on the grounds that none of them would constitute a logical basis for a solution, given that all had been rejected by one or the other side over the last 15 years.[81] Apparently, by then, the Greek veto threat had shifted the international sympathy towards the tiny Balkan country.[82]

As a last effort to bring both sides to a compromise, Nuland organized a meeting between the foreign ministers of both countries, Dora Bakoyannis and Antonio Milošoski at her residence in Brussels, outside of the UN auspice, with the presence of the US assistant secretary of state for European and Eurasian affairs, Daniel Fried. After the event both ministers stressed for the first time their "commitment" to finding a solution until NATO's Summit of Bucharest.[83] Now even Macedonian authorities seemed more inclined to compromise.[84] Then President Crvenkovski, announced:

> If during the ongoing talks we can reach a rational compromise, which from the one side will defend our ethnic identity, and from the other will enable us to receive the NATO invitation, while at the same time canceling our further EU accession obstacles, then I think that this is something that must be supported, and I personally side with the supporters. Some accuse me that with my stance I am undermining the negotiating position of the Republic of Macedonia, yet I do not agree, because we are not in the beginning, but in the final phase of the negotiations. The one who will tell me that the price is high is obliged to address the public opinion and announce an alternative scenario on how Macedonia will develop in the next ten to fifteen years.[85]

In the same spirit, Tito Petkovski, the leader of the Nova Socijaldemokratska Partija (NSDP) (New Social Democratic Party), which had recently joined the ruling coalition in response to President Crvenkovski's call for national cooperation, stated:

> I do not hide that we must proceed on an international usage name's change, with some type of addition, which in no way must put our values under question. I do not want to proceed in an auction with the name, because that will be very damaging also for the interests of the neighboring country that disputes it [...] [T]he overwhelming majority of the state and the scholars ask for a solution and for a way out, using something that does not put our identity and our cultural distinction under questioning. I think that such a solution can be found, especially if the greatest lobbyists and supporters of ours, the United States, declare that Macedonia will be safe, with a safe territorial integrity, with financial support and dynamic development. If we declare which name we support, probably there will be more terms.[86]

However, the Macedonian prime minister Nikola Gruevski seemed not to share the same optimism as President Crvenkovski and admitted his different views from Petkovski. However, Gruevski expressed optimism that there was still time "to overcome these differences and reach a solution which will benefit the country."[87] Meanwhile, the center-left Greek newspaper *To Vima* reported that the two countries were close to an agreement on the basis of the name "New Macedonia," or in Macedonian, "Nova Makedonija."[88]

The Nimetz-mediated negotiations continued in New York on March 25, 2008. Nimetz announced his final proposal of a name "with a geographic dimension, and for all purposes," and offered the name proposal and its implementation as a compromise.[89] According to the Greek media reports, Nimetz was attempting to revive his 2005 proposal, "Republic of Macedonia–Skopje."[90] The news agency for Macedonian private television station A1 reported that the full proposal was as follows: The constitutional name, in Cyrillic, Република Македонија/Republika Makedonija (Republic of Macedonia) could be used for internal purposes and that "Republic of Macedonia (Skopje)" would be used for international relations. For bilateral relations, Nimetz proposal suggested "Republic of Macedonia (Skopje)" and any countries using the state's constitutional name would be encouraged to use it, but not forced to change it. The terms "Macedonia" and "Macedonian," on their own, would be able to be used freely by both countries.[91]

The Macedonian government never issued any statement on whether it accepted or rejected the proposal.[92] The Greek minister of foreign affairs, Dora Bakoyannis, told journalists that the proposal did not meet Greece's stated objectives.[93] On the other side, the Macedonian minister of foreign affairs Antonio Milošoski stated that any reasonable solution that did not impose on the identity of ethnic Macedonians would be explored. However, Milošoski also threatened that if Greece were to veto the country's entrance into NATO, the compromise talks would be stopped.[94]

On April 3, 2008, in NATO's Summit in Bucharest, Greece presented its case on the non-invitation. NATO secretary general Jaap de Hoop Scheffer announced the mutually agreed text of the NATO members, which explained that the reason for no invitation was the inability to find solution in the name dispute. Moreover, the text offered an open invitation to the government of Skopje for new negotiations for the name under the auspices of the United Nations; expressed the wish that those negotiations start as soon as possible; and the further wish that they would conclude as soon as possible, without mentioning a specific time frame.[95] Reportedly, the Greek position was strongly supported by France and Spain. Italy, Portugal, Luxembourg, Iceland, Belgium, Hungary, Slovakia and the Netherlands also showed sympathy for the Greek concerns.[96] The US proposal for inviting the country under its UN provisional reference (FYROM) was backed by Turkey, Slovenia, the Czech Republic, Estonia, Lithuania, Denmark, Bulgaria and Norway; Germany, the United Kingdom and Canada were reported neutral. Meanwhile, the polls showed that 95 per cent of Greeks believed the veto to be appropriate, while only 1 per cent opposed it.[97] Greek minister of foreign affairs Dora Bakoyannis stated that her country would continue to promote its neighbor's NATO and EU accession as soon as the naming issue is resolved.[98]

The aftermath of the Bucharest Summit

On April 17 and 18, 2008 with his visits in Skopje and Athens respectively, Nimetz launched a new cycle of negotiations, without bringing a new proposal.[99] The following talks in New York, April 30–May 2, 2008 did not bring any new proposal. However, Nimetz launched a new proposal on October 8, 2008.[100] The new plan detailed the following elements for compromising: first, the name "Republic of Macedonia" would stay the official name inside the country in the native language; second, the name for the country in all official purposes (i.e. United Nations, EU, NATO) would be "Republic of North Macedonia" (in Macedonian, Република Северна Македонија/Republika Severna Makedonija); third, UN Security Council would suggest to third countries to use the name "Republic of North Macedonia" in official bilateral relations; fourth, the name "former Yugoslav Republic of Macedonia" would no longer be an acceptable name for the country; fifth, "Macedonia" alone could not be used by any of the two parties as an official name for the country or the region; sixth, both parties could use "Macedonia" and "Macedonian" in unofficial settings, with the precondition that they would not claim exclusive rights of any kind. Finally, the new proposal suggested that the front page of the Macedonian passports would contain the following names for the country: Republic of North Macedonia, in English; République de Macédoine du Nord, in French; and Република Македонија/Republika Makedonija in Macedonian. Also, the formula for compromise suggested that Greece would support the integration of its neighboring country into EU and NATO. Finally, both countries were to confirm that they have no territorial claims towards each other.[101]

The new proposal met different reactions in Skopje and Athens. The cabinet of President Crvenkovski, announced that Macedonia wanted "serious changes" in the proposal and that the presented set of ideas could not be a basis for the resolution of the dispute. Primer Gruevski agreed with Crvenkovski.[102] Meanwhile, the English edition of the Greek daily *Kathimerini* reported that Greek diplomats privately did welcome the proposals. However, Bakoyannis never commented on those proposals, stating only that Athens would not state its position before Skopje. Meanwhile, all major opposition parties expressed serious concerns about the proposal since it crosses the "red line" that Greece has set on a single name to be used *erga omnes*.[103]

The new proposal was leaked to the press even before either Athens or Skopje had officially responded to the proposal, and the Athenian weekly *Ethnos* published an allegedly secret diplomatic correspondence of the US State Department. The document, originally tagged as classified until 2018, supposedly detailed a deal between Washington and Skopje on the main provisions of the Nimetz proposal. The *Ethnos* reports claimed that the latest UN-sponsored set of ideas were drawn by the US Secretary of State Condoleezza Rice in June 2008 in a way that accommodated Skopje's concerns.[104] Mirroring the Greek public opinion's outrage, the opposition parties accused the government of tolerating "US interference" in the UN mediation process and called for Greece's withdrawal from the negotiations.[105] Skopje denied all claims of the existence of a secret deal with Washington, and so did Nimetz.[106] The new proposal was not well received by Bulgaria either. In June 2012, its premier, Boyko Borisov, maintained names like "Northern Macedonia" were completely unacceptable, since this geographical term would include Bulgarian regions, giving rise to territorial claims.[107]

In November 2008, Skopje brought Athens in front of the International Court of Justice (ICJ) on charges of flagrant violation of its obligations under Article 11 of the Interim Accord signed by the parties on September 13, 1995, where the alleged violation referred to the blockade by Athens to Macedonia's bid for NATO membership. Macedonia requested that Greek objections to the jurisdiction of the court should be rejected; that the court adjudge and declare that Greece had violated the obligations under the provisions of the Interim Accord, Article 11, Paragraph 1; and that the court should order Greece to immediately take all necessary steps to comply with the obligations under the above provisions and to refrain from objecting, directly or indirectly, to the Republic of Macedonia's membership in NATO and/or any other "international, multilateral and regional organizations and institutions" if the Republic of Macedonia applied for such membership under the name "the former Yugoslav Republic of Macedonia." In turn, Greece requested that the court should find that the case does not fall within the jurisdiction of the court and to reject it as inadmissible; and, if the court did find that it had jurisdiction over the case, then to find those claims as unfounded.

In its judgment on December 5, 2011, which was final and binding, without any possibility for appeal, the ICJ found that it had jurisdiction to process this case, and that Greece, by objecting to the admission of Macedonia in NATO under the UN agreed appellation, had breached its obligation under Article 11, Paragraph 1, of the Interim Accord of September 13, 1995 (Topalova 2011). The court instructed Greece to refrain from similar actions in the future.[108] Naturally Macedonia welcomed the ICJ's decision. Its foreign minister Nikola Poposki stated that Macedonia remained "strongly committed to finding a lasting, mutually acceptable solution to the difference with Greece over the name." Macedonian president Gjorge Ivanov called on Greece to comply with the court's ruling that was final and mandatory for all UN members, adding that

> [a]t this moment we don't want to think in categories winners and losers. We should work together with Greece for the sake of our common future and the future of the region. We are reaching out to Greece in the name of good neighbourly relations and friendship. We consider this ruling a positive impetus. (Topalova 2011)

Nonetheless, the Ministry of Foreign Affairs in Greece responded that they were reviewing the decision.[109] Greek prime minister Lucas Papademos said that Greece was committed to good neighborly relations with Skopje but was also calling for finding a mutually acceptable solution (Topalova 2011). The moral value coincident with the ICJ ruling notwithstanding did not carry binding obligations and could not force NATO or the EU to give a green light to Macedonia's membership application. Indeed, the EU was prompt to clarify that the court's decision did not impact any change in the EU's stance that Macedonia's accession negotiations could not begin prior to the solution of the name issue.[110]

In the next round of talks on February 11, 2009, Nimetz did not propose a new solution for the name, but it was agreed that talks should continue after elections in Greece and Macedonia, later that year. Milošoski's proposal for both countries to form a joint committee of scholars who would work on determining the historical facts of the dispute was flatly dismissed by Athens.[111] Talks continued on June 22, 2009 in Geneva under the Nimetz auspice, mainly focusing on the differences and the problematic points of the dispute. According to Nimetz, the negotiations had made some progress, which identified and discussed the issues that had so far stalled the solution process. However, both sides remained firm in their positions. The Geneva talks were followed by Nimetz's visits to Macedonia on July 6–8 and Greece on July 8–10. Later that summer, Nimetz expressed pessimism regarding the Greek response to his proposed names in his July meetings, yet stated that efforts to solve the name issue continued, even though Greece's answer was not positive. Apparently, Greece opposed any proposed solution that was only intended for use in bilateral relations, and insisted that any acceptable name must be used internationally. In late August, in a meeting with Nimetz, the Macedonian negotiator Zoran Jolevski stated that "is committed to active participation in the talks over the name and we expect a mutually acceptable solution, which will ensure preserving of the identity, dignity and integrity of the Macedonian citizens on the basis of Euro-Atlantic values and democratic principles."[112] From there negotiations were frozen because of Athens' rejection of essential points in the most recent proposal and the Greek elections in October 2009.

The Greek government under the premiership of Georgios Papandreou that emerged from the fall 2009 election seemed to be more inclined toward a compromise. In April 2010, former Greek ambassador to Macedonia Alexandros Mallias, Greek History professor Evangelis Kofos, professor and SDSM Diplomatic Council member Ljubomir Frčkoski, president of the Liberal Party Stojan Andov, journalist Borjan Jovanovski and a few other Macedonian journalists simulated talks for resolution of the name issue between Macedonia and Greece in Ohrid. The two negotiating parties agreed that Macedonia and Greece with mediation from the international community could reach an agreement and establish good ground for compromise between Mallias's recent proposal and Nimetz's proposal of 2008. The proposal included the new name of the country to be "Republic of Northern Macedonia," while the language and nation should be named "Makedonski" written in the Roman alphabet. The Macedonian experts present at the simulation believed the proposals could be feasible provided that Greece would not insist on constitutional changes, because Macedonia has already made enough concessions in 1995. Both sides agreed that the nationalistic rhetoric of the Macedonian government was undermining any solution. The experts concluded that the Macedonian government simply did not want to prepare its people for a compromise and in such conditions it would be much harder to achieve a positive outcome in the referendum that the government wished to organize on any account.[113] During the simulation talks, the Greek diplomats promised that Macedonia would be given a date for opening accession talks in June 2010 provided it accepted the proposal offered by the Greek government. In the meantime, Prime Minister Gruevski told national television that if the proposal for "Northern Republic of Macedonia" for all use was put forward by Nimetz as an official proposal for the solution of the name dispute, then the proposal would undergo a vote by referendum. Asked by a journalist about his vote, Prime Minister Gruevski said that he would vote against.[114]

On June 13, the Greek daily *Kathimerini* referred to sources claiming that Greece and Macedonia appeared to be close to a solution to their name dispute, and were converging on the use of the Vardar River to differentiate the Republic of Macedonia from Greek Macedonia. However, it never became clear whether the implementation model would have been "Republic of Macedonia of Vardar," "Republic of Vardar Macedonia," "Vardar Republic of Macedonia" or "Republic of Macedonia (Vardar)."[115] Meanwhile, organizations from the Macedonian diaspora launched a campaign placing advertisements in newspapers and billboards across Macedonia "demanding an end to all negotiations with Greece over its name."[116] Indeed, differently from the inflexible policy of his late father, Andreas Papandreou, Georgios Papandreou continued until the end of his term an approach toward the compromise. In his prime ministerial farewell speech on November 9, 2011, Papandreou listed the immediate settlement of the name issue as one of the three priorities that the next government should list (Pop 2011).

On October 5, 2012, the Greek minister of foreign affairs Dimitris Avramopoulos sent a letter to his Macedonian counterpart, Nikola Poposki, with a proposal for a bilateral memorandum as a basis for finding a solution to the name dispute. The letter showed support for the European Commission's plan according to which Skopje could start accession negotiations even before a resolution of the name dispute with Greece is found.[117] In its Enlargement Strategy and Main Challenges 2012–13, the EC suggested that a decision of the European Council to open accession negotiations would contribute to creating conditions conducive to finding such a solution. The EC emphasized its commitment to present without delay a proposal for a negotiating framework, which also took into account "the need to solve the name issue at an early stage of accession negotiations."[118]

On November 6, 2012, roughly a month after Avramopoulos' letter, Skopje reacted favorably through a letter from Macedonian minister of foreign affairs Nikola Poposki to Avramopoulos. Reportedly, Poposki welcomed the Greek intention to move the issue "decisively forward," and insisted that the Greek proposal for the two countries to sign a memorandum as a basis to unblock the name issue had come as a response to initiatives from Macedonia. Poposki explained his government's "firm desire to overcome the difference over the name," adding that this "will benefit both countries and the region as a whole."[119]

The proposal came as the EU, through its commissioner for enlargement, Štefan Füle, was stepping up pressure on both sides to solve their differences. Arguably, from the European Commission's perspective, there was a need to lift the Greek veto for Macedonia to begin EU accession talks, and put the country on a more stable track in light of growing ethnic tensions in the former Yugoslav republic. Moreover, the evolution in the Greek position toward the issue was rooted in its ambitious plans for the Western Balkans during its EU presidency in the first half of 2014. According to various reports, a compromise to the name would contain a "geographical qualifier" given that Macedonia was a geographical region that overlaps the territories of Greece, Bulgaria and the former Yugoslav republic. Diplomats have speculated whether "Northern Macedonia" or "Upper Macedonia" could be acceptable to both sides.[120] However, to the date of this writing, neither country has released any proposed formula.

In an effort to keep up the EU initiative on the name issue solution, in mid-January 2013, Commissioner Füle proposed a trilateral (EU-Greece-Macedonia) meeting to promote the signing of a memorandum of understanding between the two countries. Füle's new initiative followed a recent statement by the EU Council saying that any decision on opening accession talks for Macedonia would be based on a report by the European Commission due to be published in spring this year.[121] However, Füle's proposal met cautious welcome by both sides. Gregory Delavekouras, spokesperson for the Greek Ministry of Foreign Affairs stated that Greece is not opposed to meetings in principle, under the condition that "there be good preparation and, mainly, that a substantial result be ensured" (Marusic 2013a). Reportedly, in spite of the public silence from the Macedonian part, it seemed that the Macedonian government would have no objection to a trilateral meeting with Greece and the EU (ibid.). However, due to the fact that both parties were set to meet within the framework of the UN-led negotiations with mediator Matthew Nimetz, the Greek government considered a tripartite meeting with the EU participation unnecessary (ibid.; see also Lajmanovska 2013).

After nearly two years of separate meetings between UN mediator Matthew Nimetz and negotiators from both countries, a joint round of negotiations occurred in the UN Headquarters in New York. The UN mediator presented recommendations and ideas to both parties to consider; however, these proposals are not yet known to the general public. Expressing moderate hopes, the UN's press service has said the objective was to assess the status of the negotiations and the possibility of making headway in finding a solution to the name dispute. Meanwhile both countries and the EU needed that assessment as they were preparing for the December 2012 council, where a decision was expected on whether Macedonia would finally get a starting date for accession talks after the Council had previously rejected three consecutive positive recommendations by the European Commission.[122] Again, Greece, this time supported also by Bulgaria, managed to block the country from having a precise date for opening accession negotiations (Marusic 2012b). However, in light of a Greek inclination toward a compromise, the Council offered a hopeful message to Macedonia by not rejecting right away the EC recommendation, but promising to reassess its position:

> on the basis of a report to be presented by the Commission in Spring 2013, implementation of reforms in the context of the HLAD, as well as steps taken to promote good neighbourly relations and to reach a negotiated and mutually accepted solution to the name issue under the auspices of the UN.[123]

It seemed that the EU message served as a prompt incentive to the solution of the name dispute. On January 9–11, 2013 Nimetz visited Athens and Skopje, and followed with separate meetings with Zoran Jolevski and Adamantios Vassilakis, negotiators for Macedonia and Greece respectively, and then at a joint discussion on January 29 and 30. An optimistic Nimetz emerged from the meetings upbeat. After his meeting with the Macedonian premier Gruevski, Nimetz stated, "I do think we will reach a positive conclusion" (Marusic 2013b). Talks continued in New York on April 9, where Nimetz announced to have put forward a new proposal based on the previous feedback from both sides.

However, neither party leaked any details over the new proposal, and the wording has not been divulged, although media reports suggest it is some form of "Upper" or "Northern Republic of Macedonia" (Marusic 2013d). Also Nimetz avoided direct references to any concrete solution. Reportedly, Nimetz claimed that the new proposal reflected his attempts to refine previous ideas "and give them some new formulations that might meet the issues and objections and the problems we have had the last time around," referring to the previous round of talks held on January 29–30. Nimetz announced a new meeting "within the next few months" (Marusic 2013c) when both sides might be able to respond to the proposal.

While Macedonia's ethnic Albanians have remained by and large outside of the country's name dispute with Greece and historical quarrels with Bulgaria, such a position seems to have changed with Albania's membership to NATO. On May 14, 2009, the Bashkimi Demokratik për Integrim (BDI) (Democratic Union for Integration) again urged the government of Macedonia to find a compromise on a name dispute with Greece. Its leader, Ali Ahmeti, met with the newly elected Macedonian president Gjorge Ivanov in 2009, followed by a joint statement advocating the need for national unity to find a solution to issue. Menduh Thaçi, the leader of the opposition Partia Demokratike e Shqiptarëve (PDSh) (Democratic Party of Albanians) responded by saying that the country's new name should guarantee "the peculiarities of the Macedonian Albanians' national identity." Both ethnic Albanian leaders stood against the idea of a referendum. Thaçi stated that Albanians of Macedonia would never accept a new name in case it refers only to the Macedonians and ignores the Albanian people (ibid.).

Taking the diplomatic initiative, high-ranking ethnic Albanian politicians took advantage of their official positions to increase their role in the solution of the naming dispute. In January 2013, Macedonia's deputy-prime minister for European affairs Teuta Arifi, an ethnic Albanian, and her Greek counterpart, Theodoros Pangalos, met in Athens in an unsuccessful attempt to revive the talks. Then in early May 2013, her successor, Fatmir Besimi, also an ethnic Albanian, met Greek minister of foreign affairs Dimitris Avramopoulos in Athens (Marusic 2013d). However, those diplomatic efforts were not well received by all Macedonians. Recently, some of them feared that the geostrategic interest of the Albanians in the Balkans is a united Macedonia controlled by ethnic Albanians, and that the expanding Albanian demographic growth rates along with a concurrently shrinking Macedonian population will turn the Albanians into a majority. Speculating about the reasons of an emerging ethnic Albanian interest for Macedonia to join NATO, Slobodan Chashule, former Macedonian foreign minister stated: "[Albanians'] strategy is not Macedonia's territorial secession. They simply want it as a third Albanian state in the Balkans" (Yambaev 2011).[124]

The implications of Macedonia's international disputes to its EU membership: A consociationalist interpretation

On April 16, 2013, the European Commission released its expected report to the European Parliament and the Council on the implementation of reforms within the framework of the HLAD and promotion of good neighborly relations.[125] The report discussed two topics, both of significant concern for our consociationalist approach: its first part assessed the implementation of reforms in the context of the HLAD, examining additional progress under the headings of the HLAD agenda with an eye to the effects that the Macedonian political crisis during the winter of 2012–13 had on the country's reforms. The second part of the report assessed steps taken to promote good neighborly relations with all neighboring countries, especially with Bulgaria and Greece.

On December 24, 2012, a heated debate in Sobranie over the 2013 state budget ended with the intervention of security forces, who threw opposition parliamentarians and journalists out of the chamber. The violent intervention of the security personnel resulted in the largest opposition party, SDSM, to boycott the Sobranie and threaten the resignation of their MPs, as well as a boycott of the local elections. The two-month political stalemate that followed affected the functioning of the Sobranie, which continued to operate without the SDSM-led opposition presence, and the organization of local elections. The parties overcame the deadlock on March 1, 2013 under the energetic engagement of the EC and the European Parliament (Gardner 2013). The across-the-aisle agreement enabled a return to normal functioning of the Sobranie and the opposition's participation in the local elections. Moreover, the agreement helped the parties to reassert their commitment to key strategic priorities and reforms. Among others, the agreement required a memorandum of understanding affirming the cross-party consensus on, and commitment to, the country's strategic objective of EU and Atlantic integration and the establishment of a committee of inquiry related to the incident of the previous December in the Sobranie.[126]

With the political crisis of the winter of 2012–13, Macedonia found itself disadvantaged at both levels that the consociational practices required to be in place in order to enable the opening of EU accession negotiations. First, the domestic crisis only complicated the already exacerbated ethnic tensions in the country. The growing political divisions among ethnic Macedonians—the Albanians of Macedonia, too, remained deeply divided over politics—undermined efforts to allow the country to emerge as a single pillar/segment ready to embrace EU consociational practices in the second EU level. As a result, the EC took the Macedonian political crisis very seriously. The situation prompted Füle to intervene, paying an unscheduled visit to Skopje in January and then cancelling another scheduled visit to Skopje on February 22, arguing that it would not be appropriate to discuss accession at this point. Füle explicitly warned that the political crisis was threatening Macedonia's EU ambitions (Gardner 2013).

Second, the lingering disagreements with Greece would have kept Macedonia in the position of a "spoiler" of the EU consociational practices in the case it becomes an EU member country prior to the name dispute solution. With the latest success in the April 2013 local elections, the politics of *antikvizatzija* rewarded Gruevski's VMRO–DPMNE seven consecutive electoral victories and managed to instill a new national identity in many ethnic Macedonians. Therefore, VMRO–DPMNE could afford the potential political damages afflicted by delays in Macedonia's Euro-Atlantic integration. However, the reluctance of Macedonia to compromise sent the message that the country was not ready yet to embrace the consociationalist practices that underpin EU functioning. Although it might seem that

Greece's upper hand in the naming dispute is a technical product of EU institutional arrangements, the wide support that Greece continued to maintain in the European Council and European Parliament might be easily interpreted not simply as support for its position but as a EU rejection of Macedonia's stubbornness against any compromise.

Conclusion

The purpose of this chapter was to disentangle reforms from power struggles in Albania and domestic and international divisions of Macedonia in order to better understand the political background of institutional reforms in both countries. Also, the chapter helps to explain both the transformative power of EU membership conditionality and its limits. This book has argued that reform implementation depends on the combination of assumed preferences on the outcome of those reforms of domestic leaders and EU institutions. A careful scrutiny of the domestic and international context of reforms helps to explain domestic leaders' preferences in those reforms, as well as the potential leverage of EU membership conditionality and its limitations. It is obvious that power calculations in both countries undermine reforms. In the case of Albania, they show that power struggle undermines each country's ability to implement reforms that would make it able to act according to such practices on the EU political stage. In the case of Macedonia, identity politics undermine consociational practices at the domestic level, and uncover the unpreparedness of the country to implement consociational practices at the EU level.

Chapter 8

CONCLUSIONS

Membership conditionality continues to be a powerful tool by which international organizations (IOs) can improve the democratic standing of the countries that make up their membership. However, results vary depending on the leverage those IOs have on the country seeking membership, as well as on the intensity of conditionality itself. The EU is not simply an IO, but a successful political system, and its leverage might be greater than those of other IOs. The EU introduced membership conditionality with the signing of the Treaty of Amsterdam, 1997, and has used it ever since, with varying results, to affect policy changes in countries aspiring to its membership. Previous research has analyzed EU membership conditionality as an overarching policy aimed at steering democratization rather than as a set of policies trying to affect specific reforms. My argument employs a sectorial contextual approach to studying EU membership conditionality. The sectorial contextual approach provides a framework for explaining the effects of EU membership conditionality on specific sectorial reforms through mid-level theories. These theories view the reform outcome as a result of the interplay between EU and domestic leaders' preferences in that specific reform. Arguably, any change in actors' interests on a certain reform will alter the outcome. These preferences are context specific, and often might not match the preferences of these same actors in other reforms.

I assume that two sets of major actors affect Eastern European institutional reforms: EU institutions and domestic leaders. Such an assumption fits the highly institutionalized EU political stage and the weak institutionalization in Eastern European countries. The highly institutionalized EU makes the role of individual leaders less relevant than the activity of its institutions. Furthermore, recent EU internal reform aims at strengthening the role of EU institutions, thus shrinking even more the role of national leaders in making decisions. By contrast, the collapse of communism and its institutions in Eastern Europe created a vacuum that was filled by power-driven leaders.

Reliance on a rational choice approach facilitates the mapping of Eastern European leaders' interests in particular reforms; their policy choices reflect their power-driven agendas. However, the process tracing might confound causes with effects. In order to escape this problem I have employed a combination of analytical tools. First, I used the division of historical periods, "extraordinary politics" and "ordinary politics," as suggested by Balcerowicz (2002) in order to facilitate my categorization of leaders' interests in certain reforms during the early, revolutionary years of transformation (extraordinary politics) as positive. Identifying leaders' preferences in specific sectorial reforms as a political system settles into its own routine (ordinary politics) requires a more careful analysis. As an initial guideline I structured my analysis using the observation that governments work to enact reforms during their first half of tenure and dedicate more time and resources to power politics in their second term. In addition, I have maintained that governments are interested in enacting reforms that satisfy their constituents, but will not spend resources in reforms deemed less necessary for the country. Governments might also reverse reforms if that serves their agenda.

However, assessing EU preferences in the context of Eastern European institutional reforms is a complicated issue, since the *personalistic* decision-making style in Eastern European countries might be difficult to apply to EU institutions. EU rationale rests primarily on democratic stability, and its interests in eastward enlargement depend on the need to expand continental security without jeopardizing the internal integration of the Union.

Earlier efforts have suggested that consociational theory can help to explain the nature of the EU as a stable democracy formed by deeply divisive member states. I expand that argument by adding that any explanation of the EU interests in eastern enlargement can be facilitated by the consociational theory: if consociational practices have brought about stable democracy in the EU, they can help transform countries aspiring to EU membership. Here we have two cases. In the case of EU membership–aspiring countries with unified societies, the EU will simply encourage institutions receptive to EU consociational practices once these countries join the EU; in EU membership–aspiring countries with divided societies, the EU will institute consociational practices in order to homogenize the society into a single political body. That divided society, once it becomes a member state of the democratically stable EU, would feel even more pressured to implement consociational practices as a modus vivendi within the EU.

Revisiting the consociational theory reveals a shortcoming: the tautological relationship between the causal consociational practices and the consociational democracy as a dependent variable. The EU efforts focus on strengthening its democratic stability, and consociational practices are simply tools for encouraging that change. Therefore, in an effort to simultaneously avoid such a tautology in favor of scientific rigor, on the one hand, and gain conceptual breadth for democracy, on the other, I wish no longer to refer to the EU as a consociational democracy but as a stable democracy built primarily, though not exclusively, on consociational practices. Such an approach helps cast plausibility on my assumption that the EU rationale rests on democratic stability and that the EU employs consociational practices to obtain and maintain democratic stability.

The sectorial contextual approach and the consociational approach to the EU eastward expansion are intrinsically linked. While the latter explains why the EU nurtures institutional reforms within its borders, the former explains why institutional reforms develop the way they do. Implicitly, the consociational approach to its eastward enlargement tries to establish plausible assumptions about the source of EU interest in Eastern European institutional reforms, as well as the intensity of EU conditions in different sectorial reforms; while the sectorial contextual approach explains the outcome of the reforms when we take both domestic and foreign variables into account. The consociational approach helps us to understand the source of EU conditions and, by understanding the rationale behind these conditions, to evaluate their intensity; the sectorial contextual approach expands our understanding of and explanation for specific Eastern European institutional reforms, political preferences about these reforms and other independent structural variables that reflect the social context in which a specific reform occurs.

In this book, I have built a series of mid-level hypotheses that explain varying reform outcomes that are contingent on a combination of the EU's and domestic leaders' preferences for that reform. Specifically, I argue that common preferences by both domestic leaders and the EU in a sectorial approach are most likely to result in swift and successful reform. If domestic leaders' preferences in reform are positive but EU preferences are neutral, we still can have a successful reform. If domestic leaders' preferences in sectorial reform are neutral, but EU preferences in certain sectorial reform are positive, we likely have slow reform progress until EU membership conditionality turns domestic leaders' preferences to positive. However, if EU preferences in a certain sectorial reform are positive but domestic leaders' preferences in that reform are negative, the reform stalls until the EU membership conditionality manages to change domestic leaders' preferences in that reform. And finally, if both the EU and domestic leaders are not interested in certain reforms, no progress will happen in those sectors.

The empirical analysis shows that those hypotheses help explain the effects of EU membership conditionality in specific Albanian and Macedonian institutional reforms. I chose these countries because they represent overlooked cases in the study of membership conditionality and because, while the findings can be instructive for both these countries, they can help to explain institutional reforms in other Western Balkans countries, including Bosnia and Herzegovina, Croatia, Kosovo, Montenegro and Serbia, as well as Turkey and some European countries newly created with the demise of the Soviet Union, namely Belarus, Moldova, Ukraine and the Transcaucasia (Armenia, Azerbaijan and Georgia). Indeed, even though the EU does not currently consider the latter countries to be potential candidates, it has never ruled out their potential to become EU member countries. Their similarities help simplify the empirical analysis, while their differences help clarify the case of EU membership conditionality to an aspirant country with either a unified society or with a divided one. Moreover, the long road toward the EU provides more variations in both causal factors and reform outcomes. As I am interested primarily in the effects of EU membership conditionality in Eastern European institutional reforms, here I have focused only on pre-accession cases. Arguably, the post-accession developments show different reform dynamics from the ones that I expose here, due to changes in the configuration of a new member country's domestic political stage. In the long run, we should expect EU membership conditionality and EU accession to empower other domestic actors and interest groups aside the ruling elites (Hollyer 2010).

From other possible explanations, only the factor of ethnic homogeneity/heterogeneity seems to play a key role. Ethnic composition of a country highly determines both EU and domestic leaders' interests. It also defines the EU's prevailing preferences for stability over democracy, such as the case of Macedonia of the 1990s. Only when stability is not feasible without democracy, does the EU step in with conditioning consociational practices in order to assure that specific country's social cohesion. In countries with unified societies, the EU does not condition consociational practices per se, but offers an institutional design to facilitate a country's institutional adaptation to EU consociational practices once it acquires EU membership.

Communist legacies seem to play no role in the development of sectorial reforms. In less than two years, 1990–91, Macedonia went from one of the most decentralized political entities in Eastern Europe (such it was within Yugoslavia) to one of the most centralized ones. Even after 20 years of violent ethnic conflict that targeted the existing centralized system, and relentless pressure from the EU, Macedonia remains a more centralized country than Albania, although the latter comes from a totalitarian communist dictatorship. The same can be claimed for judicial reforms in both countries. By the same token, Macedonia inherited the Yugoslav adherence to the 1951 Geneva Convention and even some of the Yugoslav asylum system. Yet, it took the country 13 years from its independence to pass its first Law on Asylum, while Albania approved its first legislation on asylum in 1998. Similarly, we can refer to constitutional reforms: Albania's 1991 Major Constitutional Provisions provided a good stepping stone for the reforms of the 1990s, and the country acquired a brand new, liberal and highly praised constitution in 1998. Macedonia, with the inherited Yugoslav tradition of federalism and recognition on paper and in practice of a wide range of human and collective rights, passed a centralized, rigid constitution in 1991; it took a violent ethnic conflict to amend it into a more acceptable document for all its citizens.

My point is that institutional memory does not last long and leaders' current preferences prevail over those of the past. Both my case countries come from the Ottoman tradition, as both were the last territories in the Balkans to escape the Ottoman grip. This fact prevents us from properly understanding the role of the Habsburg tradition in the particular reforms that we considered here. However, inferring from the inconsistent role that the Leninist legacy has played in these reforms both in Albania and Macedonia, one can argue that both Hapsburg and Ottoman memories remain distant and historical rather than vivid institutional reminders imprinted in the societies' political consciences.

Other theories point to the relevance of human capital in conducting efficient reforms in transitional, postsocialist countries. My historical analysis shows that such concerns are overrated, and what keeps these countries from performing in their reform policies is a lack of political will rather than human capital. The Balkans have inherited high levels of literacy from communism, and their societies' zeal for education is reflected in the large number of students graduating abroad, as well as an ever-growing number of public and private higher education institutions across the Balkans. Had these countries been truly scarce in human resources, the very concept of EU membership conditionality would have been redundant, and their efforts would have been steered toward creating human capacities rather than conducting institutional reforms. However, the fact that reforms begin to progress immediately after domestic politics supports them shows that political will is a more efficient explanation for the outcomes of institutional reforms in EU membership–aspiring countries from Eastern Europe.

Reforms are often painful and frequently result in political costs for governments; hence governments are often reluctant to undertake radical reform programs. EU membership conditionality has become a powerful tool both to spur Eastern European ruling elites toward reforms and to shield them from domestic backlashes. Yet, while EU membership conditionality works through switching domestic leaders' preferences over reforms from against to for, they cannot change their mindset. Evidence from previous EU expansions in Eastern Europe shows that governments slow reforms or stop them altogether once they acquire membership. Aware of this tendency, on December 13, 2006, only days before the Bulgarian and Romanian accession scheduled for January 1, 2007, the EU established the Mechanism for Cooperation and Verification for Bulgaria and Romania (MCVBR). The EU was aware of the need for further progress in sectors related to the judicial reform, including corruption and organized crime, in these fledgling member states. In order both to facilitate their accession and safeguard the workings of its policies and institutions, the EU established MCVBR to help them address these outstanding shortcomings.

In June 2007 the EU released its first progress report on Bulgaria since the country joined the EU. The report was critical; highlighting the Bulgarian government's commitment to judicial reform and cleansing the system of corruption and organized crime, the report notes "a clear weakness in translating these intentions into results" and that "much remains to be done." The report concluded that progress "is still insufficient."[1] An interim report on progress in Bulgaria regarding judiciary reform and the fight against corruption and organized crime released in February 2008 points to the same problems.[2] Two years later, in July 2009, with no progress noticed in these sectors, the EU Commission decided to punish Bulgaria by cutting nearly half a billion Euros in funding, which effectively stopped the payments of some €250 million ($394 million) earmarked for institutional reforms.[3]

In July 2009, Romania got away without funding cuts to the judiciary, anti-corruption and anticrime sectors; although it suffered a suspension of agricultural payments worth €142 million, no linkage was made with the aforementioned sectors. In February 2009, the European Commission released its Interim Reports for Bulgaria and Romania. The report on Bulgaria acknowledges the "efforts" made by the authorities since July 2008, especially in setting up joint investigation teams composed of prosecutors, intelligence officers and policemen to fight organized crime, but argues that "convincing and tangible results" were still needed.[4] However, the report is very critical on Romania. It highlights that "[t]he pace of progress noted in the Commission's report of July 2008 has not been maintained," and that "[i]n most other areas, shortcomings identified by the Commission in July remain."[5]

Reportedly, several member states, namely Germany, France, UK, the Netherlands, Belgium, Finland, Sweden, Denmark and Austria, threatened fund cuts if the progress report scheduled for June 2009 did not document progress in these sectors (Pop 2009). Funding cuts did not happen, but these developments show how volatile progress in Eastern European institutional reforms continues to be even after they join the EU. With membership conditionality inapplicable to member countries, the Union will try to enforce compliance by using alternative coercive tools. But these developments also show how difficult and long the road toward reform in Eastern Europe would have been without EU membership conditionality. They served as red flags for EU member countries of the dangers of granting hasty membership to Eastern European countries before they appropriate EU consociational practices as normative behavior rather than just instrumentally comply with them.

Arguably, the cases of Bulgaria and Romania have changed the EU approach toward eastward expansion from an enthusiastic mood of European unification to an extremely cautious scrutiny of reform performance and sustainability. On January 8, 2013, in an interview for the Albanian television network *Top Channel*, René van der Linden, former president of the Dutch Senate, comments Netherland's refusal to give the EU status to Albania:

> It is very important to fulfil [*sic*] the Copenhagen Criteria, because we have seen countries such as Bulgaria and Romania that entered in the EU before they were ready, and this spurred many critics at the member countries. The EU candidate status for Albania will be given only if it will be deserved and when the criteria will be fulfilled. This is not something specific that is demanded only for Albania. All member countries can keep or lose their status only through merits. For the sake of the future of EU, we must follow all rules and agreements between the member countries.[6]

My research reveals both strengths and weaknesses of membership conditionality. A better awareness of those strengths and weaknesses would help to apply it more effectively. As a concept, membership conditionality might be related to a number of policy areas, and the EU and different IOs focus on different policy areas. First, membership conditionality works only when it manages to shift domestic leaders' policy preferences to compliance with policies prescribed by the EU or the IO that a country aspires to join. If the benefits of membership are higher than the domestic cost of a sectorial reform, then governments proceed with that reform. Second, conducting institutional reform under the pressure of membership conditionality might not be the perfect way to institute reforms, and often the tug of war between organizational and domestic leaders' competing policy preferences increase the cost of reforms. The best way to reform is domestic leaders' willingness to undertake them. Membership conditionality emerges when such willingness does not exist.

Moreover, membership conditionality is contingent upon the character and scope of the IO. The more an organization has a stake in a membership-aspiring country's particular sectorial reform, the more it will agitate for reform in that policy area. In turn, that character represents the single most important factor of membership conditionality's strength. The rationale for using membership conditionality as leverage rests on its power to alter policy preferences of the leaders of membership-aspiring countries. Thus, for the EU, while eastward enlargement brings the challenge of instability, membership conditionality aims at encouraging stability. Therefore, EU membership conditionality is a tool in function of that democratic stability.

This research rests on the assumption of divided elites, and from there stems the entire discourse of domestic leaders' rational political preferences. The alternative approach would have been the view that national elites are united, but were this the case the entire configuration of domestic elites' political preferences would have changed and would have likely focused more on issues on national interests, especially in the case of Macedonia. However, even in the latter case, the very fact that the EU has served as a guarantee for the national sovereignty of the country would have given the EU enough credibility to serve more as a partner than a competitor to Macedonia, hence realist/ neorealist and neoliberal theories of international bargaining and negotiations would have been inapplicable. Rather than international bargaining, the interaction of the EU with its membership-aspiring countries would have been resembled more a teacher-student relationship.

Indeed, this is the core of EU efforts toward its membership aspirants from Eastern Europe: the commissioning of consociational practices at the domestic level in order to foster domestic cohesion and help divided societies emerge as a single pillar/segment that can function as singular actors in a democratically stable political system (that is, the EU) established through consociational practices. For those unified pillars/segments to emerge, both sides of the aisles should cooperate. However, so far, the EU has focused its conditionality mainly on ruling elites, thus underestimating the very important role that political opposition could play in either fostering or undermining reforms. Simply, forays into reform remain almost impossible without the political cooperation across the aisles.

Such a task unveils the Achilles' heel of EU membership conditionality. While it can successfully switch the rationale of membership-aspiring countries' domestic ruling elites toward reform by applying the carrot-and-stick tactics, "sticks" against the political opposition might be more normative than real. Shaming, for instance, might be a means of compelling political opposition to cooperate; yet in the case of Albania's failure to implement reforms that would require a reinforced majority, the EU has not pointed to the political opposition as a major cause for the country failure to receive the candidate status. While the EU's vague language addressed the country's political elites, its uneven leverage on ruling elites indicates that they could pressure and reward only the ruling elites, thus leaving the political opposition to benefit from reform failure.

Therefore, while EU membership conditionality is a powerful tool for policy change toward securing reforms in countries that aspire to EU membership, it is undermined by conflicting preferences of domestic political elites. This conclusion argues for a new EU direction in which EU membership conditionality should focus, namely that it should expand its consociational practices in countries that aspire to its membership, especially during periods of crucial reforms as well as in the last stages of preparations to undertake further steps toward the Union. Thus, in order to increase reform efficiency and success, the EU could demand from membership-aspiring countries' governments of broaden coalitions as a way to reduce domestic political competition based on reform outcomes and to switch elites' rationale from competition to cooperation. Such cooperation would, first, make all parties interested in reform success and, second, foster a climate of bipartisan cooperation, thus further socializing domestic elites with consociational practices at home as they prepare to join the EU political stage where such practices are modus vivendi.

Appendix A

THE DEMOGRAPHIC DYNAMIC OF MACEDONIA SINCE 1981[1]

Figure 1. Population in Macedonia in 1981 by administrative units

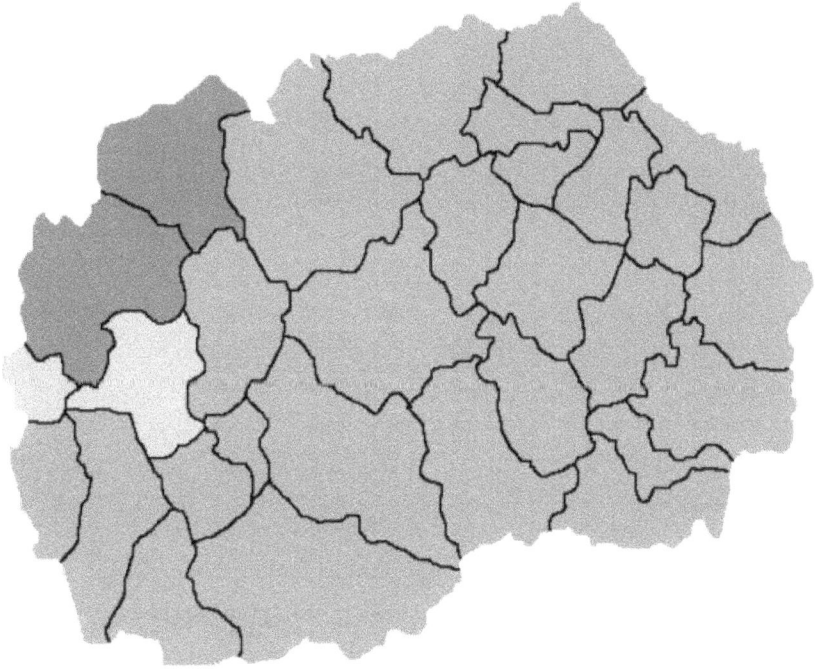

Ethnic map of the Republic of Macedonia (1981 census)
- ◓ - Macedonian majority
- ● - Albanian majority
- ○ - Mixed population

---

1 Source: Wikipedia. Online: http://en.wikipedia.org/wiki/Demographics_of_the_Republic_ of_Macedonia (accessed November 14, 2010).

Figure 2. Majority populations in Macedonia in 2002 by territory

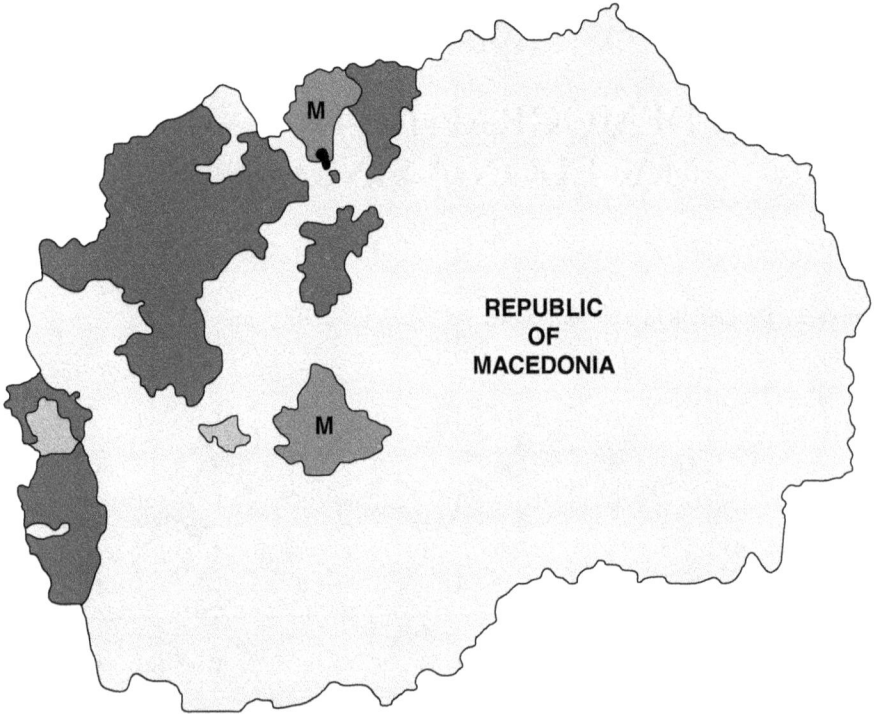

Ethnic map of the Republic of Macedonia
(based on the 2002 census municipality data)

○ Macedonians		● Albanians	
◑ Turks		⬤ Roma	
◉ Mixed population		M Relative Macedonian majority	

Figure 3. Majority populations in Macedonia in 2002 by administrative units

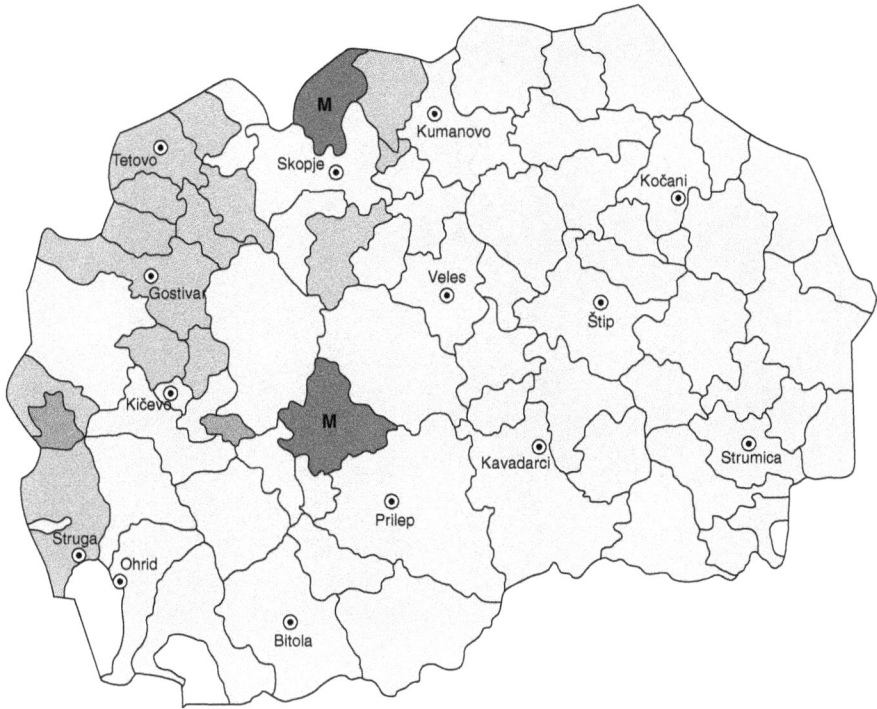

Macedonia - 2002 census

○ - Macedonian majority ◔ - Albanian majority ◕ - Turkish majority ● - Mixed

M - Relative Macedonian majority

Figure 4. Relative population of Albanians in Macedonia in 2002 by administrative units

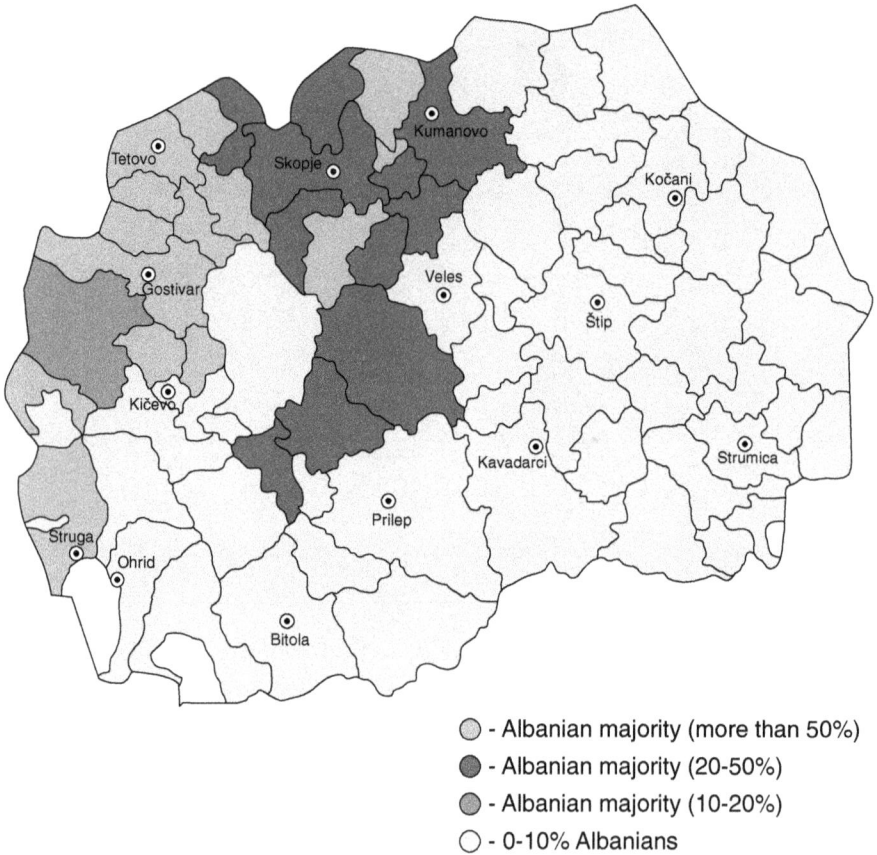

○ - Albanian majority (more than 50%)
● - Albanian majority (20-50%)
◉ - Albanian majority (10-20%)
○ - 0-10% Albanians

Appendix B

OHRID FRAMEWORK AGREEMENT

The following points comprise an agreed framework for securing the future of Macedonia's democracy and permitting the development of closer and more integrated relations between the Republic of Macedonia and the Euro–Atlantic community. This Framework will promote the peaceful and harmonious development of civil society while respecting the ethnic identity and the interests of all Macedonian citizens.

1. Basic Principles
   1.1. The use of violence in pursuit of political aims is rejected completely and unconditionally. Only peaceful political solutions can assure a stable and democratic future for Macedonia.
   1.2. Macedonia's sovereignty and territorial integrity, and the unitary character of the State are inviolable and must be preserved. There are no territorial solutions to ethnic issues.
   1.3. The multi-ethnic character of Macedonia's society must be preserved and reflected in public life.
   1.4. A modern democratic state in its natural course of development and maturation must continually ensure that its Constitution fully meets the needs of all its citizens and comports with the highest international standards, which themselves continue to evolve.
   1.5. The development of local self-government is essential for encouraging the participation of citizens in democratic life, and for promoting respect for the identity of communities.
2. Cessation of Hostilities
   2.1. The parties underline the importance of the commitments of July 5, 2001. There shall be a complete cessation of hostilities, complete voluntary disarmament of the ethnic Albanian armed groups and their complete voluntary disbandment. They acknowledge that a decision by NATO to assist in this context will require the establishment of a general, unconditional and open-ended cease-fire, agreement on a political solution to the problems of this country, a clear commitment by the armed groups to voluntarily disarm, and acceptance by all the parties of the conditions and limitations under which the NATO forces will operate.
3. Development of Decentralized Government
   3.1. A revised Law on Local Self-Government will be adopted that reinforces the powers of elected local officials and enlarges substantially their competencies in

conformity with the Constitution (as amended in accordance with Annex A) and the European Charter on Local Self-Government, and reflecting the principle of subsidiarity in effect in the European Union. Enhanced competencies will relate principally to the areas of public services, urban and rural planning, environmental protection, local economic development, culture, local finances, education, social welfare, and health care. A law on financing of local self-government will be adopted to ensure an adequate system of financing to enable local governments to fulfill all of their responsibilities.

3.2. Boundaries of municipalities will be revised within one year of the completion of a new census, which will be conducted under international supervision by the end of 2001. The revision of the municipal boundaries will be effectuated by the local and national authorities with international participation.

3.3. In order to ensure that police are aware of and responsive to the needs and interests of the local population, local heads of police will be selected by municipal councils from lists of candidates proposed by the Ministry of Interior, and will communicate regularly with the councils. The Ministry of Interior will retain the authority to remove local heads of police in accordance with the law.

4. Non-Discrimination and Equitable Representation

4.1. The principle of non-discrimination and equal treatment of all under the law will be respected completely. This principle will be applied in particular with respect to employment in public administration and public enterprises, and access to public financing for business development.

4.2. Laws regulating employment in public administration will include measures to assure equitable representation of communities in all central and local public bodies and at all levels of employment within such bodies, while respecting the rules concerning competence and integrity that govern public administration. The authorities will take action to correct present imbalances in the composition of the public administration, in particular through the recruitment of members of under-represented communities. Particular attention will be given to ensuring as rapidly as possible that the police services will generally reflect the composition and distribution of the population of Macedonia, as specified in Annex C.

4.3. For the Constitutional Court, one-third of the judges will be chosen by the Assembly by a majority of the total number of Representatives that includes a majority of the total number of Representatives claiming to belong to the communities not in the majority in the population of Macedonia. This procedure also will apply to the election of the Ombudsman (Public Attorney) and the election of three of the members of the Judicial Council.

5. Special Parliamentary Procedures

5.1. On the central level, certain Constitutional amendments in accordance with Annex A and the Law on Local Self-Government cannot be approved without a qualified majority of two-thirds of votes, within which there must be a majority of the votes of Representatives claiming to belong to the communities not in the majority in the population of Macedonia.

5.2. Laws that directly affect culture, use of language, education, personal documentation, and use of symbols, as well as laws on local finances, local elections, the city of Skopje, and boundaries of municipalities must receive a majority of votes, within which there must be a majority of the votes of the Representatives claiming to belong to the communities not in the majority in the population of Macedonia.

6. Education and Use of Languages

6.1. With respect to primary and secondary education, instruction will be provided in the students' native languages, while at the same time uniform standards for academic programs will be applied throughout Macedonia.

6.2. State funding will be provided for university level education in languages spoken by at least 20 percent of the population of Macedonia, on the basis of specific agreements.

6.3. The principle of positive discrimination will be applied in the enrolment in State universities of candidates belonging to communities not in the majority in the population of Macedonia until the enrolment reflects equitably the composition of the population of Macedonia.

6.4. The official language throughout Macedonia and in the international relations of Macedonia is the Macedonian language.

6.5. Any other language spoken by at least 20 percent of the population is also an official language, as set forth herein. In the organs of the Republic of Macedonia, any official language other than Macedonian may be used in accordance with the law, as further elaborated in Annex B. Any person living in a unit of local self-government in which at least 20 percent of the population speaks an official language other than Macedonian may use any official language to communicate with the regional office of the central government with responsibility for that municipality; such an office will reply in that language in addition to Macedonian. Any person may use any official language to communicate with a main office of the central government, which will reply in that language in addition to Macedonian.

6.6. With respect to local self-government, in municipalities where a community comprises at least 20 percent of the population of the municipality, the language of that community will be used as an official language in addition to Macedonian. With respect to languages spoken by less than 20 percent of the population of the municipality, the local authorities will decide democratically on their use in public bodies.

6.7. In criminal and civil judicial proceedings at any level, an accused person or any party will have the right to translation at State expense of all proceedings as well as documents in accordance with relevant Council of Europe documents.

6.8. Any official personal documents of citizens speaking an official language other than Macedonian will also be issued in that language, in addition to the Macedonian language, in accordance with the law.

7. Expression of Identity

    7.1. With respect to emblems, next to the emblem of the Republic of Macedonia, local authorities will be free to place on front of local public buildings emblems marking the identity of the community in the majority in the municipality, respecting international rules and usages.

8. Implementation

    8.1. The Constitutional amendments attached at Annex A will be presented to the Assembly immediately. The parties will take all measures to assure adoption of these amendments within 45 days of signature of this Framework Agreement.

    8.2. The legislative modifications identified in Annex B will be adopted in accordance with the timetables specified therein.

    8.3. The parties invite the international community to convene at the earliest possible time a meeting of international donors that would address in particular macro-financial assistance; support for the financing of measures to be undertaken for the purpose of implementing this Framework Agreement, including measures to strengthen local self-government; and rehabilitation and reconstruction in areas affected by the fighting.

9. Annexes

The following Annexes constitute integral parts of this Framework Agreement:

A. Constitutional Amendments

B. Legislative Modifications

C. Implementation and Confidence-Building Measures

10. Final Provisions

    10.1. This Agreement takes effect upon signature.

    10.2. The English language version of this Agreement is the only authentic version.

    10.3. This Agreement was concluded under the auspices of President Boris Trajkovski.

Done at Skopje, Macedonia on 13 August 2001, in the English language.

ANNEX A
CONSTITUTIONAL AMENDMENTS

Preamble

The citizens of the Republic of Macedonia, taking over responsibility for the present and future of their fatherland, aware and grateful to their predecessors for their sacrifice and dedication in their endeavors and struggle to create an independent and sovereign state of Macedonia, and responsible to future generations to preserve and develop everything that is valuable from the rich cultural inheritance and coexistence within Macedonia, equal in rights and obligations towards the common good, the Republic of Macedonia, in accordance with the tradition of the Krushevo Republic and the decisions of the Antifascist People's Liberation Assembly of Macedonia, and the Referendum of September 8, 1991, they have decided to establish the Republic of Macedonia as an independent, sovereign state, with the intention of establishing and consolidating rule of law, guaranteeing human rights and civil liberties, providing peace and coexistence, social justice, economic well-being and prosperity in the life of the individual and the community, and in this regard through their representatives in the Assembly of the Republic of Macedonia, elected in free and democratic elections, they adopt …

Article 7

(1) The Macedonian language, written using its Cyrillic alphabet, is the official language throughout the Republic of Macedonia and in the international relations of the Republic of Macedonia.

(2) Any other language spoken by at least 20 percent of the population is also an official language, written using its alphabet, as specified below.

(3) Any official personal documents of citizens speaking an official language other than Macedonian shall also be issued in that language, in addition to the Macedonian language, in accordance with the law.

(4) Any person living in a unit of local self-government in which at least 20 percent of the population speaks an official language other than Macedonian may use any official language to communicate with the regional office of the central government with responsibility for that municipality; such an office shall reply in that language in addition to Macedonian. Any person may use any official language to communicate with a main office of the central government, which shall reply in that language in addition to Macedonian.

(5) In the organs of the Republic of Macedonia, any official language other than Macedonian may be used in accordance with the law.

(6) In the units of local self-government where at least 20 percent of the population speaks a particular language, that language and its alphabet shall be used as an official language in addition to the Macedonian language and the Cyrillic alphabet. With respect to languages spoken by less than 20 percent of the population of a unit of local self-government, the local authorities shall decide on their use in public bodies.

Article 8

(1) The fundamental values of the constitutional order of the Republic of Macedonia are:
   – the basic freedoms and rights of the individual and citizen, recognized in international law and set down in the Constitution;
   – equitable representation of persons belonging to all communities in public bodies at all levels and in other areas of public life.

Article 19

(1) The freedom of religious confession is guaranteed.

(2) The right to express one's faith freely and publicly, individually or with others is guaranteed.

(3) The Macedonian Orthodox Church, the Islamic Religious Community in Macedonia, the Catholic Church, and other Religious communities and groups are separate from the state and equal before the law.

(4) The Macedonian Orthodox Church, the Islamic Religious Community in Macedonia, the Catholic Church, and other Religious communities and groups are free to establish schools and other social and charitable institutions, by ways of a procedure regulated by law.

Article 48

(1) Members of communities have a right freely to express, foster and develop their identity and community attributes, and to use their community symbols.

(2) The Republic guarantees the protection of the ethnic, cultural, linguistic and religious identity of all communities.

(3) Members of communities have the right to establish institutions for culture, art, science and education, as well as scholarly and other associations for the expression, fostering and development of their identity.

(4) Members of communities have the right to instruction in their language in primary and secondary education, as determined by law. In schools where education is carried out in another language, the Macedonian language is also studied.

Article 56

(2) The Republic guarantees the protection, promotion and enhancement of the historical and artistic heritage of Macedonia and all communities in Macedonia and the treasures of which it is composed, regardless of their legal status. The law regulates the mode and conditions under which specific items of general interest for the Republic can be ceded for use.

Article 69

(2) For laws that directly affect culture, use of language, education, personal documentation, and use of symbols, the Assembly makes decisions by a majority vote of the Representatives attending, within which there must be a majority of the votes of the Representatives attending who claim to belong to the communities not in the majority in the population of Macedonia. In the event of a dispute within the Assembly regarding the application of this provision, the Committee on Inter-Community Relations shall resolve the dispute.

Article 77

(1) The Assembly elects the Public Attorney by a majority vote of the total number of Representatives, within which there must be a majority of the votes of the total number of Representatives claiming to belong to the communities not in the majority in the population of Macedonia.

(2) The Public Attorney protects the constitutional rights and legal rights of citizens when violated by bodies of state administration and by other bodies and organizations with public mandates. The Public Attorney shall give particular attention to safeguarding the principles of non-discrimination and equitable representation of communities in public bodies at all levels and in other areas of public life.

Article 78

(1) The Assembly shall establish a Committee for Inter-Community Relations.

(2) The Committee consists of seven members each from the ranks of the Macedonians and Albanians within the Assembly, and five members from among the Turks, Vlachs, Romanies and two other communities. The five members each shall be from a different community; if fewer than five other communities are represented in the Assembly, the Public Attorney, after consultation with relevant community leaders, shall propose the remaining members from outside the Assembly.

(3) The Assembly elects the members of the Committee.

(4) The Committee considers issues of inter-community relations in the Republic and makes appraisals and proposals for their solution.

(5) The Assembly is obliged to take into consideration the appraisals and proposals of the Committee and to make decisions regarding them.

(6) In the event of a dispute among members of the Assembly regarding the application of the voting procedure specified in Article 69(2), the Committee shall decide by majority vote whether the procedure applies.

Article 84

The President of the Republic of Macedonia
  – proposes the members of the Council for Inter-Ethnic Relations.

Article 86

(1) The President of the Republic is President of the Security Council of the Republic of Macedonia.

(2) The Security Council of the Republic is composed of the President of the Republic, the President of the Assembly, the Prime Minister, the Ministers heading the bodies of state administration in the fields of security, defence and foreign affairs and three members appointed by the President of the Republic. In appointing the three members, the President shall ensure that the Security Council as a whole equitably reflects the composition of the population of Macedonia.

(3) The Council considers issues relating to the security and defence of the Republic and makes policy proposals to the Assembly and the Government.

Article 104

(1) The Republican Judicial Council is composed of seven members.

(2) The Assembly elects the members of the Council. Three of the members shall be elected by a majority vote of the total number of Representatives, within which there must be a majority of the votes of the total number of Representatives claiming to belong to the communities not in the majority in the population of Macedonia.

Article 109

(1) The Constitutional Court of Macedonia is composed of nine judges.

(2) The Assembly elects six of the judges to the Constitutional Court by a majority vote of the total number of Representatives. The Assembly elects three of the judges by a

majority vote of the total number of Representatives, within which there must be a majority of the votes of the total number of Representatives claiming to belong to the communities not in the majority in the population of Macedonia.

Article 114

(5) Local self-government is regulated by a law adopted by a two-thirds majority vote of the total number of Representatives, within which there must be a majority of the votes of the total number of Representatives claiming to belong to the communities not in the majority in the population of Macedonia. The laws on local finances, local elections, boundaries of municipalities, and the city of Skopje shall be adopted by a majority vote of the Representatives attending, within which there must be a majority of the votes of the Representatives attending who claim to belong to the communities not in the majority in the population of Macedonia.

Article 115

(1) In units of local self-government, citizens directly and through representatives participate in decisionmaking [sic] on issues of local relevance particularly in the fields of public services, urban and rural planning, environmental protection, local economic development, local finances, communal activities, culture, sport, social security and child care, education, health care and other fields determined by law.

Article 131

(1) The decision to initiate a change in the Constitution is made by the Assembly by a two-thirds majority vote of the total number of Representatives.

(2) The draft amendment to the Constitution is confirmed by the Assembly by a majority vote of the total number of Representatives and then submitted to public debate.

(3) The decision to change the Constitution is made by the Assembly by a two-thirds majority vote of the total number of Representatives.

(4) A decision to amend the Preamble, the articles on local self-government, Article 131, any provision relating to the rights of members of communities, including in particular Articles 7, 8, 9, 19, 48, 56, 69, 77, 78, 86, 104 and 109, as well as a decision to add any new provision relating to the subject matter of such provisions and articles, shall require a two-thirds majority vote of the total number of Representatives, within which there must be a majority of the votes of the total number of Representatives claiming to belong to the communities not in the majority in the population of Macedonia.

(5) The change in the Constitution is declared by the Assembly.

ANNEX B
LEGISLATIVE MODIFICATIONS

The parties will take all necessary measures to ensure the adoption of the legislative changes set forth hereafter within the time limits specified.

1. Law on Local Self-Government

   The Assembly shall adopt within 45 days from the signing of the Framework Agreement a revised Law on Local Self-Government. This revised Law shall in no respect be less favorable to the units of local selfgovernment [*sic*] and their autonomy than the draft Law proposed by the Government of the Republic of Macedonia in March 2001. The Law shall include competencies relating to the subject matters set forth in Section 3.1 of the Framework Agreement as additional independent competencies of the units of local selfgovernment [*sic*], and shall conform to Section 6.6 of the Framework Agreement. In addition, the Law shall provide that any State standards or procedures established in any laws concerning areas in which municipalities have independent competencies shall be limited to those which cannot be established as effectively at the local level; such laws shall further promote the municipalities' independent exercise of their competencies.

2. Law on Local Finance

   The Assembly shall adopt by the end of the term of the present Assembly a law on local self-government finance to ensure that the units of local self-government have sufficient resources to carry out their tasks under the revised Law on Local Self-Government. In particular, the law shall:
   - Enable and make responsible units of local self-government for raising a substantial amount of tax revenue;
   - Provide for the transfer to the units of local self-government of a part of centrally raised taxes that corresponds to the functions of the units of local self-government and that takes account of the collection of taxes on their territories; and
   - Ensure the budgetary autonomy and responsibility of the units of local self-government within their areas of competence.

3. Law on Municipal Boundaries

   The Assembly shall adopt by the end of 2002 a revised law on municipal boundaries, taking into account the results of the census and the relevant guidelines set forth in the Law on Local Self-Government.

4. Laws Pertaining to Police Located in the Municipalities

   The Assembly shall adopt before the end of the term of the present Assembly provisions ensuring:
   - That each local head of the police is selected by the council of the municipality concerned from a list of not fewer than three candidates proposed by the Ministry of the Interior, among whom at least one candidate shall belong to the community in the majority in the municipality. In the event the municipal council fails to select any of the candidates proposed within 15 days, the Ministry of the Interior shall propose a second list of not fewer than three new candidates, among

whom at least one candidate shall belong to the community in the majority in the municipality. If the municipal council again fails to select any of the candidates proposed within 15 days, the Minister of the Interior, after consultation with the Government, shall select the local head of police from among the two lists of candidates proposed by the Ministry of the Interior as well as three additional candidates proposed by the municipal council;

– That each local head of the police informs regularly and upon request the council of the municipality concerned;

– That a municipal council may make recommendations to the local head of police in areas including public security and traffic safety; and

– That a municipal council may adopt annually a report regarding matters of public safety, which shall be addressed to the Minister of the Interior and the Public Attorney (Ombudsman).

5. Laws on the Civil Service and Public Administration
The Assembly shall adopt by the end of the term of the present Assembly amendments to the laws on the civil service and public administration to ensure equitable representation of communities in accordance with Section 4.2 of the Framework Agreement.

6. Law on Electoral Districts
The Assembly shall adopt by the end of 2002 a revised Law on Electoral Districts, taking into account the results of the census and the principles set forth in the Law on the Election of Members for the Parliament of the Republic of Macedonia.

7. Rules of the Assembly
The Assembly shall amend by the end of the term of the present Assembly its Rules of Procedure to enable the use of the Albanian language in accordance with Section 6.5 of the Framework Agreement, paragraph 8 below, and the relevant amendments to the Constitution set forth in Annex A.

8. Laws Pertinent to the Use of Languages
The Assembly shall adopt by the end of the term of the present Assembly new legislation regulating the use of languages in the organs of the Republic of Macedonia. This legislation shall provide that:

– Representatives may address plenary sessions and working bodies of the Assembly in [the] languages referred to in Article 7, paragraphs 1 and 2 of the Constitution (as amended in accordance with Annex A);

– Laws shall be published in the languages referred to in Article 7, paragraphs 1 and 2 of the Constitution (as amended in accordance with Annex A); and

– All public officials may write their names in the alphabet of any language referred to in Article 7, paragraphs 1 and 2 of the Constitution (as amended in accordance with Annex A) on any official documents. The Assembly also shall adopt by the end of the term of the present Assembly new legislation on the issuance of personal documents. The Assembly shall amend by the end of the term of the present Assembly all relevant laws to make their provisions on the use of languages fully compatible with Section 6 of the Framework Agreement.

9. Law on the Public Attorney

The Assembly shall amend by the end of 2002 the Law on the Public Attorney as well as the other relevant laws to ensure:

–   That the Public Attorney shall undertake actions to safeguard the principles of non-discrimination and equitable representation of communities in public bodies at all levels and in other areas of public life, and that there are adequate resources and personnel within his office to enable him to carry out this function;
–   That the Public Attorney establishes decentralized offices;
–   That the budget of the Public Attorney is voted separately by the Assembly;
–   That the Public Attorney shall present an annual report to the Assembly and, where appropriate, may upon request present reports to the councils of municipalities in which decentralized offices are established; and
–   That the powers of the Public Attorney are enlarged:
–   To grant to him access to and the opportunity to examine all official documents, it being understood that the Public Attorney and his staff will not disclose confidential information;
–   To enable the Public Attorney to suspend, pending a decision of the competent court, the execution of an administrative act, if he determines that the act may result in an irreparable prejudice to the rights of the interested person; and
–   To give to the Public Attorney the right to contest the conformity of laws with the Constitution before the Constitutional Court.

10. Other Laws

The Assembly shall enact all legislative provisions that may be necessary to give full effect to the Framework Agreement and amend or abrogate all provisions incompatible with the Framework Agreement.

ANNEX C
IMPLEMENTATION AND CONFIDENCE-BUILDING MEASURES

1. International Support
    1.1. The parties invite the international community to facilitate, monitor and assist in the implementation of the provisions of the Framework Agreement and its Annexes, and request such efforts to be coordinated by the EU in cooperation with the Stabilization and Association Council.
2. Census and Elections
    2.1. The parties confirm the request for international supervision by the Council of Europe and the European Commission of a census to be conducted in October 2001.
    2.2. Parliamentary elections will be held by 27 January 2002. International organizations, including the OSCE, will be invited to observe these elections.
3. Refugee Return, Rehabilitation and Reconstruction
    3.1. All parties will work to ensure the return of refugees who are citizens or legal residents of Macedonia and displaced persons to their homes within the shortest

possible timeframe, and invite the international community and in particular UNHCR to assist in these efforts.

3.2. The Government with the participation of the parties will complete an action plan within 30 days after the signature of the Framework Agreement for rehabilitation of and reconstruction in areas affected by the hostilities. The parties invite the international community to assist in the formulation and implementation of this plan.

3.3. The parties invite the European Commission and the World Bank to rapidly convene a meeting of international donors after adoption in the Assembly of the Constitutional amendments in Annex A and the revised Law on Local Self-Government to support the financing of measures to be undertaken for the purpose of implementing the Framework Agreement and its Annexes, including measures to strengthen local self-government and reform the police services, to address macro-financial assistance to the Republic of Macedonia, and to support the rehabilitation and reconstruction measures identified in the action plan identified in paragraph 3.2.

4. Development of Decentralized Government

4.1. The parties invite the international community to assist in the process of strengthening local selfgovernment [*sic*]. The international community should in particular assist in preparing the necessary legal amendments related to financing mechanisms for strengthening the financial basis of municipalities and building their financial management capabilities, and in amending the law on the boundaries of municipalities.

5. Non-Discrimination and Equitable Representation

5.1. Taking into account i.a. [*sic*] the recommendations of the already established governmental commission, the parties will take concrete action to increase the representation of members of communities not in the majority in Macedonia in public administration, the military, and public enterprises, as well as to improve their access to public financing for business development.

5.2. The parties commit themselves to ensuring that the police services will by 2004 generally reflect the composition and distribution of the population of Macedonia. As initial steps toward this end, the parties commit to ensuring that 500 new police officers from communities not in the majority in the population of Macedonia will be hired and trained by July 2002, and that these officers will be deployed to the areas where such communities live. The parties further commit that 500 additional such officers will be hired and trained by July 2003, and that these officers will be deployed on a priority basis to the areas throughout Macedonia where such communities live. The parties invite the international community to support and assist with the implementation of these commitments, in particular through screening and selection of candidates and their training. The parties invite the OSCE, the European Union, and the United States to send an expert team as quickly as possible in order to assess how best to achieve these objectives.

5.3. The parties also invite the OSCE, the European Union, and the United States to increase training and assistance programs for police, including:
- professional, human rights, and other training;
- technical assistance for police reform, including assistance in screening, selection and promotion processes;
- development of a code of police conduct;
- cooperation with respect to transition planning for hiring and deployment of police officers from communities not in the majority in Macedonia; and
- deployment as soon as possible of international monitors and police advisors in sensitive areas, under appropriate arrangements with relevant authorities.

5.4. The parties invite the international community to assist in the training of lawyers, judges and prosecutors from members of communities not in the majority in Macedonia in order to be able to increase their representation in the judicial system.

6. Culture, Education and Use of Languages
6.1. The parties invite the international community, including the OSCE, to increase its assistance for projects in the area of media in order to further strengthen radio, TV and print media, including Albanian language and multi-ethnic media. The parties also invite the international community to increase professional media training programs for members of communities not in the majority in Macedonia. The parties also invite the OSCE to continue its efforts on projects designed to improve inter-ethnic relations.

6.2. The parties invite the international community to provide assistance for the implementation of the Framework Agreement in the area of higher education.

August 13, 2001

Appendix C

ANALYSIS OF THE FULFILLMENT OF THE EUROPEAN COMMISSION'S RECOMMENDATIONS TO ALBANIA, NOVEMBER 2010, ACCORDING TO 2011 AND 2012 PROGRESS REPORTS

Key Priorities	Analytical Report 2010	Progress Report 2011	Progress Report 2012
Key priority 1: Proper functioning of parliament on the basis of a constructive and sustained political dialogue among all political parties	• Political dialogue is highly confrontational and unproductive, or non-existent; • Quality of legislation passed is not of an adequate standard; • Parliament does not function as an independent institution; • Lack of effective parliamentary oversight over the executive; • Misuse of the position of parliamentary speaker on the legislative agenda; • Relatively weak parliament's structures, due to politicization of parliament's staff and frequent turnover.	• Some modest progress in parliamentary rules and practice and an increase in the parliament's administrative capacities; • Good cooperation between the ruling majority and the opposition on the Action Plan of key priorities of the opinion in the parliamentary committee for European integration; • Lack of constructive political dialogue and increased confrontational rhetoric; • Quality of legislative drafting and consultation with third parties needs to be significantly improved; • Insufficient progress regarding legislative scrutiny and the oversight function of the executive; • Lack of administrative capacity in parliament and politicization of appointments hamper the independence and professionalism of staff. **EC Conclusion: Insufficient progress**	• Dialogue and rhetoric in the parliament has improved significantly; • More constructive atmosphere was noted, in particular during committee and plenary meetings; • *It is essential that the revised parliamentary rules of procedure are adopted.*[1] **EU Conclusion: Progress has been made**
Key priority 2: Adoption of pending laws requiring a reinforced majority in parliament	• Key pieces of legislation requiring a qualified majority have not been approved.	• The adoption of laws requiring a three-fifths majority is still pending	• All pending laws requiring a reinforced three-fifth-majority vote were adopted.

	EC Conclusion: No progress made	EU Conclusion: Progress has been made
Key priority 3: Appointment of the Ombudsman and High and Constitutional Court Judges	• no progress made on the appointment of the Ombudsman • Parliament has not yet ensured an orderly hearing and a vote on Constitutional and High Court appointments, which continue to be politicized.	• Ombudsman was appointed following a transparent and merit-based selection process will public hearings, followed by a consensual vote in the parliament; • Hearing and voting process in parliament were conducted for the presidential nomination of a judge to the High Court.
• Work of the Ombudsman's Office has been hampered inter alia by the pending selection of the new Ombudsman; • Politicization of the appointment of judges to the High and Constitutional Courts, which undermines their neutrality and independence.		
Key priority 4: Reform of the electoral code in line with OSCE/ODIHR recommendations	• Electoral reform is blocked by the political stalemate and lack of political dialogue between the main parties.	• Revised electoral code was consensually adopted by Parliament on July 19.
• Electoral reform, necessary in view of upcoming local government elections, is substantially delayed.		
Key priority 5: Elections conducted in line with European and international standards	• May local elections met some of the international standards (competitiveness, transparency; peaceful voting process, media coverage); • Other international standards were not met (lengthy counting process and high controversy over the results of the Tirana mayoral election, partisan decisions by the CEC, controversy with regard to the handling of appeals by the Electoral College).	• May local elections met some of the international standards (competitiveness, transparency; positive voting day, media coverage); • Other international standards were not met (lengthy counting process and high controversy over the results of the Tirana mayoral election, partisan decisions by the CEC, controversy with regard to the handling of appeals by the Electoral College).
• June 2009 legislative elections met most international standards and were an improvement over past practices; • Shortcomings of June 2009 legislative elections should be addressed, particularly the politicization of processes such as the vote count.		

Key Priorities	Analytical Report 2010	Progress Report 2011	Progress Report 2012
		EC Conclusion: Insufficient progress	**EC Conclusion: Insufficient progress**
Key priority 6: Public administration reform	• Necessary amendments to the civil service law need to be undertaken; • Concerns remain regarding the implementation of the legal framework; • Public service is very politicized, lacks transparency in appointments and is marked by high turnover of staff.	• Some reform measures were completed (the CMD decision on structure and organization of public bodies); • Amendments to the civil service law have not been completed; • Implementation of the existing laws and administrative acts remains weak (i.e. implementation of Prime Ministerial Order setting a maximum limit of 2.5% temporary appointments in civil service positions remains poor); • Independent, merit-based and professional civil service has yet to be achieved.	• Law on the Organization and Functioning of Public Administration has been adopted; • Council of Ministers' decision on defining the structure and organization of public institutions has been implemented by 13 of the 14 ministries; • Implementation of the Law on Inspections is progressing very slowly; • Prime Minister's Order setting a maximum limit of 2.5% on temporary contracts has been considerably implemented; • Rate of execution of Civil Service Commission decisions by state institutions remains very low, even when these decisions are upheld in court and become legally binding; • Legislative and institutional framework for public administration is still marked by deficiencies; • *It is now essential to adopt the amendments to the Civil Service Law.*

	EC Conclusion: Limited progress	EU Conclusion: Progress has been made
Key priority 7: Rule of law	• Lack of a tradition of judicial independence; • Justice system suffers from corruption, lack of transparency, accountability and efficiency; • Reforming of judiciary should continue by adopting a comprehensive judicial reform strategy and key pending laws.	• Judicial reform strategy and action plan were adopted, but not the key pending laws requiring a qualified majority voting; • No further progress has been made as regards the independence and efficiency of the judiciary; • No steps have been taken to combat corruption in the judiciary, including limiting or abolishing the immunity of judges.	• Law on Administrative Courts (reinforced majority), the Law on the National Judicial Conference and the Law on the Profession of Lawyer have been adopted; • Judicial reform strategy and the relevant action plan of March 2012 have started to be implemented; • Important legislation to further strengthen the independence, accountability and efficiency of the judiciary still awaits finalization, adoption and implementation; • Good progress is reported in the fight against corruption in the judiciary, through the limitation of the immunity of judges. • *It is now essential that amendments to the Law on the High Court are adopted*

Key Priorities	Analytical Report 2010	Progress Report 2011	Progress Report 2012
Key priority 8: Anti-corruption	• Legal framework addressing GRECO recommendations should be completed; • Concerns over the unlimited immunity of certain public officials should be addressed; • Efficient implementation of the anti-corruption strategy and action plan needs to be demonstrated; • Proven track record of convictions in corruption cases should be established at all levels; • Corruption is prevalent in many areas and is a particularly serious problem	**EC Conclusion: Limited progress** • Progress was made in strengthening the legal framework by implementing Group of States against Corruption (GRECO) recommendations; • Institutional framework to combat corruption has been further developed; • Implementation of specific actions remains overall ineffective and results are insufficient; • Effective investigation of corruption is obstructed by the immunity of high public officials; • Track record of investigations, prosecutions and convictions is lacking at all levels; • Corruption prevails in many areas and continues to be a particularly serious problem.	**EC Conclusion: Moderate Progress** • Moderate progress has occurred in strengthening the legal framework, including the implementation of recommendations of the GRECO related to incrimination and political party financing; • Some progress was made, through constitutional changes, to restrict the immunity of high level public officials and judges; • No adequate track record of investigations, prosecution and convictions has been established at any levels; • Corruption is prevalent in many areas and continues to be a particularly serious problem.
Key priority 9: Fight against organized crime	• Positive results have been achieved in reform and adequate resources of the law enforcement authorities; • Fight against organized crime should be strengthened through a proactive approach and with a solid track record of convictions; • Organized crime remains a matter of concern.	**EC Conclusion: Limited progress** • Progress has been made in fighting organized crime, through good international cooperation and implementation of the "anti-mafia" law; • Efforts need to be maintained in building up of a credible track record of proactive investigations, prosecutions and conviction; • Organized crime remains a challenge.	**EC Conclusion: Moderate progress** • Some progress with international cooperation has been made. • Operational cooperation with neighboring countries, EU Member States and Europol needs to be further enhanced; • Efforts need to be stepped up on coordination between law enforcement institutions and consolidating a track record of investigations, prosecutions and convictions.

	EC Conclusion: Progress has been made	EC Conclusion: Some progress can be reported
Key priority 10: Property rights	• Piecemeal property legislation, numerous agencies with overlapping competencies and widespread corruption; • Improperly functioning land registry system; • Lack of enforcement of European Court of Human Rights judgments' against the state; • Property issue remains unresolved.	• Little visible progress in developing a comprehensive strategy for property reform; • Fragmentation of responsibilities and lack of coordination between the various institutions involved; • Legal uncertainty and a systemic risk of corruption; • Process of initial registration of immovable property has not yet been completed; • No timetable exists for enforcement of ECHR judgments regarding property rights; • Property rights remain an issue of great concern.	• Some progress was achieved in the area of property rights, notably through the adoption of a new law on registration of immovable property and through the adoption of a cross-cutting strategy and action plan; • Efficient coordination and monitoring is necessary to ensure the implementation of the strategy and consistency between the legislation in force and future initiatives; • Land registry has not yet been completed; • Former owners still have unresolved claims for compensation for and restitution of property confiscated under the communist regime.
	EC Conclusion: Little progress	EC Conclusion: Some progress
Key priority 11: Protection of human rights (women, children, Roma and anti-discrimination policies)	• Functioning of the legal and institutional framework needs to be ensured; • Framework law on children's rights needs to be adopted; • Existing strategies for gender equality and fighting domestic violence need to be effectively implemented; • Roma community constitutes the most vulnerable minority group in Albania.	• New national strategy on gender equality and the fight against domestic violence has been adopted; • Law on Protection from Discrimination has started to be implemented; • Consistent implementation of existing legislative and policy needs to be ensured; • Concerns remain over continued discrimination against certain vulnerable groups; • Roma community continues to be marginalized and lacks access to social protection and services.	• Very limited progress can be noted in enhancing the legislative and policy framework regarding respect for and protection of minorities and cultural rights; • Mandate of the State Committee for Protection of Minorities has not been enhanced; • Work has not started towards drafting a comprehensive legislation on minorities • Very limited progress was made regarding Roma inclusion

Key Priorities	Analytical Report 2010	Progress Report 2011	Progress Report 2012
		EC Conclusion: Partial progress	**EC Conclusion: Very limited progress**
Key priority 12: Improvement of treatment of the detainees in police stations, pre-trial detention and prisons	• Ill treatment in police custody and the situation of mentally ill prisoners need to be addressed.	• Some progress has been made concerning the penitentiary infrastructure; • Cases of ill treatment continue during arrest and police custody (in the aftermath of the events of January 21, 2011); • Treatment of mentally ill offenders needs to be improved.	• Progress has been made concerning the *prison system* • State Police started cooperating with two non-governmental organizations • Concerns remain over reported cases of ill-treatment and failure by police to systematically observe procedures for arrest and custody • Plans have been made for building a special medical institution for treating mentally ill offenders • Continued over use of pre-trial detention is a concern
		EC Conclusion: Some progress	**EC Conclusion: Progress has been made**

Source: Data in the first three columns (Key Priorities, Analytical Report 2010 and Progress Report 2011) are from European Movement Albania (EMA).[2] Data in the fourth column (Progress Report 2012) are from the author, following the EMA methodology.[3]

Appendix D

GEOGRAPHIC AND POLITICAL DIVISIONS OF HISTORICAL MACEDONIA

Figure 5. Geographic and political divisions of the historical Macedonia[1]

NOTES

Chapter 1 Introduction

1 Interestingly, both Leszek Balcerowicz and Laar come from politics. Balcerowicz was Poland's deputy prime minister during 1989–91 and 1997–2000; Mart Laar was prime minister of Estonia during 1991–94 and 1999–2002.

2 In its 2010 Opinion on Albania's application for membership of the European Union, the European Commission explained:

> negotiations for accession to the European Union should be opened with Albania once the country has achieved the necessary degree of compliance with the membership criteria and in particular the Copenhagen political criteria requiring the stability of institutions guaranteeing notably democracy and rule of law.

In the Opinion, the EC laid out some very specific policy prescriptions that represent the institutional threshold that Albania should achieve in order to receive the EU candidate status. Those policies are:

- Ensure the proper functioning of parliament on the basis of a constructive and sustained dialogue among all political parties.
- Pending legislation requiring a reinforced majority in parliament.
- Appoint an ombudsman, and ensure an orderly hearing and voting process in parliament for constitutional and high court appointments.
- Modify the legislative framework for elections in line with Organization for Security and Co-operation in Europe/Office for Democratic Institutions and Human Rights (OSCE/ODIHR) recommendations.
- Ensure elections are conducted in line with European and international standards.
- Complete essential steps in public administration reform including amendments to the civil service law and strengthening of the Department of Public Administration, with a view to enhancing professionalism and de-politicization of public administration and to strengthening a transparent, merit-based approach to appointments and promotions.
- Strengthen the rule of law through the adoption and implementation of a reform strategy for the judiciary, ensuring the independence, efficiency and accountability of judicial institutions.
- Effectively implement the government's anti-corruption strategy and action plan, by removing obstacles to investigations, in particular of judges, ministers and members of parliament; develop a solid track record of proactive investigations, prosecutions and convictions in corruption cases at all levels.
- Strengthen the fight against organized crime, based on threat assessment and proactive investigation, increased cooperation with regional and EU partners and better coordination of law enforcement agencies, and develop a solid track record in this area.
- Prepare, adopt and implement a national strategy and action plan on property rights following broad stakeholder consultation and taking ECtHR case law into account; this should cover restitution, compensation and legalization processes.
- Take concrete steps to reinforce the protection of human rights, notably for women, children and Roma, and to effectively implement anti-discrimination policies.

- Take additional measures to improve treatment of detainees in police stations, pre-trial detention and prisons. Strengthen the judicial follow-up of cases of ill treatment and improve the application of recommendations of the ombudsman in this field.

See European Commission, "Commission Opinion on Albania's Application for Membership of the European Union." COM (2010) 680 {SEC (2010) 1335}. Brussels. November 9, 2010. Online: http://ec.europa.eu/enlargement/pdf/key_documents/2010/package/al_opinion_2010_en.pdf (accessed March 25, 2013).

Chapter 2 A Sectorial Contextual Approach to the Effects of EU Membership Conditionality on Eastern European Institutional Reforms

1 The similarities and differences among the selected countries and institutional reforms will become even more evident in the course of tracing institutional reform processes. However, several distinct differences exist even among former Yugoslav constitutional units (six republics and two autonomous regions). One of the major differences among them is the nature of Macedonian nationalism as a Titoist creation. As the late Albanian-Macedonian intellectual and politician Arbën Xhaferi told me in an interview with him in the summer of 2009, during the Titoist Yugoslavia all nationalism was suppressed, with the exception of Macedonian nationalism. The latter was rather encouraged within the same Yugoslav nationalist logic invented by Tito: it would serve as a bulwark against Albanian, Bulgarian and Greek potential claims over Macedonia.

2 Indeed, when Rupnik (2000) develops his discussion of the Habsburg versus the Ottoman factor, he mainly focuses on the former, while the reader is invited to assume the opposite for the latter.

3 For the relevance of such a feature in selecting the countries, see Rupnik (2000).

4 The region belonged to the Ottoman Empire and was captured by Serbia during the First Balkan War, 1912, and became internationally recognized as its territory with the 1913 Treaty of London. In the interwar period, it was known as Južna Srbija (Southern Serbia) or Stara Srbija (Old Serbia). During the Second World War (between 1941–44), the Albanian-populated western territories of the Vardar Banovina, namely Pollog, were occupied by the Italian-ruled Albania, while the pro-German Bulgaria occupied the remainder. After the Second World War and the reconstitution of Titoist Yugoslavia as a federal state, the Vardar province, which was established in 1944, under the 1946 Yugoslav Constitution became a republic known as the People's Republic of Macedonia within the new Socialist Federal Republic of Yugoslavia. The name was changed to the Socialist Republic of Macedonia in the 1963 Constitution of Yugoslavia.

5 CIA World Factbook 2007. Online: https://www.cia.gov/library/publications/the-world-factbook/index.html (accessed September 3, 2010).

Chapter 3 Constitutional Reforms in Albania and Macedonia: Conditioning Consociational Practices for EU and Domestic Democratic Stability

1 Interview with Arbën Xhaferi, a member of the Sobranie and former chairman of the Democratic Party of the Albanians in Macedonia. Xhaferri stated:

Macedonia was founded as an independent republic to resolve the Balkan context of that territory between the Bulgarians, Serbs, Greeks and, inescapably, Albanians. To escape the ethnic, geopolitical, and geostrategic frictions, first was created Yugoslavia I. Then in Yugoslavia II, that friction-generating territory was transformed into the Republic of Macedonia. Now the state was created; what was needed was the nation. In that formation process, J. B. Tito elaborated the strategy of the Slavo-Macedonian mechanism. While all other nationalisms in Tito Yugoslavia were suppressed and oppressed, Macedonian nationalism was the only one that was encouraged. The cultivation of Macedonian nationalism, without repercussions and other hurdles, created among the Macedonians unrealistic and megalomaniacal aspirations which stifled the development of other peoples, especially the Albanians. Such stifling is manifested in all the realms of life: employment, culture, education, etc. During the 1980s came the prohibition of the Albanian topology, the naming of the Albanian babies with Albanian names, the elimination of classes where the lessons were conducted only in Albanian and the creation of ethnically mixed classes in only Macedonian language. (Interview with Arbën Xhaferi).

2 See for instance interviews with citizens of Macedonia conducted by Lebamoff and Ilievski (2008).

3 As the European Stability Initiative's report notes in the case of the Macedonian mix populated city of Kičevo (in Albanian Kërçovë), "[t]he majority of urban Macedonians in Kičevo have acquired secondary or higher education. Their privileged access to the education system was the key to participating in the benefits of the socialist economy, in which jobs were strictly graded according to educational requirements" (2002, 5). See European Stability Initiative, "Ahmeti's Village: The Political Economy of Interethnic Relations in Macedonia" (Skopje and Berlin, October 1, 2002). Online: http://www.esiweb.org/pdf/esi_document_id_36.pdf (accessed May 18, 2013).

4 According to the European Stability Initiative Report, "the exclusion of Albanians from the socialist sector and the benefits it offered have forced them to seek out economic strategies, chiefly labor migration and small-scale trade, which have left them much better equipped to survive the collapse of the socialist system" (ibid.).

5 A phrase from the national anthem of Macedonia.

6 Parts of this section are borrowed from a paper that I have co-authored with Arben Imami (Peshkopia and Imami 2007).

7 While the DKK stipulated the non-partisanship of the president of Albania, the constitutional amendments provided only a president who was not a chairperson of any party. With Eduart Selami as his puppet chairman of the PD, Berisha kept full control of his party.

8 Those claims were later shown to be correct as the former president of Montenegro, Momir Bulatović, confirmed in his book *Pravila Ćutanja* (The Rules of Keeping Silent, 2001). In 2006, the former president of Albania also admitted he had broken the UN embargo against Yugoslavia (OhmyNews, "Albania Smuggled Oil to Milosevic Regime," February 12, 2006. Online: http://english.ohmynews.com/articleview/article_view.asp?no=332383&rel_no=1, accessed December 15, 2013).

9 The Albanian viewers were accustomed of watching Berisha asserting on his tightly controlled national TV that his enemies' reason of existence was for him to defeat them.

10 During the presentation of his government program on July 28, 1997, the Albanian prime minister Fatos Nano stated:

"The necessity of the constitutional reform through its drafting and its approval both in Kuvend and by a referendum lies on the widely accepted fact that changes of 1992 were retrograding, while latter amendments did not manage to be framed into an organic totality. The necessity of this cornerstone is linked with reform success in other institutions, with the establishment of an independent judicial system, the implementation of an efficient decentralization of the local governance and the approval of stable electoral laws that guarantee free and fair elections" (from the Archive of the Kuvend, July 28, 1997; translated by the author).

11 Typical for Eastern European institutional reforms is the involvement of more than one international actor. Often, other IOs play role in the sectorial development besides the EU, such as the CoE, OSCE and some UN agencies. Among the state actors, the US plays a very important role especially in the Balkans, since the lack of democratic stability in the region might destabilize Kosovo, a country in which the US has invested much of its international credibility.

12 See Council of Europe, "Reply to Recommendation 1312 (1997), Doc. 8139: Honouring of Obligations and Commitments by Albania," The Committee of Ministers. Online: http://assembly.coe.int/ASP/Doc/XrefDocDetails_E.asp?FileID=8577 (accessed May 24, 2013).

The Committee of Ministers adopted it on June 4, 1998 at the 634th Meeting of the Ministers' Deputies.

13 Arben Imami, the former co-chair of the Commission for Drafting the Constitution and minister for legislative reform and relationship with the Kuvend is a colleague and friend with whom I have co-authored and published several articles on this topic (see Peshkopia and Imami 2007, 2008).

14 Organization for Security and Co-operation in Europe/Office for Democratic Institutions and Human Rights, Election Observation Mission Report, "Republic of Albania Parliamentary Elections, July 3, 2005: Final Report," Warsaw, November 7, 2005, 1. Online: http://www.osce.org/odihr/elections/albania/14487 (accessed 24 May 2013).

15 Ibid., 5.

16 Ibid., 25.

17 With the party as an impersonal candidate but also as the only possible donation recipient, there existed fewer incentives for the cronies of specific candidates to donate to party headquarters. Moreover, candidates from proportional lists have fewer incentives to individually attack candidates of other parties' lists, since that would hardly benefit them. And finally, the impact of gangs on violating Albanian electoral process is related to the tribal loyalty of the clan to its member who happens to run for office. If the candidate is located in a "safe" place in the list, gang support for him would be redundant; but if the candidate is not located in a "safe" position, gang violence might not be enough to shore him up to electoral victory.

18 This was suggested as a revision of our common paper (Peshkopia and Imami 2007) by Imami who, during the process of constitutional amendments was Premier Berisha's director of the cabinet/chief of staff.

19 See "Tragjedia e Gërdecit, rritet numri i viktimave" [The tragedy of Gërdec, increases the number of victims], *Shekulli*, March 16, 2008; "Tragjedia e Gërdecit: Arrestohen drejtori i MEICO dhe pronari i firmës" [The tragedy of Gërdec: Arrested the director of MEICO and the owner of the company], *24 Orë*, March 17, 2008.

20 For such references, for instance, see Roskin (2002) and Brown (2000).

21 See *Thessaloniki*, "EU–Western Balkans Summit Declaration," 10229/03 (Presse 163), *Thessaloniki*, June 21, 2003. Online: http://www.emins.org/sr/aktivnosti/konferencije/solun/pdf/zvanicna/deklar-e.pdf (accessed November 11, 2010). As the declaration states:

> The EU reiterates its unequivocal support to the European perspective of the Western Balkan countries. The future of the Balkans is within the European Union. The ongoing enlargement and the signing of the Treaty of Athens in April 2003 inspire and encourage the countries of the Western Balkans to follow the same successful path. Preparation for integration into European structures and ultimate membership into the European Union, through adoption of European standards, is now the big challenge ahead. The Croatian application for EU membership is currently under examination by the Commission. The speed of movement ahead lies in the hands of the countries of the region.

22 Interview with Arben Imami, by that time Albania's prime minister's chief of staff.

23 According to an anonymous source from the PD fraction in the Kuvend.

24 For the notion of constitutional nationalism and the case of Macedonia, see Robert M. Hayden (1992, 655).

25 Interview with Arbën Xhaferi, former chairman of the Democratic Party of the Albanians and member of the Sobranie.

26 In the first draft I wrote that phrase in the form of "the Macedonian case." Later, after an interview with Arbën Xhaferi of the Democratic Party of the Albanians, I realized that such an expression would presume the patronage of the ethnic Macedonians on the case. Thus, I thought it more appropriate to avoid that grammatical form unless I have to refer explicitly to other author's usage of the "Slavo-Macedonian" form. However, it was not untill I was

told by my Macedonian friends that I learned the expression Slavo-Macedonian is insulting to them, and the term "Macedonian" is the only appropriate way to address them. It was the summer of 2009, the time when the openly declared Slavic origin of the Macedonians (a position defended mainly by the political left) came under attack, and the VMRO–DPMNE inspired and construed version of the ancient Macedonian ascendancy of the contemporary Macedonians was progressing slowly but surely, in a typical Balkan, mythological way. Names such as Alexander the Great Highway and Alexander the Great Airport perplex those who remember the former president of Macedonia, Kiro Gligorov, to have asserted in the early years of the new country that Macedonians were a Slavic people. Today, one can see on the streets of Skopje, ancient Greek statues excavated in central and southern Macedonia innocuously decorating sidewalks and public parks, but serving the political purpose of establishing a new Macedonian identity. Politics underpin the entire process, since Macedonians need to confront Greece, which blocked the country's NATO membership in April 2009, in a contention over the name of the country, and which continues to block any accession negotiation of the country with the EU.

27 During my efforts to trace constitutional reform in Macedonia empirically, and, consequentially, local decentralization reform, I refer in several instances to data and their interpretation from Daskalovski's (2006) book *Walking on the Edge: Consolidating Multiethnic Macedonia 1989–2004*. Notwithstanding the lack of clarity from a linguistic standpoint, Daskalovski's book is a valuable resource of data and looks at the conflict from within. Even through Daskalovski tries to take a more balanced position, for him, ethnic inequalities in Macedonia were only "perceived." In a section that spans pages 114–30, Daskalovski wonders about the "paradox" that, while EU, NATO and US diplomats and politicians were criticizing the UÇK/NLA, they were asking the Macedonian government to show proportionality in its response to the crisis and were also urging constitutional changes in the country. Daskalovski overemphasizes security concerns over international involvement in Macedonia, but fails to see that those security concerns were threatening the very existence of Macedonia. In tune with the Macedonian mood, Daskalovski misses no opportunity to point to security threats from Kosovo, echoing Macedonian official position that, while there was nothing wrong with the Constitution of 1991 and the nation state, the Macedonian conflict was imported from Kosovo. In spite of immense evidence that Daskalovski himself offers, clearly showing that the only reason why Macedonia today still exists is international intervention to prevent its dissolution by brokering an agreement, he seems inclined to share the Macedonian official view and ubiquitous conviction that, as Xhaferi has pointed out in an interview with the author, what happened was "an international conspiracy where Albanians were only an instrument." As Xhaferi comments the constitutional amendments spurn from the Ohrid Agreement:

There are attempts in Macedonia to offer Albanians inapplicable rights. The constitution and laws provide unrestricted laws, but only verbally. The system was built so as to create psychological leverage during the implementation process as well as during the negotiations, with the Macedonian part who lacked negotiation will. This sort of perpetual intransigence negatively influenced the agreement, as well as demonstrated the lack of willingness to implement it. As such, paradoxically, this agreement exemplified the end of war by forging articles that justified inequality, namely the ethnocentric concept of state built on a multiethnic social environment. Hence, when the consensus for the concept of state to represent the multiethnic reality of Macedonia was achieved, that reflection was not optimal, due to the conviction of Macedonian negotiators that the war was an international conspiracy wherein Albanians were only an instrument. The obstructions to the implementation of the agreement come only from Macedonians. Now [in 2009] after eight years, not only the topics of the agreement concerning the representation of diversities in the concept of state are not implemented, but such agreements have been annulled or modified, that is, the official application of the Albanian language, the adequate representation, decentralization, territorial organization, the official application of the flag, the agreement for the status of former combatants in the conflict of 2001, amnesty for all the participant in that conflict, except for cases that would eventually be proceeded by the Hague Tribunal, as well as meeting the deadline for the implementation of the Ohrid Agreement, that is, year 2004. (Translated from Albanian by the author).

Moreover, following Daskalovski's course of the conflict, one reads only for government's military success; then, all of a sudden, the rebels take Aračinovo and, practically, begin the siege of the capital. Daskalovski justifies government's moderate use of force with international pleas for restraint. However, the UÇK/NLA leaders have told me that the Macedonian government spared no military resources to achieve an impossible victory. On the contrary, UÇK/NLA fighters stated that they were constrained in use of violence, since much of the conflict unfolded in Albanian heavy populated territories. As my source went on, "the reason for this nature of our struggle was that we wanted to liberate our territories from Macedonians, not occupy their territories."

28 As Lebamoff and Ilievski point out

[t]here is evidence that newly independent Republic of Macedonia was constructed in a manner that protects Macedonian ethno-national identity. While ethnic Albanians have kin states of Albania and Kosovo, the Republic of Macedonia is considered critical to the protection and nurturance of the Macedonian ethno-nation by ethnic Macedonians. Yet Albanian Macedonians were fearful of repression and second-class citizen status if the new state remained defined in Macedonian ethno-nationalist terms, particularly since they were (at Macedonian independence in 1991, and today) underrepresented in public employment, higher education, the sciences, the military and law enforcement, and white-collar professions. (Lebamoff and Ilievski 2008, 8)

29 *Borba*, October 17, 1990, 4, cited by Hayden (1992).

30 Interview with Arbën Xhaferi.

31 Lebamoff and Ilievski cite the former deputy prime minister Vasil Tupurkovski recounting in an interview, "Macedonian political elites did not accept the idea of reaching an 'historical agreement with our ethnic Albanians'" (Lebamoff and Ilievski 2008, 15).

32 In a conversation with the deputy speaker of the Sobranie and PPD chairman Abdurraman Aliti in 1995, Aliti offered a very similar explanation for the reason of Albanian participation in the Macedonian political system. He emphasized Albanian fears that an unstable Macedonia would have been an attractive lure for the militaristic Serbia; and also expressed his confidence that participating in the system would be better to improve the position of the Albanians in the Macedonian society. The events that followed proved him only partially right.

33 "*Me punue brenda sistemit*" [working within the system] was the political doctrine of the Albanian politics in Macedonia during the 1990s.

34 According to Marko (2004), the number of Albanian judges increased from 1.7 per cent of the total judges in 1991 to 8.7 per cent in 1996; the number of Albanian Macedonian students increased from the share of 6.4 per cent that they had at the University of Prishtina in 1991, to 15.7 per cent in the Macedonian universities in the 1997–98 academic year. In an interview in the summer of 1995, the Albanian deputy minister of education of Macedonia Hasan Jashari revealed that the number of the Albanian high schools have increased from five to nineteen (Sejdiaj 1998, 214).

35 Albanians boycotted the referendum for independence held on September 8, 1991, as well as the population censuses of 1992 and 1994.

36 For instance, on March 31, 1992, up to 40,000 Albanians demonstrated in the Macedonian capital Skopje, asking the international community not to recognize Macedonia as an independent country "until the state grants Macedonian Albanians the right to autonomy in regions and villages where ethnic Albanians make up the majority" (Daskalovski 2006, 68). Moreover, at a December 1992 press conference, one of the leaders of the PPD-PDK alliance,

Muhamed Halili, warned that if Macedonian elites did not change policy the Albanians would seek to achieve their ends "through acts of civil disobedience" (Daskalovski 2006, 69); as for the Albanian project of political autonomy, I have already mentioned their symbolic act of declaration of independence in an unrecognized referendum in January 1992, as well as the formal act of the declaration of the Albanian Autonomous Republic of Illyrida in the southwestern Macedonian city of Struga, April 1992.

37 When, during my conversations with Abdurraman Aliti from 1994–96, the latter gave me the long list of Albanian complaints, I asked him whether or not they had a chance to explain this situation to the Macedonian elites and foreign officials, Aliti asserted "many times." The same answer of the same question has been given to me during my exchanges and interviews with Arbën Xhaferi.

38 The Weapons Affair is one of the murkiest spots in Macedonia's recent history, and a deep scar in the interethnic relations in the post-Yugoslav Macedonia. In late September 1993, nine ethnic Albanians, including Macedonia's then deputy minister of defense Hysen Haskaj and deputy minister of health Imer Imeri, both from the PPD, were arrested; in January of the next year, the secretary general of PPD Mitat Emini was added to the list of arrests, all of them charged with conspiracy to organize armed gangs. The passionate involvement of the Albanian government in accusing Emini as a betrayer of the Albanian cause, and Albania's PD involvement in restructuring and, consequentially, splitting the PPD, continues to remain a mystery for those who were attentively following the Macedonian developments in the early 1990s. A trial was staged in 1994, and an ethnic-Macedonian-dominated court found all of them guilty and sentenced them with jail time ranging from five to eight years. In an interview several years after he had served his one-year jail sentence, Fiqiri Sejdiaj cites Emini to maintain that the so-called armed gangs were in fact self-organized Albanian villagers in the border of Macedonia with then Serbian occupied Kosova who were trying to defend themselves against incursions of Arkan and Šešelj paramilitaries who were in the business of terrorizing and looting Albanian villages throughout Kosova and, apparently, northwest Macedonia as well (Sejdiaj 1998, 91–108). An Interpol-wanted thug, Željko Ražnatović Arkan led paramilitaries throughout the Yugoslav wars, focusing more on terrorizing civilians and looting than real fighting. Arkan was indicted by the Criminal Tribunal for former Yugoslavia (ICTY), but was assassinated before he could stand trial in 2000. The radical Serbian politician and paramilitary leader Vojislav Šešelj is currently standing trail in The Hague. Moreover, reportedly, in June 1992, the Macedonian police discovered in the Albanian inhabited-village of Radolishta on the Ohrid lake, near the border with Albania, "a cache full with illegal weapons, explosives, ammunitions and paramilitary uniforms" (Daskalovski 2006, 68). On July 22, 1998, three bombs exploded in three different Macedonian cities: Skopje, Kumanovo and Priljep. The Kosovo Liberation Army claimed responsibility for all the three explosions which caused only material damages (Daskalovski 2006, 74).

39 Sometimes, authors use the mysterious term "foreign mercenaries" to refer to members of UÇK/KLA and UÇK/NLA; yet, during my frequent contacts with political and military leaders of both UÇK/KLA and UÇK/NLA, they have credibly dismissed any involvement of foreign fighters in the Albanian insurgency in both Kosovo and Macedonia.

40 There is a widespread tendency to consider the Macedonian crisis as a spillover of the Kosovo War (Lebamoff and Ilievski 2008; Ilievski 2007; Ragaru 2007; Daskalovski 2006; Micheva 2005; Brunnbauer 2002; Schneckener 2002), along with the recognition that the way it was built, the Macedonian stability could not last long. However, the emphasis on what Mincheva (2009) calls "the emergence of a transborder non-state actor" (ETMS) as a causal factor of the Macedonian conflict might be misleading. As the historical analysis in this chapter shows, the Albanian ETMS is more an effect than a cause of the conflict; the long list of complaints among the Albanians in Macedonia over at least two decades of Macedonian independence and the reluctance of the Macedonians to recognize them and accept Albanians as a constitutive part of the country generated and perpetuated frustrations that occasionally burst

in demonstrations and open public defiance to the Macedonian dominated government. As Mincheva (2009) claims, ETMS might not be a "useful unit of analysis," as it tries to shift too much of a causality on the external factors.

41 These messages ranged from "we don't want to endanger Macedonia's stability and integrity, but we will fight a guerrilla war until we have won our basic rights, until we are accepted as equal people in Macedonia" to statements asserting that the UÇK/NLA was fighting for an "independent, separate Albanian state of Western Macedonia" (Ilievski 2007, 7).

42 By early June 2001, the UÇK/NLA had taken control of the Albanian-inhabited village of Aračino that overlooked Skopje. While the move did not represent any major military success, since the village lacked the presence of any security forces, it represented a major psychological and public relation success for the UÇK/NLA: in matter of months, its units managed to reach the gates of the capital, and also put some of the country's main industries within the range of their mortars. Government's military efforts to recapture the village failed after meeting fierce resistance. On June 11, an EU and US brokered ceasefire was announced, but it was violated on June 22 as government troops pushed to gain the village. Their unsuccessful military operation ended again as the chief of EU common foreign and security policy Javier Solana brokered another ceasefire. On June 25, the US personnel of the KFOR observed the withdrawal of Albanian fighters from Aračino. When several months later I asked one of the political leaders of the UÇK/NLA about the reasons of their withdrawal from Aračino, the commander, who wished to remain anonymous, told me that in no way would Albanian fighters oppose US demands and denied any leverage of Solana brokerage: "Some high-ranking US militaries came to us and asked us to leave the village because our presence was interfering with their mission in Kosovo. Although Aračino is besides the highway that connects Skopje with Prishtina, we could not understand how our presence in Aračino was interfering with NATO operations in Kosovo, but we did not want even remotely of being accused as disturbing NATO after all the help that they have given to Albanians of Kosovo" (personal interview, in June 2009).

43 See Wikisource, "Executive Order 13219 of 26 June 2001: Blocking Property of Persons Who Threaten International Stabilization Efforts in the Western Balkans." Online: http://en.wikisource.org/wiki/Executive_Order_13219 (accessed November 13, 2010).

44 European Union, "Presidency Conclusions of the Stockholm European Council, 23–24 March 2001." Online: http://www.consilium.europa. eu/uedocs/cms_data/docs/pressdata/en/ec/00100-r1.%20ann-r1.en1.html (accessed 13 November 2010).

45 In the period between November 2005 and December 2009, the Mission of the European Union acted as a single representative of the European Commission and the Council of Ministers of the European Union stemming from the double function of Ambassador Erwan Fouéré, being both European Union special representative and head of the Delegation of the European Commission. With the implementation of the Lisbon Treaty on December 1, 2009, the EU was represented in Macedonia by the Delegation of the European Union, as foreseen by the Treaty of Lisbon. The EU high representatives ever since the establishment of the office have been as follows: Alain le Roy (October 19, 2001–October 30, 2002), Alexis Brouhns (November 1, 2002–January 31, 2004), Soren Jessen-Petersen (February 1, 2004–August 31, 2004), Michael Sahlin (September 1, 2004–October 30, 2005) and Erwan Fouéré (November 1, 2005–August 21, 2011). Fouéré was appointed both head of the Delegation of the European Commission and EUSR, following the fusion of the former office for the implementation of the Ohrid Agreement with the EC Delegation (Ragaru 2007, 9, note 12). François Léotard served as a EU high representative from June 29, 2001–October 29, 2001, before the office was actually opened.

46 As Ragaru writes,

> Amnesty for the former insurgents and refugee returns were amongst the issues that provoked heated controversies in the months following the end of the infighting. Despite President Boris Trajkovski's (VMRO–DPMNE) firm commitment to the Ohrid process,

political tensions remained high until the September 2002 parliamentary elections that saw the victory of the (more moderate) Social-Democratic Alliance (SDSM) and the formation of a coalition in which the Albanians were represented by the Union for Democratic Integration (DUI), an Albanian party initiated in June 2002 by former NLA chief, Ali Ahmeti. With some of Macedonia's most flamboyant nationalists out of office—former Interior minister, Ljube Boškovski, former Prime Minister, Ljubčo Georgievski [*sic*]—the implementation of the Ohrid Accords [*sic*] went smoother [...] at least until decentralization and redistricting were put on the agenda in 2003–2004. (Ragaru 2007, 10)

47 See International Crisis Group, "Macedonia: No Room for Complacency," ICG Europe Report No. 149, October 2003, 23. Online: http://www.crisisgroup.org/library/documents/ europe/49_macedonia_no_room_for_complacency.pdf (accessed October 3, 2010); cf. Marko 2004, n53.

48 I have found corroborations of this argument among Macedonian and Albanian students from the Sts Cyril and Methodius University in Skopje and the Southeast European University in Tetovo during my field research for various projects in the summers of 2009 and 2010.

49 The drafted preamble read:

The citizens of the Republic of Macedonia, taking over responsibility for the present and future of their fatherland, aware and grateful to their predecessors for the sacrifice and dedication in their endeavors and struggle to create an independent and sovereign state of Macedonia, and responsible to future generations to preserve and develop everything that is valuable from the rich cultural inheritance and coexistence within Macedonia, equal rights and obligations towards the common good—the Republic of Macedonia [...] have decided to establish the Republic of Macedonia [...] (Ilievski 2007, 21)

50 Council of Europe, "The Former Yugoslav Republic of Macedonia." Online: http://www. venice.coe.int/webforms/events/default.aspx?id=279 (accessed October 11, 2009).

51 The draft of Article 19 reads:
1. The freedom of religious confession is guaranteed.
2. The right to express one's faith freely and publicly, individually or with others is guaranteed.
3. The Macedonian Orthodox Church, the Islamic Religious Community in Macedonia, The Catholic Church, and other religious communities and groups are separate from the state and equal before the law.
4. The Macedonian Orthodox Church, the Islamic Religious Community in Macedonia, the Catholic Church, and other religious communities and groups are free to establish schools and other social and charitable institutions, by way of procedure regulated by law. (Daskalovski 2006, 164)

52 According to data from the UNDP–Kapital Center for Development Research (2003) survey, the percentage of citizens having "much confidence" or being "somewhat confident" in their parties relative to those having "no confidence at all" or being "somewhat not confident" are for SDSM 51% to 45%, BDI 21% to 74%, VMRO–DPMNE 18% to 78% and PDSh 16% to 80% respectively.
    Moreover, the life of Albanians in Macedonia was not considered unbearable by all Albanians. In a report for the *Independent*, Justin Hugger (2001) referred to an Albanian who did not support the Albanian armed rebellion for the following reason: "Things were getting better. There has been an improvement in our rights over the past year." But, after the events in Tearce, Hugger claims there were heavy-handed police raids in Albanian areas, and opinion began to harden. Meanwhile, an Albanian who supported the armed rebellion said, "It's not one big thing that's influencing the people. It's a long story of little things building up that makes them sympathetic to the men in the hill." As the report follows, "It's that we're not

allowed to have our names in Albanian in our passports. It's that we feel discrimination against us everywhere."

As the UN special envoy to the Balkans Carl Bilt has noted,

> In terms of human rights, as in the economy, Macedonia is a star by Balkans standards. It is nonsense to compare the Albanians' situation here with Kosovo. They have an Albanian party in the coalition government. Western Macedonia is de facto run by Albanians.

Following this comment, Bilt considered the conflict as "an internal Albanian dispute" adding that "[t]he people in the hills' argument is with Xhaferi, not the Macedonians."

See Justin Huggler, "My Father Was a Fighter. It Is in Albanian Blood. I Am Not Afraid. We Will Fight," *Independent*, March 19, 2001. Online: http://www.independent.co.uk/news/world/europe/my-father-was-a-fighter-it-is-in-albanian-blood-i-am-not-afraid-we-will-fight-687996.html (accessed 28 September 2010).

53 Interpreting it from a constitutional perspective, Marko notes that

> This new formula reintroduces the mix of the nation state and state-nation concepts, but in a quite different way than in 1991 or even under the communist constitution of 1974. In contrast even to the constitution of 1974, Macedonia is no longer called the nation state of the Macedonian people and others (nationalities). Instead, both citizens and ethnic groups, all of them called peoples, are declared "constituent" forces in the process of state formation. Hence, the inequality between the bearers of rights of the Macedonian nation and citizens of other groups under the constitution of 1991 has now been balanced on two levels. First, all members of all the peoples are (equal) citizens, and, secondly, all ethnic groups including the majority population are recognized as (equal) communities by designating them peoples. Nevertheless, the preamble has returned to the concept of group equality without, however, giving the nation state concept priority. In comparison to the constitutions of other ex-Yugoslav republics such as Slovenia, Croatia, Serbia and Bosnia-Herzegovina, which all give preference to the respective majority nation(s), this new mix in the preamble of the Macedonian Constitution can indeed be called the formula for a "multiethnic" state and society requiring the development of multiple identities. With this new formula the term "Macedonia" is no longer exclusively connected to Slav Macedonians and hence allows for the development of a feeling of belonging to this state and its society for the other ethnic communities too. This will also facilitate the chance to overcome the exclusive ethno-national identities which dominate in particular among members of the Albanian Macedonian community ("auto-ghettoization") and to develop the required multiple identity both with the ethnic community and the state. (Marko 2004, 9)

54 However, in particular Turks are put under pressure to assimilate into the Albanian Macedonian community where the Albanian Macedonian are in the majority. See International Crisis Group, "Macedonia: No Room For Complacency," 23.

55 According to interviews with Abdurraman Aliti and Arbën Xhaferi.

56 A rational interpretation of "sticks and carrots" would help to see leaders' preferences adjusted accordingly.

Chapter 4   Local Decentralization Reform

1 For the undemocratic, Communist Party controlled, centralist, economically dependent, ideological, and vertical characteristics of the Eastern European local government during the communist period, see Coulson (1995); Elander (1997); Illés (1993); Illner (1992, 1992).

2 For instance, Tanas Tanasoski, a Macedonian local official in the southern city of Ohrid, told me that most of the Macedonian local officials accept the lack of decentralization insofar as it serves to preserve the territorial integrity of the country and the unitary character of the state.

Later in the interview, Tanasoski pointed out that most Macedonians see local decentralization as a step toward federalization and the eventual separation of the country.

3 Interview with Arbën Xhaferi.

4 The National Strategy of Decentralization and Local Autonomy was prepared during 1999, based on wide political participation. The National Committee on Decentralization composed of governmental members and local government representatives was the political organism that led the strategy.

5 For more details, see Council of Ministers of the Republic of Albania, "Decision for the Approval of the Strategy for Decentralization and Local Autonomy," No. 651, December 12, 1999.

6 During that period, the Kuvend approved a law package that included Law on Taxes System in the Republic of Albania, No. 8435, December 28, 1998; Law on Taxes Procedure in the Republic of Albania, No. 8560, December 22, 1999; Electoral Code of the Republic of Albania, No. 8609, May 8, 2000; Law on the Organization and Functioning of the Local Governing, No. 8652, July 31, 2000; Law on Territorial and Administrative Organization in the Republic of Albania, No. 8653, July 31, 2000; Law on the Organization and Functioning of the Tirana Municipality, No. 8657, July 31, 2000.

7 These issues are: central government–local authorities' consultation mechanisms (Article 4.6 Of ECLSG); the purpose of the administrative control (Article 8.2); and the main focus of the financial autonomy as defined by the Charter such as financial resources (Article 9.1).

8 ECLSG, Article 8.3.

9 For figures on Albanian local government revenues and expenditures, see Albanian Decentralization Progress Report 2000, Tirana: Urban Institute, and Institute for Contemporary Studies, October 2001.

10 Interview with Artan Hoxha, president of Institute for Contemporary Studies.

11 Interview with Arben Imami, minister of local government and decentralization, September 2001–April 2002.

12 *Shekulli*, "Shalsi: Qeveria të na Kalojë Ujësjellësin" [Shalsi: The government should transfer to us the water company], *Shekulli*, October 29, 2006.

13 A notes that explains its meaning reads,

> The ratings reflect the consensus of Freedom House, its academic advisors and the author(s) of this report. The opinions expressed in this report are those of the author(s). The ratings are based on a scale of 1 to 7, with 1 representing the highest level of democratic progress and 7 the lowest. The Democracy Score is an average of ratings for the categories tracked in a given year. (Bushati 2009, 47)

14 The ratings follow a quarter-point scale. Changes in ratings are based on events during the study year in relation to the previous year. Minor to moderate developments typically warrant a positive or negative change of a quarter (0.25) to a half (0.5) point. Significant developments typically warrant a positive or negative change of three-quarters (0.75) to a full (1.0) point. It is rare that the rating in any category will fluctuate by more than a full point (1.0) in a single year. The ratings process in Freedom House's (2005b) "Nations in Transit 2005" involved four steps:

1. Authors of individual country reports suggested preliminary ratings in all seven categories covered by the study.

2. The US and CEE–NIS (Central and Eastern Europe–Newly Independent States) academic advisers evaluated the ratings and reviewed reports for accuracy, objectivity, and completeness of information.

3. Report authors were given the opportunity to dispute any revised rating that differed from the original by more than 0.5 point.

4. Freedom House refereed any disputed ratings and, if the evidence warranted, considered further adjustments. Final editorial authority for the ratings rested with Freedom House.

15 European Commission, Albania 2011, Progress Report, 9. Online: http://ec.europa.eu/enlargement/pdf/key_documents/2011/package/al_rapport_2011_en.pdf, 10 (accessed February 10, 2013).

16 Congress of Local and Regional Authorities, Congress President Calls on Albanian Authorities to Fully Comply with Provisions of the European Local Self-Government Charter [Press Release 025(2006)], January 17, 2006.

17 Freedom House, "Country Report 2008: Albania." Online: http://www.freedomhouse.org/template.cfm?page=47&nit=443&year=2008 (accessed November 22, 2010).

18 Ibid.

19 Ibid.

20 Ibid.

21 Ibid.

22 Finally, the PD managed to depose Edi Rama from his mayoral seat when, in the local elections of May 8, 2011, the PD candidate Lulëzim Basha prevailed with around 100 votes in a process that involved much politicking and a long legal process to reach a final decision.

23 LajmiiFundit, "Berisha ka bllokuar financimet e huaja për bashkitë e majta" [Berisha has blocked foreign funding for left-wing municipalities], LajmiiFundit.com, April 10, 2010. Online: http://www.lajmifundit.com/lajmet/ekonomia/te-tjera/5168-berisha-ka-bllokuar-financimet-e-huaja-per-bashkite-e-majta (accessed November 18, 2010).

24 World Bank, Camille Nuamah, Country Manager of the World Bank Office in Albania [Press Release], April 10, 2010. Online: http://web.worldbank.org/WBSITE/EXTERNAL/COUNTRIES/ECAEXT/ALBANIAEXTN/0,,contentMDK:22533723~menuPK:301417~pagePK:2865066~piPK:2865079~theSitePK:301412,00.html (accessed November 18, 2010).

25 Shekulli, "Vendorët, Rama: Të tërhiqet Ligji për Taksat, merr 'Rob' Bashkitë" [The bill on taxes must be withdrawn: "Takes hostage" municipalities], Shekulli, November 6, 2010. Online: http://www.shekulli.com.al/2010/11/06/vendoret-berishes-terhiq-ligjin-e-taksave.html (accessed November 19, 2010). See also Shekulli, "Rama: Protesta, Qeveria po kap 'Rob' Bashkitë e Komunat Opozitare" [Rama: Protest, the government is "taking hostage" the opposition municipalities], Shekulli, November 10, 2010; "Rama: Protestë Kundër Talebanizmit të Qeverisë [Rama: Protest against the Talibanization of the government]," Shekulli, November 11, 2010.

26 Ibid.

27 Shekulli, "Olldashi: Do Prishim Planin Rregullues të Tiranës" [Olldashi: Will undo the urban plan of Tirana], Shekulli, November 14, 2010. Online: http://www.shekulli.com.al/2010/11/14/olldashi-do-prishim-planin-rregullues-te-tiranes.html (accessed November 19, 2010).

28 Organization for Security and Co-operation in Europe, Report by the Head of the OSCE Presence in Albania to the OSCE Permanent Council, September 9, 2010. Online: http://www.osce.org/documents/pia/2010/09/45985_en.pdf (accessed November 18, 2010).

29 Ibid.

30 European Commission, Albania 2011 Progress Report, 9.

31 As the EC's Albania 2011 Progress Report notes, "The decentralization reform process was adversely affected by the difficult relationship between central and local government" (ibid.).

32 European Commission, Albania 2012 Progress Report, 9. Online: http://ec.europa.eu/enlargement/pdf/key_documents/2012/package/al_rapport_2012_en.pdf (accessed February 10, 2013).

33 The opinion comments on the following policy areas:
   1. Political criteria: democracy (constitution and legislative frameworks, parliamentary, political dialogue, elections), rule of law (reform of the judiciary, fight against corruption, organized crime), human rights and respect for minorities;
   2. Economic criteria.
   See European Commission, "Commission Opinion on Albania's Application for Membership of the European Union." COM (2010) 680 {SEC (2010) 1335}. Brussels. November 9, 2010. Online: http://ec.europa.eu/enlargement/pdf/key_documents/2010/package/al_opinion_2010_en.pdf (accessed March 25, 2013).

34 Ibid.

35 Law on Territorial Division of the Republic of Macedonia and Determination of the Areas of the Local Self-Government Units, *Official Gazette of the Republic of Macedonia*, No. 49/1996.

36 Institute for Regional and International Studies, "The Process of Decentralization in Macedonia: Prospects for Ethnic Conflict Mitigation, Enhanced Representation, Institutional Efficiency and Accountability" (Sofia–Skopje, 2006), 9. Online: http://www.iris-bg.org/f/macedonia2.pdf (accessed May 26, 2007).

37 Ibid., 11.

38 Center for Economic Analysis, CEA Comments on the EBDR 2006 Strategy for the Republic of Macedonia [Press Release], 2006. Online: http://www.cea.org.mk/Documents/Press_release_EBRD_strategy_2006.pdf (accessed May 26, 2006).

39 *Official Gazette of the Republic of Macedonia*, No. 5/2002.

40 See also International Crisis Group, "Macedonia: No Room For Complacency," ICG Europe Report No. 149, October 2003. Online: http://www.crisisgroup.org/library/documents/europe/49_macedonia_no_room_for_complacency.pdf (accessed October 3, 2010); cf. Marko 2004, n53.

41 Reliefweb, "Macedonia – Parliament: Law on Local Self-Government Adopted," January 25, 2002. Online: http://www.reliefweb.int/rw/rwb.nsf/db900sid/ACOS-64C3N4?OpenDocument&Click= (accessed October 11, 2010).

42 As Brunnbauer (2002) reveals, it was the first vote that applied the double majority (Badinter) principle. Out of the 93 present MPs, 85 voted "for," four "against" and four refrained. According to Amendment 16 to the Macedonian Constitution, the Law on Local Self-Government can be approved with a qualified majority of two-thirds of votes, within which there must be a majority of the votes of MPs, who belong to the communities not in the majority population of Macedonia. Out of 27 such MPs, 19 voted "for," granting five votes more than the necessary 14; see previous note.

43 See Reliefweb, "Boucher: Law on Local Self-Government Opens the Door for Donor Conference," January 25, 2002. Online: http://www.reliefweb.int/rw/rwb.nsf/db900sid/ACOS-64C3N4?OpenDocument&Click= (accessed October 11, 2010).

44 *Official Gazette of the Republic of Macedonia*, No. 5/2002. As Richard Boucher, a spokesman for the Department of State stated, "We acclaim the adoption of the agreement between leaders of the major political parties in Macedonia and we think it is a big step forward towards implementation of the Framework Agreement." "Boucher: Law on Local Self-Government Opens the Door for Donor Conference," January 25, 2002. Online: http://www.reliefweb.int/rw/rwb.nsf/db900sid/ACOS-64C3N4?OpenDocument&Click= (accessed October 11, 2010).

45 The number of laws to be adapted range from 44 (ICC 2003) to 250 in Freedom House (2004b, 421); cf. Marko 2004, n69.

46 As ICG notes, the IMF appears to fear the impact of decentralization on central budgetary control; the prospect of multiple municipalities running up debt is a worst-case scenario for the Fund and drives much of its caution. See International Crisis Group, "Macedonia: No Room for Complacency."

47 Ibid.

48 International Crisis Group, "Macedonia: Not Out of the Woods Yet," Europe Briefing No. 37, February 25, 2005. Online: http://www.refworld.org/docid/425e8ce84.html (accessed May 18, 2013).

49 See also United Nations Development Programme (UNDP), "National Human Development Report 2004, FYR Macedonia: Decentralization for Human Development." Online: http://www.undp.org.mk/datacenter/publications/documents/nhdr2004EngFP1.pdf (accessed November 26, 2010).

50 See also International Crisis Group, "Macedonia: No Room for Complacency."

51 Ibid.

52 Ibid., 20.

53 Another think tank, the Macedonian Center for International Cooperation, stated that "the process which resulted in the proposed local government re-organization was non-transparent;

it disregarded the principles of public involvement, openness, and sincerity towards the citizens, which are all necessary while generating such crucial changes" (Daskalovski 2006, 211). Similar objections were voiced from the Macedonian Helsinki Committee, reminding the government that, since decentralization aims to satisfy citizens' needs and interests, it "should begin and end with active participation of citizens through their common will" (Daskalovski 2006, 211). Meanwhile, reportedly, the draft was also criticized by local decentralization experts who opposed the adjunction of the large ethnic Albanian villages of Saraj and Kondovo surrounding Skopje to the capital city in order to increase the municipality's ethnic Albanian population to above 20 per cent, thus making Albanian the city's second official language. In addition, the southern city of Struga, where ethnic Albanians were slightly shy of the 50 per cent majority, was slated to absorb some surrounding ethnic Albanian villages. Additionally, the draft anticipated that the municipality of Kičevo, located in western part of the country, which barely contained a Macedonian majority, would be expanded to surrounding ethnic Albanian villages in order to ensure an Albanian majority in the newly created municipality. Experts stated that adding a population of 30,000 rural habitants to 30,000 city dwellers would be impractical and unproductive. They also pointed to seven other municipalities that had been enlarged, noting that this had resulted in "seriously compromise[ing] the possibility for citizens to participate actively in the decision making process" (Daskalovski 2006, 211).

    See also the Report of Helsinki Committee of Human Rights of the Republic of Macedonia "Decentralization and Sustainable Development," 2004. The Committee also pointed to other cases, where ethnicity seems to be the sole factor influencing the decision on municipal boundaries, [that] failed to meet the criteria of the municipal unit set by the Law on Decentralization itself. In 13 such cases, the condition that a municipality has more than 5,000 inhabitants to secure sufficient economic and financial and human resources to perform its new prerogatives has been clearly overlooked. Finally, objections were raised to the erasing of the municipal status of some municipalities, which, regardless of their capacity to function as such lost their autonomy in order to alter the ethnic composition of other units. (cf. Daskalovski 2006, 211)

54 Indeed, it is clear that ethnic considerations underpin the territorial division legislated according to the August 2003 Law. As Ragaru outlines some details:

    The 2004 redistricting process was thus bound to be marred with "ethnic" considerations and afterthoughts, as were debates over the previous Macedonian territorial organization in 1996. In 2004, both sides knew what they were doing when the SDSM tried to guarantee that the road to the international airport located 7 km east of Struga near the lakeshore would remain in an ethnic Macedonian municipality or when they negotiated the delimitation of Skopje districts so as to guarantee that the Cyril and Methodius University, although on the side of the Vardar where Albanians now tend to predominate, would remain in Centar municipality, where ethnic Macedonians prevail. Similarly, the Albanian BDI was fully aware of the impact of drawing some Albanian villages and the city of Struga together. By giving ethnic Albanians a relative majority, they guaranteed that the next mayor would be Albanian, and indeed in March 2005 Ramiz Merko (DUI) was elected at the head of the enlarged municipality. Locally, his policies have been understood as primarily targeting his Albanian constituency— including an ill-fated initiative for placing a memorial to the murdered municipal councilor, Nura Mazar [sic], a.k.a. Commander Struga, an alledged [sic] former NLA member (the decision was adopted without applying the "Badinter rule," as stipulated by the 2002 Law on Self-Government). (Ragaru 2007, 25)

55 The events resulting from the election of Struga's mayor from Ahmeti's BDI, Ramiz Merko, in the local elections of March 2005 justify these fears. As Ragaru notes,

    Many an [sic] ethnic Macedonian feel uneasy with recent changes within the municipality, such as extensive personnel reshuffle in ethnic institutions and renaming of streets, squares, buildings with Albanian names. Some feel Struga is now following the path Tetovo earlier undertook—a path toward ethnic homogenization. (Ragaru 2007, 26)

56 European Stability Initiative (ESI), "Ahmeti's Village: The Political Economy of Interethnic Relations in Macedonia," Skopje and Berlin, October 1, 2002. Online: http://www.esiweb.org/pdf/esi_document_id_36.pdf (accessed May 18, 2013).

57 As the Macedonians feared, Kičevo and Struga both went to the ethnic Albanians in the March–April 2013 local elections in Macedonia, after they were joined by Zajas and Velešta respectively.

58 The November 7 referendum question (cf. Marko 2004, 16) reads as follows: "Are you for the territorial organization of the local self-government (the municipalities and City of Skopje) as determined by the Law on Territorial Division of the Republic of Macedonia and Determination of the Law on Local Self-Government Units?" (*Official Gazette of the Republic of Macedonia* No. 49/1996) and the Law on the City of Skopje (*Official Gazette of the Republic of Macedonia* No. 49/1996).
— For
— Against"

59 See UNDP, "National Human Development Report 2004."

60 Organization for Security and Co-operation in Europe/Office for Democratic Institutions and Human Rights, "Former Yugoslav Republic of Macedonia, 7 November 2004 Referendum," Warsaw, February 2, 2005. Online: http://www.osce.org/documents/odihr/2005/02/4221_en.pdf (accessed October 21, 2010).

61 International Crisis Group, "Macedonia: Not Out of the Woods Yet."

62 Ibid., 3.

63 Ibid.

64 Ibid.

65 Ibid.

66 Ibid.

67 Freedom House, Country Report 2008: Macedonia. Online: http://www.freedomhouse.org/template.cfm?page=17&nit=160&year=2008 (accessed November 22, 2010).

68 European Commission, The Former Yugoslav Republic of Macedonia 2011 Progress Report, 9. Online: http://ec.europa.eu/enlargement/pdf/key_documents/2011/package/mk_rapport_2011_en.pdf (accessed February 10, 2013).

69 For instance, the European Commission's Former Yugoslav Republic of Macedonia 2011 Progress Report notes those developments as follows:

> The Law on management of state-owned land was adopted and entered into force in July 2011. Capacity-building programmes are being implemented to assist municipalities in the areas of property tax administration, human resources and financial control. Financial affairs units were established in three more municipalities; 52 municipalities established internal audit units and in 46 municipalities an internal auditor is operating. More than 1000 municipal civil servants have been trained, and progress was made in implementing annual training programmes.
>
> However, four of the six municipalities which remain in phase 1 of the decentralisation process have sizeable debts, and two lack financial management capacity. Additional efforts are needed in order to prepare them for moving to phase 2. Blocked accounts remain a problem for municipalities in both phases 1 and 2. Mechanisms to address the significant disparities in delivery of public services are limited, and rural and small municipalities are especially disadvantaged. Some municipalities remain weak in the areas of monitoring or enforcing collection of the property tax.

See European Commission, The Former Yugoslav Republic of Macedonia 2011 Progress Report. Online: http://ec.europa.eu/enlargement/pdf/key_documents/2011/package/mk_rapport_2011_en.pdf (accessed February 10, 2013).

70 European Commission, The Former Yugoslav Republic of Macedonia 2012 Progress Report, 8. Online: http://ec.europa.eu/enlargement/pdf/key_documents/2012/package/mk_rapport_2012_en.pdf (accessed 10 February 10, 2013).

71 Introducing the sectorial report on local decentralization, the most recent EC's progress reports on Macedonia begins with a variation of the following sentence: "Decentralisation of government, a key element of the Ohrid Framework Agreement, continued" (ibid.).

72 The Ohrid Agreement on local decentralization reads as follows:

  3. Development of Decentralized Government

  3.1. A revised Law on Local Self-Government will be adopted that reinforces the powers of elected local officials and enlarges substantially their competencies in conformity with the Constitution (as amended in accordance with Annex A) and the European Charter on Local Self-Government, and reflecting the principle of subsidiarity in effect in the European Union. Enhanced competencies will relate principally to the areas of public services, urban and rural planning, environmental protection, local economic development, culture, local finances, education, social welfare, and health care. A law on financing of local self-government will be adopted to ensure an adequate system of financing to enable local governments to fulfill all of their responsibilities.

  3.2. Boundaries of municipalities will be revised within one year of the completion of a new census, which will be conducted under international supervision by the end of 2001. The revision of the municipal boundaries will be effectuated by the local and national authorities with international participation.

  3.3. In order to ensure that police are aware of and responsive to the needs and interests of the local population, local heads of police will be selected by municipal councils from lists of candidates proposed by the Ministry of Interior, and will communicate regularly with the councils. The Ministry of Interior will retain the authority to remove local heads of police in accordance with the law.

73 European Commission, "Communication from the Commission to the Council and the European Parliament "Enlargement Strategy and Main Challenges 2010–2011," COM (2010) 660 final. Online: http://ec.europa.eu/enlargement/press_corner/key-documents/reports_nov_2010_en.htm (accessed November 23, 2010).

74 This fact has been asserted to me especially by the former chairman of the PPD and deputy speaker of the Sobranie Abdurrahman Aliti, and the former chairman of the PDSh and member of the Sobranie Arbën Xhaferi.

75 Freedom House, "Nations in Transit 2012." Online: http://www.freedomhouse.org/report/nations-transit/nations-transit-2012 (accessed February 10, 2010).

Chapter 5   Judicial Reforms

1 European Commission, "Commission Opinion on Albania's Application for Membership of the European Union." COM (2010) 680 {SEC (2010) 1335}. Brussels. November 9, 2010. Online: http://ec.europa.eu/enlargement/pdf/key_documents/2010/package/al_opinion_2010_en.pdf (accessed March 25, 2013).

2 Rule of Law Working Group, "Introduction," DG Enlargement–Donor Coordination Conference, Brussels, October 23–24, 2008. Online: http://ec.europa.eu/enlargement/pdf/donor_conference/16_dcf_working_group_rule_of_law_en.pdf (accessed November 8, 2010).

3 For a review on the connection between democratic consolidation and successful economic reform with independent judiciaries that protect political and property rights, as well as the contribution of the courts to policymaking and the investigation of abuses of power in several West European democracies, see Linz and Stepan 1996, 10–15; Shapiro and Stone 1994; Nelken 1996.

4 Organization for Security and Co-operation in Europe Presence in Albania, Legal Sector Report for Albania 2004, 1. Online: http://www.osce.org/documents/pia/2004/02/2117_en.pdf (accessed May 22, 2007).

5 Ibid.

6 The Venice Commission, "Opinion on the Albanian Law on the Organization of the Judicial," Strasbourg, December 4, 2005. Online: http://www.venice.coe.int/docs/1995/CDL(1995)074rev-e.asp (accessed May 17, 2007). As the Commission notes,

> One of the effects of the adoption of the Law on the Organisation of the Judicial in April 1992 was to abrogate a prior ordinary Law on the Status of Magistrates, applicable to both judges and prosecutors. That law contained detailed provisions on the rights and duties of magistrates, including extensive procedural and substantive safeguards against arbitrary removal from office.

7 OSCE, Legal Sector Report, 1.

8 I reached such a conclusion from my conversations and exchanges with other colleagues during my own participation in Albanian politics as a member of the Kuvend, 1991–92 and 1992–96.

9 Personally, I remember the "Tirana Court incident," May 1992, when then president Sali Berisha went to the Tirana District Court and, in a speech, tried to steer the judges on how to rule.

10 The Venice Commission, "Opinion on the Albanian Law." As the opinion states,

> [I]t was clearly the intention of the statutory scheme established by Chapter VI that similar implementing legislation be introduced—Article 5 provides that the organisation of the courts is to be regulated by law; Article 10 provides that the circumstances and procedures for the removal of judges from office should be provided for by law; furthermore, it is not consistent with international standards for legal guarantees of judicial independence, which Article 10 also pledges to respect, that questions of judicial qualification, appointment, transfer and discipline be left unregulated by either the Constitution or an Act of Parliament.

11 Ibid.

12 Ibid.

13 As the Organization for Security and Co-operation in Europe's Legal Sector Report 2004 notes,

> A number of new judges were assigned to the courts in 1994 after taking a controversial six-month special course and then completing the "correspondence" system at the Law Faculty in Tirana on an accelerated basis (six more months) The 1997 predecessor to the Judicial Power Law [Law No. 8265, On the Organization of Justice in the Republic of Albania, December 18, 1997] would have removed these judges from their other positions, but after additional controversy, the Judicial Power Law repealed the earlier law, while requiring a one-time competency test for all first instance judges with less than ten years of judicial experience [Judicial Power Law, Article 48]. This test took place in 1999, and of the judges who participated, four failed but one was re-tested and passed. The three who failed, and over 30 who refused to take the examination, were discharged. Now, nine years after the six-month courses and eight years after many of its graduates were appointed to judicial positions, the judges interviewed generally reported that those graduates who remain as judges have been well integrated into the system.

See Organization for Security and Co-operation in Europe, "Presence in Albania 2004," Legal Sector Report for Albania 2004, 18 . Online: http://www.osce.org/documents/pia/2004/02/2117_en.pdf (accessed May 22, 2007).

14 Council of Europe and the European Union, "Second Joint Programme between the European Union and the Council of Europe for the Promotion of Legal System Reform in Albania, Final Report, Restricted GR-EDS(98)5," February 2, 1998.

15 World Bank, Report No. 19915-ALB: Project Appraisal Document, March 1, 2000. Online: http://www-wds.worldbank.org/external/default/WDSContentServer/IW3P/IB/2000/04/07/000094946_00030805302144/Rendered/INDEX/multi_page.txt (accessed May 18, 2007).

16 The Albanian Government Program, July 2002. Tirana, Albania. Archives of the *Kuvendi i Shqipërisë*.

17 Interview with Arben Imami who held two ministerial positions in the 1997–2001 coalition (minister of legislative reform and relations with the Kuvend (1997–99); and minister of justice (2000–2001); in the 2001–2005 coalition was minister of local government and decentralization (2001–2002); and in the 2009–13 government held the position of minister of defense.

18 Ibid.

19 Ibid. Related to the situation of the judicial during this period, Organization for Security and Co-operation in Europe suggested that,

> [A] more transparent system should be adopted for assigning cases. At the moment there is no special law, nor a united sub-statutory act, specifying how lots for assigning court cases are drawn. [...] There is no legislative guidance for the transfer of judges and no criteria for their promotion [...]. The Judges who were interviewed occasionally reported instances of undue pressure from other branches of the government to make particular decisions, especially in cases when the State was a party.

See OSCE Presence in Albania. "Legal Sector Report for Albania," 2004, 18. Online: http://www.osce.org/documents/pia/2004/02/2117_en.pdf (accessed May 18, 2007).

In the same line, the EU observed that,

> despite some institutional and legal measures such as Standing Rules of Minister of Justice for the Judicial Administration, the judicial administration still enjoys a low level of remuneration and poor working conditions. Concerning the above issues, the legal framework does not offer clear and detailed rules for the mission, tasks and the relationship of judicial administration with the justice system and the third parties.

See European Union. "Increasing Transparency and Improvement of Management of Criminal and Civil Judicial Processes," 2004.

20 Commission of the European Communities, Albania: Stabilisation and Association Report 2004, 1. Online: http://www.delalb.ec.europa.eu/en/documents_march_2004/Country_report_Albanie_04_03_29_Final.pdf (accessed May 19, 2007).

21 Freedom House, Study: Slow and Uneven Progress in Balkan Democratization [Press Release], April 26, 2004. Online: http://www.freedomhouse.org/media/pressre1/042604.htm (accessed May 19, 2007).

22 Human Rights Watch, "Human Rights and Armed Conflict," Human Rights Watch World Report 2004, 4. Online: http://www.essex.ac.uk/armedcon/story_id/humanrightswatchworldreport2004.pdf (accessed May 24, 2013).

23 Parliamentary Assembly of the Council of Europe, "Resolution 1377 Honouring of Obligations and Commitments by Albania, 2004," Online: http://assembly.coe.int/Main.asp?link=/Documents/AdoptedText/ta04/ERES1377.htm (accessed May 20, 2007).

24 These interests can be considered negative because, while there existed a high awareness in the Albanian society about the need for judiciary reform admitted and reiterated by all political and societal actors, the Albanian government did not undertake the necessary measures to conduct such reform. The awareness of the need for judicial reforms in the country remains in stark contrast with Albanian society's inexistent sensibility related to the asylum reform. In the latter, I have evaluated domestic leaders' interest as inexistent (0).

25 The Council of the European Union, "Council Decision of January 30 on Principles, Priorities, and Conditions Contained in the European Partnership with Albania and Repealing Decision 2004/5/19/EC," 2006/54/EC, 2006. Online: http://eur-lex.europa.eu/smartapi/cgi/sga_doc?smartapi!celexplus!prod!CELEXnumdoc&numdoc=306D0054&lg=en (accessed May 20, 2007).

26 Parliamentary Assembly of the Council of Europe, "Resolution 1538: Honouring of Obligations and Commitments by Albania, 2007." Among the recommendations directed to the Albanian government are:

1. Take into account Council of Europe expert advice on draft amendments to the law on the organization of the judiciary in order to strengthen the independence and professionalism of judges;

2. Address the problem of remuneration of judges and increase the budget for the judicial;

3. Adopt legislation on the status, recruitment, competencies and remuneration of courts' administrative staff;

4. Continue the training of judges and prosecutors through the Magistrates' School and provide for competitive examinations for new appointments;

5. Take into account Council of Europe expert advice on the Law on the Organization of the Office of the Prosecutor and introduce a system for the evaluation of prosecutors as was recently done for judges.

27 Commission of the European Communities, Albania 2005 Progress Report {SEC (2005) 1421}, Brussels, November 9, 2005. Online: http://ec.europa.eu/enlargement/archives/ pdf/key_documents/2005/package/sec_1421_final_progress_report_al_en.pdf (accessed November 29, 2010).

28 EURALIUS (European Assistance to the Albanian Justice System) is a project funded by the European Union under the Albania CARDS 2002 program, which was conducted by the Ministry of Justice of Austria to implement the project in a consortium with the Ministries of Justice of Germany and Italy. EURALIUS began in 2005 and ended in 2010. Online: http:// www.euralius.org.al/php/index.php?lang=1&page=1 (accessed May 28, 2007).

29 EURALIUS, "Background Information for Designing the Future Court Branches and for Selecting a Possible Pilot Court for Court Merging," 2007. Online: http://www.euralius.org. al/reccomendations/eng/Microsoft_Word_Background_information_for_designing_the.pdf (accessed May 28, 2007).

30 Freedom House, Country Report 2008: Albania. Online: http://www.freedomhouse.org/ template.cfm?page=47&nit=443&year=2008 (accessed November 25, 2010).

31 Ibid.

32 Freedom House, Country Report 2007: Albania, Online: http://www.freedomhouse.org/ template.cfm?page=47&nit=414&year=2007 (accessed November 25, 2010).

33 Commission of the European Communities, Albania 2006 Progress Report {SEC (2006) 1383}, Brussels, November 8, 2006. Online: http://ec.europa.eu/enlargement/pdf/key_ documents/2006/nov/al_sec_1383_en.pdf (accessed November 29, 2010).

34 Commission of the European Communities, Albania 2006 Progress Report. As the report goes on:

> The proposed new Law on the Judicial does not address three long-standing shortfalls: improving the independence and constitutional protection of judges, improving the pay and status of the administrative staff of the judicial system (who are not civil servants) and the appropriate division of competences between the judicial inspectorates of the High Council of Justice and the Ministry of Justice. The two inspectorates currently divide work informally. The proposed provisions for the transparent assignment of cases to judges will require implementing legislation to establish objective rules. A system for the evaluation of prosecutors is not yet in place. Implementation of a planned reorganisation of district courts is needed to improve efficiency, but has not yet begun. Many courts still lack adequate space for courtrooms, judges' offices, archives and equipment. Co-operation between the police and the judicial generally remains poor. The Bailiff Service remains hindered in executing judgments by lack of funds, unclear court decisions, and the refusal of many state organisations to meet their judgment obligations.

See Commission of the European Communities, Albania 2006 Progress Report, {SEC (2006) 1383}, Brussels, November 8, 1. Online: http://ec.europa.eu/enlargement/pdf/key_ documents/2006/nov/al_sec_1383_en.pdf (accessed November 29, 2010).

35 Freedom House, Country Report 2008: Albania.

36 Ibid.

37 According to the Freedom House (2008) report:

> Some of the terminated judges challenged the HCJ decision before the high court [sic], which declared the terminations unconstitutional, and in October 2008, these judges were reappointed to the courts that had taken over the jurisdiction of the dissolved courts.

38 Freedom House, Country Report 2008: Albania. See also EURALIUS, "Recommendations on Different Models of Reorganization of District Courts."

39 Ibid.

40 The exact phrase is "crime world." This should be considered a serious accusation for any prosecutor. However, in the case of the Albanian language, the phrase is often rhetorical, used to discharge unwanted public servants.

41 Freedom House, Country Report 2008: Albania. See also Decision 26/2006 of the Constitutional Court of Albania. Online: http://www.gjk.gov.al/ (accessed November 27, 2010).

42 Statement made by Member of the Kuvend Spartak Ngjela, on the November 5, 2007 plenary session on the dismissal of the prosecutor general from the Albanian parliament; also see Interview with Spartak Ngjela, *TV Vizion Plus*, November 5, 2007 (cited in Freedom House, Country Report 2008: Albania).

43 The history of Albanian prosecutors general since the fall of the communist regime abounds with dismissals, resignations and judgments by the Constitutional Court that have never been enforced. Yet, overall relations between the government and the High Council of Justice have improved with the election of President Topi and the replacement of High Council of Justice deputy chairman Ilir Panda with Kreshnik Spahiu (Freedom House, Country Report 2008: Albania). See also Rulings of the Constitutional Court No. 75/2002, No. 76/2002, No. 18/2003, No. 26/2006; and Commission of the European Communities, Albania 2007 Progress Report.

44 American Bar Association–Central European and Eurasian Law Initiative, "Judicial Reform Index for Albania, 2008," vol. 4, December 2008, v. Online: http://www.abanet.org/rol/publications/albania_jri_iv_12_2008_en.pdf (accessed November 27, 2010). As the report summarized the progress and regress of the Albanian judicial reform, it noted that

> Of the 30 factors analyzed in the JRI, the correlations assigned for two factors (judicial associations and objective judicial advancement criteria) improved since 2006, while two factors (guaranteed tenure and publication of judicial decisions) suffered a decline. Overall, a total of seven factors, including those relating to training of judicial candidates and sitting judges, judicial jurisdiction over human rights cases, appellate process, budgetary process, judicial immunity, and professional associations, were rated positive in 2008, while 19 factors received neutral correlations. The remaining four factors, including those related to improper influence in judicial decision-making, enforcement powers of the courts, public access to court proceedings, and publication of judicial decisions, continue to carry negative correlations.

45 Ibid.

46 Commission of the European Communities. Albania 2007 Progress Report, 10.

47 As the Freedom House (2008) report explains:

> The Parliament's subcommittee on justice reform brings together Representatives of justice institutions and international institutions to filter all legal initiatives prior to sending them to the laws committee for adoption and later to the plenary session of the assembly. Yet the subcommittee met officially only once in 2008. Still, its creation marks a salutary step forward—the government ignores its existence in preparing and adopting laws in the area of justice—in the lawmaking process in Albania.

48 Ibid.

49 Ibid.

50 Ibid.

51 Commission of the European Communities, Albania 2008 Progress Report {SEC (2008) 2692 final}, Brussels, November 11, 2008. Online: http://ec.europa.eu/enlargement/pdf/press_corner/key-documents/reports_nov_2008/albania_progress_report_en.pdf (accessed November 29, 2010).

52 Ibid.

53 See *Fletorja Zyrtare e Republikës së Shqipërisë* [Official gazette of the Republic of Albania], 116: August 18, 2011. "Për Miratimin e Strategjisë Ndërsektoriale të Drejtësisë dhe të Planit të Veprimit të Saj" [On the approval of the judicial intersectorial strategy and its action plan], July 20, 2011. Online: http://www.justice.gov.al/spaw2/uploads/files/File/Legjislacioni_Brendshem_Web/Strategjia_Ndersektoriale_Plani_Veprimit.pdf (accessed February 12, 2013).

54 Embassy of the United States in Tirana, Delays in Approving Law on Administrative Courts Jeopardizes Continuation of USG Assistance for Administrative Courts [Press Release], September 27, 2010. Online: http://tirana.usembassy.gov/10pr_0927.html (accessed November 28, 2010).

55 Commission of the European Communities, Albania 2009 Progress Report {SEC (2009) 1337/3}, Brussels, October 14, 2009. Online: http://ec.europa.eu/delegations/albania/documents/eu_albania/2009_progress_report_en.pdf (accessed November 29, 2010).

56 Embassy of the United States in Tirana, "Delays in Approving Law."

57 *Shekulli*, "Gjykata Administrative, SHBA: Afati për Fondin, Deri në Janar 2011 [The administrative court, the US: The deadline for the fund until January 2011]," *Shekulli*, October 29, 2010. Online: http://www.shekulli.com.al/2010/10/29/ambasadoret-e-be-se-takojne-ramen-dhe-berishen.html (accessed November 28, 2010).

58 Ibid.

59 Ibid.

60 European Commission, Communication from the Commission to the Council and the European Parliament "Enlargement Strategy and Main Challenges 2010–2011, COM (2010) 660 final. Online: http://ec.europa.eu/enlargement/press_corner/key-documents/reports_nov_2010_en.htm (accessed November 23, 2010).

61 European Commission. Albania 2011 Progress Report {SEC (2011) 1205 final}, Brussels, October 12, 2011, 9. Online: http://ec.europa.eu/enlargement/pdf/key_documents/2011/package/al_rapport_2011_en.pdf (accessed February 10, 2013)

62 Ibid.

63 Ibid., 11.

64 See for instance *Tirana Observer*, "PD–PS Arrijnë më në Fund një Marrëveshje" [PD–PS finally reach an agreement], *Tirana Observer*, November 15, 2011. Online: http://www.tiranaobserver.al/2011/11/15/pd-ps-arrijne-me-ne-fund-nje-marreveshje/ (accessed February 12, 2013).

65 European Commission, Albania 2012 Progress Report {SWD (2012) 334 final}, Brussels, October 10, 2012, 11. Online: http://ec.europa.eu/enlargement/pdf/key_documents/2012/package/al_rapport_2012_en.pdf (accessed February 10, 2013).

66 Ibid.

67 *Shqiptarja*, "Ngrihet Gjykata Administrative: pr/ligji Miratohet Unanimisht" [The administrative court set to be established: The law passes unanimously], *Shqiptarja*, May 3, 2012. Online: http://www.shqiptarja.com/politike/2732/ngrihet-gjykata-administrative-pr-ligji-miratohet-unanimisht-78743.html (accessed February 14, 2013).

68 Panorama Online, "Miratohet me 128 Vota Ligji për Konferencën Gjyqësore" [The law on the judicial conference was adopted with 128 votes], Panorama Online, July 27, 2012. Online: http://www.panorama.com.al/2012/07/27/miratohet-me-128-vota-ligji-per-konferencen-gjyqesore/ (accessed February 14, 2013). As the report concludes:

    moderate progress has been made in addressing judicial reforms, which is a key priority of the Opinion. The judicial reform strategy and the relevant action plan of March 2012 have started to be implemented. The Law on Administrative Courts, the Law on the National Judicial Conference, and the Law on the Profession of Lawyer have been adopted. Steps have been taken to restrict the immunity of judges. The new private bailiff system is operational. However, important legislation to further strengthen the independence, accountability and efficiency of the judiciary still awaits finalisation, adoption and implementation. In this respect, it is now essential that amendments to the Law on the High Court are adopted. Court organisation, transparency, case backlogs, and the rate of enforcement of decisions continue to raise concern for the efficiency of the judiciary, as does budget allocation. The proceedings to shed light on the events of the 21 January 2011 need to be completed through a credible judicial process. Good progress is reported in the fight against corruption in the judiciary, through the limitation of the immunity of judges. Albania needs to further accelerate the implementation of the judicial reform strategy in order to ensure the independence, efficiency and accountability of its judicial institutions.

69 EURALIUS stated as its objective:

> To facilitate, through the building of the required capacities within the Ministry of Justice and the Judicial, the development of a more independent, impartial, efficient, professional, transparent and modern justice system in Albania, therefore contributing to the restoring of people's confidence in their institutions and to the consolidation of democracy and rule of law in the country, as required by the Stabilisation and Association process with the EU.

See "European Assistance Mission to the Justice System (EURALIUS II) in Albania." Online: https://www.devex.com/projects/tenders/european-assistance-mission-to-the-justice-system-euralius-ii-in-albania/43223 (accessed January 13, 2013).

EURALIUS was a project funded by the EU under the Albania CARDS 2002 Programme. The Contractor of the Grant Agreement No. 2005/103284, which is the basis of the EURALIUS, is the Ministry of Justice of Austria, which implemented the project in cooperation with the Ministries of Justice of Germany and Italy. The implementation of the project started on June 13, 2005 and was designed for an initial period of two years, but was later extended until 2010. EURALIUS was led by Gerald Colledani, vice-president of the Court of Appeal of Innsbruck, Austria, and it consisted in a total of 25 personnel, of which 9 were non-Albanian and 16 were Albanian citizens.

70 This approach also explains the complexity of EU assistance to Albania where its assistance to the judicial reform is often intertwined with assistance to police, border control, anti-corruption policies and the asylum and immigration system. In its "Resolution on the Conclusion of the Stabilisation and Association Agreement between the European Communities and their Member States and the Republic of Albania," the European Parliament notes that it "underlines the importance of the Union's assistance missions for capacity building and welcomes the results achieved by the police assistance mission (PAMECA), customs assistance mission (EU–CAFAO Albania) and the judicial assistance mission (EURALIUS); taking into account the extensiveness and complexity of the fight against organised crime in the Western Balkans, calls on the Commission to substantially increase and strengthen EU assistance in the police (PAMECA) and rule of law (EURALIUS) area..." See European Parliament, "Resolution on the Conclusion of the Stabilisation and Association Agreement between the European Communities and Their Member States and the Republic of Albania," August 29, 2006. Online: http://www.europarl.europa.eu/sides/getDoc.do?pubRef=-//EP//TEXT+TA+P6-TA-2006-0344+0+DOC+XML+V0//EN (accessed May 28, 2007).

71 Freedom House, Country Report 2007: Albania. Online: http://www.freedomhouse.org/template.cfm?page=47&nit=414&year=2007 (accessed November 25, 2010).

72 American Bar Association–Central European and Eurasian Law Initiative, "Judicial Reform Index for Albania, 2006," vol. 3. Online: http://www.abanet.org/rol/docs/albania-jri-volume-3.pdf (accessed November 30, 2010).

73 Freedom House, Country Report 2003: Macedonia. Online: http://www.freedomhouse.org/template.cfm?page=47&nit=242&year=2003 (accessed December 1, 2010).

74 American Bar Association–Central European and Eurasian Law Initiative, "Judicial Reform Index for Macedonia."

75 Ibid.

76 See, for instance, Freedom House, Country Report 2005: Macedonia. Online: http://www.freedomhouse.org/template.cfm?page=47&nit=364&year=2005 (accessed December 1, 2010).

77 Freedom House, Country Report 2003: Macedonia. Online: http://www.freedomhouse.org/
template.cfm?page=47&nit=242&year=2003 (accessed December 1, 2010).

78 See ibid.; also BBC News, "Macedonia Minister 'Shoots Three,'" BBC News, May 15, 2002.
Online: http://news.bbc.co.uk/2/hi/europe/1989547.stm (accessed December 2, 2010).

Moreover, Boškovski was indicted in 2003 by the Crvenkovski government for staging the
assassination of six Pakistanis and one Indian illegal immigrant in March 2002, and exposing
them to the media and public opinion as Islamic terrorists who wanted to attack Macedonian
institutions and foreign embassies in the country. After collecting enough evidence, the
successor government brought charges against him. However, Boškovski fled the country and
hid in Croatia. Boškovski had dual Croatian and Macedonian citizenship. See BBC News,
"Fake Shoot-out, Minister Flees," BBC News, May 8, 2004. Online: http://news.bbc.co.uk/2/
hi/europe/3696781.stm (accessed December 2, 2010).

In another case, during the national elections of September 2002, which VMRO–DPMNE
lost to SDSM, special police troops called Lions, loyal to Boškovski, "raided the printing company
which produced the election's ballot papers, and minister of the interior Ljube Boškovski said
500,000 of the papers had been burned." However, Macedonia's Electoral Commission denied
the allegations, saying that "the numbers of ballot papers and registered voters were the same."
See BBC News, "Fraud Row Clouds Macedonia Poll," BBC News, September 19, 2002. Online:
http://news.bbc.co.uk/2/hi/europe/2267742.stm (accessed December 2, 2010).

Boškovski has been one of two Macedonian citizens to be tried in the International Criminal
Court for Former Yugoslavia (ITCY). On August 12, 2001 a special police unit under the
command of Jovan Tarčulovski raided the Albanian village of Ljuboten, north of the capital
Skopje. During the raid, 7 villagers had been killed, 14 houses burned and tens of others
residents reportedly harassed in police stations around Skopje. According to the charges, the
victims were innocent civilians, and the destroyed houses were not military targets. On July 10,
2002, after a year in session, the ICTY at The Hague pronounced its verdict in the case of
the two indicted officials from Macedonia. Boškovski was acquitted. Police commander Jovan
Tarčulovski was sentenced to 12 years.

In spite, or because, of allegations that Boškovski has been in Ljuboten directing the police
operation himself, Boškovski is hailed as a hero among segments of Macedonian society. Reportedly,
a small government delegation went from Skopje to Hague to support the indicted officials during
pronunciation of the verdict, comprising the ministers of justice, the interior and transportation,
as well as some members of the Sobranie. They had brought Boškovski back to Skopje on a small
government plane the next day. Boškovski was received as a hero. Premier Nikola Gruevski greeted
him at the airport, together with a crowd of fans. As Macedonian custom would have it, Boškovski
was offered bread and salt. Music, general euphoria and T-shirts with his name abounded. His
first act, as Boškovski stepped down from the plane, was to kiss the ground. Boškovski said, "After a
difficult time, a Macedonian Golgotha we had to go through, I have another responsibility. To take
care of the family of our brother Jovan Tarčulovski. To help all we can."

The Macedonian government officially welcomed the verdict releasing Boškovski, and so did
his party. The opposition, SDSM, and the two major Albanian parties, the BDI and the PDSh,
did not issue reactions. However, families of victims from Ljuboten were horrified by the acquittal
of Boškovski. Reportedly Qani Jashari, the father of two men who were killed in the raid said:
"This is a scandal." The brother of the victims, Afet Jasari, said the Jasharis had nothing more to
look for in Macedonia.

Risto Karajkov describes Boškovski's time of glory as follows:

Mr. Boškovski has been on the front pages since his return. Cameras followed him
to his native village of Celopek. Crowds greeted him at a concert he attended with
his wife in Ohrid. Some papers have already hinted that the office of the President is
vacant next year. Incumbent Branko Crvenkovski has recently said he would not run
again. Mr. Boškovski has not said much about going back to politics. He said he would
wait for the trial to fully end first. (Karajkov 2008)

Boškovski's legal problems did not end there. When Boškovski fled to Croatia from Macedonia back in 2004, Croatian authorities arrested him in connection with the controversial case of Raštanski Lozja. The trial for Raštanski Lozja took place during a time of severe political upheaval in Macedonia and the accused were eventually acquitted. But Croatia pressed charges against Boškovski, who had already fled there. The trial in the northwest Croatian city of Pula was postponed several times due to the defendant's failure to appear before the Court. Including detention time in Croatia before he was sent to The Hague, the former minister had already stayed behind bars for over four years. According to Hague rules, detainees are not entitled to compensation in a case of acquittal.

See also *SETimes*, "Croatia Postpones Murder Trial of Former Macedonian Interior Minister," *SETimes*, February 4, 2009. Online: http://www.setimes.com/cocoon/setimes/xhtml/en_GB/features/setimes/newsbriefs/2009/02/04/nb-03 (accessed December 2, 2010).

For a political portrait of Boškovski and his relationship with former premier Georgievski, see Georgievski (2002).

79 Freedom House, Country Report 2003: Macedonia.
80 Freedom House, Country Report 2005: Macedonia.
81 Freedom House, Country Report 2004: Macedonia. Online: http://www.freedomhouse.org/template.cfm?page=47&nit=339&year=2004 (accessed December 1, 2010).
82 Ibid.
83 The Macedonian judicial system was confronted with inefficiency. In 2004 alone, more than a million legal cases were processed in the Macedonian courts. In March 2005, the total number of pending cases was 730,700; among these, 296,000 were decisions that needed to be implemented and 227,000 were "misdemeanor" cases. The average duration of a civil proceeding was nine and a half months in the first instance and over seventy days for an appeal, and criminal cases duration was also nine and a half months. The judiciary's insufficient infrastructure and lack of resources were also serious problems (ibid.).
84 Ibid.
85 Freedom House, Country Report 2006: Macedonia. Online: http://www.freedomhouse.org/template.cfm?page=47&nit=395&year=2006 (accessed December 1, 2010).
86 The Judicial Council consists of seven individuals appointed by a parliamentary commission and proposes the appointment, dismissal and disciplinary decisions concerning judges, with such decisions then taken up by the Sobranie. Since members of the Judicial Council are selected by a simple majority of votes in the Parliament, the governing coalition effectively has control over the appointment of both. See Freedom House, Country Report 2006: Macedonia.
87 Ibid.
88 Freedom House, Country Report 2007: Macedonia. Online: http://www.freedomhouse.org/template.cfm?page=47&nit=429&year=2007 (accessed December 1, 2010).
89 Ibid.
90 European Commission, "Communication from the Commission to the Council and the European Parliament, Former Yugoslav Republic of Macedonia 2006," Progress Report {SEC (2006) 1387}, Brussels, November 8, 2008. Online: http://ec.europa.eu/enlargement/pdf/key_documents/2006/nov/fyrom_sec_1387_en.pdf (accessed December 4, 2010).
91 Ibid.
92 Freedom House, Country Report 2008: Macedonia. Online: http://www.freedomhouse.org/template.cfm?page=47&nit=460&year=2008 (accessed December 1, 2010).
93 European Commission, "Communication from the Commission to the Council and the European Parliament Former Yugoslav Republic of Macedonia 2007," Progress Report {SEC (2007) 1432}, Brussels, November 6, 2007. Online: http://ec.europa.eu/enlargement/pdf/key_documents/2007/nov/fyrom_progress_reports_en.pdf (accessed December 4, 2010). As the report notes, "Overall, steps were undertaken to gradually address the deficiencies of the judicial system. However, a number of delays were encountered, notably as regards the appointments to the Judicial Council and the reform of the prosecution service."

94 European Commission, "Communication from the Commission to the European Parliament and the Council. The Former Yugoslav Republic of Macedonia 2009," Progress Report {SEC (2009)}, Brussels, November 4, 2009. Online: http://ec.europa.eu/enlargement/pdf/key_documents/2009/mk_rapport_2009_en.pdf (accessed December 4, 2010).

95 OSCE, Spillover Monitor Mission to Skopje. "Legal Analysis: Independence of the Judicial," November 2009.

96 European Commission, "Former Yugoslav Republic of Macedonia 2009," Progress Report.

97 European Commission, "Communication from the Commission to the Council and the European Parliament Enlargement Strategy and Main Challenges 2010–2011," COM (2010) 660 final. Online: http://ec.europa.eu/enlargement/press_corner/key-documents/reports_nov_2010_en.htm (accessed November 23, 2010).

98 For instance, Taseski (2010, 1) assesses that "Macedonia badly failed on the assessment from the European Commission."

99 Those laws and by-laws include the removal of the minister of justice's voting rights on the Judicial Council along with the abolition of the ex officio participation on the Council of Public Prosecutors; the enactment of a reform package consisting of a new Criminal Procedure Code (to begin implementation in November 2012); and amendments to the Law on Courts, the Law on the Judicial Council, the Law on Administrative Disputes (amended in order to establish a High Administrative Court, July 2011, with jurisdiction to decide on appeals against decisions of the Administrative Court), the Law on the Court Budget, the Law on the Court Service and the Law on Litigation (September 2011). See European Commission, The Former Yugoslav Republic of Macedonia 2011, Progress Report, {SEC (2011) 1203 final}, Brussels, October 12, 2011, 13. Online: http://ec.europa.eu/enlargement/pdf/key_documents/2011/package/mk_rapport_2011_en.pdf (accessed February 10, 2013).

100 Ibid.

101 European Commission, The Former Yugoslav Republic of Macedonia 2012 Progress Report {SWD (2012) 332 final}, Brussels, October 10 2012, 10. Online: http://ec.europa.eu/enlargement/pdf/key_documents/2012/package/mk_rapport_2012_en.pdf (accessed February 17 2013); emphasis added.

102 See for instance, *Albanian Times*, "Macedonian Government and Opposition Agree on Judicial Reforms," *Albanian Times*, July 7, 2007. Online: http://www.albaniantimes.com/2007/07/albanian-times-macedonian-government.html (accessed February 17, 2013).

103 Lydia Brashear (1997) offers a recount of her work as an attorney with ABA–CEELI in Skopje, 1995. Brashear mentions the EU's ECPHARE Programme only as a donor.

104 European Commission, "CARDS Assistance Programme: Former Yugoslav Republic of Macedonia 2002–2006."

105 European Commission, Albania 2012 Progress Report.

106 European Commission, "Communication from the Commission to the European Parliament and the Council. The Former Yugoslav Republic of Macedonia 2009," Progress Report.

107 European Commission, "The Former Yugoslav Republic of Macedonia 2012 Progress Report," 10.

Chapter 6   Asylum Reforms

1 As Byrne, referring to Anagnost (2000, 396), points out,

> For the CEEC and Baltic states, not only have their own ministry officials not had any influence in the creation of the *acquis*, that they now must implement, but with the notable exception of Lithuania, the asylum offices in applicant states are excluded from the formal asylum discussion under the accession process, which is tightly controlled by Ministry officials. (Byrne 2003, 334).

However, this was not the case of Albania in 2001–2002 when I led the Albanian asylum system. The ZpR that I led was in charge of leading asylum policies and I have participated in the Albania–EU negotiations/progress assessment on behalf of the OfR.

2 I was appointed national commissioner for refugees/director of the Office for Refugees on October 4, 2001. I still remember how surprised people were when I told them that I was the person in charge to grant asylum to foreigners in Albania. It was difficult for Albanians to comprehend that anyone would choose Albania as his place of refuge.

3 The Constitution of Albania. Online: www.kqz.org.al (accessed December 2004).

4 Only in 2003 did the government take over a small number of expenses, including employees' stipends, but funds for legal assistance continue to be out of the question.

5 Such agreements have been highlighted by then UNHCR Ruud Lubbers, when the latter proposed the EU "prong" of his three-pronged approach to a global solution of the refugee situation. Lubbers explains his proposal as follows:

> Under the "EU prong", the UNHCR proposes separating out groups that are misusing the system, namely asylum seekers from countries that produce hardly any genuine refugees. These asylum seekers would be sent to one or more reception centres somewhere within the EU, where their claims would be rapidly examined by joint EU teams. Those judged not to have any sort of refugee claim would be sent straight home.
>
> The limited number of recognised refugees among them would be shared between the EU states. There should be a strict time limit for the entire process. Readmission agreements between the EU and the rejected asylum seekers' home countries must be reached in advance so that people are not detained for months or years simply because they cannot be deported. (Lubbers 2003)

Indeed, Lubbers's EU prong became the blueprint of EU efforts to build a common European asylum system; see, for instance, Thielemann (2003). Moreover, note Lubbers's remarks in the following quote:

> I am pleased that these proposals have found an echo in a recent communication published by the European Commission at the request of member states. The dialogue is continuing at the EU summit in Thessaloniki. We should not miss this opportunity to put in place a more balanced and equitable approach that safeguards the protection of refugees, promotes solutions and restores public confidence in asylum systems. This is one of the most urgent policy challenges confronting Europe today. (Lubbers 2011)

6 I was appointed Albania's Komisioner Kombëtar për Refugjatë and Drejtor i Zyrës për Refugjatë [National Commissioner for Refugees and Director of the Office for Refugees] on October 4, 2001, and arrived in the ZpR the same day. My superior, the minister of local government, told me flatly that the ZpR was his last priority and that the government wanted me to deal with it on my own. I discovered that my predecessor, who had left his job for another position with the Ministry of Justice, had withdrawn $40,000 without explanation, thus leaving the entire institution without cash in its bank account. Indeed, the annual budget of the ZpR was a transferred fund from the UNHCR BoT, and represented a combination of UNHCR and EU contributions, while the Albanian government contributed only with the facility, an ugly workplace patched together among the ruins of a rundown Chinese fair building from the early 1970s. It took three months for the MPVD to send an audit team only to reconfirm the embezzlement of the previous commissioner. Aware of the embezzlement, the UNHCR BoT decided to include the ZpR personnel in its payroll and directly financing its daily operations, rather than transferring additional funds to ZpR's bank account. It is easy to perceive the frustration of public servants who operated within the administrative framework of a government agency but were financially dependent from an international organization.

The MLGD never pressed charges against the former commissioner, a member of the ruling Socialist Party. In February 2002, in a government organization, the minister of local government and decentralization, Arben Imami, from the Albanian Democratic Alliance who had initiated the ZpR's audit was replaced with Et'hem Ruka of the Socialist Party. The affiliation of both Ruka and my predecessor with the Socialist Party and both their adherence with then embattled prime minister Fatos Nano's entourage explain why the former commissioner was able to get away with embezzlement.

7 Pre-screening was a policy strongly supported by the UNHCR; it reflected the concern of then UNHCR Ruud Lubbers to engage in disentangling the mixed flows of refugees entering the EU territories. Such mixed flows are said to contain both refugees and economic migrants. Lubbers's approach reflected its awkward compromise with the governments of some EU member countries who happened to be major donors of the UNHCR and were facing serious domestic challenges from both limited resources to deal with high numbers of asylum applications and a growing tide of anti-immigration mood reflected both as public opinion and rise of anti-immigration parties and politicians. See, for instance, Lubbers (2002, 2004).

8 European Commission, "Commission Opinion on Albania's Application for Membership of the European Union." COM (2010) 680 {SEC (2010) 1335}. Brussels. November 9, 2010. Online: http://ec.europa.eu/enlargement/pdf/key_documents/2010/package/al_opinion_2010_en.pdf (accessed March 25, 2013).

9 Personal communication with Ali Rasha, former director of the Refugee Reception Center, 2010. According to Rasha, the asylum-seeker reception center in Babrru hosts few families from the Kosovar refugee wave of 1999 (a total of 12–13 persons). The staff of the center counts 15 staffers and 6 policemen.

10 Commission of the European Communities, Albania 2006 Progress Report, COM (2006) 649 final, November 8, 2006. Online: http://www.delalb.ec.europa.eu/en/news/al_sec_1383_en.pdf (accessed February 2011).

11 Ibid.

12 As Lubbers writes:

It is essential that such an initiative takes place within the EU's borders. Reception centres then would be bound by EU legal standards. That is important not only to safeguard the human rights of people being assessed but also because it would reduce the legal obstacles states would face if the centres were located outside the EU. The accusation of burden-shifting would not arise. (Lubbers 2003)

13 During our efforts to keep the ZpR alive in 2001–2002, we bowed to the UNHCR pressure to implement a pre-screening policy and, given the time of the beginning of its implementation, it was a unique procedure in dealing with migration fluxes. During my meetings with Albanian officials of the MPO, including then Minister Ilir Gjoni, I learned that the Albanian government had neither knowledge nor opinion about this topic. It was perhaps my position in the politics of the country or the minister's inclination to deal with refugee topics—he worked for the UNHCR BoT before he became minister—that allowed us contacts with local officials, but it did not promise any institutional engagement from his ministry. From the entire government of Albania, only its vice prime minister, Skënder Gjinushi, who was also minister of social affairs and assistance showed some interests on the asylum policies, mainly in issues that affect social aspects of refugee protection.

14 Personal communication with Ali Rasha, former director of the Refugee Reception Center, 2010.

15 Furthermore, the Commission emphasized that

By-laws are required to implement the 2003 Law on local integration and family reunion, in particular to allow development of a system for local integration of refugees. Albania's protection regime for those granted asylum remains weak, especially its judicial aspects. Staff changes as a result of the restructuring of the directorate for nationality and refugees have continued to hinder its capacity and delay decision-making. Reduced capacity led to shortcomings in implementation of the action plans for asylum and for management of asylum cases. Further training is required. Coordination with the national migration system is at an early stage. Improved coordination with the border police is required in order to implement the pre–screening system properly. The expertise of the staff running new asylum centres remains weak. The impact of readmission agreements on asylum system capacity has not yet been properly evaluated. In general, Albania has partially met its targets in the field of asylum.

See Commission of the European Communities, Albania 2007 Progress Report {SEC (2007) 1429}, Brussels, November 6, 2007. Online: http://ec.europa.eu/enlargement/pdf/key_documents/2007/nov/fyrom_progress_reports_en.pdf (accessed December 4, 2010).

16 Website of the Albanian Ministry of Foreign Affairs. Online: http://www.mfa.gov.al/index.php?option=com_content&view=article&id=5596%3Amlv-ja-dhe-liberalizimi-i-vizave&catid=64%3Amlv-ja-dhe-liberalizimi-i-vizave&Itemid=65&lang=en (accessed March 2011); see also Visa Liberalization with Albania Roadmap. Online: http://www.esiweb.org/pdf/White%20List%20Project%20Paper%20-%20Roadmap%20Albania.pdf (accessed March 2011).

17 Commission of the European Communities, Commission Staff Working Document: Albania 2008 Progress Report {SEC (2008) 2692}, Brussels, November 5.

18 European Commission, Albania 2011 Progress Report, COM (2011) 666 final, Brussels, October 12, 2011, 55. Online: http://ec.europa.eu/enlargement/pdf/key_documents/2011/package/al_rapport_2011_en.pdf (accessed March 1, 2013).

19 European Commission, Albania 2012 Progress Report, COM (2012) 600 final {SWD (2012) 334 final}, Brussels, October 10, 2012, 56. Online: http://ec.europa.eu/enlargement/pdf/key_documents/2012/package/al_rapport_2012_en.pdf (accessed March 1, 2013).

20 Commission of the European Communities, Former Yugoslav Republic of Macedonia: Stabilisation and Association Report {SEC (2002) 342}, Brussels, April 4, 2002.

21 Ibid.

22 In its 2003 Association and Stabilization Report, the European Commission points out that:
[t]he temporary protection regime applied to the refugees does not meet EU and international standards (2,756 according to the UNHCR). A proper legislation on Asylum, based on international and EC standards, should be adopted without further delay in order to give them a clearer status.

Later, the report repeats the same sentence as the 2002 Report when it asks the Macedonian government to
[a]dopt a new asylum law, including adoption of the secondary legislation and improved capacity to process asylum applications, establish an independent second instance.

Curiously, a footnote for this sentence explains: "Recommendations included in the 2002 SAP Report, basically not implemented." See Commission of the European Communities, Former Yugoslav Republic of Macedonia: Stabilisation and Association Report {SEC (2003) 342}, Brussels, March 26, 2003.

23 Commission of the European Communities, Analytical Report for the Opinion on the Application from the Former Yugoslav Republic of Macedonia for EU Membership {SEC (2005) 1425}, Brussels, November 9, 2005, 32.

24 Ibid. In 2005, the European Commission highlights the fact that "so far very few have been recognized as refugees, and most applicants have been granted humanitarian protection which is a status with limited entitlements and duration."

25 Ibid.

26 See Commission of the European Communities, Analytical Report for the Opinion on the Application from the Former Yugoslav Republic of Macedonia for EU Membership; and Commission Opinion on the Application from the Former Yugoslav Republic of Macedonia for Membership of the European Union, COM (2005) 562. Brussels, November 9, 2005.

27 European Council, "Council Decision of 30 January 2006 on the Principles, Priorities and Conditions Contained in the European Partnership with the Former Yugoslav Republic of

Macedonia and Repealing Decision 2004/518/EC," *Official Journal of the European Union*, February 7, 2006.

28 As the report mentions,

> There have been no significant developments in the field of asylum. The implementing legislation for the Law on Asylum and Temporary Protection is still missing. The Law still lacks provisions for subsidiary protection. Further legislative alignment and administrative strengthening are necessary. In this area the former Yugoslav Republic of Macedonia is moderately advanced.

See Commission of European Communities, The Former Yugoslav Republic of Macedonia 2006, Progress Report {SEC (2006) 1387}, Brussels, November 8, 2006.

29 Explicitly, the report notes that

> [a]mendments to the law on asylum and temporary protection have been adopted. The amendments take account of the provisions of the qualification directive, which also regulates subsidiary protection. However, the provisions concerning subsidiary protection will not apply until 1 July 2008. Asylum procedures are not yet fully in line with European standards, and proper implementation of the law has still not been ensured, especially as regards issuing identity documents for people covered by the law, decision making, and the appeals procedure. The handbook on reception centres for asylum-seekers has been published. The reception centre is not yet operational and the administrative capacity remains weak. A central database for aliens, covering asylum, migration and visas, has not yet been developed. There is still a lack of staff, proper equipment and budgetary support. In this area the country is not yet sufficiently prepared.

See Commission of European Communities, The Former Yugoslav Republic of Macedonia 2007, Progress Report {SEC (2007) 1432}, Brussels, November 6, 2007.

30 "Roadmap on Visa Free Travel for all Citizens of the Former Yugoslav Republic of Macedonia," May 8, 2008. Online: http://europa.eu/rapid/pressReleasesAction.do?reference=IP/08/724 (accessed March 13, 2011); also "Visa Libcralisation with the Former Yugoslav Republic of Macedonia." Online: http://www.esiweb.org/pdf/White%20List%20Project%20Paper%20-%20Roadmap%20Macedonia.pdf (accessed March 3, 2011).

31 The report concludes that "[i]n this area, legislative alignment is advanced and development of the administrative capacity is well on track." However, the report also notes that

> asylum procedures are not yet fully in line with European standards. The identity documents stipulated in the implementing legislation were still not being issued to people covered by the law. The decision-making procedures and appeals system require further improvement. Amendments to the Law on asylum and temporary protection, notably in the area of subsidiary protection, have yet to be enacted. The authorities have still not fully taken over from the international community responsibility for providing financial and material assistance for asylum seekers. There is still a lack of properly trained staff, proper equipment and adequate budgetary support.

See Commission of European Communities, The Former Yugoslav Republic of Macedonia 2008, Progress Report {SEC (2008) 2695}, Brussels, November 5, 2008.

32 However, the report also points to hovering problems:

> Amendments to the Law on Asylum and Temporary Protection were adopted, but the law is still not fully aligned with the *acquis*. The provisions concerning subsidiary protection were applied. The administrative court, which has jurisdiction over refugee cases previously handled by the Supreme Court, is operational, but there are some shortcomings in its decision making, notably in appeal cases […]. The administrative court needs to be given powers by law to conduct independent judicial review of the substance of asylum decisions. Further efforts are required by the authorities to take on full responsibility for providing financial and material assistance for refugees and asylum seekers. The administrative capacity has improved. Identity documents have started to be issued, though at a slow pace. However, asylum procedures are still not

fully in line with European standards. A central database for aliens, covering asylum, migration and visas, will have to be developed.

See Commission of European Communities, The Former Yugoslav Republic of Macedonia 2009, Progress Report {SEC (2009) 1335}, Brussels, October 14, 2009.

33 See Commission of European Communities, The Former Yugoslav Republic of Macedonia 2009, Progress Report {SEC (2010) 1332}, Brussels, November 9, 2010.

34 European Commission, The Former Yugoslav Republic of Macedonia 2011, Progress Report {SEC (2011) 1203 final}, Brussels, October 12, 2011, 65. Online: http://ec.europa.eu/enlargement/pdf/key_documents/2011/package/mk_rapport_2011_en.pdf (accessed March 2, 2013).

35 Ibid.

36 *Official Gazette of the Republic of Macedonia*, No. 150, October 18, 2010.

37 Government of the Republic of Macedonia, "National Program for Adoption of the *Acquis Communautaire*, 2012: Revisions," 320. Online: http://www.sep.gov.mk/content/Dokumenti/EN/NPAA2012-NarativePart-VersionEN.pdf (accessed March 3, 2013).

38 European Commission, The Former Yugoslav Republic of Macedonia 2012, Progress Report, COM (2012) 600 final {SWD (2012) 332 final}, Brussels, October 10, 2012, 56. Online: http://ec.europa.eu/enlargement/pdf/key_documents/2012/package/mk_rapport_2012_en.pdf (accessed March 3, 2013).

39 I visited the Vizbegovo reception center in July 2012, and the accounts of its director matched what I experienced when I was the head of Albania's asylum system in 2001–2002. Similar to Albanian officials, the asylum authorities in Macedonia recount many instances when illegal migrants abuse the asylum system. Most of the asylum seekers do not stay until the end of the RSD and leave the shelter, allegedly in an attempt to continue their journey northward.

During my visit in the summer of 2012, along with my colleague Steve Voss and the companionship of Orhan Ibrahimi, the representative of the constituency in Sobranie, in the Albanian-inhabited villages of the Kumanovo municipality, right across the Serbian border, I met Afghan refugees returning to the Vizbegovo Reception Center after they had failed to cross the border to Serbia or have been caught by Serbian forces in mainland Serbia and where returned to the country from which they had declared to have entered Serbia.

40 Assembly of the Republic of Macedonia, "Draft-Law on Asylum and Temporary Protection Debated in the National Council," News from the Assembly of the Republic of Macedonia, No. 27, November/December 2012. Online: http://www.sobranie.mk/WBStorage/Files/JPCNo27.pdf (accessed March 3, 2013).

41 *Official Journal of the European Union*, "Regulation (EU) No. 439/2010 of the European Parliament and of the Council of 19 May 2010 establishing a European Asylum Support Office," May 29, 2009.

42 For ERF see *Official Journal of the European Union*, "Council Decision of 28 September 2000 establishing a European Refugee Fund," October 6, 2000; for EASO see *Official Journal of the European Union*, "Regulation (EU) No. 439/2010 of the European Parliament and the Council of 19 May 2010 Establishing a European Asylum Support Office," May 29, 2010; and for the Dublin II, see *Official Journal of the European Union*, "Council Regulation (EC) No. 343/2003 of 18 February 2003 Establishing the Criteria and Mechanisms for Determining the Member State Responsible for Examining an Asylum Application Lodged in One of the Member States by a Third-Country National," February 25, 2003.

43 See for instance *Official Journal of the European Union*, "Joint Action of 27 April 1998 Adopted by the Council on the Basis of Article K.3 of the Treaty on European Union, Concerning the Financing of Specific Projects in Favour of Asylum-Seekers and Refugees (98/305/JHA)," May 9, 1998.

44 Council of the European Union, "Common Statement by Belgium, Hungary, Poland, Denmark and Cyprus on Immigration and Asylum," 17223/10, November 30, 2010.

45 *Official Journal of the European Union*, "Opinion of the European Economic and Social Committee on 'The Added Value of a Common European Asylum System both for Asylum Seekers and for the EU Member States' (Exploratory Opinion) (2011/C 44/03)," February 11, 2011.

46 Ibid.

47 "Council Directive 2004/83/EC of 29 April 2004 on minimum standards for the qualification and status of third country nationals or stateless persons as refugees or as persons who otherwise need international protection and the content of the protection granted." See *Official Journal of the European Union, September 30, 2004.*

48 "Opinion," *Official Journal of the European Union*, February 11, 2011.

49 European Commission, Agenda 2000: For a Stronger and Wider Union, COM (97) 2000 final, July 13, 1997, Bulletin of the European Union, Supplement 5/97.

50 In spite of the theoretical approach, some scholars consider the asylum and immigration issue in the EU to be a matter of security; some others consider it an economic issue. See Messina and Thouez (2002); Peshkopia (2005a, 2005b, 2005c); Busch (1999); Lavenex (2001; 1999: 115–24; 1998: 275); Lavenex and Uçarer (2002: 75); Lindstrom (2003).

51 See *Official Journal of the European Union*, "Agreement between the European Community and the Former Yugoslav Republic of Macedonia on the Readmission of Persons Residing without Authorization," December 19, 2007.

52 See also *Deutche Welle*, "Albania Submits bid for European Union Membership," *Deutche Welle*, April 28, 2009.

53 European Commission, Albania 2012, Progress Report, COM (2012) 600 final {SWD (2012) 334 final}, Brussels, October 10, 2012, 56. Online: http://ec.europa.eu/enlargement/pdf/key_documents/2012/package/al_rapport_2012_en.pdf (accessed March 1, 2013).

54 In the summer of 2012, along with my colleague Steve Voss, I visited Serbia's Asylum Protection Center, Group 484, and UNHCR in Belgrade, Serbia, as well as Young Lawyers of Macedonia Association and UNHCR in Skopje, Macedonia, only to learn that the phenomenon of asylum-seeker disappearance, which I have described in several articles (Peshkopia 2005a, 2005b, 2005c, 2005d) has been a common feature of other Balkan countries' asylum systems as well. In those countries, I found colleagues who, like myself when I was heading the Albanian Office for Refugees, felt helpless knowing that the asylum systems in their countries were being abused by illegal migrants, and asylum workers had turned to be instruments of such an abuse.

55 See, for instance, Embassy of Norway in Skopje, "Asylum Applications from Serbia, Macedonia and Montenegro are to be Processed Within 48 Hours." Online: http://www.norway.org.mk/Embassy/visas/News/visa_notification/ (accessed March 12, 2011); Norwegian Directorate for Immigration, "Asylum Applications from Serbia, Macedonia and Montenegro is Processed in 48 Hours," March 11, 2010. Online: http://www.udi.no/Norwegian-Directorate-of-Immigration/News/2010/Asylum-applications-from-Serbia-Macedonia-and-Montenegro-is-processed-in-48-hours/ (accessed March 12, 2011); EUbusiness, "EU Faces 'Alarming' Rise in Serbia, Macedonia Asylum Seekers," EUbusiness, October 10, 2010. Online: http://www.eubusiness.com/news-eu/immigration-serbia.6mh (accessed March 2011); Expatica, "Failed Asylum Seekers Return Home to Serbia, Macedonia," Expatica, December 3, 2010. Online: http://www.expatica.com/be/news/local_news/Failed-asylum-seekers-return-home-to-Serbia_-Macedonia--_60984.html (accessed March 13, 2011); Euractiv, "Europe Hit by Scores of Western Balkan Asylum Seekers," Euractiv. Online: http://www.euractiv.com/en/enlargement/europe-hit-scores-western-balkan-asylum-seekers-news-498992 (accessed March 2011).

Chapter 7   Beyond Reforms

1 Council of the European Union, 3210th Council Meeting, General Affairs [Press Release], December 11, 2012. Online: http://www.consilium.europa.eu/ueDocs/cms_Data/docs/pressData/EN/genaff/134235.pdf (accessed February 7, 2013).

2   Radio Free Europe/Radio Liberty, "Albania Receives EU Candidate Status, with Conditions," Radio Free Europe/Radio Liberty, October 10, 2012. Online: http://www.rferl.org/content/european-union-albania-bosnia-kosovo/24735102.html (accessed February 7, 2013).

3   BalkanInsight, "EU Urges Free and Fair Albania Elections," BalkanInsight, February 5, 2013. Online: http://www.balkaninsight.com/en/article/eu-urges-for-free-and-fair-elections-in-albania (accessed February 7, 2013).

4   Council of the European Union, 3210th Council Meeting, General Affairs [Press Release].

5   European Commission, "Commission Opinion on Albania's Application for Membership of the European Union." COM (2010) 680 {SEC (2010) 1335}. Brussels. November 9, 2010.   Online: http://ec.europa.eu/enlargement/pdf/key_documents/2010/package/al_opinion_2010_en.pdf (accessed March 25, 2013).

6   Top Channel, "Prishet 'Magjia' e Politikës" [The "magic" of politics spoiled], Top Channel, November 14, 2011. Online: http://www.top-channel.tv/artikull.php?id=222782 (accessed March 29, 2013).

7   Gazeta Tema, "'Ngrin' Konsensusi për Ligjet mes PS-së dhe PD-së" ["Freezes" the PD–PS consensus over the laws], Gazeta Tema, January 12, 2012. Online: http://www.gazetatema.net/web/2012/01/12/ngrin-konsensusi-per-ligjet-mes-ps-se-dhe-pd-se/ (accessed March 29, 2013).

8   Shqiptarja, "Këshilli i Qarkut të Fierit, ja Pretendimet e PD dhe PS" [Council of the Fier Region, the claims of the PD and PS], Shqiptarja, November 14, 2012. Online: file:///C:/Users/Ridvan/Documents/Shqiptarja.com%20-%20K%C3%ABshilli%20i%20qarkut%20t%C3%AB%20Fierit,%20ja%20pretendimet%20e%20PS%20dhe%20PD.htm   (accessed March 29, 2013).

9   Interview with Skënder Minxhozi, Editor-in-Chief of the MAPO magazine, Tirana.

10 Gazeta Tema, "PS: Nuk Tërhiqemi nga Fier. Ligjet jo Vetëm të Miratohen, por edhe të Zbatohen" [We will not give up on Fieri: We seek not only the adoption but also implementation of laws], Gazeta Tema, November 24, 2012. Online: http://www.gazetatema.net/web/2012/11/24/ps-nuk-terhiqemi-nga-fieri-ligjet-jo-vetem-te-miratohen-por-edhe-te-zbatohen (accessed April 17, 2013).

11 Koha Jonë, "Imuniteti, Xhafa Anulon Tërheqjen e Edi Ramës" [Immunity, Xhafa cancels Rama withdrawal], Koha Jonë, September 9, 2012. Online: http://www.kohajone.com/html/artikull_64786.html (accessed April 7, 2013).

12 BalkanWeb, "Halimi: Të Miratohen Ligjet me 3/5, Përmirësojnë Legjislacionin" [Halimi: The 3/5 laws should be adopted, they improve legislation], BalkanWeb, November 2, 2012. Online: http://www.balkanweb.com/bw_lajme2.php?IDNotizia=108271&NomeCategoria=shqiperi&Titolo=halimi-te-miratohen-ligjet-me-3-5-permiresojne-legjislacionin&IDCategoria=2685 (accessed April 7, 2013).

13 Shekulli, "Statusi, Topalli: 'Po të mos na Duheshin Votat Tuaja, nuk do t'ju Lutesha'" [The Status, Topalli: "If we did not need your votes, I would have not begged you"], Shekulli, November 15, 2012. Online: http://shekulli.com.al/web/p.php?id=8346&kat=88 (accessed April 17, 2013).

14 Panorama, "Meta fton Berishën dhe Ramën: Të Lëmë pas të Shkuarën dhe të Miratojmë 3 Ligjet e Integrimit" [Meta calls on Berisha and Rama: Let's leave the past behind and adopt the three laws], Panorama, May 2, 2013. Online: http://www.panorama.com.al/2013/05/02/meta-fton-berishen-dhe-ramen-te-miratojme-3-ligjet/ (accessed May 14, 2013).

15 Gazeta Tema, "Rama: I Votojmë 3 Ligjet Nëse Hyjnë në Fuqi pas Zgjedhjeve" [Rama: We vote the three laws if they enter to force after the elections], Gazeta Tema, May 3, 2013. Online: http://www.gazetatema.net/web/2013/05/03/rama-i-votojme-3-ligjet-nese-hyjne-ne-fuqi-pas-zgjedhjeve/ (accessed May 14, 2013).

16 Economist, "Macedonia's Prime Minister: A Profile of Gruevski," Economist, August 12, 2011. Online: http://www.economist.com/blogs/easternapproaches/2011/08/macedonias-prime-minister (accessed April 8, 2013).

17 In an appearance before journalists during his visit in Tirana in 1992, President Gligorov asserted that the Macedonians "are Slavs" who have no connections with Alexander the Great because, in his words, the Macedonians "arrived here in the 6th Century after Christ." See an extract from the interview on http://www.youtube.com/watch?v=o_gjBAhak18 (accessed April 8, 2013); also, *Telegraph*, "Kiro Gligorov," *Telegraph*, January 9, 2012. Online: http://www.telegraph.co.uk/news/obituaries/9003397/Kiro-Gligorov.html (accessed April 8, 2013).

President Gligorov reiterated this position consistently. Reportedly, in early 1992, Gligorov stated: "We are Slavs who came to this area in the sixth century [...] We are not descendants of the ancient Macedonians," *Foreign Information Service Daily Report*, Eastern Europe, February 26, 1992, 35 (quoted in James Mayfield, "Are the Modern Slavic Macedonians Descended from the Greeks and Alexander the Great?" Online: http://euroheritage.net/macedoniaalexander.shtml (accessed April 11, 2013)). Elsewhere, President Gligorov asserted: "We are Macedonians but we are Slav Macedonians. That's who we are! We have no connection to Alexander the Greek and his Macedonia [...] Our ancestors came here in the 5th and 6th century." See *Toronto Star*, "Interview with FYROM'S President Mr. Kiro Gligorov," March 15, 1992.

This attitude toward Macedonian history and identity was a mainstream position during the 1990s. Thus, Gyordan Veselinov, a Macedonian diplomat, was quoted by the *Ottawa Citizen* in 1999 as stating, "We are not related to the northern Greeks who produced leaders like Philip and Alexander the Great. We are a Slav people and our language is closely related to Bulgarian [...] There is some confusion about the identity of the people of my country." See *Ottawa Citizen*, "Interview with Gyordan Veselinov, FYROM's Ambassador to Canada," February 24, 1999.

18 Fakulteti.mk, "Ke se Gradi Spomenik na Majka Tereza Povisok od Voinot na Konj [Mother Theresa monument will be built higher than the Warriors on a Horse]," Fakulteti.mk, June 29, 2012. Online: http://bukvar.mk/news/kje-se-gradi-spomenik-na-majka-tereza-povisok-od-voinot-na-konj?newsid=9SxW (accessed April 8, 2013).

19 European Commission, The Former Yugoslav Republic of Macedonia 2012 Progress Report, COM (2012) 600 final {SWD (2012) 332 final}, Brussels, October 10, 2012, 19. Online: http://ec.europa.eu/enlargement/pdf/key_documents/2012/package/mk_rapport_2012_en.pdf (accessed March 3, 2013).

20 Quoted in Georgievski 2009.

21 Ibid.

22 Personal communication with Arbën Xhaferi, former chairman of the Partia Demokratike e Shqiptarëve (PDSh) (Democratic Party of the Albanians) and member of the Sobranie, May 2012.

23 *New York Times*, "Shame On Greece: Messing With Macedonia," *New York Times*, April 3, 2008. Online: http://theboard.blogs.nytimes.com/2008/04/03/shame-on-greece-messing-with-macedonia/ (accessed April 15, 2013).

24 Quoted in Georgievski 2009.

25 Ibid.

26 Ibid.

27 Ibid.

28 Ibid.

29 Ibid.

30 EurActiv, "Bulgaria Vetoes Macedonia's EU Accession Talks," EurActiv, November 2, 2012. Online: http://www.euractiv.com/enlargement/bulgaria-vetoes-macedonia-eu-acc-news-515809 (accessed May 1, 2013).

31 EurActiv, "Macedonia warms to Greek name solution initiative," EurActiv, November 8, 2012. Online: http://www.euractiv.com/enlargement/macedonia-warms-greek-name-solut-news-515915 (accessed April 9, 2013).

32 See also Radio B92, "Amnesty International urges release of Bishop Jovan," Radio B92, January 17, 2005. Online: http://www.b92.net/eng/news/old_archive-article.php?yyyy=2004&mm=01&dd=17&nav_category=12&nav_id=26480 (accessed April 9, 2013).

33 On January 27, 2004, the Court of Bitola sentenced the Serbian Orthodox Bishop Marko (Kimev) and a monk, Sasko Velkov, with the fine of 8,500 Macedonian dinars each (€139/$175), for participating in a baptism held on July 20, 2003 in St Demetherios' Church in Bitola. See F18News, "Macedonia: Orthodox Monk and Bishop Fined, and another Bishop still Jailed," F18News, January 28, 2004. Online: http://www.forum18.org/Archive.php?article_id=238 (accessed April 9, 2013).

34 Ibid.

35 Quoted in Bojarovski (2005).

36 Ibid.

37 Radio B92, "SPC Bishop in Favor of Macedonian Autocephaly," Radio B92, October 23, 2013. Online: http://www.b92.net/eng/news/society-article.php?yyyy=2012&mm=10&dd=23&nav_id=82789 (accessed April 9, 2013).

38 Ibid.

39 *Kosovapress*, "Dačić: We Do Not Have Territorial Claims on Macedonia," *Kosovapress*, January 29, 2013. Online: http://www.kosovapress.com/?cid=2,83,159290 (accessed April 9, 2013).

40 "Recognition of States – Annex 2: Declaration on Yugoslavia," Extraordinary EPC Ministerial Meeting, Brussels, December 16, 1991. Online: http://207.57.19.226/journal/Vol4/No1/art7.html (accessed April 15, 2013).

41 *New Europe: The European Weekly Issue*, "Macedonia Enlarged," *New Europe: The European Weekly* 802, October 6, 2008. Also, Shayne Mooney, TV coverage of the Greek Macedonian Rally in Melbourne, 1994. Online: http://www.youtube.com/watch?v=ykte79YCOsA (accessed April 15, 2013).

42 European Council in Lisbon, "Conclusions of the Presidency, Annex II," 43, June 26–27, 1992. Online: http://www.europarl.europa.eu/summits/lisbon/li2_en.pdf (accessed April 15, 2013).

43 United Nation, Former Yugoslavia – UNPROFOR, Department of Public Information, August 31, 1996. Online: http://www.un.org/Depts/DPKO/Missions/unprof_b.htm (accessed April 15, 2013).

44 United Nations, "Repertoire of the Practice of the Security Council Twelfth Supplement 1993–1995, Chapter VII: Practice Relative to Recommendations to the General Assembly Regarding Membership in the United Nations 1993–1995," January 25, 1993 Online: http://www.un.org/fr/sc/repertoire/93-95/93-95_7.pdf (accessed April 15, 2013).

45 Ibid.

46 United Nation, United Nations Security Council Resolution 817, April 7, 1993. Online: http://www.nato.int/ifor/un/u930407a.htm (accessed April 15, 2013).

47 "Admission of the former Yugoslav Republic of Macedonia to Membership in the United Nations," United Nations General Assembly Resolution 225, April 8, 1993. Online: http://www.un.org/documents/ga/res/47/a47r225.htm (accessed April 15, 2013).

48 "Repertoire of the Practice of the Security Council Twelfth Supplement 1993–1995."

49 Ibid.

50 Hellenic Resources Network, "Interim Accord between the Hellenic Republic and the FYROM," Hellenic Resources Network, September 13, 1995. Online: http://www.hri.org/docs/fyrom/95-27866.html (accessed April 18, 2013).

51 See, for instance, the Agreement on a Five-Year Development Cooperation Programme 2002–2006 between the Government of the Party of the First Part to the Interim Accord, September 13, 1995 and the Government of the Party of the Second Part to the Interim Accord, September 13, 1995. Online: http://lj.rossia.org/users/bbb/2008/08/18/ (accessed April 18, 2013).

52 See also Hellenic Republic, Ministry of Foreign Affairs, "FYROM Name Issue." Online: http://www.mfa.gr/en/fyrom-name-issue/ (accessed April 18, 2013); BBC News, "Greece Considers Macedonia Name," BBC News, April 8, 2005. Online: http://news.bbc.co.uk/2/hi/europe/4425249.stm (accessed April 18, 2013); Kathimerini, "Interview of FM Ms. D. Bakoyannis with journalist D. Antoniou," October 14, 2007. Online: http://www.greekembassy.org/Embassy/content/en/Article.aspx?office=6&folder=24&article=21836 (accessed April 18, 2013).

53 United States Department of State, Bureau of Democracy, Human Rights, and Labor, Country Reports on Human Rights Practices 2005, March 9, 2006. Online: http://www.state.gov/j/drl/rls/hrrpt/2005/61651.htm (accessed April 24, 2013).

54 National Bank of the Republic of Macedonia, Annual Report 2003. Online: http://www.nbrm.mk/WBStorage/Files/AI_Annual_Report_2003_ang.pdf (accessed April 23, 2013).

55 *Economist*, "Macedonia's Referendum: A Narrow Squeak," *Economist*, November 11, 2004. Online: http://www.economist.com/node/3387806/print?story_id=3387806 (accessed April 23, 2004).

56 See BBC News, "Greece Considers Macedonia Name"; and also Nikolovski, "Nimitz Proposal For Macedonia's Name Sparks Debate."

57 OneWorld Southeast Europe, "Matthew Nimitz Will Not Present a New Proposal on the Name," OneWorld Southeast Europe. Online: http://see.oneworld.net/article/view/120536/1/ (accessed April 23, 2013).

58 *Kathimerini*, "A Stir over Name of Skopje's Airport," *Kathimerini*, December 29, 2006. Online: http://www.vmacedonianews.com/2006/12/stir-over-name-of-skopjes-airport.html (accessed April 23, 2013).

59 MacedoniaDaily, "Nimetz's talks in Athens included 'Alexander the Great,'" MacedoniaDaily, January 13, 2007. Online: http://macedoniadaily.blogspot.com/2007/01/nimetz-talks-in-athens-included.html (accessed April 23, 2013).

60 SETimes, "Karamanlis: Greece to Veto Macedonia's EU, NATO Bids if Name Issue Not Resolved," SETimes, September 7, 2007. Online: http://www.setimes.com/cocoon/setimes/xhtml/en_GB/newsbriefs/setimes/newsbriefs/2007/09/07/nb-06 (accessed April 23, 2013); Embassy of Greece, Washington, DC, "Answer of FM Ms. D. Bakoyannis Regarding the FYROM Name Issue," August 29, 2006. Online: http://www.greekembassy.org/embassy/content/en/Article.aspx?office=10&folder=24&article=18371 (accessed April 23, 2013); and "Interview with Greek Foreign Minister Dora Bakoyannis," *Dnevnik*, October 28, 2006. Online: http://archive.is/ofP2 (accessed April 23, 2013).

61 See Embassy of Greece, "Answer of FM Ms. D. Bakoyannis" and "Interview with Greek Foreign Minister Dora Bakoyannis."

62 *To Vima*, "Ολόκληρο το κείμενο της πρότασης Νίμιτς" [Olokliro to kimeno tis protasis Nimits] [The whole text of the Nimetz proposal," *To Vima*, February 21, 2008. Online: http://www.tovima.gr/relatedarticles/article/?aid=228676 (accessed April 23, 2013).

63 Ibid.

64 In.gr, "Στην Αθήνα τη Δευτέρα ο γγ του ΝΑΤΟ με φόντο το αδιέξοδο στο θέμα της ΠΓΔΜ" [Stin Athina ti Dheftera o gi tou NATO me Fonto to Adhieksodho sto Thema tis PGDM] [NATO Secretary in Athens on Monday after FYROM Issue Deadlock], In.gr, March 2, 2008. Online: http://archive.in.gr/news/reviews/article.asp?lngReviewID=830577&lngItemID=878422 (accessed April 23, 2013); also Skai News, "Στην Αθήνα με 'μήνυμα' ο Σέφερ" [Stin Athina me "minima" o Sefer] [Scheffer in Athens with a "message"]. Skai News, March 2, 2008. Online: http://www.skai.gr/news/politics/article/75029/Στην-Αθήνα-με-μήνυμα-ο-Σέφερ (accessed April 23, 2013).

65 Ant1 News, "Ώρα μηδέν για το Σκοπιανό" [Ora Midhen gia to Skopiano] [Time zero for the Skopjan issue], Ant1 News, November 27, 2011. Online: http://www.antinews.gr/2011/11/27/135640 (accessed April 23, 2013); In.gr, "Στην Αθήνα τη Δευτέρα ο γγ του ΝΑΤΟ

με φόντο το αδιέξοδο στο θέμα της ΠΓΔΜ" [Stin Athina ti Dheftera o gi tou NATO me Fonto to Adhieksodho sto Thema tis PGDM] [NATO Secretary in Athens on Monday after FYROM issue deadlock], In.gr. Online: http://archive.in.gr/news/reviews/article.asp?lngReview ID=830577&lngItemID=878422 (accessed May 25, 2013).

66 Such was, for instance, the rally in Thessaloniki of the LAOS, which brought about 2,000 people to the streets in early November 2011. See "Macedonia's Referendum: A Narrow Squeak."

67 See Ant1 News, "Ώρα μηδέν για το Σκοπιανό" [Ora midhen gia to Skopiano] [Time zero for the Skopjan issue]; In.gr, "Στην Αθήνα τη Δευτέρα ο γγ του NATO με φόντο το αδιέξοδο στο θέμα της ΠΓΔΜ" [Stin Athina ti Dheftera o gi tou NATO me Fonto to Adhieksodho sto Thema tis PGDM] [NATO secretary in Athens on Monday after FYROM issue deadlock].

68 Skai News, "Ενημέρωση ΠΑΣΟΚ για την πρόταση Νίμιτς" [Briefing PASOK on Nimetz's proposal], Skai News, February 20, 2008. Online: http://www.skai.gr/news/politics/article/74086/Ενημέρωση-ΠΑΣΟΚ-για-την-πρόταση-Νίμιτς (accessed April 23, 2013).

69 Skai News, "Μη λύση σημαίνει μη πρόσκληση" [Mi Lisi Simeni mi Prosklisi] [No solution equals no invitation]. Skai News, February 29, 2008. Online: http://www.skai.gr/player/TV/?mmid=74870 (accessed April 23, 2013).

70 BBC News, "Macedonia Urged to Solve Name Row," BBC News, March 4, 2008. Online: http://news.bbc.co.uk/2/hi/europe/7276524.stm (accessed April 24, 2013).

71 Skai News, "Παραμένει το χάσμα" [Parameni to hasima] [The gap remains], Skai News, March 5, 2008. Online: http://www.skai.gr/news/politics/article/75294/Παραμένει-το-χάσμα (accessed April 24, 2013); BalkanInsight, "EU Warns Over Macedonia 'Name'," BalkanInsight, March 3, 2008. Online: http://old.balkaninsight.com/en/main/news/8393/?tpl=297 (accessed April 24, 2013).

72 See "Παραμένει το χάσμα" [Parameni to hasima] [The gap remains]. Indeed, as earlier anticipated, on March 6, 2008, in the NATO Summit of Foreign Ministers in Brussels, Greek minister Dora Bakoyannis announced that:

> as regards the former Yugoslav Republic of Macedonia […] unfortunately, the policy followed by our neighboring country in its relations with Greece, on the one side with intransigence and on the other with a logic of nationalist and irredentist actions tightly connected with the naming issue, does not allow us to maintain a positive stance, as we did for Croatia and Albania. […] As long as there is no such solution, Greece will remain an insuperable obstacle to the European and Euro-Atlantic ambition of FYROM.

See Skai News, "Η Ελλάδα ανυπέρβλητο εμπόδιο" [Greece, an insuperable obstacle], Skai News, March 7, 2008. Online: http://www.skai.gr/news/politics/article/75394/Η-Ελλάδα-ανυπέρβλητο-εμπόδιο (accessed April 23, 2013); also Skai News Video, "Λύση ή Βέτο" [Lisi i Veto] [Solution or veto], Skai News Video, video of Bakoyannis's press interview after the summit, March 6, 2008. Online: http://www.skai.gr/player/TV/?mmid=75389 (accessed April 24, 2013).

73 Skai News, "Επαφές στα Σκόπια" [Epafes sta Skopia] [Contacts in Skopje], Skai News, March 8, 2008. Online: http://www.skai.gr/news/politics/article/75520/Επαφές-στα-Σκόπια (accessed April 24, 2013).

74 Reuters, "Albanian Party Threatens to Bring Down Macedonian Govt," bdnews24/Reuters, March 12, 2008. Online: http://dev-bd.bdnews24.com/details.php?id=96214&cid=1 (accessed April 24, 2013).

75 Skai News, "Νέοι Ελιγμοί" [Nei eligmi] [New tactics], Skai News, March 13, 2008. Online: http://www.skai.gr/news/politics/article/75990/Νέοι-ελιγμοί (accessed April 24, 2013).

76 Skai News, "Στηρίζουν Γκρουέφκσι" [Stirizoun Gkrouefski] [They support Gruevski], Skai News, March 15, 2008. Online: http://www.skai.gr/news/world/article/76105/Στηρίζουν-Γκρουέφκσι (accessed April 24, 2013).

77 Nooz, "Μιλοσόσκι: Η εντολή του Νίμιτς παραμένει ως έχει" [Milososki: I entoli tou Nimits parameni os egi] [Nimetz's order remains unchanged], Nooz, March 11, 2008. Online: http://www.nooz.gr/page.ashx?pid=9&aid=281213 (accessed April 27, 2013); also In.gr, "Ισχύει η εντολή Νίμιτς" [Isini i Entoli] [Nimetz's Order], In.gr, March 11, 2013. Online: http://news.in.gr/greece/article/?aid=881231 (accessed April 27, 2013).

78 Skai News, "Ξεκίνησαν οι Συνομιλίες" [Xekinsan i Sinomilies] [The talks began], Skai News, March 17, 2008. Online: http://www.skai.gr/news/politics/article/76251/Ξεκίνησαν-οι-συνομιλίες (accessed April 27, 27, 2013).

79 Skai News, "Αισιόδοξος ο Νιμιτς" [Esiodhoksos o Nimits] [Nimetz is optimistic], Skai News, March 17, 2008. Online: http://www.skai.gr/news/politics/article/76261/Αισιόδοξος-ο-Νίμιτς (accessed April 27, 2013).

80 Utrinski Vestnik, "По Виена Нимиц е поголем оптимист за името" [Po Viena Nimis e Pogolem optimist za Imeto] [After Vienna Nimetz is a bigger optimist about the name], Utrinski Vestnik, March 17, 2013. Online: http://www.utrinski.com.mk/?ItemID=A169B25801FA6C4F9D16CBD7B56A8E94 (accessed April 27, 2013).

81 Skai News, "'Όχι' από Σκόπια στις προτάσεις Νίμιτς" [Ohi apo Skopia Stis Protasis Nimits] ["No" from Skopje to Nimetz proposals], Skai News, March 21, 2008. Online: http://archive.is/Jtkm (accessed April 27, 2013).

82 Skai News, "Εντατικές διαπραγματεύσεις για το όνομα" [Entatikes Dhiapragmatevsis gia to Onoma] [Intense negotiations for the name], Skai News, March 18, 2008. Online: http://www.skai.gr/news/politics/article/76333/Εντατικές-διαπραγματεύσεις-για-το-όνομα (accessed April 27, 2013).

83 Skai News, "'Δέσμευση' για το όνομα" [Dhesmensi gia to Onoma] ["Commitment" for the name], Skai News, March 21, 2013. Online: http://www.skai.gr/news/politics/article/76459/Δέσμευση-για-το-όνομα (accessed April 27, 2013); also Skai News, "Νέος γύρος συνομιλιών για το όνομα" [Neos giros sinomilion gia to onoma] [New Round of talks for the name]. Skai News, March 22, 2008. Online: http://www.skai.gr/news/politics/article/76552/ Νέος-γύρος-συνομιλιών-για-το-όνομα (accessed April 27, 2013).

84 Skai News, "Σύσκεψη για το όνομα στα Σκόπια" [Siskepsi gia to onoma sta Skopia] [Meeting for the name in Skopje], Skai News, March 23, 2013. Online: http://www.skai.gr/news/politics/article/76555/Σύσκεψη-για-το-όνομα-στα-Σκόπια (accessed April 27, 2013).

85 In.gr, "Ενισχύονται οι φωνές στο εσωτερικό της ΠΓΔΜ για ένα 'λογικό συμβιβασμό' στην ονομασία" [Enihionte I fones sto esoteriko tis PGDM gia ena:'logiko simvivasmo"] [Voices within FYROM for a "logical compromise" are louder], In.gr, March 22, 2008. Online: http://news.in.gr/greece/article/?aid=884242 (accessed April 27, 2013); Skai News, "Σύσκεψη για το όνομα στα Σκόπια" [Siskepsi gia to onoma sta Skopia] [Meeting for the name in Skopje].

86 Ibid.

87 Ibid.

88 To Vima, "Πιθανή συμφωνία στο 'Νέα Μακεδονία'" [Pithani simfonia sto "Nea Makedhonia"] [Possible agreement on "New Macedonia"], To Vima, March 21, 2008. Online: http://www.tovima.gr/relatedarticles/article/?aid=231535 (accessed April 27, 2008).

89 Skai News, "Όνομα με γεωγραφική διάσταση" [Onoma me geografiki dhiastasi] [Name with a geographic dimension], Skai News, March 25, 2008. Online: http://www.skai.gr/news/politics/article/76795/Όνομα-με-γεωγραφική-διάσταση (accessed April 27, 2008).

90 Skai News, "Νέα ονομασία" [Nea Onomasia] [New name], Skai News, January 12, 2009. Online: http://www.skai.gr/news/politics/article/106993/Νέα-συνάντηση-για-την-ονομασία (accessed April 27, 2013).

91 Ibid.

92 *Dvevnik*, "Посредникот Нимиц Понуди Компромис За Името: Последен предлог Republic of Macedonia (Skopje)" [Posrednikot Nimits Ponudi Kompromis za Imeto: Posleden Predlog Republic of Macedonia Skopje] [Mediator Nimetz has offered a compromise: Last suggestion Republic of Macedonia (Skopje)], *Dvevnik*, March 26, 2008. Online: http://www.dnevnik.com.mk/default.asp?ItemID=3D4385183F07B24789E9107CC34B92D6 (accessed May 1, 2013).

93 *Ethnos*, "Δεν ικανοποιεί την Ελλάδα η πρόταση" [Dhen Ikanopii tis Elladha i Protasi] [The proposal does not satisfy Greece], *Ethnos*, March 26, 2008. Online: http://www.ethnos.gr/article.asp?catid=22767&subid=2&pubid=728559 (accessed April 30, 2013); *Dnevnik*, "Бакојани: Новиот предлог е далеку од целите на Грција" [Bakojani: Noviot Predlog e Daleku od Tselite na Grtsija] [Bakoyannis: The new proposal is far from the goals of Greece], *Dnevnik*, March 26, 2008. Online: http://www.dnevnik.com.mk/?ItemID=D90837CFC3404943AE129F6EA109D015 (accessed May 1, 2013).

94 *Dnevnik*, "Македонија подготвена за разумен компромис" [Makedonia Podgotvena za Razumen Kompromis] [Macedonia prepared for a reasonable compromise], *Dnevnik*, March 25, 2008. Online: http://www.dnevnik.com.mk/?ItemID=CB70AA00FAC7D646B80D0DC4222FB699 (accessed April 30, 2013); *Vest*, "Грчко вето ќе ги прекине преговорите" [Grcko Veto keg i Prekine Pregovorite] [Greek veto to suspend negotiations], *Vest*, March 26, 2008. Online: http://star.vest.com.mk/default.asp?id=149257&idg=8&idb=2333&rubrika=Makedonija (accessed May 1, 2013).

95 "NATO 2008 Bucharest summit, Bucharest Summit Declaration Issued by the Heads of State and Government participating in the meeting of the North Atlantic Council in Bucharest on April 3, 2008." Online: http://www.nato.int/cps/en/natolive/official_texts_8443.htm (accessed April 30, 2013); Skai News, "Νέα δεδομένα μετά το βέτο" [Nea Dhedhomena Meta to Veto] [New situation after veto], Skai News, April 3, 2008. Online: http://www.skai.gr/news/politics/article/77661/Νέα-δεδομένα-μετά-το-βέτο (accessed April 30, 2013); In.gr, "Πρόσκληση μόνο εάν βρεθεί λύση για την ονομασία, αποφάσισε το NATO για την ΠΓΔΜ" [Prosklisi Mono ean Vrethi Lisi gia Onomasia, Apofasise to NATO] [Invitation only if solution is found for the name, NATO decided on FYROM], In.gr, April 3, 2008. Online: http://news.in.gr/greece/article/?aid=887873 (accessed April 30).

96 *Eleftherotypia*, "Η επιμονή Μπους και η αλληλεγγύη των Ευρωπαίων στην Ελλάδα" [I epimoni Bous ke i Allilevgin ton Evropeon stin Elladha] [Bush's insistence and the European support to Greece], *Eleftherotypia*, April 4, 2008. Online: www.enet.gr/online/online_text/c=110,dt=04.04.2008,id=86594016 (accessed May 5, 2013); *Eleftherotypia*, "Άρνηση, χωρίς χρονοδιάγραμμα και με ήπιες αντιδράσεις" [Arnisi, Horis Hronodhiagramma ke me ipies Antidhrasis] [Refusal, without time frame and with moderate reactions], *Eleftherotypia*, April 3, 2008. Online: archive.enet.gr/online/online_text/c=110,dt=03.04.2008,id=15246048 (accessed May 5, 2013).

97 Skai News, "Σωστό το βέτο για το 95%" [Sosto to veto to 95%] [Veto Correct for 95%], Skai News, April 6, 2008. Online: http://www.skai.gr/news/politics/article/77905/Σωστό-το-βέτο-για-το-95- (accessed April 30, 2013).

98 *The Washington Times*, "In the Name of a Common Future," *The Washington Times*, April 29, 2008. Online: http://www.washingtontimes.com/news/2008/apr/29/in-the-name-of-a-common-future (accessed April 30, 2013).

99 Skai News, "Συνεχίζονται οι διαπραγματεύσεις" []Sinehizonte i dhiagravmatensis] [Negotiations continue], Skai News, April 11, 2008. Online: http://www.skai.gr/news/politics/article/78533/Συνεχίζονται-οι-διαπραγματεύσεις (accessed April 30, 2013).

100 *Dnevnik*, "Интегралната верзија на предлог-документот од медијаторот Нимиц" [Integralnata Verzija na Predlog-Dokumentot od Memedijatorot] [Comprehensive version on name-documents by mediator Nimetz], *Dnevnik*, October 9, 2008. Online: http://www.dnevnik.com.mk/?ItemID=9CE7EEBB4F0F6841AA320398A021C61E (accessed April 30,

2013); Aristotelia Peloni, "Παράθυρο για διπλή ονομασία" [Parathiro gia Dhipli Onomasia] [A window for double naming], *Ta Nea*, October 10, 2008. Online: http://www.tanea.gr/news/greece/article/1403491/?iid=2 (accessed April 30, 2013).

101 Ibid.

102 MacedoniaDaily, "Macedonia wants serious changes in the latest proposal," MacedoniaDaily, October 11, 2008. Online: http://macedoniadaily.blogspot.com/2008/10/macedonia-wants-serious-changes-in.html (accessed April 30, 2013).

103 In.gr, "Επιφυλάξεις από την Αντιπολίτευση για την 'κόκκινη γραμμή' στις ιδέες Νίμιτς" [Epifilaksis apo tin Antipolitevsi gia tin "Kokkini Grammi" stis Idhees Nimits] [Concerns from the opposition for "red line" on ideas Nimetz], In.gr, October 10, 2010. Online: http://news.in.gr/greece/article/?aid=945957&lngDtrID=244 (accessed April 30, 2013).

104 *Ethnos*, "'Θα τα περάσουμε όλα σιωπηλά'" ["Tha ta Perasoume ola Siopila"] ["We will get everything through quietly"], *Ethnos*, October 19, 2008. Online: http://www.ethnos.gr/article.asp?catid=22767&subid=2&pubid=1738592 (accessed April 30, 2013); Nikos Meletis, "Οι ιδέες ήταν τελικά της Ράις" [I Idhees Itan Telika tis Rais] [The ideas were ultimately Rice's], In.gr, October 19, 2008. Online: http://www.ethnos.gr/article.asp?catid=22767&subid=2&pubid=1738592 (accessed April 30, 2013).

105 In.gr, "Αποκάλυπτη παρέμβαση" [Apokalipsti Parembasi] [Blatant interference], In.gr, October 19, 2008. Online: http://www.ethnos.gr/article.asp?catid=22767&subid=2&pubid=1742569 (accessed April 30, 2013).

106 BalkanInsight, "Macedonia Denies 'Secret Work' with US," BalkanInsight, October 20, 2008. Online: http://old.balkaninsight.com/en/main/news/14100/?tpl=297 (accessed April 30, 2013); George Gilson, "Nimetz Denies US Influence," Helleniccomserve, October 31, 2008. Online: http://www.helleniccomserve.com/nimetzdeniesusinfluence.html (accessed April 30, 2013).

107 Novinite, "Bulgaria Says No to FYROM Becoming 'Northern Macedonia,'" Novinite, June 8, 2012. Online: http://www.novinite.com/view_news.php?id=140079 (accessed April 30, 2013).

108 International Court of Justice, "The Court finds that Greece, by objecting to the admission of the former Yugoslav Republic of Macedonia to NATO, has breached its obligation under Article 11, paragraph 1, of the Interim Accord of 13 September 1995." Press Release, No. 2011/37. December 5, 2011. Online: http://www.icj-cij.org/docket/files/142/16841.pdf (accessed April 30, 2013).

109 BBC News, "ICJ Rules Greece 'Wrong' to Block Macedonia's Nato Bid," BBC News, December 5, 2011. Online: http://www.bbc.co.uk/news/world-europe-16032198 (accessed April 30, 2013).

110 *Economist*, "Call It What You Want: A Legal Victory for Macedonia Looks Hollow," *Economist*, December 10, 2011. Online: http://www.economist.com/node/21541400 (accessed April 30, 2013).

111 MINA–Macedonian International News Agency, "Greek FM Rejects Milososki Offer, Disputes Macedonian Identity," MINA–Macedonian International News Agency, March 30, 2009. Online: http://macedoniaonline.eu/content/view/6164/45/ (accessed April 30, 2013).

112 MacedoniaDaily, "Macedonian Negotiator Meets Nimetz," MacedoniaDaily, August 21, 2009. Online at: http://macedoniadaily.blogspot.com/2009_08_01_archive.html (accessed August 19, 2013).

113 The Free Library, "Prime Minister Refuses Erga Omnes Name Issue Solution, Opposition and Greek Diplomats Simulate Talks," The Free Library, April 26, 2010. Online: http://www.thefreelibrary.com/Prime+minister+refuses+Erga+Omnes+name+issue+solution,+opposition+and...-a0225503814 (accessed April 30, 2013).

114 Ibid.

115 EurActiv, "Macedonia to Add 'Vardar' to Its Name," EurActiv, June 16, 1010. Online: http://www.euractiv.com/enlargement/macedonia-add-vardar-name-news-495266 (accessed May 1, 2013); A. Papapostolou, "Towards an Agreement for the Name 'Macedonia of Vardar," *Greek Reporter*, June 14, 2010. Online: http://greece.greekreporter.com/2010/06/14/towards-an-agreement-for-the-name-%C2%ABmacedonia-of-vardar%C2%BB/ (accessed May 1, 2013).

116 The campaign was organized by the Macedonian Human Rights Movement International (MHRMI) and the Australian Macedonian Human Rights Committee (AMHRC). Online: http://www.mhrmi.org/our_name_is_macedonia/ (accessed May 1, 2013).

117 Reportedly, Avramopoulos's letter stated: "I hope you will also agree with the recent assessment of the European Commission that a decision of the European Council to open accession negotiations would contribute to creating the conditions conductive to finding a solution to the name issue, under the auspices of the United Nations." See EurActiv, "Macedonia Warms to Greek Name Solution Initiative."

118 European Commission, "Enlargement Strategy and Main Challenges 2012–2013," COM (2012) 600 final, Brussels, October 10, 2012. Online: http://ec.europa.eu/enlargement/pdf/key_documents/2012/package/strategy_paper_2012_en.pdf (accessed May 1, 2013).

119 EurActiv, "Macedonia Warms to Greek."

120 Ibid.

121 The Council of the European Union's Press Release of December 11, 2012 read:

With a view to a possible decision of the European Council to open accession negotiations with the former Yugoslav Republic of Macedonia, the Council will examine, on the basis of a report to be presented by the Commission in Spring 2013, implementation of reforms in the context of the HLAD, as well as steps taken to promote good neighbourly relations and to reach a negotiated and mutually accepted solution to the name issue under the auspices of the UN. In this perspective, the Council will assess the report during the next Presidency. Provided that the assessment is positive, the Commission will be invited by the European Council to: (1) submit without delay a proposal for a framework for negotiations with the former Yugoslav Republic of Macedonia, in line with the European Council's December 2006 conclusions and established practice; (2) carry out the process of analytical examination of the EU *acquis* beginning with the chapters on the judiciary and fundamental rights, and justice, freedom and security. The Council takes note of the intention of the Commission to conduct all the necessary preparatory work in this respect.

See Council of the European Union, 3210th Council Meeting, General Affairs [Press Release], 17439/12, PRESSE 517, PR CO 73, 22, Brussels, December 11, 2012. Online: http://www.consilium.europa.eu/ueDocs/cms_Data/docs/pressData/EN/genaff/134235.pdf (accessed May 1, 2013); also Marusic (2013a).

122 MINA–Macedonian International News Agency, "UN Mediator Nimetz to Meet with Jolevski and Vassilakis in New York," MINA–Macedonian International News Agency, November 20, 2012. Online: http://macedoniaonline.eu/content/view/22247/45/ (accessed May 5, 2013).

123 3210th Council Meeting, General Affairs [Press Release]; see also Gerald Knaus, "Macedonia and the Council of the EU Conclusions," BalkanInsight, December 13, 2012. Online: http://www.balkaninsight.com/en/blog/eu-council-conclusions-on-macedonia-impor tant-step-forward (accessed May 5, 2013).

124 A June 2012 survey in Macedonia (Table 7.1) highlights the different sensibilities of various ethnic groups in Macedonia as related to possible compromises over the country's name.

Table 7.1. Question: Are you for or against changing the name of the Republic of Macedonia with a geographical qualifier in terms that Macedonia will be immediately admitted into the EU and NATO?

	Ethnicity						
	Macedonian	Albanian	Turk	Roma	Serb	Other	Total
For	16.1%	81.5%	66.7%	40.0%	37.5%	53.8%	34.2%
Against	80.8%	15.4%	27.8%	60.0%	62.5%	46.2%	62.8%
I don't know/No answer	3.1%	3.1%	5.6%				3.0%
	100%	100%	100%	100%	100%	100%	100%

Source: Survey conducted in June 2013 from the Macedonian polling agency rating under the request of Blagoja Markovski. Courtesy of Blagoja Markovski.

125 European Commission, "Report from the Commission to the European Parliament and the Council, the Former Yugoslav Republic of Macedonia: Implementation of Reforms within the Framework of the High Accession Dialogue and Promotion of Good Neighbourly Relations," COM (2013) 205 final, Strasbourg, April 16, 2013. Online: http://ec.europa.eu/enlargement/pdf/key_documents/2013/mk_spring_report_2013_en.pdf (accessed May 7, 2013).

126 European Commission, "Implementation of Reforms within the Framework of the High Accession Dialogue and Promotion of Good Neighbourly Relations."

Chapter 8   Conclusions

1 European Commission, Report from the Commission to the European Parliament and the Council on Bulgaria's Progress on Accompanying Measures Following Accession, COM (2007) 377 final, Brussels, June 27, 2007. Online: http://eur-lex.europa.eu/LexUriServ/LexUriServ. do?uri=COM:2007:0377:FIN:EN:PDF (accessed April 4, 2011).

2 European Commission, Interim Report on Progress in Bulgaria with Judiciary Reform and the Fight against Corruption and Organised Crime. Online: http://europa.eu/rapid/pressReleasesAction.do?reference=MEMO/08/73&format=HTML&aged=0&language=EN&guiLanguage=en (accessed April 4, 2011).

3 Other financial cuts include €115 million in funding chiefly meant for highway construction. A freeze was also imposed on €121 million for Bulgaria's agricultural sector. Deutsche Welle, "EU Cuts Funding to Bulgaria for Failing to Fight Organized Crime," Deutsche Welle, July 23, 2008. Online: http://www.dw-world.de/dw/article/0,,3507068,00.html (accessed April 5, 2011).

4 Interim Report from the Commission to the European Parliament and the Council on Progress in Bulgaria under the Co-operation and Verification Mechanism, COM (2009) 69 final, Brussels, February 2, 2009. Online: http://ec.europa.eu/dgs/secretariat_general/cvm/docs/bulgaria_report_20090212_en.pdf (accessed April 4, 2011).

5 The report concludes that
> It will be crucial for Romania to achieve significant, irreversible progress by [the Progress Report scheduled for June 2009]. Romania must demonstrate the existence of an autonomously functioning, stable judiciary which is able to detect and sanction corruption and preserve the rule of law. This means in particular adopting the remaining laws needed to modernise the legal system and showing through an expeditious treatment of high-level corruption cases that the legal system is capable of implementing the laws in an independent and efficient way.

European Commission, "Romania under the Co-operation and Verification Mechanism," February 2, 2009, 3. Online: http://eur-lex.europa.eu/LexUriServ/LexUriServ. do?uri=COM:2009:0070:FIN:EN:PDF (accessed April 5, 2011).

6 Top Channel, "Van der Linden: Albania, Cautious with Elections," Top Channel, January 8, 2013. Online: http://www.top-channel.tv/english/artikull.php?id=7976&ref=fp (accessed April 7, 2013).

Appendix C   Analysis of the Fulfillment of the European Commission's Recommendations to Albania, November 2010, According to 2011 and 2012 Progress Reports

1 Italicized letters denote the (three) reform areas that the European Council Meeting of December 2012 made conditions for granting Albania EU candidate status.
2 European Movement Albania, "12 Key Priorities for Albania: Where Do We Stand?" October 2011. Online: http://www.em-al.org/skedaret/1-EMA%20Policy%20Brief%20-%2012%20 Key%20Priorities%20EN.pdf (accessed February 12, 2013).
3 European Commission, Albania 2012 Progress Report, COM (2012) 600 final {SWD (2012) 334 final}, Brussels, 10 October 2012, 56. Online: http://ec.europa.eu/enlargement/pdf/ key_documents/2012/package/al_rapport_2012_en.pdf (accessed March 21, 2013).

Appendix D   Geographic and Political Divisions of Historical Macedonia

1. Source: Wikipedia. Online: http://en.wikipedia.org/wiki/Macedonia_naming_dispute (accessed April 9, 2013).

REFERENCES

24 Orë. 2008. "Tragjedia e Gërdecit: Arrestohen drejtori i MEICO dhe pronari i firmës" [The tragedy of Gërdec: Arrested the director of MEICO and the owner of the company]. *24 Orë*, March 17.

_____. 2008. "Judicial Reform Index for Albania, 2008," vol. 4. Online: http://www.abanet.org/rol/publications/albania_jri_iv_12_2008_en.pdf (accessed November 27, 2010).

Acton, John. 1862. *Essays on Freedom and Power*. London: Thames and Hudson.

Ager, Dennis E. 1997. *Language, Community and the State*. Bristol: Intellect Books.

Albanian Decentralization Progress Report 2000. 2001. Tirana: Urban Institute, and Institute for Contemporary Studies.

The Albanian Government Program. July 2002.

Albanian Ministry of Foreign Affairs. 2010. "Agreement on Visa Facilitation (AVF) and Visa Liberalization." 13 July. Online: http://www.mfa.gov.al/index.php?option=com_content&view=article&id=5596%3Amlv-ja-dhe-liberalizimi-i-vizave&catid=64%3Amlv-ja-dhe-liberalizimi-i-vizave&Itemid=65&lang=en (accessed March 27, 2011).

Albanian Times. 2007. "Macedonian Government and Opposition Agree on Judicial Reforms." *Albanian Times*, July 7. Online: http://www.albaniantimes.com/2007/07/albanian-times-macedonian-government.html (accessed February 17, 2013).

Allison, Graham T. and Kalypso Nicolàeidis. 1997. *The Greek Paradox: Promise vs. Performance*. Cambridge, MA: MIT Press.

American Bar Association–Central European and Eurasian Law Initiative. 2006. "Judicial Reform Index for Albania, 2006," vol. 3. Online: http://www.abanet.org/rol/docs/albania-jri-volume-3.pdf (accessed November 30, 2010).

Anagnost, Stephan. 2000. "Challenges Facing Asylum System and Asylum Policy Development in Europe: Preliminary Lessons Learned from Central European and Baltic States (CEBS)." *International Journal of Refugee Law* 12: 380–400.

Anastasakis, Othon. 2008. "The EU's Political Conditionality in the Western Balkans: Towards a More Pragmatic Approach." *Southeast European and Black Sea Studies* 8: 365–77.

Anastasakis, Othon and Dimitar Bechev. 2003. "EU Conditionality in South East Europe: Bringing Commitment to the Process." Paper of the South East European Studies Programme, European Studies Centre, St Antony's College, University of Oxford.

Anderson, Benedict. 1993. "The New World Disorder." *New Left Review* 193: 3–14.

Andeweg, Rudy B. 2000. "Consociational Democracy." *Annual Review of Political Science* 3: 509–36.

Ant1 News. 2011. "Ώρα μηδέν για το Σκοπιανό" [Ora Midhen gia to Skopiano] [Time zero for the Skopjan issue]. Ant1 News, November 27. Online: http://www.antinews.gr/2011/11/27/135640 (accessed April 23, 2013).

Antoniou, D. 2007. "Interview of FM Ms. D. Bakoyannis." *Kathimerini*, October 14. Online: http://www.greekembassy.org/Embassy/content/en/Article.aspx?office=6&folder=24&article=21836 (accessed April 18, 2013).

Assembly of the Republic of Macedonia. 2012. "Draft-Law on Asylum and Temporary Protection Debated in the National Council." News from the Assembly of the Republic of Macedonia, No. 27. November/December. Online: http://www.sobranie.mk/WBStorage/Files/JPCNo27.pdf (accessed March 3, 2013).

Athanasopoulos, Aggelos. 2008. "Αναζητούν συμβιβασμό με 'Νέα Μακεδονία'" [Seeking a compromise with "New Macedonia"]. *To Vima*, March 19. Online: http://www.tovima.gr/relatedarticles/article/?aid=231390 (accessed April 27, 2013).

Balalovska, Kristina, Alessandro Silly and Mario Zucconi. 2002. *Minority Politics in Southeast Europe: The Crisis of Macedonia.* Ethnobarometer Working Paper Series. Rome: Ethnobarometer

Balcerowicz, Leszek. 2002. "Understanding Postcommunist Transitions." In *Democracy after Communism*, edited by Larry Diamond and Marc F. Plattner, 63–77. Baltimore and London: Johns Hopkins University Press.

Baldersheim, Harald, Michal Illner, Audun Offerdal, Lawrence Rose and Pawel Swianiewics, eds. 1996. *Local Democracy and the Process of Transformation in East-Central Europe*. Boulder, San Francisco and Oxford: Westview Press.

BalkanInsight. 2008a. "EU Warns over Macedonia 'Name.'" BalkanInsight, March 3. Online: http://old.balkaninsight.com/en/main/news/8393/?tpl=297 (accessed April 24, 2013).

———. 2008b. "Macedonia Denies 'Secret Work' with US." BalkanInsight, October 20. Online: http://old.balkaninsight.com/en/main/news/14100/?tpl=297 (accessed April 30, 2013).

———. 2013. "EU Urges Free and Fair Albania Elections." BalkanInsight, February 5. Online: http://www.balkaninsight.com/en/article/eu-urges-for-free-and-fair-elections-in-albania (accessed February 7, 2013).

BalkanWeb. 2012. "Halimi: Të Miratohen Ligjet me 3/5, Përmirësojnë Legjislacionin" [Halimi: The 3/5 laws should be adopted, they improve legislation]. BalkanWeb, November 2. Online: http://www.balkanweb.com/bw_lajme2.php?IDNotizia=108271&NomeCategoria=shqiperi &Titolo=halimi-te-miratohen-ligjet-me-3-5-permiresojne-legjislacionin&IDCategoria=2685 (accessed April 7, 2013).

Barry, Brian. 1975a. "Review Article: Political Accommodation and Consociational Democracy." *British Journal of Political Science* 5: 477–505.

———. 1975b. "The Consociational Model and Its Dangers." *European Journal of Political Research* 3: 393–412.

Bartilow, Horace. 1997. *The Debt Dilemma: IMF Negotiations in Jamaica, Grenada and Guyana*. London and Basingstoke: Macmillan Education.

BBC News. 2002. "Macedonia Minister 'Shoots Three.'" BBC News, May 15. Online: http://news.bbc.co.uk/2/hi/europe/1989547.stm (accessed December 2, 2010).

———. 2002. "Fraud Row Clouds Macedonia Poll." BBC News, September 19. Online: http://news.bbc.co.uk/2/hi/europe/2267742.stm (accessed December 2, 2010).

———. 2004. "Fake Shoot-out, Minister Flees." BBC News, May 8. Online: http://news.bbc.co.uk/2/hi/europe/3696781.stm (accessed December 2, 2010).

———. 2005. "Greece Considers Macedonia Name." BBC News, April 8. Online: http://news.bbc.co.uk/2/hi/europe/4425249.stm (accessed April 18, 2013).

———. 2008. "Macedonia Urged to Solve Name Row." BBC News, March 4. Online: http://news.bbc.co.uk/2/hi/europe/7276524.stm (accessed April 24, 2013).

———. 2011. "ICJ Rules Greece 'Wrong' to Block Macedonia's Nato Bid." BBC News, December 5. Online: http://www.bbc.co.uk/news/world-europe-16032198 (accessed April 30, 2013).

Bellou, Fotini, Theodore A. Couloumbis and Theodore C. Kariotis, 2003. *Greece in the Twentieth Century*. London: Routledge.

Berend, Ivan T. 2005. "Democracy and Ethnic Diversity: The Case of Central and Eastern Europe." In *Political Democracy and Ethnic Diversity in Modern European History*, 32–48. Stanford: Stanford University Press.

Berg-Schlosser, Dirk and Jeremy Mitchell. 2000. "Introduction." In *Conditions of Democracy in Europe, 1919–39*, edited by Dirk Berg-Schlosser and Jeremy Mitchell, 1–39. Houndmills: Macmillan.

Berisha, Sali. 2006. "Speech at the Conference for the Donors' Activity Coordination in Decentralization and Local Government." Conference for the Donors' Activity Coordination in Decentralization and Local Government, Tirana, May 8–9.

Bertotto, Marco. 2003. "Curbing the Number of Asylum Claimants: In How Far is a Stricter Approach the Solution?" Lecture in the International Seminar for Experts, European Migration and Refugee Policy: New Developments. Cicero Foundation, Great Debates Series. Rome, November 13.

Bethlehem, Daniel L. and Marc Weller. 1997. The "Yugoslav" Crisis in International Law. Cambridge: Cambridge University Press.

Bhagwati, Jagdish. 2005. In Defense of Globalization. Oxford: Oxford University Press.

Bideleux, Robert and Richard Taylor. 1996. European Integration and Disintegration: East and West. London: Routledge.

Bird, Richard M., Robert D. Ebel and Christine I. Wallich. 1996. "Fiscal Decentralization: From Command to Market." In Decentralization of the Socialist State: Intergovernmental Finance in Transition Economies, edited by Richard M. Bird, Robert D. Ebel, and Christine I. Wallich, 1–68. Brookfield: Ashgate.

Bluhm, William T. 1967. Theories of the Political System. Englewood Cliffs: Van Nostrand.

Bogaards, Matthijs. 1998. "The Favourable Factors for Consocional Democracy: A Review." European Journal of Political Research 33: 475–96.

Bogdani, Mirela. 2008. "Aplikimi në BE, Pacipëri dhe Mashtrim" [Application for the EU, shamelessness and deception]. Shekulli, April 2.

Bojarovski, Zoran. 2005. "Pro-Serb Revolt Rocks Macedonian Church." Institute for War and Peace Supporting. February 21. Online: http://iwpr.net/report-news/pro-serb-revolt-rocks-macedonian-church (accessed April 9, 2013).

Brashear, Lydia. 1997. "A Year in the Balkans: Macedonia and the Rule of Law." Human Rights 24: 18. Online: http://www.abanet.org/irr/hr/winter97/brashear.html (accessed December 5, 2010).

Brunnbauer, Ulf. 2002. "The Implementation of the Ohrid Agreement: Ethnic Macedonian Resentments." Journal of Ethnopolitics and Minority Issues in Europe 1: 1–24.

Brusis, Martin. 2005. "The Instrumental Use of European Union Conditionality: Regionalization in the Czech Republic and Slovakia." East European Politics and Societies 19: 291–316.

Bulíř, Aleš and Timothy Lane. 2002. "Aid and Fiscal Management." IMF Working Paper WP/02/112. Washington, DC: International Monetary Fund.

Bunce, Valerie. 1999. "The Political Economy of Postsocialism." Slavic Review 58: 756–93.

_____. 2000a. "Postsocialisms." In Between Past and Future: The Revolutions of 1989 and Their Aftermath, edited by Sorin Antohi and Vladimir Tismaneanu, 122–52. Budapest: Central European University Press.

_____. 2000b. Subversive Institutions: The Design and the Destruction of the Socialism and the State. Cambridge: Cambridge University Press.

_____. 2003. "Rethinking Recent Democratization: Lessons from the Postcommunist Experience." World Politics 55: 167–92.

Busch, Nicholas. "Asylum and Immigration Policies of the EU." Paper presented in the International Seminar EU: Area of Justice or Orwellian Nightmare? University of Tampere, October 13, 1999.

Bush, George W. 2003. "Statement on the Situation in Macedonia." March 23. Online: http://www.presidency.ucsb.edu/ws/index.php?pid=45952 (accessed 1 October 2009).

Bushati, Ditmir. 2009. "Albania." Freedom House. Online: http://www.freedomhouse.org/uploads/nit/2009/Albania-final.pdf (accessed November 21, 2010).

Butenschøn, Nils. A. 1985. "Conflict Management in Plural Societies: The Consociational Democracy Formula." Scandinavian Political Studies 8: 85–103.

Byrne, Rosemary. 2002. "Future Perspectives: Accession and Asylum in an Expanded European Union." In The New Asylum Countries? Migration Control and Refugee Protection in an Enlarged European Union, edited by Rosemary Byrne, Gregor Noll, and J. Vedsted-Hansen. 373–422. The Hague: Kluwer.

_____. 2003. "Harmonization and Burden Redistribution in the Two Europes." *Journal of Refugee Studies* 16: 336–58.

Byrne, Rosemary, Gregor Noll and J. Vedsted-Hansen. 2002a. "Western European Asylum Policies for Export: The Transfer of Protection and Defection Formulas to Central Eastern Europe and the Baltics." In *The New Asylum Countries? Migration Control and Refugee Protection in an Enlarged European Union*, edited by Rosemary Byrne, Gregor Noll, and J. Vedsted-Hansen, 5–28. The Hague: Kluwer.

_____. 2002b. "Tranformation of Asylum in Europe." In *The New Asylum Countries? Migration Control and Refugee Protection in an Enlarged European Union*, edited by Rosemary Byrne, Gregor Noll, and J. Vedsted-Hansen, 423–31. The Hague: Kluwer.

Cameron, David R. 2003. "The Challenges of Accession." *East European Politics and Societies* 17: 24–41.

Carothers, Thomas. 2006. "The Rule of Law Revival." In *Promoting the Rule of Law Abroad: In Search of Knowledge*, edited by Thomas Carothers, 3–13. Washington, DC: Carnegie Endowment for International Peace.

Center for Economic Analysis. 2006. "CEA Comments on the EBDR 2006 Strategy for the Republic of Macedonia." Press Release. Online: http://www.cea.org.mk/Documents/Press_release_EBRD_strategy_2006.pdf (accessed May 26, 2006).

Checkel, Jeffrey T. 2000. "Compliance and Conditionality." ARENA Working Papers WP 00/18. University of Oslo.

Chehabi, H. E. 1980. "The Absence of Consociationalism in Sri Lanka." *Plural Societies* 11(4): 55–85.

Chryssochoou, Dimitris N. 1994. "Democracy and Symbiosis in the European Union: Towards a Confederal Consociation?" *West European Politics* 17(4): 1–14.

CIA World Factbook. 2007. Online: https://www.cia.gov/library/publications/the-world-factbook/index.html (accessed September 3, 2010).

Commission of the European Communities. 2002. Former Yugoslav Republic of Macedonia: Stabilisation and Association Report. {SEC (2002) 342}. Brussels. April 4.

_____. 2003. Former Yugoslav Republic of Macedonia: Stabilisation and Association Report. {SEC (2003) 342}. Brussels. March 26.

_____. 2004. Albania: Stabilisation and Association Report 2004. Online: http://www.delalb.ec.europa.eu/en/documents_march_2004/Country_report_Albanie_04_03_29_Final.pdf (accessed May 19, 2007).

_____. 2005a. Albania 2005 Progress Report. {SEC (2005) 1421}. Brussels. November 9. Online: http://ec.europa.eu/enlargement/archives/pdf/key_documents/2005/package/sec_1421_final_progress_report_al_en.pdf (accessed November 29, 2010).

_____. 2005b. Analytical Report for the Opinion on the Application from the Former Yugoslav Republic of Macedonia for EU Membership. {SEC (2005) 1425}. Brussels. November 9.

_____. 2005c. Commission Opinion on the Application from the Former Yugoslav Republic of Macedonia for Membership of the European Union. COM (2005) 562. Brussels. November 9.

_____. 2006a. Albania 2006 Progress Report. {SEC (2006) 1383}. Brussels. November 8. Online: http://ec.europa.eu/enlargement/pdf/key_documents/2006/nov/al_sec_1383_en.pdf (accessed November 29, 2010).

_____. 2006b. The Former Yugoslav Republic of Macedonia 2006 Progress Report. {SEC (2006) 1387}. Brussels. November 8.

_____. 2007a. Commission Staff Working Document: Albania 2007 Progress Report. {SEC (2007) 1429}. Brussels. November 6.

_____. 2007c. The Former Yugoslav Republic of Macedonia 2007 Progress Report. {SEC (2007) 1432}. Brussels. November 6.

_____. 2008a. The Former Yugoslav Republic of Macedonia 2008 Progress Report. {SEC (2008) 2695}. Brussels. November 5.

_____. 2008b. Albania 2008 Progress Report. {SEC (2008) 2692 final}. Brussels. November 11. Online: http://ec.europa.eu/enlargement/pdf/press_corner/key-documents/reports_nov_2008/albania_progress_report_en.pdf (accessed November 29, 2010).

_____. 2009a. Albania 2009 Progress Report. {SEC (2009) 1337/3}. Brussels. October 14. Online: http://ec.europa.eu/delegations/albania/documents/eu_albania/2009_progress_report_en.pdf (accessed November 29, 2010).

_____. 2009b. The Former Yugoslav Republic of Macedonia 2009 Progress Report. {SEC (2009) 1335}. Brussels, October 14.

_____. 2009c. "Communication from the Commission to the European Parliament and the Council. The Former Yugoslav Republic of Macedonia 2009." Progress Report. {SEC (2009)}. Brussels. November 4. Online: http://ec.europa.eu/enlargement/pdf/key_documents/2009/mk_rapport_2009_en.pdf (accessed December 4, 2010).

_____. 2010. The Former Yugoslav Republic of Macedonia 2009 Progress Report. {SEC (2010) 1332}. Brussels. November 9.

Congress of Local and Regional Authorities. 2006. "Congress President Calls on Albanian Authorities to Fully Comply with Provisions of the European Local Self-Government Charter." Press Release 025(2006). January 17.

Connor, Walker. 1967. "Self-Determination: The New Phase." *World Politics* 20: 30–53.

Constitution of Albania. Online: www.kqz.org.al (accessed December 2004).

Constitutional Court the Republic of Albania. 2002. "Vendimi Përfundimtar i Gjykatës Nr. 75/2002" [Final ruling of the court No. 75/2002]. April 19. Online: http://www.gjk.gov.al/templates/NEModules/kerkese_list/konsulto.php?id_kerkesa_vendimi= 431&language=Lng1 (accessed September 7, 2013).

_____. 2002. "Vendimi Përfundimtar i Gjykatës Nr. 76/2002" [Final ruling of the court No. 76/2002]. April 25. Online: http://www.gjk.gov.al/templates/NEModules/kerkese_list/konsulto.php?id_kerkesa_vendimi= 432&language=Lng1 (accessed September 7, 2013).

_____. 2003. "Vendimi Përfundimtar i Gjykatës Nr. 18/2003" [Final ruling of the court No. 18/2003]. May 14. Online: http://www.gjk.gov.al/templates/NEModules/kerkese_list/konsulto.php?id_kerkesa_vendimi= 476&language=Lng1 (accessed September 7, 2013).

_____. 2006. "Vendimi Përfundimtar i Gjykatës Nr. 26/2006" [Final ruling of the court No. 26/2006]. April 12. Online: http://www.gjk.gov.al/templates/NEModules/kerkese_list/konsulto.php?id_kerkesa_vendimi=543&language=Lng1 (accessed September 7, 2013).

Costa, Oliver and Paul Magnette. 2003. "The European Union as a Consociation? A Methodological Assessment." *West European Politics* 26(3): 1–18.

Coulson, Andrew, ed. 1995. *Local Government in Eastern Europe: The Rebirth of Local Democracy.* Cheltenham: Edward Elgar.

Council of Europe. 2001. "The Former Yugoslav Republic of Macedonia." July 10. Online: http://www.venice.coe.int/webforms/events/default.aspx?id=279 (accessed October 11, 2009).

_____. 1997. "Reply to Recommendation 1312, Doc. 8139: Honouring of Obligations and Commitments by Albania." The Committee of Ministers. Online: http://assembly.coe.int/ASP/Doc/XrefDocDetails_E.asp?FileID=8577 (accessed May 24, 2013).

_____. 2006. "Council Decision of January 30 on Principles, Priorities, and Conditions Contained in the European Partnership with Albania and Repealing Decision 2004/5/19/EC," 2006/54/EC. Online: http://eur-lex.europa.eu/smartapi/cgi/sga_doc?smartapi!celexplus!prod!CELEXnumdoc&numdoc=306D0054&lg=en (accessed May 20, 2007).

Council of Europe and the European Union. 1998. Second Joint Programme between the European Union and the Council of Europe for the Promotion of Legal System Reform in Albania, Final Report. Restricted GR-EDS(98)5. February 2.

Council of the European Union. 2010. "Common Statement by Belgium, Hungary, Poland, Denmark and Cyprus on Immigration and Asylum." 17223/10. November 30.

_____. 2012. "3,210th Council Meeting, General Affairs." Press Release. December 11. Online: http://www.consilium.europa.eu/ueDocs/cms_Data/docs/pressData/EN/genaff/134235.pdf (accessed February 7, 2013).

Council of Ministers of the Republic of Albania. 1999. "Decision for the Approval of the Strategy for Decentralization and Local Autonomy." No. 651. December 12.

Crawford, Beverly and Arend Lijphart, eds. 1997. *Liberalization and Leninist Legacies: Comparative Perspectives on Democratic Transitions*. Berkeley: University of California Press.

Daalder Hans. 1971. "On Building Consociational Nations: The Cases of the Netherlands and Switzerland." *International Social Science Journal* 23: 355–70.

_____. 1974. "The Consociational Democracy Theme." *World Politics* 26: 604–21.

_____. 1989. "Ancient and Modern Pluralism in the Netherlands." Working Paper Series, No. 22. Cambridge, MA: Central European Studies, Harvard University.

Danforth, Loring. 1995. *The Macedonian Conflict*. Princeton: Princeton University Press.

Daskalovski, Židas. 2006. *Walking on the Edge: Consolidating Multiethnic Macedonia, 1989–2004*. Chapel Hill: Globic Press.

_____. 2009. "Macedonia." Freedom House. Online: http://www.freedomhouse.org/uploads/nit/2009/Macedonia-final.pdf (accessed November 22, 2010).

_____. 2010. "Macedonia." Freedom House. Online: http://www.freedomhouse.org/images/File/nit/2010/NIT-2010-Macedonia-proof-II.pdf (accessed November 22, 2010).

Davies, Catriona. 2011. "Is Macedonia's Capital Being Turned into a Theme Park?" CNN, October 10. Online: http://edition.cnn.com/2011/10/04/world/europe/macedonia-skopje-2014/index.html (accessed April 8, 2013).

Dekmeijian, Richard H. 1978. "Consociational Democracy in Crisis: The Case of Lebanon." *Comparative Politics* 10: 251–65.

Deutche Welle. 2008. "EU Cuts Funding to Bulgaria for Failing to Fight Organized Crime." July 23. Online: http://www.dw-world.de/dw/article/0,,3507068,00.html (accessed April 2011).

_____. 2009. "Albania Submits Bid for European Union Membership." *Deutche Welle*, April 28.

Dew, Edward. 1972. "Surinam: The Test of Consociationalism." *Plural Societies* 3(4): 3–17.

Di Palma, Giuseppe. 1990. *To Craft Democracies: An Essay on Democratic Transition*. Berkeley: University of California Press.

Diamond, Larry and Marc Plattner. 1994. "Introduction." In *Nationalism, Ethnic Conflict, and Democracy*, edited by Larry Diamond and Marc F. Plattner, 3–22. Baltimore and London: Johns Hopkins University Press.

Dimitrova, Antoaneta, ed. 2004. *Driven to Change: The European Union's Enlargement Viewed from the East*. Manchester: Manchester University Press.

Dix, Robert H. 1980. "Consociational Democracy: The Case of Colombia." *Comparative Politics* 12: 303–21.

Dnevnik. 2006. "Interview with Greek Foreign Minister Dora Bakoyannis." *Dnevnik*, October 28. Online: http://archive.is/ofP2 (accessed April 23, 2013).

_____. 2008a. "Македонија подготвена за разумен компромис" [Makedonia Podgotvena za Razumen Kompromis] [Macedonia prepared for a reasonable compromise]. *Dnevnik*, March 25. Online: http://www.dnevnik.com.mk/?ItemID=CB70AA00FAC7D646B80D0DC4222FB699 (accessed April 30, 2013).

_____. 2008b. "Бакојани: Новиот предлог е далеку од целите на Грција" [Bakojani: Noviot Predlog e Daleku od Tselite na Grtsija] [Bakoyannis: The new proposal is far from the goals of Greece]. *Dnevnik*, March 26. Online: http://www.dnevnik.com.mk/?ItemID=D90837CFC340 4943AE129F6EA109D015 (accessed May 1, 2013).

_____. 2008c. "Посредникот Нимиц Понуди Компромис За Името: Последен предлог Republic of Macedonia (Skopje)" [Posrednikot Nimits Ponudi Kompromis za Imeto: Posleden Predlog Republic of Macedonia Skopje] [Mediator Nimetz has offered a compromise: Last suggestion

Republic of Macedonia (Skopje)]. *Dvevnik*, March 26. Online: http://www.dnevnik.com.mk/default.asp?ItemID=3D4385183F07B24789E9107CC34B92D6 (accessed May 1, 2013).

———. 2008d. "Интегралната верзија на предлог-документот од медијаторот Нимиц" [Integralnata Verzija na Predlog-Dokumentot od Memedijatorot] [Comprehensive version on name-documents by mediator Nimetz]. *Dnevnik*, October 9. Online: http://www.dnevnik.com.mk/?ItemID=9CE7EEBB4F0F6841AA320398A021C61E (accessed April 30, 2013).

Easterly, William. 2002. *The Elusive Quest for Growth: Economists' Adventures and Misadventures in the Tropics*. Cambridge, MA, and London: MIT Press.

———. 2006. *White Man's Burden: Why the West's Efforts to Aid the Rest Have Done So Much Ill and So Little Good*. New York: Penguin Press.

Economist. 2004. "Macedonia's Referendum: A Narrow Squeak." *Economist*, November 11. Online: http://www.economist.com/node/3387806/print?story_id=3387806 (accessed April 23, 2004).

———. 2011a. "Macedonia's Prime Minister: A Profile of Gruevski." *Economist*, August 12. Online: http://www.economist.com/blogs/easternapproaches/2011/08/macedonias-prime-minister (accessed April 8, 2013).

———. 2011b. "Call It What You Want: A Legal Victory for Macedonia Looks Hollow." *Economist*, December 10. Online: http://www.economist.com/node/21541400 (accessed April 30, 2013).

Elander, Ingemar. 1997. "Between Centralism and Localism: On the Development of Local Self-Government in Post-socialist Europe." *Environment and Planning C: Government and Policy* 15: 143–59.

Eleftherotypia. 2008a. "Άρνηση, χωρίς χρονοδιάγραμμα και με ήπιες αντιδράσεις" [Arnisi, Horis Hronodhiagramma ke me ipies Antidhrasis] [Refusal, without time frame and with moderate reactions]. *Eleftherotypia*, April 3. Online: archive.enet.gr/online/online_text/c=110,dt=03.04.2008,id=15246048 (accessed May 5, 2013).

———. 2008b. "Η επιμονή Μπους και η αλληλεγγύη των Ευρωπαίων στην Ελλάδα" [I epimoni Bous ke i Allilevgin ton Evropeon stin Elladha] [Bush's insistence and the European support to Greece]. *Eleftherotypia*, April 4. Online: www.enet.gr/online/online_text/c=110,dt=04.04.2008,id=86594016 (accessed May 5, 2013).

Elster, Jon, Claus Offe and Ulrich K. Preuss. 1998. *Institutional Design in Post-communist Societies: Rebuilding the Ship at Sea*. Cambridge: Cambridge University Press.

Embassy of Greece, Washington, DC. 2006. "Answer of FM Ms. D. Bakoyannis Regarding the FYROM Name Issue." August 29. Online: http://www.greekembassy.org/embassy/content/en/Article.aspx?office=10&folder=24&article=18371 (accessed April 23, 2013).

Embassy of Norway in Skopje. "Asylum Applications from Serbia, Macedonia and Montenegro Are to Be Processed Within 48 Hours." Online: http://www.norway.org.mk/Embassy/visas/News/visa_notification/ (accessed March 12, 2011).

Embassy of the United States in Tirana. 2010. "Delays in Approving Law on Administrative Courts Jeopardizes Continuation of USG Assistance for Administrative Courts." Press Release. September 27. Online: http://tirana.usembassy.gov/10pr_0927.html (accessed November 28, 2010).

ESIWeb. 2008. "Visa Liberalisation with the Former Yugoslav Republic of Macedonia." European Sustainability Initiative. Online: http://www.esiweb.org/pdf/White%20List%20Project%20Paper%20-%20Roadmap%20Macedonia.pdf (accessed March 3, 2011).

Ethnos. 2008a. "Δεν ικανοποιεί την Ελλάδα η πρόταση" [Dhen Ikanopii tis Elladha i Protasi] [The proposal does not satisfy Greece]. Ethnos, March 26. Online: http://www.ethnos.gr/article.asp?catid=22767&subid=2&pubid=728559 (accessed April 30, 2013).

———. 2008b. "Απροκάλυπτη παρέμβαση" [Apokalipsti Parembasi] [Blatant interference]. Ethnos, October 19. Online: http://www.ethnos.gr/article.asp?catid=22767&subid=2&pubid=1742569 (accessed April 30, 2013).

_____. 2008c. "'Θα τα περάσουμε όλα σιωπηλά'" ["Tha ta Perasoume ola Siopila"] ["We will get everything through quietly"]. Ethnos, October 19. Online: http://www.ethnos.gr/article.asp?catid=22767&subid=2&pubid=1738592 (accessed April 30, 2013).

EurActiv. 2010a. "Europe Hit by Scores of Western Balkan Asylum Seekers." EurActiv, May 3. http://www.euractiv.com/en/enlargement/europe-hit-scores-western-balkan-asylum-seekers-news-498992 (accessed March 2011).

_____. 2010b. "Macedonia to Add 'Vardar' to Its Name." EurActiv, June 16. Online: http://www.euractiv.com/enlargement/macedonia-add-vardar-name-news-495266 (accessed May 1, 2013).

_____. 2012a. "Macedonia Warms to Greek Name Solution Initiative." EurActiv, November 8. Online: http://www.euractiv.com/enlargement/macedonia-warms-greek-name-solut-news-515915 (accessed April 9, 2013).

_____. 2012b. "Bulgaria Vetoes Macedonia's EU Accession Talks." EurActiv, November 2. Online: http://www.euractiv.com/enlargement/bulgaria-vetoes-macedonia-eu-acc-news-515809 (accessed May 1, 2013).

EUbusiness. 2010. "EU Faces 'Alarming' Rise in Serbia, Macedonia Asylum Seekers." EUbusiness, October 10. Online: http://www.eubusiness.com/news-eu/immigration-serbia.6mh (accessed March 2011).

European Commission. 1991. "Recognition of States – Annex 2: Declaration on Yugoslavia." Extraordinary EPC Ministerial Meeting, Brussels. December 16. Online: http://207.57.19.226/journal/Vol4/No1/art7.html (accessed April 15, 2013).

_____. 1992. "Europe and the Challenge of Enlargement." Bulletin of the European Communities, Supplement 3/92: 19.

_____. 1997. "Agenda 2000: For a Stronger and Wider Union." COM (97) 2000 final. July 13. Bulletin of the European Union, Supplement 5/97: 39–42.

_____. 2006a. "CARDS Assistance Programme: Former Yugoslav Republic of Macedonia 2002–2006." Online: http://ec.europa.eu/enlargement/pdf/financial_assistance/cards/publications/fyrom_strategy_paper_en.pdf (accessed August 5, 2013).

_____. 2006b. "Communication from the Commission to the Council and the European Parliament, Former Yugoslav Republic of Macedonia 2006 Progress Report." {SEC (2006) 1387}. Brussels. November 8. Online: http://ec.europa.eu/enlargement/pdf/key_documents/2006/nov/fyrom_sec_1387_en.pdf (accessed December 4, 2010).

_____. 2007a. "Communication from the Commission to the Council and the European Parliament, Former Yugoslav Republic of Macedonia 2007 Progress Report." {SEC (2007) 1432}. Brussels. November 6. Online: http://ec.europa.eu/enlargement/pdf/key_documents/2007/nov/fyrom_progress_reports_en.pdf (accessed December 4, 2010).

_____. 2007b. "Report from the Commission to the European Parliament and the Council on Bulgaria's Progress on Accompanying Measures Following Accession." COM (2007) 377 final. Brussels. June 27. Online: http://eur-lex.europa.eu/LexUriServ/LexUriServ.do?uri=COM:2007:0377:FIN:EN:PDF (accessed April 3, 2011).

_____. 2008a. "Roadmap on Visa Free Travel for all Citizens of the Former Yugoslav Republic of Macedonia." May 8. Online: http://europa.eu/rapid/pressReleasesAction.do?reference=IP/08/724 (accessed March 21, 2011).

_____. 2008b. "Communication from the Commission to the Council and the European Parliamen, Former Yugoslav Republic of Macedonia 2008." Progress Report. {SEC (2007) 2695}. Brussels. November 5. Online: http://ec.europa.eu/enlargement/pdf/press_corner/key-documents/reports_nov_2008/ the_former_yugoslav_republic_of_macedonia_progress_report_en.pdf (accessed December 4, 2010).

_____. 2009a. "Communication from the Commission to the European Parliament and the Council, The Former Yugoslav Republic of Macedonia 2009." Progress Report. {SEC

(2009) 1335/3}. Brussels. October 14. Online: http://vorige.nrc.nl/redactie/Europa/voortgangsrapporten2009/macedonie.pdf (accessed August 5, 2013).

_____. 2009b. "Interim Report from the Commission to the European Parliament and the Council on Progress in Bulgaria under the Co-operation and Verification Mechanism." COM (2009) 69 final. Brussels. February 2. Online: http://ec.europa.eu/dgs/secretariat_general/cvm/docs/bulgaria_report_20090212_en.pdf (accessed April 3, 2011).

_____. 2009c. "Interim Report from the Commission to the European Parliament and the Council on Progress in Romania under the Co-operation and Verification Mechanism." COM (2009) 70 final. Brussels. February 2, 2009. Online: http://ec.europa.eu/dgs/secretariat_general/cvm/docs/romania_report_20090212_en.pdf (accessed April 3, 2011).

_____. 2010a. "Commission Opinion on Albania's Application for Membership of the European Union." COM (2010) 680 {SEC (2010) 1335}. Brussels. November 9. Online: http://ec.europa.eu/enlargement/pdf/key_documents/2010/package/al_opinion_2010_en.pdf (accessed March 25, 2013).

_____. 2010b. "Communication from the Commission to the Council and the European Parliament: Enlargement Strategy and Main Challenges 2010–2011." COM (2010) 660 final. Online: http://ec.europa.eu/enlargement/press_corner/key-documents/reports_nov_2010_en.htm (accessed November 23, 2010).

_____. 2011a. Albania 2011 Progress Report. {SEC (2011) 1205 final}. Brussels. October 12. Online: http://ec.europa.eu/enlargement/pdf/key_documents/2011/package/al_rapport_2011_en.pdf (accessed February 10, 2013).

_____. 2011b. The Former Yugoslav Republic of Macedonia 2011 Progress Report. {SEC (2011) 1203 final}. Brussels. October 12. Online: http://ec.europa.eu/enlargement/pdf/key_documents/2011/package/mk_rapport_2011_en.pdf (accessed March 2, 2013).

_____. 2012a. Albania 2012 Progress Report. COM (2012) 600 final {SWD (2012) 334 final}. Brussels. October 10. Online: http://ec.europa.eu/enlargement/pdf/key_documents/2012/package/al_rapport_2012_en.pdf (accessed March 1, 2013).

_____. 2012b. The Former Yugoslav Republic of Macedonia 2012 Progress Report. {SWD (2012) 332 final}. Brussels. October 10. Online: http://ec.europa.eu/enlargement/pdf/key_documents/2012/package/mk_rapport_2012_en.pdf (accessed February 17, 2013).

_____. 2012c. "Enlargement Strategy and Main Challenges 2012–2013." COM (2012) 600 final. Brussels. October 10. Online: http://ec.europa.eu/enlargement/pdf/key_documents/2012/package/strategy_paper_2012_en.pdf (accessed May 1, 2013).

_____. 2013. "Report from the Commission to the European Parliament and the Council, the Former Yugoslav Republic of Macedonia: Implementation of Reforms within the Framework of the High Accession Dialogue and Promotion of Good Neighbourly Relations." COM (2013) 205 final. Strasbourg. April 16. Online: http://ec.europa.eu/enlargement/pdf/key_documents/2013/mk_spring_report_2013_en.pdf (accessed May 7, 2013).

European Council. 2006. "Council Decision of 30 January 2006 on the Principles, Priorities and Conditions Contained in the European Partnership with the Former Yugoslav Republic of Macedonia and Repealing Decision 2004/518/EC." *Official Journal of the European Union* February 7.

European Council in Lisbon. 1992. "Conclusions of the Presidency, Annex II." 43. June 26–27. Online: http://www.europarl.europa.eu/summits/lisbon/li2_en.pdf (accessed April 15, 2013).

European Movement Albania. 2011. "12 Key Priorities for Albania: Where Do We Stand?" October. Online: http://www.em-al.org/skedaret/1-EMA%20Policy%20Brief%20-%2012%20Key%20Priorities%20EN.pdf (accessed February 12, 2013).

European Parliament. 2006. "Resolution on the Conclusion of the Stabilisation and Association Agreement between the European Communities and Their Member States and the Republic of Albania." August 29. Online: http://www.europarl.europa.eu/sides/getDoc.do?pubRef=-//EP//TEXT+TA+P6-TA-2006-0344+0+DOC+XML+V0//EN (accessed May 28, 2007).

European Stability Initiative. 2002. "Ahmeti's Village: The Political Economy of Interethnic Relations in Macedonia." Skopje and Berlin, October 1. Online: http://www.esiweb.org/pdf/esi_document_id_36.pdf (accessed May 18, 2013).

European Union. 2001. "Presidency Conclusions of the Stockholm European Council, 23–24 March 2001." Online: http://www.consilium.europa.eu/uedocs/cms_data/docs/pressdata/en/ec/00100-r1.%20ann-r1.en1.html (accessed 13 November 2010).

_____. 2008. "Interim Report on Progress in Bulgaria with Judiciary Reform and the Fight against Corruption and Organised Crime." February 4. Online: http://europa.eu/rapid/pressReleasesAction.do?reference=MEMO/08/73&format=HTML&aged=0&language=EN&guiLanguage=en (accessed April 2011).

Expatica. 2010. "Failed Asylum Seekers Return Home to Serbia, Macedonia." Expatica, December 3. Online: http://www.expatica.com/be/news/local_news/Failed-asylum-seekers-return-home-to-Serbia_-Macedonia--_60984.html (accessed March 13, 2011).

F18News. 2004. "Macedonia: Orthodox Monk and Bishop Fined, and Another Bishop Still Jailed." F18News, January 28. Online: http://www.forum18.org/Archive.php?article_id=238 (accessed April 9, 2013).

Fakulteti.mk. 2012. "Ke se Gradi Spomenik na Majka Tereza Povisok od Voinot na Konj" [Mother Theresa monument will be built higher than the Warriors on a Horse]. Fakulteti.mk, June 29. Online: http://bukvar.mk/news/kje-se-gradi-spomenik-na-majka-tereza-povisok-od-voinot-na-konj?newsid=9SxW (accessed April 8, 2013).

Feijen, Liv. 2007. "Asylum Conditionality: Development of Asylum Systems in the Western Balkans in the Context of the European Union's External Dimension." *ERA Forum* 8: 459–509.

Finer, Samuel E., ed. 1966. *Vilfredo Pareto: Sociological Writings*. London: Pall Mall Press.

Fish, Steven M. 1998a. "The Determinants of Economic Reform in the Post-Communist World." *East European Politics and Societies* 12: 31–78.

_____. 1998b. "Democratization's Requisites: The Postcommunist Experience." *Post-Soviet Affairs* 14: 212–47.

_____. 1999. "Postcommunist Subversion: Social Science and Democratization in East Europe and Eurasia." *Slavic Review* 58: 794–823.

Fletorja Zyrtare e Republikës së Shqipërisë. 2011. "Për Miratimin e Strategjisë Ndërsektoriale të Drejtësisë dhe të Planit të Veprimit të Saj" [On the approval of the judicial intersectorial strategy and its action plan]. *Fletorja Zyrtare e Republikës së Shqipërisë* [Official gazette of the Republic of Albania] 11 (August 18): 4,579–626. Online: http://www.justice.gov.al/spaw2/uploads/files/File/Legjislacioni_Brendshem_Web/Strategjia_Ndersektoriale_Plani_Veprimit.pdf (accessed February 12, 2013).

Foucault, Michel. 1994. "Governmentality." In *The Essential Foucault: Selections from Essential Works of Foucault, 1954–1984*, edited by Paul Rabinow and Nikolas Rose, 201–22. New York and London: New Press.

Frashëri, Hektor. 1995. "Addendum the Opinion on the Albanian Law on the Organization of the Judicial." Tirana. December 7. Online: http://www.venice.coe.int/docs/1995/CDL(1995)074add-e.asp (accessed May 17, 2007).

The Free Library. 2010. "Prime Minister Refuses Erga Omnes Name Issue Solution, Opposition and Greek Diplomats Simulate Talks." The Free Library, April 26. Online: http://www.thefreelibrary.com/Prime+minister+refuses+Erga+Omnes+name+issue+solution,+opposition+and...-a0225503814 (accessed April 30, 2013).

Freedom House. 2003. "Country Report 2003: Macedonia." Online: http://www.freedomhouse. org/template.cfm?page=47&nit=242&year=2003 (accessed December 1, 2010).

———. 2004a. "Country Report 2004: Macedonia." Online: http://www.freedomhouse.org/ template.cfm?page=47&nit=339&year=2004 (accessed December 1, 2010).

———. 2004b. "Study: Slow and Uneven Progress in Balkan Democratization." Press Release. April 26. Online: http://www.freedomhouse.org/media/pressre1/042604.htm (accessed May 19, 2007).

———. 2005a. "Country Report 2005: Macedonia." Online: http://www.freedomhouse.org/ template.cfm?page=47&nit=364&year=2005 (accessed December 1, 2010).

———. 2005b. "Nations in Transit 2005." Online: http://www.freedomhouse.eu/nitransit/2006/ methodology.pdf (accessed March 2, 2011).

———. 2006. "Country Report 2006: Macedonia." Online: http://www.freedomhouse.org/ template.cfm?page=47&nit=395&year=2006 (accessed December 1, 2010).

———. 2007a. "Country Report 2007: Albania." Online: http://www.freedomhouse.org/ template.cfm?page=47&nit=414&year=2007 (accessed November 25, 2010).

———. 2007b. "Country Report 2007: Macedonia." Online: http://www.freedomhouse.org/ template.cfm?page=47&nit=429&year=2007 (accessed December 1, 2010).

———. 2008a. "Country Report 2008: Albania." Online: http://www.freedomhouse.org/ template.cfm?page=47&nit=443&year=2008 (accessed November 22, 2010).

———. 2008b. "Country Report 2008: Macedonia." Online: http://www.freedomhouse.org/ template.cfm?page=47&nit=460&year=2008 (accessed November 22, 2010).

———. 2012. "Nations in Transit 2012." Online: http://www.freedomhouse.org/report/nations-transit/nations-transit-2012 (accessed February 10, 2010).

Frowein, Jochen A. and Rüdiger Wolfrum. 1998. *Max Planck Yearbook of United Nations Law 1997*. Leiden: Martinus Nijhoff Publishers.

Füle, Štefan. 2012. "Start of the High Level Accession Dialogue with the Government of the Former Yugoslav Republic of Macedonia." March 15. Online: http://ec.europa.eu/ commission_2010-2014/fule/headlines/news/2012/03/20120315_en.htm (accessed February 7, 2013).

Gabel, Matthew. 1998. "The Endurance of Supranational Governance: A Consociational Interpretation of the European Union." *Comparative Politics* 30: 463–75.

Gallagher, Tom. 2005. *The Balkans in the New Millennium: In the Shadow of War and Peace*. London: Routledge.

Gardner, Andrew. 2013. "EU Ends Macedonian Deadlock." EuropeanVoice, March 2. Online: http://www.europeanvoice.com/article/2013/march/eu-ends-macedonian-deadlock/76563. aspx (accessed May 13, 2013).

Garton Ash, Timothy. 2001. "Is There a Good Terrorist?" *New York Review of Books*, November 1. Online: http://www.nybooks.com/articles/archives/2001/nov/29/is-there-a-good-terrorist/ ?pagination=false (accessed 13 November 2010).

Gazeta Tema. 2012a. "'Ngrin" Konsensusi për Ligjet mes PS-së dhe PD-së" ["Freezes" the PD–PS consensus over the laws]. *Gazeta Tema*, January 12. Online: http://www.gazetatema.net/ web/2012/01/12/ngrin-konsensusi-per-ligjet-mes-ps-se-dhe-pd-se/ (accessed March 29, 2013).

———. 2012b. "PS: Nuk Tërhiqemi nga Fieri. Ligjet jo Vetëm të Miratohen, por edhe të Zbatohen" [We will not give up on Fier: We seek not only the adoption but also implementation of laws]. *Gazeta Tema*, November 24. Online: http://www.gazetatema.net/web/2012/11/24/ ps-nuk-terhiqemi-nga-fieri-ligjet-jo-vetem-te-miratohen-por-edhe-te-zbatohen (accessed April 17, 2013).

———. 2013. "Rama: I Votojmë 3 Ligjet Nëse Hyjnë në Fuqi pas Zgjedhjeve" [Rama: We vote the three laws if they enter to force after the elections]. *Gazeta Tema*, May 3. Online: http://

www.gazetatema.net/web/2013/05/03/rama-i-votojme-3-ligjet-nese-hyjne-ne-fuqi-pas-zgjedhjeve/ (accessed May 14, 2013).

Georgievski, Boris. 2009. "Ghosts of the Past Endanger Macedonia's Future." Balkan Traveller, October 27. Online: http://www.balkantravellers.com/en/read/article/1558 (accessed April 8, 2013).

Georgievski, Dejan. 2002. "Fratello Dove Sei? Un Profilo del Ministro Macedone Boskovski" [Brother where are you? A portrait of the Macedonian Minister Boškovski]. *Osservatorio Balkani*, June 5. Online: http://old.osservatoriobalcani.org/article/articleview/940/1/46/ (accessed December 2, 2010).

Gerrits, André W. M. and Dirk Jan Wolffram, eds. 2005. *Political Democracy and Ethnic Diversity in Modern European History*. Stanford: Stanford University Press.

Gerskovits, Béla. 1998. *The Political Economy of Protest and Patience: Political and Economic Reforms in Eastern Europe and Latin America*. Budapest: Central European University Press.

Gheciu, Alexandra. 2005. "Security Institutions as Agents of Socialization? NATO and the 'New Europe.'" *International Organization* 59: 973–1,012.

Gilson, George. 2008. "Nimetz Denies US Influence." Helleniccomserve, October 31. Online: http://www.helleniccomserve.com/nimetzdeniesusinfluence.html (accessed April 30, 2013).

Gjipali, Gledis. 2010. "Albania." Nations in Transit 2010, edited by Freedom House, 49–64. Online: http://www.freedomhouse.org/images/File/nit/2010/NIT-2010-Macedonia-proof-II.pdf (accessed 28 November, 2010).

Goldsmith, M. 1992. "The Future of British Local Government: Old Wine; Even Older Bottles?" Paper presented at the Fourth Copenhagen Conference on the Future of Local Government, Stege, Denmark, January 31–February 2.

Goldstein, Judith. 1996. "International Law and Domestic Institutions: Reconciling North American 'Unfair' Trade Laws." *International Organization* 50(4): 541–64.

———. 1998. "International Institutions and Domestic Politics: GATT, WTO, and the Liberalization of International Trade." In *The WTO as an International Organization*, edited by Anne O. Krueger, 133–52. Chicago: University of Chicago Press.

Gourevitch, Peter. 1978. "The Second Image Reversed: The International Sources of Domestic Politics." *International Organization* 32: 881–912.

Government of the Republic of Macedonia. 2012. "National Program for Adoption of the *Aquis Communautaire*, 2012: Revisions." Online: http://www.sep.gov.mk/content/Dokumenti/EN/NPAA2012-NarativePart-VersionEN.pdf (accessed March 3, 2013).

Grabbe, Heather. 1999. "A Partnership for Accession? The Implications of EU Conditionality for the Central and East European Applicants." Robert Schuman Center Working Paper 12/99, European University Institute.

———. 2001. "How Does Europeanization Affect CEE Governance? Conditionality, Diffusion and Diversity." *Journal of European Public Policy* 8: 1,013–31.

———. 2002. "European Union Conditionality and the 'Acquis Communautaire.'" *International Political Science Review* 23(3): 249–68.

———. 2003. "Europeanization Goes East: Power and Uncertainty in the EU Accession Process." In *The Politics of Europeanization*, edited by Kevin Featherstone and Claudio M. Radaelli, 303–30. Oxford: Oxford University Press.

GreekNews. 2008. "Karamanlis: 'No Solution Means No NATO Invitation to Skopje.'" GreekNews, February 25. Online: http://www.greeknewsonline.com/?p=8149 (accessed April 23, 2013).

Grugel, Jean, ed. 1999. *Democracy without Borders: Transnationalization and Conditionality*. London: Routledge.

Haggard, Stephan and Robert R. Kaufman. 1995. *The Political Economy of Democratic Transition*. Princeton: Princeton University Press.

Hahn, J. G. von. 2005. *Albanesische Studien*. Ann Arbor: University of Michigan Press.

Haughton, Timothy J. and Darina Malová. 2002. "Making Institutions in Central and Eastern Europe, and the Impact of Europe." *West European Politics* 25(2): 101–20.

Hayden, Robert M. 1992. "Constitutional Nationalism in the Formerly Yugoslav Republics." *Slavic Review* 51: 654–73.

Hellenic Republic, Ministry of Foreign Affairs. "FYROM Name Issue." Online: http://www.mfa.gr/en/fyrom-name-issue/ (accessed April 18, 2013).

Hellenic Resources Network. 1995. "Interim Accord between the Hellenic Republic and the FYROM." Hellenic Resources Network, September 27. Online: http://www.hri.org/docs/fyrom/95-27866.html (accessed April 18, 2013).

Henderson, Karen, ed. 1999. *Back to Europe: Central and Eastern Europe and the European Union*. London: UCL Press.

Heritier, Adrienne. 2001. "Differential Responses to European Policies: A Comparison." In *Differential Europe: The European Union Impact on National Policymaking*, edited by Adrienne Héritier, Dieter Kerwer, Christoph Knill, Dirk Lehmkuhl, Michael Teutsch and A. C. Douillet, 257–94. Boulder: Rowman and Littlefield.

Hibou, Béatrice. 2002. "The World Bank: Missionary Deeds (and Misdeeds)." In *Exporting Democracy: Rhetoric Versus Reality*, edited by Peter Schraeder, 173–92. Boulder and London: Lynne Rienner Publisher.

Higley, John, Judith Kullberg and Jan Pakuski. 2002. "The Persistence of Communist Elites." In *Democracy after Communism*, edited by Larry Diamond and Marc F. Plattner, 33–47. Baltimore and London: Johns Hopkins University Press.

Hislope, Robert. 2005. "When Being Bad Is Good: Corrupt Exchange in Divided Societies." Paper presented in the Postcommunist States and Societies: Transnational and National Politics Conference. Maxwell School, Syracuse University, September 30–October 1.

Hix, Simon. 1999. *The Political System of the European Union*. Basingstoke: Macmillan.

Hollyer, James R. 2010. "Conditionality, Compliance, and Domestic Interests: State Capture and EU Accession Policy." *Review of International Organizations* 5: 387–431.

Horowitz, Donald L. 1985. *Ethnic Groups in Conflict*. Berkeley and Los Angeles: University of California Press.

Howard, Marc M. 2003. *The Weakness of Civil Society in Post-Communist Europe*. Cambridge: Cambridge University Press.

Hoxha, Artan. 2002. *Local Self-Government and Decentralization Case of Albania: History, Reforms and Challenges*. Tirana: Institute for Contemporary Studies.

Hugger, Justin. 2001. "My Father Was a Fighter. It Is in Albanian Blood. I Am Not Afraid. We Will Fight." *Independent*, March 19. Online: http://www.independent.co.uk/news/world/europe/my-father-was-a-fighter-it-is-in-albanian-blood-i-am-not-afraid-we-will-fight-687996.html (accessed September 28, 2010).

Hughes, James, Gwendolyn Sasse, and Claire Gordon. 2003a. "EU Enlargement and Power Asymmetries: Conditionality and the Commission's Role in Regionalization in Central and Eastern Europe." ESRC One Europe or Several? programme working paper no. 49. Brighton: University of Sussex.

_____. 2003b. "EU Enlargement, Europeanization and the Dynamics of Regionalization in the CEECs." In *The Regional Challenge in Central and Eastern Europe: Territorial Restructuring and European Integration*, edited by Michael Keating and James Hughes, 69–88. Brussels: Peter Lang.

Human Rights Watch. 2004. "Human Rights and Armed Conflict." Human Rights Watch World Report 2004. Online: http://www.essex.ac.uk/armedcon/story_id/humanrightswatchworldreport2004.pdf (accessed May 24, 2013).

Huntington, Samuel. 1991. *The Third Wave: Democratization in the Late Twentieth Century*. Norman: Oklahoma University Press.

Huyse, Lucien. 1970. *Passiviteit, Pacificatie en Verzuiling in de Belgische Politiek: Een Sociologische Studie* [Passivity, pacification and pillarization in Belgian politics: A sociological study]. Antwerp: Standaard Wetenschappelijke Uitgeverij.

Hysi, Vasilika. 2004. "Organized Crime in Albania: The Ugly Side of Capitalism and Democracy." *Studies of Organized Crime* 4: 537–62.

Ilievski, Zoran. 2007. "Country Specific Report: Conflict Settlement Agreement Macedonia." Bolzano, Italy: European Academy. Online: http://www.eurac.edu/en/research/institutes/imr/Documents/23_Macedonia.pdf (accessed 18 May 2013).

Ilijevski, Klimentina, Maja Nedelkovska, Aneta Risteska and Valentina Stojancevska. 2012. "Macedonian Culture Strategy: Milestone or Wish List?" BalkanInsight, November 15. Online: http://www.balkaninsight.com/en/article/macedonian-culture-strategy-milestone-or-wish-list (accessed April 8, 2013).

Illner, Michal. 1992. "Municipalities and Industrial Paternalism in a 'Real Socialist' Society." In *Changing Territorial Administration in Czechoslovakia: International Viewpoints*, edited by P. Dorstál, M. Illner, J. Kára and M. Barlow, 39–47. Amsterdam: University of Amsterdam, Charles University and the Czechoslovak Academy of Sciences.

———. 1993. "Continuity and Discontinuity: Political Change in a Czech Village after 1989." *Czechoslovak Sociological Review* (special issue): 79–81.

———. 1997. "The Territorial Dimension of Public Administration Reforms in East-Central Europe." *Polish Sociological Review* 1: 23–45.

———. 1998. "Territorial Decentralization: An Obstacle to Democratic Reform in Central and Eastern Europe?" In *The Transfer of Power: Decentralization in Central and Eastern Europe*, edited by Jonathan D. Kimball, 7–42. Budapest: Local Government and Public Service Reform Initiative.

Imami, Arben. 1998. "Report in Kuvend on the Albanian Constitutional Draft." Archive of the Kuvend. November.

In.gr. 2008a. "Στην Αθήνα τη Δευτέρα ο γγ του ΝΑΤΟ με φόντο το αδιέξοδο στο θέμα της ΠΓΔΜ" [Stin Athina ti Dheftera o gi tou NATO me Fonto to Adhieksodho sto Thema tis PGDM] [NATO secretary in Athens on Monday after FYROM issue deadlock]. In.gr, March 2. Online: http://archive.in.gr/news/reviews/article.asp?lngReviewID=830577&lngItemID=878422 (accessed April 23, 2013).

———. 2008b. "Ενισχύονται οι φωνές στο εσωτερικό της ΠΓΔΜ για ένα 'λογικό συμβιβασμό' στην ονομασία" [Enihionte I fones sto esoteriko tis PGDM gia ena "logiko simvivasmo"] [Voices within FYROM for a "logical compromise" are louder]. In.gr, March 22. Online: http://news.in.gr/greece/article/?aid=884242 (accessed April 27, 2013).

———. 2008c. "Πρόσκληση μόνο εάν βρεθεί λύση για την ονομασία, αποφάσισε το ΝΑΤΟ για την ΠΓΔΜ" [Prosklisi Mono ean Vrethi Lisi gia Onomasia, Apofasise to NATO] [Invitation only if solution is found for the name, NATO decided on FYROM]. In.gr, April 3. Online: http://news.in.gr/greece/article/?aid=887873 (accessed April 30).

———. 2010. "Επιφυλάξεις από την Αντιπολίτευση για την 'κόκκινη γραμμή' στις ιδέες Νίμιτς" [Epifilaksis apo tin Antipolitevsi gia tin "Kokkini Grammi" stis Idhees Nimits] [Concerns from the opposition for "red line" on ideas Nimetz]. In.gr, October 10. Online: http://news.in.gr/greece/article/?aid=945957&lngDtrID=244 (accessed April 30, 2013).

———. 2013. "Ισχύει η εντολή Νίμιτς" [Isini i Entoli] [Nimetz's order]. In.gr, March 11. Online: http://news.in.gr/greece/article/?aid=881231 (accessed April 27, 2013).

Institute for Regional and International Studies. 2006. "The Process of Decentralization in Macedonia: : Prospects for Ethnic Conflict Mitigation, Enhanced Representation, Institutional Efficiency and Accountability." Institute for Regional and International Studies. Sofia–Skopje. Online: http://www.iris-bg.org/f/macedonia2.pdf (accessed May 26, 2006).

———. 2006. "The Process of Decentralization in Macedonia: Prospects for Ethnic Conflict Mitigation, Enhanced Representation, Institutional Efficiency and Accountability." Institute for Regional and International Studies. Sofia–Skopje. Online: http://www.iris-bg.org/f/macedonia2.pdf (accessed May 26, 2007).

International Crisis Group. 2003. "Macedonia: No Room For Complacency." ICG Europe Report No. 149, October. Online: http://www.crisisgroup.org/library/documents/europe/49_macedonia_no_room_for_complacency.pdf (accessed October 3, 2010).

_____. 2005. "Macedonia: Not Out of the Woods Yet." Europe Briefing No. 37, February 25. Online: http://www.refworld.org/docid/425e8ce84.html (accessed May 18, 2013).

International Court of Justice. 2011. "The Court finds that Greece, by objecting to the admission of the former Yugoslav Republic of Macedonia to NATO, has breached its obligation under Article 11, paragraph 1, of the Interim Accord of 13 September 1995." Press Release No. 2011/37. December 5. Online: http://www.icj-cij.org/docket/files/142/16841.pdf (accessed April 30, 2013).

Janos, Andrew C. 2005. "Democracy and Multinationality in East Central Europe." In *Political Democracy and Ethnic Diversity in Modern European History*, edited by André W. M. Gerrits and Dirk Jan Wolffram, 94–110. Stanford: Stanford University Press.

Jeffries, Ian. 2003. *The Former Yugoslavia at the Turn of the Twenty-First Century*. London: Routledge.

Johnson, Janet Buttolph and H. T Reynolds. 2008. *Working with Political Science Research Methods*. 6th edition. Washington, DC: C. Q. Press.

Johnston, Alastair Iain. 2001. "Treating Institutions as Social Environment." *International Studies Quarterly* 45: 487–515.

Karajkov, Risto. 2008. "Boškovski Walks Free." *Osservatorio Balcani e Caucaso*, July 23. Online: http://www.balcanicaucaso.org/eng/Regions-and-countries/Macedonia/Boskovski-Walks-Free (accessed December 2, 2010).

_____. 2010. "Macedonia: Stuck in the Waiting Room," *Osservatorio Balcani and Caucaso*, June 14. Online: http://www.balcanicaucaso.org/eng/Regions-and-countries/Macedonia/Macedonia-Stuck-in-the-Waiting-Room (accessed March 3, 2011).

Karl, Terry Lynn and Philippe C. Schmitter. 1991. "Modes of Transition in Latin America, Southern and Eastern Europe." *International Social Science Journal* 43: 269–84.

Kathimerini. 2006. "A Stir over Name of Skopje's Airport." *Kathimerini*, December 29. Online: http://www.vmacedonianews.com/2006/12/stir-over-name-of-skopjes-airport.html (accessed April 23, 2013).

Kaufman, Stuart J. 2001. *Modern Hatreds: The Symbolic Politics of Ethnic War*. Ithaca, NY and London: Cornell University Press.

Kelley, Judith G. 2004a. "International Actors on the Domestic Scene: Membership Conditionality and Socialization by International Institutions." *International Organization* 58: 425–57.

_____. 2004b. *Ethnic Politics in Europe: The Power of Norms and Incentives*. Princeton: Princeton University Press.

Kentrotis, Kyriakos. 1996. "Echoes from the Past: Greece and the Macedonian Controversy." In *Mediterranean Politics*, edited by Richard Gillespie, 85–103. New York: Fairleigh Dickinson University Press.

King, Gary, Robert O. Keohane and Sidney Verba. 1994. *Designing Social Inquiry: Scientific Inference in Qualitative Research*. Princeton: Princeton University Press.

Knaus, Gerald. 2012. "Macedonia and the Council of the EU Conclusions." BalkanInsight, December 13. Online: http://www.balkaninsight.com/en/blog/eu-council-conclusions-on-macedonia-important-step-forward (accessed May 5, 2013).

Knorr, Klaus. 1977. "International Economic Leverage and Its Uses." In *Economic Issues and National Security*, edited by Klaus Knorr and Frank Trager, 99–126. Lawrence: University Press of Kansas.

Koha Jonë. 2012. "Imuniteti, Xhafa Anulon Tërheqjen e Edi Ramës" [Immunity, Xhafa cancels Rama withdrawal]. Koha Jonë, September 9. Online: http://www.kohajone.com/html/artikull_64786.html (accessed April 7, 2013).

Koliopoulos, John S. and Thanos Veremis. 2002. *Greece: From 1821 to the Present*. London: C. Hurst and Co.

Kopecký, Petr and Cass Mudde. 2000. "What Has Eastern Europe Taught Us about the Democratization Literature (and Vice Versa)?" *European Journal of Political Research* 37: 517–39.

Kosovapress. 2013. "Dačić: We Do Not Have Territorial Claims on Macedonia." Kosovapress, January 29. Online: http://www.kosovapress.com/?cid=2,83,159290 (accessed April 9, 2013).

Kubicek, Paul J. 2003. *The European Union and Democratization*. London, New York: Routledge.

Laar, Mart. 2002. "Estonia's Success Story." In *Democracy after Communism*, edited by Larry Diamond and Marc F. Plattner, 78–83. Baltimore and London: Johns Hopkins University Press.

Lajmanovska, Biljana. 2013. "Greece Prefers to Continue the UN-Mediated Process with Macedonia." *SETimes*, January 24. Online: http://www.setimes.com/cocoon/setimes/xhtml/en_GB/features/setimes/features/2013/01/24/feature-01 (accessed May 7, 2013).

LajmiiFundit. 2010. "Berisha ka bllokuar financimet e huaja për bashkitë e majta" [Berisha has blocked foreign funding for left-wing municipalities]. LajmiiFundit, April 10. Online: http://www.lajmifundit.com/lajmet/ekonomia/te-tjera/5168-berisha-ka-bllokuar-financimet-e-huaja-per-bashkite-e-majta (accessed November 18, 2010).

Lambert, Hélène. 2006. "The EU Asylum Qualification Directive, Its Impact on the Jurisprudence of the United Kingdom and International Law." *International Comparative Law Quarterly* 55: 161–92.

Lauterpacht, E. and C. J. Greenwood, eds. 1993. *International Law Reports Vol. 93*. Cambridge: Grotius Publications Ltd.

Lavenex, Sandra. 1998. "Asylum, Immigration and Central-Eastern Europe: Challenges to EU Enlargement." *European Foreign Affairs Review* 3: 275–94.

_____. 1999. *Safe Third Countries: Extending the EU Asylum and Immigration Policies to Central and Eastern Europe*. Budapest and New York: Central European University Press.

_____. 2001. "The Europeanization of Refugee Policies: Normative Challenges and Institutional Legacies." *Journal of Common Market Studies* 39: 851–74.

Lavenex, Sandra and Emek Uçarer, eds. 2002. *Migration and the Externalities of European Integration*. Lanham: Lexington Books.

Lebamoff, Mary Frances Rosett and Zoran Ilievski. 2008. "The Ohrid Framework Agreement in Macedonia: Neither Settlement nor Resolution of Ethnic Conflict?" Paper presented at the International Studies Association Conference, San Francisco, California, March 26–29.

Lehmbruch, Gerhard. 1967. *Proporzdemokratie: Politisches System und Politische Kultur in der Schwa und in Oesterreich* [Proportional democracy: Political system and political culture in Switzerland and Austria]. Tübingen: Mohr.

_____. 1968. "Konkordanzdemokratien im Politischen System der Schweiz." *Politische Vierteljahresschrift* 9: 443–59.

_____. 1974. "A Non-Competitive Pattern of Conflict Management in Liberal Democracies: The Case of Switzerland, Austria and Lebanon." In *Consociational Democracy: Political Accommodation in Segmented Societies*, edited by K. D. McRae, 90–7. Toronto: McClelland and Stewart.

_____. 1975. "Consociational Democracy in the International System." *European Journal of Political Research* 3: 377–91.

Lijphart, Arend. 1968. "Typologies of Democratic Systems." *Comparative Political Studies* 1: 3–44.

_____. 1969. "Consociational Democracy." *World Politics* 21: 207–25.

_____. 1975. *The Politics of Accommodation. Pluralism and Democracy in the Netherlands*. 2nd edition. Berkeley: University of California Press.

_____. 1977. *Democracy in Plural Societies; A Comparative Exploration*. New Haven and London: Yale University Press.

_____. 1984. *Democracies: Patterns of Majoritarian and Consensus Government in Twenty-One Countries*. New Haven and London: Yale University Press.

_____. 1985. *Power-Sharing in South Africa*. Berkeley: Institute of International Studies, University of California. Policy Papers in International Affairs, No. 24.

_____. 1996a. "The 'Framework' Proposal for Northern Ireland and the Theory of Powersharing." *Government and Opposition* 31: 267–74.

_____. 1996b. "The Puzzle of Indian Democracy: A Consociational Reinterpretation." *American Political Science Review* 90: 258–68.

_____. 1999. *Patterns of Democracy: Government Forms and Performance in Thirty-Six Countries.* New Haven: Yale University Press.

_____. 2004. "Constitutional Design for Divided Societies." *Journal of Democracy* 15(2): 96–109.

Lewis, Paul. 1993. "Compromise Likely to Take Macedonia into UN." *New York Times,* January 26. Online: http://www.nytimes.com/1993/01/26/world/compromise-likely-to-take-macedonia-into-un.html (accessed April 15, 2013).

Lijphart, Arend and Carlos H. Waisman, eds. 1996. *Institutional Design in New Democracies: Eastern Europe and Latin America.* Boulder: Westview Press.

Lili, Ylber. 2009. *Maqedonia në Darën e Krizave* [Macedonia in the pincers of crises]. Tetovo: Tringa.

Lindstrom, Channe. 2003. "Addressing the Root Causes of Forced Migration: A European Union Policy of Containment?" Working Paper No. 11. University of Oxford, Refugee Studies Center.

Linz, Juan L. and Alfred Stepan. 1996. *Problems of Democratic Transition and Consolidation: Southern Europe, South America, and Post-Communist Europe.* Baltimore and London: Johns Hopkins University Press.

Lipset, Seymour Martin. 1959. "Some Social Requisites of Democracy: Economic Development and Political Legitimacy." *American Political Science Review* 53: 69–105.

_____. 1960. *Political Man: The Social Bases of Politics.* Garden City, NY: Doubleday.

_____. 1968. *Revolution and Counterrevolution: Change and Persistency in Social Structures.* New York: Basic Books.

Lipset, Seymour Martin and Reinhard Bendix. 1959. *Social Mobility in Industrial Society.* Berkeley: University of California Press.

Loomis, A., L. Davis and S. Broughton. 2001. "Politics and Identity in Macedonia: Intrinsic versus Extrinsic Understandings." Paper presented at the Conference Macedonia—Macedonians: Changing Contexts in the Changing Balkans, London, June 14–16.

Lozny, Ludomir R. 2011. *Comparative Archaeologies: A Sociological View of the Science of the Past.* New York: Springer.

Lubbers, Ruud. 2002. "Tackling the Causes of Asylum." *Guardian,* June 23. Online: http://www.guardian.co.uk/society/2002/jun/23/immigrationandpublicservices.immigration (accessed March 25, 2011).

_____. 2003. "Put an End to Their Wandering." *Guardian,* June 20. Online: http://www.guardian.co.uk/politics/2003/jun/20/immigration.immigrationandpublicservices (accessed March 1, 2011).

_____. 2004. "Make Asylum Fair, Not Fast." *Guardian,* November 3. Online: http://www.guardian.co.uk/world/2004/nov/03/eu.immigrationandpublicservices (accessed March 25, 2011).

Lustick, Ian S. 1997. "Lijphart, Lakatos, and Consociationalism." *World Politics* 50: 88–117.

MacedoniaDaily. 2007. "Nimetz's Talks in Athens Included 'Alexander the Great.'" MacedoniaDaily, January 13. Online: http://macedoniadaily.blogspot.com/2007/01/nimetz-talks-in-athens-included.html (accessed April 23, 2013).

_____. 2008. "Macedonia Wants Serious Changes in the Latest Proposal." MacedoniaDaily, October 11. Online: http://macedoniadaily.blogspot.com/2008/10/macedonia-wants-serious-changes-in.html (accessed April 30, 2013).

_____. 2009. "Macedonian Negotiator Meets Nimetz." MacedoniaDaily, August 21. Online: http://macedoniadaily.blogspot.com/2009_08_01_archive.html (accessed August 19, 2013).

Macedonian Human Rights Movement International and the Australian Macedonian Human Rights Committee. n.d. "Our Name Is Macedonia." Online: http://www.mhrmi.org/our_name_is_macedonia/ (accessed May 1, 2013).

Maleska, Mirjana. 1998. "Rizikot na Demokratijata: Sluchajot na Makedonia" [Risks of democracy: The Macedonian case]. In *Godoshnik na Institutot za Socjalno Pravno Politichki Istrazhuvanja*. Skopje: Annual of Institute for Social, Legal and Political Research.

Mansfield, Edward D. and Jon C. Pevehouse. 2006. "Democratization and International Organization." *International Organization* 60: 137–67.

Marena, Jakin. 2013. "Meta Prish Koalicionin me Berishën, ja Biseda Sekrete" [Meta quits ruling coalition with Berisha, their secret conversation]. Shqiptarja, April 2. Online: http://www.shqiptarja.com/politike/2732/meta-prish-koalicionin-me-berishen-ja-biseda-sekrete-150014.html (accessed May 14, 2013).

Marko, Joseph. 2004. "The Referendum on Decentralization in Macedonia in 2004: A Litmus Test for Macedonia's Interethnic Relations." *European Yearbook for Minority Issues* 4: 695–721.

Marusic, Sinisa Jakov. 2012a. "Skopje 2014: The New Face of Macedonia." BalkanInsight, May 11. Online: http://www.balkaninsight.com/en/gallery/skopje-2014 (accessed April 8, 2013).

———. 2012b. "Bulgaria and Greece Block Macedonia's EU Talks." BalkanInsight, December 12. Online: http://www.balkaninsight.com/en/article/bulgaria-joins-greece-in-blocking-macedonia-s-eu-bid (accessed May 5, 2013).

———. 2013a. "Greece, Macedonia Positive." BalkanInsight, January 17. Online: http://www.balkaninsight.com/en/article/brussels-opts-closer-insight-in-to-macedonia-name-talks (accessed May 1, 2013).

———. 2013b. "Fresh Macedonia 'Name' Talks Start in New York." BalkanInsight, January 29. Online: http://www.balkaninsight.com/en/article/fresh-round-of-macedonia-name-talks-in-new-york (accessed May 5, 2013).

———. 2013c. "Nimetz Floats New Macedonia 'Name' Proposal." BalkanInsight, April 10. Online: http://www.balkaninsight.com/en/article/nimetz-tables-fresh-macedonia-name-proposal (accessed May 7, 2013).

———. 2013d. "Macedonian, Greek Leaders Hold Rare Direct Meeting." BalkanInsight, May 8. Online: http://www.balkaninsight.com/en/article/macedonian-eu-integration-discussed-in-athens (accessed May 11, 2013).

Mastnak, Tomaž. 2005. "The Reinvention of Civil Society: Through the Looking Glass of Democracy." *Archives of European Sociology* 44: 323–55.

Mayfield, James. 2011. "Are the Modern Slavic Macedonians Descended from the Greeks and Alexander the Great?" *History of Macedonia*, January 2. Online: http://euroheritage.net/macedoniaalexander.shtml (accessed April 11, 2013).

McGarry, John and S. J. R. Noel. 1989. "The Prospects for Consociational Democracy in South Africa." *Journal of Commonwealth and Comparative Politics* 27: 3–22.

McNeil, Donald G. Jr. 2001. "NATO Conditionally Approves Troops for Macedonia." *New York Times*, August 22.

Meletis, Nikos. 2008. "Οι ιδέες ήταν τελικά της Ράις" [I Idhees Itan Telika tis Rais] [The ideas were ultimately Rice's]. Ethnos, October 19. Online: http://www.ethnos.gr/article.asp?catid=22767&subid=2&pubid=1738592 (accessed April 30, 2013).

Messina, Anthony M. and C. V. Thouez. 2002. "The Logics and Politics of an European Immigration Regime." In *West European Immigration and Immigrant Policy in the New Century*, edited by Anthony M. Messina, 97–122. London: Praeger.

MINA–Macedonian International News Agency. 2009. "Greek FM Rejects Milososki Offer, Disputes Macedonian Identity." MINA–Macedonian International News Agency, March 30. Online: http://macedoniaonline.eu/content/view/6164/45/ (accessed April 30, 2013).

Mincheva, Lyubov. 2009. "The Albanian Ethnoterritorial Separatist Movement: Local Conflict, Regional Crisis." *Nationalism and Ethnic Politics* 15: 211–36.

Mill, John Stuart. (1861) 1958. *Considerations on Representative Government*. New York: Liberal Arts Press.

Milne, Robert S. 1981. *Politics in Ethnically Bipolar Societies*. Vancouver: University of British Columbia Press.

Mishler, William and Richard Rose. 1997. "Trust, Distrust, and Skepticism: Popular Evaluation of Civil and Political Institutions in Post-Communist Societies." *Journal of Politics* 59: 418–51.

Misirkov, Krste. 1903. *Za Makedonckite Raboti* [On Macedonian matters]. Sofia: Pečatnica na "Liberalnije Ključ."

Moravcsik, Andrew and Milada Anna Vachudová. 2003. "National Interests, State Power, and EU Enlargement." *East European Politics and Societies* 17: 42–57.

———. 2005. "Preferences, Power and Equilibrium: The Causes and Consequences of EU Enlargement." In *The Politics of European Union Enlargement: Theoretical Approaches*, edited by Frank Schimmelfenning and Ulrich Sedelmeier, 198–211. London: Routledge.

Morrison, John and Beth Crosland. 2001. "The Trafficking and Smuggling of Refugees: The End Game in European Asylum Policy?" Working Paper No. 39, New Issues in Refugee Research, UNHCR.

Nardulli, Peter, ed. 2008. *Domestic Perspectives on Contemporary Democracy*. Champaign: University of Illinois Press.

National Bank of the Republic of Macedonia. "Annual Report 2003." Online: http://www.nbrm.mk/WBStorage/Files/AI_Annual_Report_2003_ang.pdf (accessed April 23, 2013).

Nelken, David. 1996. "A Legal Revolution? The Judges and Tangentopoli." In *The New Italian Republic: From the Fall of the Berlin Wall to Berlusconi*, edited by Stephen Gundle and Simon Parker, 191–205. London: Routledge.

New Europe: The European Weekly Issue. 2008. "Macedonia Enlarged." *New Europe: The European Weekly* 802, October 6.

Newman, Saul. 1996. *Ethnoregional Conflict in Democracies: Mostly Ballots, Rarely Bullets.* Westport, CT and London: Greenwood Press.

New York Times. 2008. "Shame on Greece: Messing with Macedonia." *New York Times*, April 3. Online: http://theboard.blogs.nytimes.com/2008/04/03/shame-on-greece-messing-with-macedonia/ (accessed April 15, 2013).

Nikolovski, Zoran. 2013. "Nimitz Proposal for Macedonia's Name Sparks Debate." *SETimes*, April 14. Online: http://www.setimes.com/cocoon/setimes/xhtml/en_GB/features/setimes/features/2005/04/14/feature-02 (accessed April 18, 2013).

Nodia, Ghia. 2001. "The Impact of Nationalism." *Journal of Democracy* 12(4): 27–34.

———. 2002. "The Impact of Nationalism." In *Democracy after Communism*, edited by Larry Diamond and Marc. F. Plattner, 201–8. Baltimore and London: Johns Hopkins University Press.

Noll, Gregor. 2000. *Negotiating Asylum: The EU Acquis, Extraterritorial Protection and the Common Market of Deflection.* The Hague: Kluwer.

———. 2003. "Risky Games? A Theoretical Approach to Burden-Sharing in the Asylum Field." *Journal of Refugee Studies* 16: 236–52.

Nooz. 2008. "Μιλοσόσκι: Η εντολή του Νίμιτς παραμένει ως έχει" [Milososki: I entoli tou Nimits parameni os egi] [Nimetz's order remains unchanged]. Nooz, March 11. Online: http://www.nooz.gr/page.ashx?pid=9&aid=281213 (accessed April 27, 2013).

Norwegian Directorate for Immigration. 2010. "Asylum Applications from Serbia, Macedonia and Montenegro Is Processed in 48 Hours." March 11. Online: http://www.udi.no/Norwegian-Directorate-of-Immigration/News/2010/Asylum-applications-from-Serbia-Macedonia-and-Montenegro-is-processed-in-48-hours/ (accessed March 12, 2011).

Noutcheva, Gergana. 2006. "EU Conditionality, State Sovereignty and the Compliance Patterns of Balkan States." Paper presented at the 3rd Pan-European Conference on EU Politics European Consortium for Political Research, Bilgi University, Istanbul, September 21–23.

Novinite. 2012. "Bulgaria Says No to FYROM Becoming 'Northern Macedonia.'" Novinite, June 8. Online: http://www.novinite.com/view_news.php?id=140079 (accessed April 30, 2013).

Nyiri, Pal, J. Toth and Maryellen Fullerton, eds. 2001. *Diasporas and Politics.* Budapest: Centre for Migration and Refugee Studies.

O'Donnell, Guillermo and Philippe Schmitter. 1986. *Transition from Authoritarian Rule: Tentative Conclusions about Uncertain Democracies.* Baltimore: Johns Hopkins University Press.

O'Donnell, Guillermo, Philippe Schmitter and Laurence Whitehead, eds. 1986. *Transition from Authoritarian Rule: Southern Europe*. Baltimore: Johns Hopkins University Press.

O'Dwyer, Conor. 2006. "Reforming Regional Governance in East Central Europe: Europeanization or Domestic Politics as Usual?" *East European Politics and Societies* 20: 219–53.

O'Leary, B. 1989. "The Limits to Coercive Consociationalism in Northern Ireland." *Political Studies* 37: 562–88.

Official Gazette of the Republic of Macedonia. 2002. No. 5.

_____. 2004. "Law on Territorial Division of the Republic of Macedonia and Determination of the Areas of the Local Self-Government Units." *Official Gazette of the Republic of Macedonia*, No. 49/1996.

_____. 2010. No. 150. October 18.

Official Journal of the European Union. 1998. "Joint Action of 27 April 1998 Adopted by the Council on the Basis of Article K.3 of the Treaty on European Union, Concerning the Financing of Specific Projects in Favour of Asylum-Seekers and Refugees (98/305/JHA)." May 9. Online: http://eur-lex.europa.eu/LexUriServ/LexUriServ.do?uri=CELEX:31998F0305:EN:HTML (accessed September 7, 2013).

_____. 2000. "Council Decision of 28 September 2000 Establishing a European Refugee Fund." October 6. Online: http://www.refworld.org/docid/3ae6b3b34.html (accessed September 7, 2013).

_____. 2003. "Council Regulation (EC) No 343/2003 of 18 February 2003 Establishing the Criteria and Mechanisms for Determining the Member State Responsible for Examining an Asylum Application Lodged in One of the Member States by a Third-Country National." February 25. Online: http://www.refworld.org/docid/3e5cf1c24.html (accessed September 7, 2013).

_____. 2007. "Agreement between the European Community and the Former Yugoslav Republic of Macedonia on the Readmission of Persons Residing without Authorization." December 19. Online: http://eur-lex.europa.eu/LexUriServ/LexUriServ.do?uri=OJ:L:2007:334:0007:0024:EN:PDF (accessed September 7, 2013).

_____. 2009. "Regulation (EU) No. 439/2010 of the European Parliament and of the Council of 19 May 2010 Establishing a European Asylum Support Office." May 29.

_____. 2010. "Regulation (EU) No. 439/2010 of the European Parliament and of the Council of 19 May 2010 Establishing a European Asylum Support Office." May 29. Online: http://eur-lex.europa.eu/LexUriServ/LexUriServ.do?uri=OJ:L:2010:132:0011:0028:EN:PDF (accessed September 7, 2013).

_____. 2011. "Opinion of the European Economic and Social Committee on 'the Added Value of a Common European Asylum System both for Asylum Seekers and for the EU Member States' (Exploratory Opinion) (2011/C 44/03)." February 11. Online: http://eur-lex.europa.eu/LexUriServ/LexUriServ.do?uri=OJ:C:2011:044:0017:0022:EN:PDF (accessed September 7, 2013).

OneWorld Southeast Europe. "Matthew Nimitz Will Not Present a New Proposal on the Name." OneWorld Southeast Europe. Online: http://see.oneworld.net/article/view/120536/1/ (accessed April 23, 2013).

Organization for Security and Co-operation in Europe. "Presence in Albania 2004." Legal Sector Report for Albania 2004. Online: http://www.osce.org/documents/pia/2004/02/2117_en.pdf (accessed May 22, 2007).

_____. 2010. Report by the Head of the OSCE Presence in Albania to the OSCE Permanent Council. September 9. Online: http://www.osce.org/documents/pia/2010/09/45985_en.pdf (accessed November 18, 2010).

Organization for Security and Co-operation in Europe/Office for Democratic Institutions and Human Rights. 2005. Former Yugoslav Republic of Macedonia, November 7, 2004 Referendum. Warsaw. February 2. Online: http://www.osce.org/documents/odihr/2005/02/4221_en.pdf (accessed October 21, 2010).

_____. 2005. OSCE/ODIHR Election Observation Mission Report, July 3.

_____. 2005. Election Observation Mission Report. "Republic of Albania Parliamentary Elections, July 3, 2005: Final Report." Warsaw. November 7. Online: http://www.osce.org/odihr/elections/albania/14487 (accessed 24 May 2013).

Osmanczyk Edmund J. 2002. "Macedonia, Former Yugoslav Republic of." In *Encyclopedia of the United Nations and International Agreements*, edited by Anthony Mango, 1,355. London: Routledge.

Ottawa Citizen. 1999. "Interview with Gyordan Veselinov, FYROM's Ambassador to Canada." February 24.

Palmer, Stephen E. and Robert R. King. 1971. *Yugoslav Communism and the Macedonian Question.* Hamden: Archon Books.

Panorama. 2012. "Miratohet me 128 Vota Ligji për Konferencën Gjyqësore" [The law on the judicial conference was adopted with 128 votes]. Panorama, July 27. Online: http://www.panorama.com.al/2012/07/27/miratohet-me-128-vota-ligji-per-konferencen-gjyqesore/ (accessed February 14, 2013).

Panorama. 2013. "Meta fton Berishën dhe Ramën: Të Lëmë pas të Shkuarën dhe të Miratojmë 3 Ligjet e Integrimit" [Meta calls on Berisha and Rama: Let's leave the past behind and adopt the three laws]. Panorama, May 2. Online: http://www.panorama.com.al/2013/05/02/meta-fton-berishen-dhe-ramen-te-miratojme-3-ligjet/ (accessed May 14, 2013).

Papapostolou, A. 2010. "Towards an Agreement for the Name 'Macedonia of Vardar.'" *Greek Reporter,* June 14. Online: http://greece.greekreporter.com/2010/06/14/towards-an-agreement-for-the-name-%C2%ABmacedonia-of-vardar%C2%BB/ (accessed May 1, 2013).

Pappalardo, Adriano. 1979. "Le Condizioni della Democrazia Consociativa: Una Critica Logica ed Empirica" [The conditions of consociational democracy: A logical and empirical critique]. *Rivista Italiana di Scienza Politica* 9: 367–445.

_____. 1981. "The Conditions for Consociational Democracy: A Logical and Empirical Critique." *European Journal of Political Research* 9: 365–90.

Parliamentary Assembly of the Council of Europe. 2004. "Resolution 1377 Honouring of Obligations and Commitments by Albania, 2004." April 29. Online: http://assembly.coe.int/Main.asp?link=/Documents/AdoptedText/ta04/ERES1377.htm (accessed May 20, 2007).

_____. 2007. "Resolution 1538: Honouring of Obligations and Commitments by Albania, 2007." January 25. Online: http://assembly.coe.int/Main.asp?link=/Documents/AdoptedText/ta07/ERES1538.htm (accessed September 7, 2013).

Peloni, Aristotelia. 2008. "Παράθυρο για διπλή ονομασία" [Parathiro gia Dhipli Onomasia] [A window for double naming]. *Ta Nea,* October 10. Online: http://www.tanea.gr/news/greece/article/1403491/?iid=2 (accessed April 30, 2013).

Perry, Duncan M. 1997. "The Republic of Macedonia: Finding Its Way." In *Politics, Power, and the Struggle for Democracy in South-East Europe,* edited by Karen Dawisha and Bruce Perrot, 228–9. Cambridge: Cambridge University Press.

Peshkopia, Ridvan. 2005a. "Asylum Capacity Building in the Balkans: A Rational Answer to Leaders; Concerns." *Albanian Journal of Politics* 1: 25–53.

_____. 2005b. "Albania-Europe's Reluctant Gatekeeper." *Forced Migration Review* 23: 35–36.

_____. 2005c. "Asylum in the Balkans: European Union and United Nations High Commissioner for Refugees Assistance to Balkan Countries for Establishing Asylum Systems." *Southeast European and Black Sea Studies* 5: 213–41.

_____. 2005d. "The Limits of Conditionality." *Southeast European Politics* 6: 44–55.

_____. 2008a. "In Search of the Private, Public, and Counterpublic: Modernity, Postmodernity, and Postsocialism." *New Political Science* 30: 23–47

_____. 2008b "Albania and the Balkan Route" Paper presented in the Conference on Albanian Societies in Transition, New York, December 19–20.

_____. 2010. "A Ghost from the Future: The Postsocialist Myth of Capitalism and the Ideological Suspension of Potsmodernity." *Theoria: A Journal of Political and Social Theory* 124: 23–53.

Peshkopia, Ridvan and Arben Imami. 2007. "Institutional Reforms, Domestic Needs, and Membership Conditionality: The Case of the Albanian Institutional Reforms." Paper presented at the 65th Annual Midwest Political Science Association Conference, Chicago, April 12–15.

———. 2008. "Between Elite Compliance and State Socialisation: The Abolition of the Death Penalty in Eastern Europe." *International Journal of Human Rights* 12: 353–72.

Peshkopia, Ridvan and D. Stephen Voss. 2011. "The Balkan Route." Working Paper. Universum College Kosovo and University of Kentucky.

Petkovski, Mihail, Goce Petreski and Trajko Slaveski. 1992. "Stabilization Efforts in the Republic of Macedonia." *RFE/RL Research Report* 2(3): 34–7.

Pevehouse, Jon C. 2002. "Democracy from the Outside-In? International Organizations and Democratization." *International Organization* 56: 515–49.

Phillips, John. 2004. *Macedonia: Warlords and Rebels in the Balkans*. London: I. B. Tauris.

Pop, Valentina. 2009. "Bulgaria, Romania Risk More EU Aid Cuts." EUObserver, February 2. Online: http://euobserver.com/9/27599 (accessed April 4, 2011).

———. 2011. "Greek Government Collapse Not Helping Macedonia." EUObserver, November 9. Online: http://euobserver.com/enlargement/114224 (accessed May 1, 2013).

Prewitt, Kenneth and Alan Stone. 1973. *The Ruling Elites: Elite Theory, Power, and American Democracy*. New York: Harper and Row.

Pridham, Geoffrey. 1994. *Building Democracy? The International Dimension of Democratization in Eastern Europe*. London: Leicester University Press.

———. 2000. *The Dynamics of Democratization: A Comparative Approach*. London: Continuum.

Przeworski, Adam. 1991. *Democracy and Market: Political and Economic Reforms in Eastern Europe and Latin America*. Cambridge: Cambridge University Press.

Putnam, Robert D. 1988. "Diplomacy and Domestic Politics: The Logic of Two-Level Games." *International Organization* 42: 427–60.

Rabushka, Alvin and Kenneth A. Shepsle. 1972. *Politics in Plural Societies: A Theory of Democratic Instability*. Columbus: Charles Merrill.

Radio B92. 2005. "Amnesty International Urges Release of Bishop Jovan." Radio B92, January 17. Online: http://www.b92.net/eng/news/old_archive-article.php?yyyy=2004&mm=01&dd=17&nav_category=12&nav_id=26480 (accessed April 9, 2013).

———. 2013. "SPC Bishop in Favor of Macedonian Autocephaly." Radio B92, October 23. Online: http://www.b92.net/eng/news/society-article.php?yyyy=2012&mm=10&dd=23&nav_id=82789 (accessed April 9, 2013).

Radio Free Europe/Radio Liberty. 2012. "Albania Receives EU Candidate Status, with Conditions." Radio Free Europe/Radio Liberty, October 10. Online: http://www.rferl.org/content/european-union-albania-bosnia-kosovo/24735102.html (accessed February 7, 2013).

Ragaru, Nadège. 2007. "Macedonia: Between Ohrid and Brussels." Paris: CÉRIUM: Centre d'Études et de Recherches Internationals.

Reisinger, William M. 1997. "Establishing and Strengthening Democracy." In *Democratic Theory and Post-Communist Change*, edited by Robert D. Grey, 54–78. Upper Saddle River: Prentice Hall.

Reliefweb. 2002. "Boucher: Law on Local Self-Government Opens the Door for Donor Conference." January 22. Online: http://www.reliefweb.int/rw/rwb.nsf/db900sid/ACOS-64C3N4?OpenDocument&Click= (accessed October 11, 2010).

———. "Macedonia – Parliament: Law on Local Self-Government Adopted." January 25. Online: http://www.reliefweb.int/rw/rwb.nsf/db900sid/ACOS-64C3N4?OpenDocument&Click= (accessed October 11, 2010).

Reuters. 2008. "Albanian Party Threatens to Bring Down Macedonian Govt." bdnews24/Reuters, March 12. Online: http://dev-bd.bdnews24.com/details.php?id=96214&cid=1 (accessed April 24, 2013).

Rhodio, Guido and Jean-Claude Van Cauwenberghe. 2006. "Recommendation 201 (2006) on Local and Regional Democracy in Albania." Council of Europe, The Congress of Local and

Regional Authorities. Online: https://wcd.coe.int/ViewDoc.jsp?id=1053995&Site=COE (accessed November 23, 2010).

Risse, Thomas, Stephen C. Ropp and Kathryn Sikkink. 1999. *The Power of Human Rights: International Norms and Domestic Change*. Cambridge: Cambridge University Press.

Rogowski, Ronald and Lois Wasserspring. 1969. "Legitimacy and Stability in Corporatist Societies." Paper delivered in the 1969 Annual Meeting of American Political Science Association, Washington, DC, September 2–6.

Rose, Richard. 1995. "Freedom as a Fundamental Value." *International Social Science Journal* 145: 454–71.

Rose, Richard, William Mishler and Christian Haerpfer. 1998. *Democracy and Its Alternatives: Understanding Post-Communist Societies*. Baltimore: Johns Hopkins University Press.

Rothchild, Donald. 1970. "Ethnicity and Conflict Resolution." *World Politics* 22: 597–616.

Roudometof, Victor. 1996. "Nationalism and Identity Politics in the Balkans: Greece and the Macedonian Question." *Journal of Modern Greek Studies* 14(2): 253–301.

_____. 2002. *Collective Memory, National Identity, and Ethnic Conflict*. Westport, CT: Greenwood Publishing Group.

Roussis, Nikos. 2008. "Βρήκαν τοίχο τα Σκόπια στο Συμβούλιο της Ευρώπης" [Vrikan tigo ta Skopia sto simvoulio tis Evropis] [Skopje hits a stone wall at the Council of Europe]. *Eleftherotypia*, January 22. Online: http://archive.enet.gr/online/online_text/c=110,dt=22.01.2008,id=10870080 (accessed April 24, 2013).

Rule of Law Working Group. 2008. "Introduction," DG Enlargement–Donor Coordination Conference, Brussels, October 23–24. Online: http://ec.europa.eu/enlargement/pdf/donor_conference/16_dcf_working_group_rule_of_law_en.pdf (accessed November 8, 2010).

Rupnik, Jacques 1999. "The Postcommunist Divide." *Journal of Democracy* 10: 57–62.

_____. 2000. "On Two Models of Exit from Communism: Central Europe and the Balkans." In *Between Past and Future: The Revolutions of 1989 and Their Aftermath*, edited by Sorin Antohi and Vladimir Tismaneanu, 14–24. Budapest and New York: Central European University Press.

_____. 2002. "The Postcommunist Divide." In *Democracy after Communism*, edited by Larry Diamond and Marc F. Plattner, 103–8. Baltimore and London: Johns Hopkins University Press.

Rusi, Iso. 2004. "From Army to Party: The Politics of NLA." International Relations and Security Network. Available Online: http://www.isn.ethz.ch/isn/Digital-Library/Publications/Detail/?ots591=0c54e3b3-1e9c-be1e-2c24-a6a8c7060233&lng=en&id=44474 (accessed May 18, 2013).

Rustow, Dankwart. 1970. "Transitions to Democracy: Toward a Dynamic Model." *Comparative Politics* 2: 337–63.

Sachs, Jeffrey D. 2005. *The End of Poverty: Economic Possibilities for Our Time*. London: Penguin Books.

Saideman, Stephen M. and R. William Ayres. 2007. "Pie Crust Promises and the Sources of Foreign Policy: The Limited Impact of Accession and the Priority of Domestic Constituencies." *Foreign Policy Analysis* 3(3): 189–210.

Santiso, Carlos. 2001. "Good Governance and Aid Effectiveness: The World Bank and Conditionality." *Georgetown Public Policy Review* 7: 1–22.

van Schendelen, M. P. C. M. 1984. "The Views of Arend Lijphart and Collected Criticism." *Acta Politica* 19: 19–55.

Schimmelfenning, Frank. 2005. "Strategic Calculation and International Socialization: Membership Incentives, Party Constellations, and Sustained Compliance in Central and Eastern Europe." *International Organization* 59: 827–60.

_____. 2007. "European Regional Organizations, Political Conditionality, and Democratic Transformation in Eastern Europe." *East European Politics and Societies* 21: 126–41.

Schimmelfenning, Frank and Ulrich Sedelmeier. 2005. "Introduction." In *The Politics of European Union Enlargement: Theoretical Approaches*, edited by Frank Schimmelfenning and Ulrich Sedelmeier, 3–30. London and New York: Routledge.

Schmitter, Phillipe. 1996. "The Influence of the International Context upon the Choice of National Institutions and Policies in Neo-Democracies." In *The International Dimension of Democratization*, edited by Laurence Whitehead, 26–54. Oxford: Oxford University Press.

Schneckener, Ulrich. 2002. "Developing and Applying EU Crisis Management: Test Case Macedonia." 4 ECMI Working Paper.

Schöpflin, György. 1993. *Politics in Eastern Europe 1945–1992*. Oxford: Blackwell.

Sedelmeier, Ulrich. 2005. "Sectorial Dynamics of EU Enlargement: Advocacy, Access and Alliances in a Composite Policy." In *The Politics of European Union Enlargement: Theoretical Approaches*, edited by Frank Schimmelfenning and Ulrich Sedelmeier, 237–57. London and New York: Routledge.

Sejdiaj, Fiqiri. 1998. *Maqedonia Si e Kam Njohur* [Macedonia as I have known it]. Tirana: Dituria.

Selami, Agim and Sonja Risteska. 2009. "Public Administration Reform in Macedonia with Particular Focus on Decentralization Process." *Analytica* 7–8(3): 1,306–14.

SETimes. 2007. "Karamanlis: Greece to Veto Macedonia's EU, NATO Bids if Name Issue Not Resolved." SETimes, September 7. Online: http://www.setimes.com/cocoon/setimes/xhtml/en_GB/newsbriefs/setimes/newsbriefs/2007/09/07/nb-06 (accessed April 23, 2013).

———. 2009. "Croatia Postpones Murder Trial of Former Macedonian Interior Minister." SETimes, February 4. Online: http://www.setimes.com/cocoon/setimes/xhtml/en_GB/features/setimes/newsbriefs/2009/02/04/nb-03 (accessed December 2, 2010).

Sewell, David and Christine I. Wallich. 1996. "Fiscal Decentralization and Intergovernmental Relations in Albania. In *Decentralization of the Socialist State: Intergovernmental Finance in Transition Economies*, edited by Richard M. Bird, Robert D. Ebel, and Christine I. Wallich, 251–80. Brookfield: Ashgate.

Shapiro, Martin and Alec Stone. 1994. "The New Constitutional Politics of Europe." *Comparative Political Studies* 26: 397–420.

Shekulli. 2006. "Shalsi: Qeveria të na Kalojë Ujësjellësin" [Shalsi: The government should transfer to us the water company]. *Shekulli*, October 29.

———. 2008. "Tragjedia e Gërdecit, rritet numri i Viktimave" [The tragedy of Gërdec, increases the number of victims]. *Shekulli*, March 16.

———. 2010a. "Gjykata Administrative, SHBA: Afati për Fondin, Deri në Janar 2011" [The administrative court, the US: The deadline for the fund until January 2011]. *Shekulli*, October 29. Online: http://www.shekulli.com.al/2010/10/29/ambasadoret-e-be-se-takojne-ramen-dhe-berishen.html (accessed November 28, 2010).

———. 2010b. "Vendorët, Rama: Të Tërhiqet Ligji për Taksat, merr 'Rob' Bashkitë" [The bill on taxes must be withdrawn: "Takes hostage" municipalities]. *Shekulli*, November 6. Online: http://www.shekulli.com.al/2010/11/06/vendoret-berishes-terhiq-ligjin-e-taksave.html (accessed November 19, 2010).

———. 2010c. "Rama: Protesta, Qeveria po kap 'Rob' Bashkitë e Komunat Opozitare" [Rama: Protest, the government is "taking hostage" the opposition municipalities]. *Shekulli*, November 10.

———. 2010d. "Rama: Protestë Kundër Talebanizmit të Geverisë" [Rama: Protest against the Talebinization of the government]. *Shekulli*, November 11.

———. 2010e. "Olldashi: Do Prishim Planin Regullues të Tiranës" [Olldashi: Will undo the urban plan of Tirana]. *Shekulli*, November 14. Online: http://www.shekulli.com.al/2010/11/14/olldashi-do-prishim-planin-rregullues-te-tiranes.html (accessed November 19, 2010).

———. 2012. "Statusi, Topalli: 'Po të mos na Duheshin Votat Tuaja, nuk do t'ju Lutesha'" [The status, Topalli: "If we did not need your votes, I would have not begged you"]. *Shekulli*, November 15. Online: http://shekulli.com.al/web/p.php?id=8346&kat=88 (accessed April 17, 2013).

Shkëmbi, Adi. 2008. "OSBE dhe KE: Dakort me ndryshimet Kushtetuese" [OSCE and EC: We agree with the constitutional amendments]. *Panorama*, April 23.

Shoup, Brian. 2008. *Conflict and Cooperation in Multi-Ethnic States: Institutional Incentives, Myths, and Counter-Balancing.* London and New York: Routledge.

Shqiptarja. 2012a. "Ngrihet Gjykata Administrative: Pr/ligji Miratohet Unanimisht" [The administrative court set to be established: The law passes unanimously]. *Shqiptarja*, May 3. Online: http://www.shqiptarja.com/politike/2732/ngrihet-gjykata-administrative-pr-ligji-miratohet-unanimisht-78743.html (accessed February 14, 2013).

———. 2012b. "Këshilli i Qarkut të Fierit, ja Pretendimet e PD dhe PS" [Council of the Fier region, the claims of the PD and PS]. *Shqiptarja*, November 14. Online: file:///C:/Users/Ridvan/Documents/Shqiptarja.com%20-%20K%C3%ABshilli%20i%20qarkut%20t%C3%AB%20 Fierit,%20ja%20pretendimet%20e%20PS%20dhe%20PD.htm (accessed March 29, 2013).

Skai News. 2008a. "Ενημέρωση ΠΑΣΟΚ για την πρόταση Νίμιτς" [Briefing PASOK on Nimetz's proposal]. Skai News, February 20. Online: http://www.skai.gr/news/politics/article/74086/Ενημέρωση-ΠΑΣΟΚ-για-την-πρόταση-Νίμιτς (accessed April 23, 2013).

———. 2008b. "Μη λύση σημαίνει μη πρόσκληση" [Mi Lisi Simeni mi Prosklisi] [No solution equals no invitation]. Skai News, February 29. Online: http://www.skai.gr/player/TV/?mmid=74870 (accessed April 23, 2013).

———. 2008c. "Στην Αθήνα με 'μήνυμα' ο Σέφερ" [Stin Athina me "minima" o Sefer] [Scheffer in Athens with a "message"]. Skai News, March 2. Online: http://www.skai.gr/news/politics/article/75029/Στην-Αθήνα-με-μήνυμα-ο-Σέφερ (accessed April 23, 2013).

———. 2008d. "Παραμένει το χάσμα" [Parameni to hasima] [The gap remains]. Skai News, March 5. Online: http://www.skai.gr/news/politics/article/75294/Παραμένει-το-χάσμα (accessed April 24, 2013).

———. 2008e. "Η Ελλάδα ανυπέρβλητο εμπόδιο" [Greece, an insuperable obstacle]. Skai News, March 7. Online: http://www.skai.gr/news/politics/article/75394/Η-Ελλάδα-ανυπέρβλητο-εμπόδιο (accessed April 23, 2013).

———. 2008f. "Επαφές στα Σκόπια" [Epafes sta Skopia] [Contacts in Skopje]. Skai News, March 8. Online: http://www.skai.gr/news/politics/article/75520/Επαφές-στα-Σκόπια (accessed April 24, 2013).

———. 2008g. "Νέοι Ελιγμοί" [Nei eligmi] [New tactics]. Skai News, March 13. Online: http://www.skai.gr/news/politics/article/75990/Νέοι-ελιγμοί (accessed April 24, 2013).

———. 2008h. "Στηρίζουν Γκρουέφκσι" [Stirizoun Gkrouefski] [They support Gruevski]. Skai News, March 15. Online: http://www.skai.gr/news/world/article/76105/Στηρίζουν-Γκρουέφκσι (accessed April 24, 2013).

———.2008i. "Ξεκίνησαν οι Συνομιλίες" [Xekinsan i Sinomilies] [The talks began]. Skai News, March 17. Online: http://www.skai.gr/news/politics/article/76251/Ξεκίνησαν-οι-συνομιλίες (accessed April 27, 2013).

———. 2008j. "Αισιόδοξος ο Νιμιτς" [Esiodhoksos o Nimits] [Nimetz is optimistic]. Skai News, March 17. Online: http://www.skai.gr/news/politics/article/76261/Αισιόδοξος-ο-Νίμιτς (accessed April 27, 2013).

———. 2008k. "Εντατικές διαπραγματεύσεις για το όνομα" [Entatikes Dhiapragmatevsis gia to Onoma] [Intense negotiations for the name]. Skai News, March 18. Online: http://www.skai.gr/news/politics/article/76333/Εντατικές-διαπραγματεύσεις-για-το-όνομα (accessed April 27, 2013).

———. 2008l. "Όνομα με γεωγραφική διάσταση" [Onoma me geografiki dhiastasi] [Name with a geographic dimension]. Skai News, March 25. Online: http://www.skai.gr/news/politics/article/76795/Όνομα-με-γεωγραφική-διάσταση (accessed April 27, 2008).

———. 2008m. "'Οχι' από Σκόπια στις προτάσεις Νίμιτς" [Ohi apo Skopia Stis Protasis Nimits] ["No" from Skopje to Nimetz proposals]. Skai News, March 21. Online: http://archive.is/Jtkm (accessed April 27, 2013).

———. 2008n. "Νέος γύρος συνομιλιών για το όνομα" [Neos giros sinomilion gia to Onoma] [New round of talks for the name]. Skai News, March 22. Online: http://www.skai.gr/news/politics/article/76552/ Νέος-γύρος-συνομιλιών-για-το-όνομα (accessed April 27, 2013).

_____. 2008o. "Νέα δεδομένα μετά το βέτο" [Nea Dhedhomena Meta to Veto] [New situation after veto]. Skai News, April 3. Online: http://www.skai.gr/news/politics/article/77661/Νέα-δεδομένα-μετά-το-βέτο (accessed April 30, 2013).

_____. 2008p. "Σωστό το βέτο για το 95%" [Sosto to Veto to 95%] [Veto correct for 95%]. Skai News, April 6. Online: http://www.skai.gr/news/politics/article/77905/Σωστό-το-βέτο-για-το-95- (accessed April 30, 2013).

_____. 2008q. "Συνεχίζονται οι διαπραγματεύσεις" [Sinehizonte i dhiagravmatensis] [Negotiations continue]. Skai News, April 11. Online: http://www.skai.gr/news/politics/article/78533/Συνεχίζονται-οι-διαπραγματεύσεις (accessed April 30, 2013).

_____. 2009. "Νέα ονομασία" [Nea onomasia] [New name]. Skai News, January 12. Online: http://www.skai.gr/news/politics/article/106993/Νέα-συνάντηση-για-την-ονομασία (accessed April 27, 2013).

_____. 2013a. "'Δέσμευση' για το όνομα" [Dhesmensi gia to Onoma] ["Commitment" for the name]. Skai News, March 21. Online: http://www.skai.gr/news/politics/article/76459/Δέσμευση-για-το-όνομα (accessed April 27, 2013).

_____. 2013b. "Σύσκεψη για το όνομα στα Σκόπια" [Siskepsi gia to onoma sta Skopia] [Meeting for the name in Skopje]. Skai News, March 23. Online: http://www.skai.gr/news/politics/article/76555/Σύσκεψη-για-το-όνομα-στα-Σκόπια (accessed April 27, 2013).

Skai News Video. 2008. "Λύση ή Βέτο" [Lisi i Veto] [Solution or veto]. Skai News Video. March 6. Online: http://www.skai.gr/player/TV/?mmid=75389 (accessed April 24, 2013).

Skålner, Lars S. 2005. "Geopolitics and the Eastern Enlargement of the European Union." In *The Politics of European Union Enlargement: Theoretical Approaches*, edited by Frank Schimmelfenning and Ulrich Sedelmeier, 213–34. London and New York: Routledge.

Smelser, Neil J. and Seymour Martin Lipset, eds. 1966. *Social Structure and Mobility in Economic Development*. Chicago: Aldine Publishing Company.

Smith, Karen E. 2003. "The European Union: A Distinctive Actor in International Relations." *Brown Journal of World Affairs* 9: 103–13.

_____. 1997. "Paradoxes of European Foreign Policy: The Instruments of European Union Foreign Policy." EUI Working Paper No. 97/68, Badia Fiesolana.

Smolar, Aleksander. 2002. "Civil Society after Communism." In *Democracy after Communism*, edited by Larry Diamond and Marc F. Plattner, 48–62. Baltimore: Johns Hopkins University Press.

Sokolaj, Trashgim. 2007. "Ngec Shkrirja e Gjykatave e Prokurorive" [Stalls the merge of courts and prosecutor offices]. Panorama, May 28. Online: http://www.panorama.com.al/ (accessed May 28, 2007).

Spraos, John. 1986. "IMF Conditionality: Ineffectual, Inefficient, Mistargeted." Princeton Essays in International Finance, No. 166.

Stavenhagen, Rodolfo. 1996. *Ethnic Conflicts and the Nation State*. Houndmills: Macmillan Press; New York: St. Martin's Press.

Steiner, Jürg. 1970. *Gewaltlose Politik und Kulturelle Vielfalt: Hypothesen Entwickelt am Beispiel der Schweiz*. Bern and Stuttgart: Paul Haupt.

_____. 1974. *Amicable Agreement versus Majority Rule: Conflict Resolution in Switzerland*. Chapel Hill: University of North Carolina Press.

_____. 1981a. "Consociational Democracy and Beyond." *Comparative Politics* 13: 339–54.

_____. 1981b. "Research Strategies beyond Consociational Democracy." *Journal of Politics* 43: 1,241–50.

_____. 1987. "Consociational Democracy as a Policy Recommendation: The Case of South Africa." *Comparative Politics* 19: 361–72.

Stiglitz, Joseph E. 2002. *Globalization and Its Discontents*. New York and London: W. W. Norton and Company.

Stojanovska, Marina. 2009. "Biljali: Macedonia's Ethnic Balance at Risk." SETimes, June 8. Online: https://www.google.com/#hl=en&gs_rn=11&gs_ri=psy-ab&tok=Pq1qpr6B0JNz6J

82Mg9xoQ&cp=43&gs_id=6&xhr=t&q=Biljali%3A+Macedonia's+ethnic+balance+at+risk
&es_nrs=true&pf=p&output=search&sclient=psy-ab&oq=Biljali:+Macedonia's+ethnic+bala
nce+at+risk&gs_l=&pbx=1&bav=on.2,or.r_qf.&bvm=bv.45645796,d.Yms&fp=9a411b6da0
7ee78a&biw=1366&bih=667 (accessed April 24, 2013).

Stola, Dariusz. 2001. "Two Kinds of Quasi-Migration in the Middle Zone: Central Europe as a
Space for Transit Migration and Mobility for Profit." In *Patterns of Migration in Central Europe*,
edited by Claire Wallace and Dariusz Stola, 84–104. London: Palgrave Macmillan.

Taleski, Misko. 2010. "Macedonia's Thorny Path to the EU." SETimes, September 16. Online:
http://www.setimes.com/cocoon/setimes/xhtml/en_GB/features/setimes/features/
2010/09/16/feature-02 (accessed October 5, 2010).

Taseski, Filip. 2010. "Macedonia's Judicial Reforms: A Rocky Path toward Accountability and
Independence." *Analytical* 3: 1–12.

Taylor, Paul. 1991. "The European Community and the State: Assumptions, Theories and
Propositions." *Review of International Studies* 17: 109–25.

_____. 1996. *The European Union in the 1990s*. Oxford: Oxford University Press.

_____. 1998. "Consociationalism and Federalism as Approaches to International Integration."
In *Frameworks for International Cooperation*, edited by A. J. R. Groom and Paul Taylor, 172–84.
London: Pinter.

Telegraph. 2012. "Kiro Gligorov," *Telegraph*, January 9. Online: http://www.telegraph.co.uk/news/
obituaries/9003397/Kiro-Gligorov.html (accessed April 8, 2013).

Thessaloniki. 2003. "EU–Western Balkans Summit Declaration" 10229/03 (Presse 163). *Thessaloniki*,
June 21. Online: http://www.emins.org/sr/aktivnosti/konferencije/solun/pdf/zvanicna/
deklar-e.pdf (accessed November 11, 2010). eu/enlargement/enlargement_process/
accession_process/how_does_a_country_join_the_eu/sap/thessaloniki_summit_en.htm
(accessed September 28, 2010).

Thielemann, Eiko. 2003. "Between Interests and Norms: Explaining Burden-Sharing in the
European Union." *Journal of Refugee Studies* 16: 254 73.

_____. 2008. "The Future of the Common European Asylum System: In Need of a More
Comprehensive Burden-Sharing Approach." *European Policy Analysis* 1 (February): 1–8.

Tindigarukayo, Jimmy K. 1989. "The Viability of Federalism and Consociationalism in Cultural
Plural Societies of Post-Colonial States: A Theoretical Exploration." *Plural Societies* 19: 41–54.

Tirana Observer. 2011. "PD–PS Arrijnë më në Fund një Marrëveshje" [PD–PS finally reach an
agreement]. *Tirana Observer*, November 15. Online: http://www.tiranaobserver.al/2011/11/15/
pd-ps-arrijne-me-ne-fund-nje-marreveshje/ (accessed February 12, 2013).

Tismaneanu, Vladimir. 1995. *Political Culture and Civil Society in Russia and New States of Eurasia*.
Armonk, New York and London: M. E. Sharpe.

_____. 2000. "Fighting for the Public Sphere: Democratic Intellectuals Under Postsocialism." In
Between the Past and Future: The Revolutions of 1989 and Their Aftermath, edited by Sorin Antohi and
Vladimir Tismaneanu, 153–71. Budapest and New York: Central European University Press.

Top Channel. 2011. "Prishet 'Magjia' e Politikës" [The "magic" of politics spoiled]. Top Channel,
November 14. Online: http://www.top-channel.tv/artikull.php?id=222782 (accessed March
29, 2013).

_____. 2013. "Van der Linden: Albania, Cautious with Elections." Top Channel, January 8. Online:
http://www.top-channel.tv/english/artikull.php?id=7976&ref=fp (accessed April 7, 2013).

Topalova, Evelina. 2011. "Macedonia Wins a Battle but Not the War in Name Dispute with
Greece." EUInside, December 11. Online: http://www.euinside.eu/en/news/macedonia-has-
won-a-battle-but-not-the-war-in-the-name-issue-with-greece (accessed April 30, 2013).

Toronto Star. 1992. "Interview with FYROM'S President Mr. Kiro Gligorov." *Toronto Star*, March 15.

To Vima. 2008. "Ολόκληρο το κείμενο της πρότασης Νίμιτς" [Olokliro to kimeno tis protasis Nimits]
[The whole text of the Nimetz proposal]. *To Vima*, February 21. Online: http://www.tovima.
gr/relatedarticles/article/?aid=228676 (accessed April 23, 2013).

_____. 2008. "Πιθανή συμφωνία στο 'Νέα Μακεδονία'" [Pithani simfonia sto "Nea Makedhonia"] [Possible agreement on "New Macedonia"]. *To Vima*, March 21. Online: http://www.tovima. gr/relatedarticles/article/?aid=231535 (accessed April 27, 2008).

Trajkov, Goran. 2008. "VMRO–DPMNE and DUI Form Ruling Coalition in Macedonia." SETimes, July 8. Online: http://www.setimes.com/cocoon/setimes/xhtml/en_GB/features/ setimes/features/2008/07/08/feature-02 (accessed December 5, 2010).

Trajkovski, Miki. 2012. "Bulgaria May Block Macedonia's EU Accession." SETimes, November 13. Online: http://www.setimes.com/cocoon/setimes/xhtml/en_GB/features/setimes/ features/2012/11/13/feature-03 (accessed April 9, 2013).

Tsebelis, George. 1990. "Elite Interaction and Constitution Building in Consociational Democracies." *Journal of Theoretical Politics* 2(1): 5–29.

Turncock, David. 2003. *The Human Geography of East Central Europe*. London: Routledge.

United Nation. 1993a. United Nations Security Council Resolution 817. April 7. Online: http:// www.nato.int/ifor/un/u930407a.htm (accessed April 15, 2013).

_____. 1993b. "Admission of the Former Yugoslav Republic of Macedonia to Membership in the United Nations," United Nations General Assembly Resolution 225, April 8. Online: http:// www.un.org/documents/ga/res/47/a47r225.htm (accessed April 15, 2013).

_____. 1993c. "Repertoire of the Practice of the Security Council Twelfth Supplement 1993– 1995, Chapter VII: Practice Relative to Recommendations to the General Assembly Regarding Membership in the United Nations 1993–1995." January 25. Online: http://www.un.org/fr/ sc/repertoire/93-95/93-95_7.pdf (accessed April 15, 2013).

_____. 1995. "Agreement on a Five-Year Development Cooperation Programme 2002–2006 between the Government of the Party of the First Part to the Interim Accord, September 13, 1995 and the Government of the Party of the Second Part to the Interim Accord." September 13. Online: http://lj.rossia.org/users/bbb/2008/08/18/ (accessed April 18, 2013).

_____. 1996. "Former Yugoslavia – UNPROFOR." Department of Public Information. August 31. Online: http://www.un.org/Depts/DPKO/Missions/unprof_b.htm (accessed April 15, 2013).

United Nations Development Programme (UNDP). 2004. "FYR Macedonia: Decentralization for Human Development." National Human Development Report 2004. Online: http:// www.undp.org.mk/datacenter/publications/documents/nhdr2004EngFP1.pdf (accessed November 26, 2010).

United States Department of State, Bureau of Democracy, Human Rights, and Labor. 2006. Country Reports on Human Rights Practices 2005. March 9. Online: http://www.state.gov/j/ drl/rls/hrrpt/2005/61651.htm (accessed April 24, 2013).

Utrinski Vesnik. 2013. "По Виена Нимиц е поголем оптимист за името" [Po Viena Nimis e Pogolem optimist za Imeto] [After Vienna Nimetz is a bigger optimist about the name]. Utrinski Vesnik, March 17. Online: http://www.utrinski.com.mk/?ItemID=A169B25801FA6 C4F9D16CBD7B56A8E94 (accessed April 27, 2013).

Vachudová, Milada Anna. 2001. "The Leverage of International Institutions on Democratizing States: Eastern Europe and the European Union." European University Working Papers, Florence, Italy.

Vasilis, Hiotis. 2007. "Εγώ δεν είπα ποτέ τη λέξη βέτο" [Ego then ipa Pote ti Leksi Veto] [I never used the word veto]. *To Vima*, September 11. Online: http://www.tovima.gr/politics/ article/?aid=212742 (accessed April 23, 2013).

Venice Commission. 2005. "Opinion on the Albanian Law on the Organization of the Judicial." Strasbourg. December 4. Online: http://www.venice.coe.int/docs/1995/CDL(1995)074rev-e. asp (accessed May 17, 2007).

Verdery, Katherine. 2000. "Privatization as Transforming Persons." In *Between Past and Future: The Revolutions of 1989 and the Struggle for Democracy in Central and Eastern Europe*, edited by Sorin Antohi and Vladimir Tismaneanu, 175–97. Budapest: Central European University Press.

Vest. 2008. "Грчко вето ќе ги прекине преговорите" [Grcko Veto keg i Prekine Pregovorite] [Greek veto to suspend negotiations]. *Vest*, March 26. Online: http://star.vest.com.mk/default.asp?id= 149257&idg=8&idb=2333&rubrika=Makedonija (accessed May 1, 2013).

Vreeland, James Raymond. 2003. *The IMF and Economic Development.* Cambridge: Cambridge University Press.

Wallace, Claire and Dariusz Stola. 2001. *Patterns of Migration in Central Europe.* Basingstoke: Palgrave-Macmillan.

Washington Times. 2008. "In the Name of a Common Future." *Washington Times*, April 29. Online: http://www.washingtontimes.com/news/2008/apr/29/in-the-name-of-a-common-future (accessed April 30, 2013).

Waterfield, Bruno. 2009. "Albania to Apply for EU Membership." *Telegraph*, April 27.

Weiler, J., U. R. Haltern and F. C. Mayer. 1995. "European Democracy and Its Critique." *West European Politics* 18(3): 4–39.

Welsh, Helga A. 1994. "Political Transitions in Central and Eastern Europe." *Comparative Politics* 26: 379–94.

Wikipedia. 2013."Demographics of the Republic of Macedonia." Last modified: September 12, 2013. Online: http://en.wikipedia.org/wiki/Demographics_of_the_Republic_of_Macedonia.

_____. 2013. "Macedonia Naming Dispute." Last modified: October 4, 2013. Online: http:// en.wikipedia.org/wiki/Macedonia_naming_dispute.

Wikisource. 2013. "Executive Order 13,219 of 26 June 2001: Blocking Property of Persons Who Threaten International Stabilization Efforts in the Western Balkans." Last modified: June 19, 2013. Online: http://en.wikisource.org/wiki/Executive_Order_13219.

Whitehead, Laurence. 1996. "Three International Dimensions of Democratization." In *The International Dimension of Democratization*, edited by Laurence Whitehead, 3–25. Oxford: Oxford University Press.

World Bank. 1981. *Accelerated Development in Sub-Saharan Africa: An Agenda for Action.* Washington, DC: World Bank.

_____. 1989. *Sub-Saharan Africa: From Crisis to Sustainable Growth.* Washington, DC: World Bank.

_____. 1992. *Governance and Development.* Washington, DC: World Bank.

_____. 1996. World Development Report. Oxford: Oxford University Press.

_____. 1997. World Development Report. Oxford: Oxford University Press.

_____. 2000. Report No. 19,915-ALB: Project Appraisal Document. March 1. Online: http:// www-wds.worldbank.org/external/default/WDSContentServer/IW3P/IB/2000/04/07/00 0094946_00030805302144/Rendered/INDEX/multi_page.txt (accessed May 18, 2007).

_____. 2010. "Camille Nuamah, Country Manager of the World Bank Office in Albania." Press Release. April 10. Online: http://web.worldbank.org/WBSITE/EXTERNAL/COUNTRIES/ ECAEXT/ALBANIAEXTN/0,,contentMDK:22533723~menuPK:301417~pagePK:286506 6~piPK:2865079~theSitePK:301412,00.html (accessed November 18, 2010).

Yambaev, Mikhail. 2011. "Will Macedonia Become the Third Albanian State in the Balkans?" Strategic Culture Foundation, March 11. Online: http://www.strategic-culture.org/ pview/2011/03/11/will-macedonia-become-the-third-albanian-state.html (accessed May 11, 2013).

Zimmermann, Warren. 1999. *The Origins of a Catastrophe: Yugoslavia and Its Destroyers.* New York: Three Rivers Press.

Zogaj, Preç. 1996. *Rënia e Zgjedhjeve* [Elections' downfall]. Tirana: Dita.

Zürn, Michael and Jeffrey T. Checkel. 2005. "Getting Socialized to Build Bridges: Constuctivism and Rationalism, Europe and the Nation-State." *International Organization* 59: 1,045–79.

INDEX

www.ingramcontent.com/pod-product-compliance
Lightning Source LLC
Chambersburg PA
CBHW022347280326
41935CB00007B/110